STUDIES IN IMPERIALISM

General Editor: Andrew S. Thompson

Founding Editor: John M. MacKenzie

When the 'Studies in Imperialism' series was founded by Professor John M. MacKenzie more than twenty-five years ago, emphasis was laid upon the conviction that 'imperialism as a cultural phenomenon had as significant an effect on the dominant as on the subordinate societies'. With well over a hundred titles now published, this remains the prime concern of the series. Cross-disciplinary work has indeed appeared covering the full spectrum of cultural phenomena, as well as examining aspects of gender and sex, frontiers and law, science and the environment, language and literature, migration and patriotic societies, and much else. Moreover, the series has always wished to present comparative work on European and American imperialism, and particularly welcomes the submission of books in these areas. The fascination with imperialism, in all its aspects, shows no sign of abating, and this series will continue to lead the way in encouraging the widest possible range of studies in the field. 'Studies in Imperialism' is fully organic in its development, always seeking to be at the cutting edge, responding to the latest interests of scholars and the needs of this ever-expanding area of scholarship..

The relic state

MANCHESTER
1824

Manchester University Press

SELECTED TITLES AVAILABLE IN THE SERIES

BORDERS AND CONFLICT IN SOUTH ASIA
The Radcliffe boundary commission and the partition of Punjab
Lucy P. Chester

CONQUERING NATURE IN SPAIN AND ITS EMPIRE, 1750–1850
Helen Cowie

MISSIONARIES AND THEIR MEDICINE
A Christian modernity for tribal India
David Hardiman

WELSH MISSIONARIES AND BRITISH IMPERIALISM
The Empire of Clouds in North-East India
Andrew J. May

THE COLONISATION OF TIME
Ritual, routine and resistance in the British Empire
Giordano Nanni

The relic state

ST FRANCIS XAVIER AND THE POLITICS OF RITUAL IN PORTUGUESE INDIA

Pamila Gupta

MANCHESTER UNIVERSITY PRESS
Manchester and New York

distributed in the United States exclusively by
Palgrave Macmillan

Published by MANCHESTER UNIVERSITY PRESS
ALTRINCHAM STREET, MANCHESTER M1 7JA, UK
and ROOM 400, 175 FIFTH AVENUE, NEW YORK, NY 10010, USA
www.manchesteruniversitypress.co.uk

Distributed in the United States exclusively by
PALGRAVE MACMILLAN, 175 FIFTH AVENUE, NEW YORK, NY 10010, USA

Distributed in Canada exclusively by
UBC PRESS, UNIVERSITY OF BRITISH COLUMBIA,
2029 WEST MALL, VANCOUVER, BC, CANADA V6T 1Z2

British Library Cataloguing-in-Publication Data
A catalogue record for this book is available from the British Library

Library of Congress Cataloging-in-Publication Data applied for

ISBN 978 0 7190 9061 5 *hardback*

First published 2014

Typeset in Trump Medieval by
Koinonia, Manchester
Printed in Great Britain by
TJ International Ltd, Padstow

for Padma

CONTENTS

LIST OF FIGURES

All illustrations are from the author's own collection

GENERAL EDITOR'S INTRODUCTION

It is a particular pleasure to introduce this volume to the Studies in Imperialism series. This series has long had a commitment to comparative imperialism, to interdisciplinary studies, and to radical approaches to phenomena associated with European empire in the East and elsewhere. Pamila Gupta's book magnificently embraces all of these. It is a study of Portuguese imperialism, in which the historical health of the state is reflected in the treatment and constructions of the body of St Francis Xavier over a period of five centuries. It constitutes a notable contribution to historical anthropology, carefully analysing the extraordinary historical moments in which the reputation and corporeal presence of the Jesuit saint has been used to reflect the alleged sanctity of the Portuguese Estado da Índia during its high point in the era of 'Golden Goa' in the sixteenth and seventeenth centuries; then its decline in the face of Dutch and British competition, all reflecting the dynamic balance between church and state and the intricate relationship among the various organs of the Roman Catholic Church and royal politics. But of course there was an additional factor in this complex situation – the geographical, cultural, and ethnic contexts of India itself, in which Indians were excluded in the original acts of ritualization, but were later included, both as Christians and as Hindus and Muslims. In the nineteenth century, the Portuguese confronted the manner in which their empire was, like the body of Xavier itself, seriously contracting. And they set about a policy of attempting to resurrect the imperial state through the further reinstitution of the ritualization of the saint. And they reinvigorated the same policy as late as 1952, continuing to argue that Goa was an overseas province of Portugal. But it was of course a hopeless cause. Ultimately, the Portuguese enclaves were finally extinguished in the Indian invasion of 1961. Yet again the body of Xavier played a symbolic part.

Gupta describes the process of the shift from church to state in the manipulation of the body of Xavier as a form of secularization. By the time I myself 'encountered' St Francis Xavier, this secularization had taken a further twist. Xavier had shifted from being a source of veneration, albeit observed by actors in the imperial drama and by eyewitness travellers, into an object of historical curiosity for tourists. My visit to Velha Goa took place thirty-five years ago, in March 1978, and by then the Church of Bom Jesus had become an Ancient Monument under the Archaeological Survey of India. I travelled with my trusty *Murray's Guide to India*, which I used in order to get a flavour of the reactions of imperial travellers. In the 1919 edition, I read that Old Goa 'is now, literally, a city of ruins, with a population of 155 inhabitants, and is so hidden from view by the foliage of the jungle which has occupied it that the stranger approaches it unawares ... In the midst of all this ruin Goa remains a city of magnificent churches, four or five ranking as first class and in a perfect state of preservation.' I also read that the coffin of St Francis weighed '600 marks of silver' and 'is unlocked by three keys, in the keeping of the Governor, the Archbishop, and the Administrator of the Convent'. I immediately recognized an intriguing balance here between church and state symbolizing both the synergies and tensions of Portuguese royal and Catholic imperialism. Turning to my diary, I find that I wrote that the church of Bom Jesus and the other ecclesiastical buildings were 'all deserted'. I decided to leave Bom Jesus to the last, as a climax, and was pounced upon by a Hindu guide (probably unofficial). He was persistent, so I gave in, and he took me to the 'best place' to see 'the incorruptible head of St Francis in his casket', the lights being turned on to show me better. Like the sceptical late seventeenth-century Scot Alexander Hamilton, I wrote that it looked like a poor case of embalming or mummification. I was then taken upstairs to the Art Gallery to see the paintings of Dom Martin depicting the life of the saint.

Many years later, now reading Pamila Gupta's fascinating book, I am struck by striking parallels with a study of my own (though there are of course differences too). In the past few years, I have published a number of articles dealing with the relationship between David Livingstone and British imperialism in Africa. I too have been more interested in the copious 'afterlife' than in the life. Livingstone's body, though not 'incorrupted', was crudely embalmed by his African followers and, like Xavier's, this body proceeded on a journey which matched that of its owner in life. Like Xavier's, it came to be surrounded by ritual, the transfer from Africa to Britain on a Royal Navy vessel, the grand reception in Southampton, the progress across the country, the medical examination of the remains, concentrating on the arm wounded by an encounter with a lion many years before, then the formal and national ritualization of the funeral in Westminster Abbey. Although the body was interred (in a central place in the nave where visitors and worshippers would walk over it), nonetheless Livingstone was repeatedly invested with the powers that had been attributed to Xavier – he became the patron saint of British imperialism in Africa. He was seen as 'sanctifying' through his alleged heroic qualities, moral force, and martyrdom the creation of British colonies. This took a variety of forms.

His reputation animated other explorers to follow him; he enthused colonial administrators to emulate his principles; but above all his body (in effect) was used as an inspiration for large numbers of missionaries of a wide variety of Christian denominations. As with Xavier, he inspirationally lived on through a number of biographies. In the twentieth century he too was 'resurrected'. He became, as I have described it, a 'Protestant saint' with the relics (artefacts rather than body parts) gathered together for the creation of his 'birthplace' museum. As with St Francis, print culture and the industrial production of 'souvenirs' helped to spread his fame, as did statues, stamps, magic lantern slides, and films. Later it was even suggested that he was admired by African nationalists. Moreover, he and Xavier shared a great irony. Xavier was a Spaniard appropriated by the Portuguese for their imperial purposes. Livingstone was a Scot similarly appropriated by the English, although later reappropriated by the Scots as part of their new sense of cultural identity. Though the lives of Xavier and of Livingstone were separated by a period of more than three hundred years, both reflected the tendencies of churches and states to use heroic and saintly figures to further their causes, emphasized by the fortification of myth through repeated ceremonial and ritual. The fourth centenary of Xavier's death was celebrated in Goa in 1952. Sixty years later, I became an eyewitness of the ritual surrounding the bicentennial of Livingstone's birth in Westminster Abbey in March 2013. On that occasion, the supposed postcolonial significance of Livingstone was symbolized by the presence of the President of Malawi. Moreover, the lives of Xavier and Livingstone intersected in the ambitions of nineteenth-century imperialism. Livingstone visited Angola and Mozambique. He was influential (and later his reputation was used for the same purpose) in the shrinkage of Portuguese claims upon Africa.

Pamila Gupta has used a tremendous range of sources in the pursuit of her study together with her own intimate knowledge of Goa. She has repeatedly laid emphasis on, and carefully analysed, eyewitness accounts. She has also been influenced by a range of theoretical ideas derived from writings about the Portuguese Empire, on church history, sainthood, mythic commemorations, and the modern practice of historical anthropology. The result is a richly textured and highly rewarding book that may stimulate many parallel thoughts – as it has done for me.

John M. MacKenzie

ACKNOWLEDGEMENTS

It was the image of St Francis Xavier's corpse as it lies in Goa today that guided me through the conceptualization and writing of this book. My first fieldwork trip to Goa (summer 1997) was made possible by a Social Science Research Council Pre-dissertation Fellowship. Archival research in Portugal (1998–9) was made possible by financial support from Fulbright IIE and the Luso-American Educational Commission. Here I would like to thank the various staffs at the Torre do Tombo, the Arquivo Histórico Ultramarino, the Biblioteca Nacional, the Brotéria, and the Biblioteca da Sociedade de Geografia de Lisboa. Archival research and fieldwork in Goa (1999–2000) was made possible by financial support from the American Institute for Indian Studies Dissertation Research Fellowship (AIIS). Here I would like to thank the various staffs at the Xavier Center of Historical Research, the Central Library, the Archaeological Survey of India (Goa branch), the library at Goa University and the State Archives of Goa. Lilia Maria D'Souza, of the Xavier Centre of Historical Research, was invaluable in helping me to locate Xavier in the (Jesuit) archives. The many people who generously shared their 'stories' of Goa's patron saint with me not only helped give life to my project on death, but kept me in touch with what really mattered. Finally, the close friendships of Rukshana, Naz, Ricard, and Rhea, Heta and Rajesh and Sangeeta made my experience of living in Goa unforgettable.

The guidance of Professors Tom Patterson, Niyi Akinnaso, and Peter Rigby and the financial support of a Future Faculty Fellowship from Temple University provided a nurturing environment to initially pursue graduate studies in anthropology. Here I thank Jason S. Greenberg for exploring the visual with me and Meena Khandelwal for making my first visit to Goa possible. Together, the professors and graduate students affiliated with the Joint Program in Anthropology and History at the University of Michigan provided a vibrant intellectual community that continued, albeit in a different form, at Columbia University. Most of all, I would like to thank the members of my dissertation committee at Columbia University for their scholarly depth and expertise: Professors Nicholas Dirks, Brinkley Messick, Partha Chatterjee, Sanjay Subrahmanyam, and Gauri Viswanathan. A special thanks to Nick for being my adviser and introducing me to the field of historical anthropology and to Brinkley for teaching me to see the richness of ethnographic description. The Graduate School of Arts and Sciences and a Morton H. Fried Memorial Fellowship at Columbia University provided funds to support the writing-up phase of the dissertation. Remaining mistakes are my own.

My parents provided love and support throughout this entire process. Nor would the completion of this book have been possible without the infamous 'Downtown Dissertation Writing Group' in New York city: Ilana Feldman, Rachel Heiman, Mani Limbert, Brian Mooney, and Karen Strassler; they collectively provide much needed coffee, warmth, and support during the writing phase (2000–4). I give a special thanks to Marco, who will always remind me of Goa and who patiently stood by me when I was trying to complete the seemingly impossible task of finishing a never-ending dissertation, and who dared to take me on an adventure to South Africa, one I am still living.

Here in Johannesburg, I would like to thank numerous friends and colleagues associated with Wits University and WISER (Wits Institute for Social and Economic Research), my intellectual space and home: Deborah Posel, Achille Mbembe, Isabel Hofmeyr, Sarah Nuttall, Ashlee Neser, Jon Hyslop, Irma du Plessis, Michael Titlestad, Julia Hornberger, Jon Soske, and Ronit Frenkel.

Special thanks go to Craig MacKenzie, who helped me edit an unmanageable thesis into a concise book, Hannah Chapelle Wojciehowski for her continued interest in my work, Nandini Chaturvedula and Anjali Arondekar for their expert advice, and, finally, to Michael Pearson who always had faith in my little (big) book. I want to thank my editor Emma Brennan at Manchester University Press for seeing the potential in my work, and for her patience along the editorial process, the anonymous reviewer of my manuscript appointed by Manchester, and finally the editors for the Studies in Imperialism series, which gave my book a home. Lastly, I want to thank Juan for helping me to see the nuances of words and images, and Padma for making me smile every day.

For the illustrations included in this book, I have made every effort to trace the holder of the copyright to this remarkable set of posters that were commissioned in conjunction with Xavier's past expositions. I have also searched the archives in Goa for copies and/or additional information on them but to no avail. Presumably, these posters were sold or distributed during the days of his expositions. I would like to thank the owner of the small photo and frame shop in Panjim who in September 1999 took an interest in my research and sold me the few copies he had available.

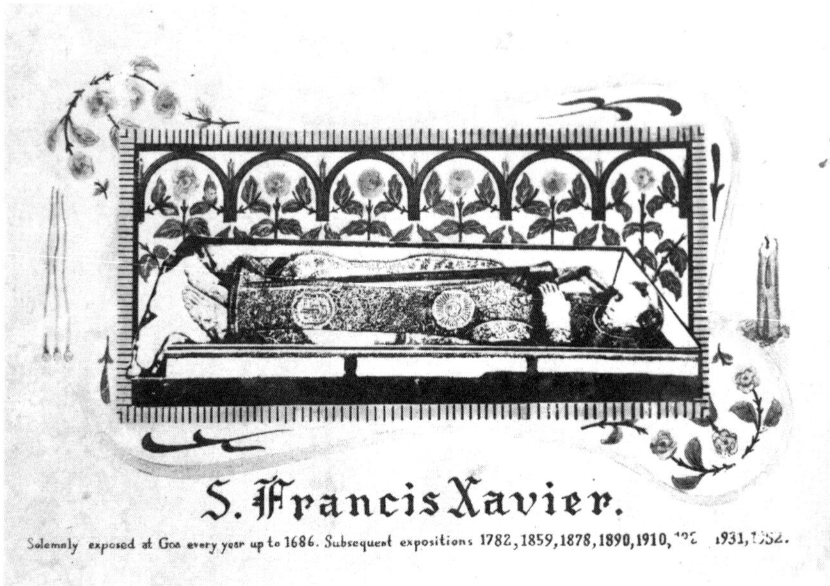

Figure 1 Souvenir, St Francis Xavier Exposition, 1952

CHAPTER ONE

Introduction: the relic state

> Relic: 1. object interesting because of its age or association; 2. part of a deceased holy person's remains, etc., kept out of reverence; 3. surviving custom or belief from past age; 4. memento or souvenir; 5. fragments, ruins, etc. (in plural) – *The Oxford American Desk Dictionary and Thesaurus*, 2001[1]

On 18 December 1961, a colonial government's attempts to quietly remove a saint's corpse from the location where he had lain in state for over four hundred and fifty years, periodically exposed for public veneration, were thwarted; if it hadn't been for members of this same public, Portuguese colonial officials would reportedly have taken the 'sacred remains' of Goa's Apostle and Defender, São Francisco Xavier, with them when they were forced to leave by Indian troops bent on liberating this colonial enclave (1510–1961) located in the midst of a newly independent nation-state (1947).

That the Estado da Índia desired the removal of Xavier's body from Goa as a last colonial act suggests his crucial role (both in life and death) in defining their form of rule. That Xavier was the founder of the Society of Jesus in India reinforces the intimate connections between conquest and conversion that defined the Portuguese enterprise in India. That the public were rumoured to have prevented his 'theft' from Goa illuminates the diversity of meanings attached to this colonial body by those subjected to Portuguese rule, and their crucial role in defining and delimiting colonial practices. That the Portuguese had preceded and outlasted the British in India suggests the longevity and distinctiveness of their colonial rule and the complexity of the larger context within which the Portuguese maintained their Asian empire centred at Goa. That Xavier's corpse – in spite of its very real physical decay over time – not only was displayed by the Estado da Índia in 1961 but was repeatedly exposed for public view at crucial historical junctures throughout its duration (1554, 1624, 1782, 1859, 1952) reveals an investment in Catholic saint veneration to enact and represent colonial and missionary power during moments of crisis or anxiety. That the sources for this 'story' concerning this last-minute attempt to remove Xavier's corpse from Goa at its moment of decolonization are not found solely in government archives illuminates the value of a variety of source materials less bounded by the state to access the changing character of Portuguese colonialism in India. Lastly, that this last colonial display in 1961 reflects all of these historical processes highlights the potential of using the repeated ritualization of Xavier's corpse as a window on to the Portuguese colonial state and Jesuit missionary processes over a four-hundred-year period.

This book takes the idea of a 'relic state' – as a material condition and discursive formation that is applicable to both São Francisco Xavier and the Estado da Índia, which changes over time, and is evidenced in ritual – as its starting point. I set up this conceptual framework in order to suggest a relationship between the figure of a saint and that of a colonial state, one where a story of mutation is echoed in both sites, and where death (of a saint) is used to revitalize life (of a state) through repeated display. Here the architecture of ritual gets folded into many forms of governmentality, religiosity, spirituality, and affect at different historical moments to suit differing agendas, collective and individual. In the following sections I lay out some of the general contours of this historical anthropology project; they in turn will illuminate some of the principal theoretical and methodological concerns and interventions underpinning this body of work.

Colonial and postcolonial studies: 'provincializing' Portugal

One of the most compelling questions about the Portuguese Empire in India is not why it died out when it did, but rather how it endured as long as it did. Combining historical and anthropological approaches to studying the (colonial) state allows me to delve into this set of complex issues, as well as to participate in the larger postcolonial project of 'provincializing' Portugal (Europe).[2] Also, this book brings the Portuguese into the sightlines of colonial historiographies of South Asia in more vivid and yet unsettling ways. First, rather than view the Portuguese in Goa as simply a story of imperial decline, I look at its obverse, as one of survival and dynamism.[3] Thus, one of the intentions of this book is to trace the changing character of Portuguese statehood through the figure of Xavier, suggesting that it was its adaptability to dramatically different circumstances that allowed it to evolve over

Figure 2 Souvenir of the Exposition of St Francis Xavier, Goa, 1952

a four-hundred-and-fifty-year period. I conceptualize the Estado da Índia as five distinct entities at five different historical moments or 'clusters',[4] drawing upon a corpus of source materials to develop a series of general characterizations of colonial governmentality, which in turn help to contextualize each set of ritual practices. I suggest that in 1554 the burgeoning Portuguese colonial state largely functioned as a tenuous system of networks – a string of colonial outposts in Asia –whereas by 1624 it had reached the pinnacle of its success – Goa Dourada (Golden Goa) – and was just beginning to show signs of its fading glory, not least in response to the entrance of other colonial powers on to the India scene. In 1782 the Estado da Índia was closely linked to changes in the metropole owing to its increasingly involuted character. By 1859, the Portuguese colonial state was fast becoming a 'client state' of the British, its survival largely dependent on unofficial commerce. In 1952 the Estado da Índia was operating as an 'overseas province' of Portugal in the midst of an independent Indian nation-state. Finally, in 1961, Xavier was a potent symbol of power and endurance in the midst of an Indian nation-state bent on liberating itself from the last of its colonial vestiges; hence the Portuguese investment in holding on to him. This book harnesses the biography of a saint to simultaneously tell the biography of a (colonial) state.

Anthropological approaches to studying the state have suggested that, conceptually, it is both an illusory object of study and a set of concrete institutions; it is simultaneously personalized and impersonal, distant and localized, orderly and disordered, and in a continuous process of construction.[5] Thus, to understand state processes, according to the anthropologists Thomas Hansen and Finn Stepputat, requires one to 'study how the state tries to make itself real and tangible through symbols, texts, and iconography, but also that one move beyond the state's own prose, categories, and perspective and study how the state appears in everyday and localized forms'.[6] My contribution to this expanding area of postcolonial studies that examines the state (and the archive it produces) from an 'ethnographic' perspective is to examine Portuguese colonial and missionary practices and institutions as they are manifest in the localized form of ritual activity at five different historical moments.[7] The story of how Xavier's corpse is managed, handled and displayed across five centuries tells us much about the changing character of the colonial state in charge of overseeing these ritual processes.

My exclusive focus on Xavier allows me to problematize the categories of 'church' and 'state' as well as explore the overlapping ideologies of conquest and conversion,[8] since, in his role as a missionary, Goa's patron saint acted as an agent of both at the local level. In Portuguese

India, within the space of ritual, the church is represented at various moments by multiple institutions (the Archdiocese, the Vatican, the Padroado, the Propaganda, the Inquisition, etc.) and religious orders (the Jesuits, Franciscans, Augustinians, Oratorians, etc.), operating individually and jointly.[9] Neither do these church organizations function harmoniously, for, as my analysis will show, there were always tensions between and among organizations and individuals. Nor do these church organs operate neatly within the boundaries of colonial states and nation-states; rather, linguistic and cultural differences are often blurred, adding yet another layer of complexity to our understanding of the 'church' in Portuguese India over the *longue durée*. Meanwhile, the state is represented through kings and queens, viceroys and governor generals – the personality of each no doubt shaping the kind of power he or she wields – and colonial state organizations (the senate, high court, etc.).[10] I both trace governmental changes in Portugal (monarchy, republicanism, dictatorship) and explore 'tensions of empire' between metropole (Portugal) and colony (Goa) as well as between additional colonial powers operating in India (British, Dutch, and French).[11] I look more closely at what was happening in the larger Indian and European contexts at the same time that Xavier's corpse was being put on display in Goa. Highlighting the histories of these various relationships not only indicates the intricacies of the 'state' as it operated in Portuguese India over five centuries – including the impact these other colonial governmentalities had on the changing shape of the Estado da Índia – but, most importantly, reveals how the Estado da Índia adapted to shifting contexts as a means for change and continuity.

I also explore, through the spectacle of Xavier, the multiple ways that 'church' and 'state' structure and are structured by one another over time. That is, for each ritual moment, I explore the imbrication of Jesuit missionary and Portuguese colonial processes. I suggest that in 1554 the Jesuits operated under the umbrella of a burgeoning colonial state. At the same time that both missionaries and colonial officials were carving out their respective roles and relationships, the Jesuits in particular harnessed Xavier's death to their missionary cause – whereas by 1624 the Jesuits and the Estado da Índia were jointly involved in implementing certain colonial and missionary practices such that Xavier's canonization reflected the successes of both. At the same time, Portugal was subsumed under the Spanish Crown (1580–1640), which, in turn, caused internal tensions, including between Portuguese and Spanish Jesuits operating from Goa. By 1782, the Portuguese monarchy, under the guidance of the Marquis de Pombal, had instigated liberal reforms in an effort to curb church power. First on his agenda had been the expulsion of the Jesuits (1759), a religious order whose monetary worth and power in Goa exceeded that of the Estado da Índia. By 1859 the Jesuits had been allowed to return to India, but were slow to return to the site of Xavier's corpse under a period of Portuguese constitutionalism. The year 1952 witnessed the full integration of the Jesuits in Goa under the Salazar dictatorship, a regime taking Catholicism under its wing in order to promote the uniqueness of Goa's Catholic Portuguese 'culture' in the face of impending decolonization.

Lastly, this book opens up a space to understand the distinct global nature of Portuguese imperialism. It is through the figure and corpse of Xavier that I am able to reveal Goa's crucial role, starting as early as the sixteenth century and continuing up until the end of Portuguese colonial rule in the mid-twentieth century, as a centre and stopping-off point for a variety of colonial officials, missionaries, and travellers from a variety of backgrounds, many of whom witnessed Xavier's ritualization at different historical moments before returning to Europe or other (Portuguese) colonial outposts. Not only was Portuguese India intimately linked to other colonial and missionary projects throughout its duration, both within and outside South Asia (Cochin, Daman, Diu, Sri Lanka, Sancian, Malacca, Macao, Brazil, Mozambique, and Angola), but comparison was central to colonial knowledge production in Goa. I show the ways in which other forms of colonialism (predominantly British, but also Dutch and French) in India indelibly shaped the uniquely Portuguese colonial experience for both colonizer and colonized.

Indo-Portuguese studies: 'problematizing' India

Both despite and because of the particular history and historiography of British colonialism in South Asia, the history of the Portuguese Empire has received far less scholarly attention, particularly outside the field of maritime (Indian Ocean) studies. The Estado da Índia has been largely characterized as an early modern phenomenon, such that after the British ascendancy on Indian soil starting in the eighteenth century the Portuguese are either largely left out of the historical narrative on India or are studied in isolation, even as they are importantly marked by 'difference'.[12] Thus, by focusing on the marginalized Portuguese case prior to, during, and after the period of British colonial rule, I problematize the category of 'India' by showing its historical complexity as a 'notion' and 'nation'.[13]

This study makes both a contribution and an intervention in the growing field of Indo-Portuguese studies, building on the foundations laid by numerous historians, but also moving the field in different directions by infusing historical analysis with an anthropological perspective. While it was a British historian – Charles Boxer – who was at the forefront in documenting the history of the Estado da Índia, he also set it up conceptually as a 'seaborne' empire (fifteenth to seventeenth century), which, in turn, indirectly resulted in the relative isolation of the Portuguese within a separate field of maritime studies.[14] While I suggest that an emphasis on trade was the first step in understanding the role of the Portuguese in India, it simultaneously constrained this field of study early on by setting up the Portuguese investment in India as operating in contradistinction to the British Empire, which was conceptualized as a 'land-based' empire (eighteenth to twentieth century).[15] This conceptual gap led to the increasing separation of these two areas of study, when in fact their histories (and historiographies) are far from disparate.

While Indo-Portuguese studies has never completely moved away from this enduring legacy, several historians have called for a more land-based approach to viewing Portuguese statehood in India, one that looks beyond Portugal's role in shaping trade routes in the Indian Ocean.[16] A group of historians writing in the 1980s to the 1990s started to fill in this gap, demonstrating that the Estado da Índia had a profound impact on Goan society at both the macro and micro levels of politics, economics, culture, and religion up until its demise in the twentieth century, and which endures in the postcolonial phase.[17]

This study continues this historiographical trend, demonstrating that to understand the role of the Portuguese one must examine the complex issue of territoriality – which, again, I address by way of an anthropological focus on ritual as actively involved in the production of the 'local' – in order to expand our view of the Estado da Índia as operating not in isolation but rather as connected to India's larger history.[18] Adopting a wider historical lens allows us to see that by 1554 the Portuguese were engaged in negotiations with several Indian dynasties (Bijapur, Vijayanagar, Mughal), whereas in 1624 they were protecting Goa from the colonial incursions of the Dutch in particular, but also the British and French. By 1782 not only had the Society of Jesus become an enemy of the state but both the Marathas and Tipu Sultan had repeatedly threatened the Estado da Índia. In 1859 the Portuguese had to prevent the British from turning Goa into a dependency even as they had occupied it earlier (1799–1813) to stave off a French Napoleonic invasion. By 1952 Salazar was forced to defend Portugal's colonial position in Goa against a post-Partition Indian government and a growing Goan independence movement with close ties to Bombay. The book not only traces the history of these contentious relationships as they are evidenced in the space of ritual, but offers an alternative perspective on the changing character of Portuguese statehood by documenting the transformation of Xavier into a *spiritual* leader that the Estado da Índia repeatedly relied on to intervene in territorial crises involving these different enemies of state. This viewpoint, in turn, offers a different understanding of the tenacity of the Estado da Índia over a four-hundred-and-fifty-year period.

A group of historians of the Catholic church in Goa have contributed important studies that help us to realize the impact that missionaries have had on religious, cultural, and linguistic practices at the local level, suggesting that things both stayed the same and were very much transformed.[19] However, few studies have dealt with the complex relationship of missionaries to the colonial state, a gap evidenced at an 'Indo-Portuguese History' conference that I attended during fieldwork in Goa in 1999,[20] and an area that surprisingly, more than ten years later, still remains a lacuna. This book makes an intervention in this area by examining the history and role of the Society of Jesus as operating under the umbrella of the Estado da Índia and as manifest in the space of ritual. I follow their rise in power (1554) through their apogee (1624), expulsion (1782), and quiet return to India (1859) and then Goa (1952). Thus, by adopting a wider framework – one that traces the history of the Jesuits through state processes and vice versa – I bridge the gap between conquest and conversion at a historiographical level in the hopes of opening up a dialogue between historians of Portuguese colonialism and historians of the Catholic church in India.

The anthropologist Rosa Maria Perez has argued recently (2012) that for Goa 'the work that still needs to be done is the analysis of colonial society, which was far more stratified and complex than we like to assume, and some members of which were given limited access to certain privileges which were denied to others, just as it happened with the colonized'.[21] An emergent and emerging group of scholars working on Indo-Portuguese history and culture have taken seriously Perez's call and contributed an exciting array of rich studies, those focused on new topics such as print cultures or the history of medicine in colonial Goa as well as those focused on re-examining specific time frames in light of particular themes such as corruption.[22] Thus, while I am very much indebted to this new scholarship, I also move the discussion in a different direction. I offer a combined anthropological and historical breadth not found in the extant literature. I also gesture towards something distinct in that my focus on the *longue durée* of Portuguese colonialism in India and through the constant of Xavier's corpse and ritualization suggests a carryover from the colonial to the postcolonial that is perhaps less surprising but significant, showing a continuity of both periods in turn. This returns us to a land-based discussion of Goan history (as opposed to the more familiar recourse to the maritime model) and deepens our understanding of Goa today. This is one of the key interventions of this body of work.

Ritual studies: implementing 'practice'

Anthropological approaches to the study of ritual, all indebted to the legacies of Emile Durkheim and Max Weber,[23] have emphasized different aspects of what has increasingly become labelled an 'overdetermined' concept.[24] Ritual has been analysed as a site for social bonding – 'communitas' – as well as for the assertion of power and acts of resistance.[25] Ritual also involves the exchange of words and things, and is a central site for acts of communication and symbolism, for the harnessing of technologies, and for exhibiting the 'hazards' of representation.[26] Additional approaches have showcased the human body as a site for multiple levels of ritual activity.[27] Very often embedded in studies of ritual are larger theories of how society changes or stays the same, and how society maintains or resists authority.

One of the aims of this book is to infuse ritual analysis with a sense of history, power, and agency by exploring both the cultivation of political and religious order through the process of ritualization[28] and the mutability of ritual activity such that the decaying corpse of a missionary-turned-saint remains its centrepiece over a four-hundred-year period. The manner by which he (or it) is exposed by church and state as a form of colonial control dramatically also shifts in correspondence with the larger historical context surrounding him, including the role of a changing attendant public in altering the form and content of ritual. For each of the five moments of display that comprise this study, I pay close attention to the various types of ritual practices that take place at the site of Xavier's body (colonial vernaculars so to speak), including the political, economic, and religious motivations underlying the staging of each of these events. I document the transformation of Xavier's ritualization from a small-scale Catholic religious feast day celebration organized by Jesuit missionaries (1554) into an elaborate canonization celebration organized jointly by church and state (1624), and, finally, into a series of large-scale state expositions organized by colonial officials that take place at regular centenary intervals (1782, 1859, 1952), culminating in the last-minute staged exposition of 1961. Here the display of Xavier's corpse acts a representational playing field for the multiple sites of contestation within the colonial and missionary governance of Goa. Each moment of display also shows the many hybrid forms that Xavier's body must occupy to fit ritual, and in turn, how such hybrid forms infect ritualization each and every time. Here we must remember how much ritual potentially stands for in these expressive scenes of presentation.

I also use ritual as my central focus to make a case for understanding the often-overlooked messianic component of Portuguese colonialism that was the byproduct of involution, and functioned ideologically as a coping method, the spiritual counter-balancing the material.[29] At the same time that Portuguese colonial officials and Jesuit missionaries looked to Xavier, turning him into an effective religious figurehead and political agent through his repeated ritualization, they increasingly chose to defend their empire centred at Goa in terms of its spiritual value, looking for their salvation (and thus continued material investment) in the continued 'miraculousness' of Xavier in death. Here interestingly, ritual gets dislodged from its typical non-Western form and emplaced within a longer and fascinating story of colonial and missionary messianism. The chronological ordering of the multiple ritual moments is also key to understanding the changing ideological form of messianism that the Estado da Índia increasingly adopts and adapts over time.

My particular approach to the study of ritual is through the lens of 'practice'.[30] Examining ritual through the lens of practice does not exclude other ways of understanding ritualized activity; instead, ritual appears as a process rather than an objective achievement, at the same time offering insight into formations and techniques of colonial and missionary rule. 'Practice' also focuses our attention on the repetitive authorization of ritual, rather than on an imagined moment of stable authority. This is a crucial point for exploring the multiple displays of Xavier's corpse both as separate ritual events and as imbricated historical processes wherein the colonial state increasingly relies on Xavier to legitimate its own rule, the increased frequency of Xavier's public exposures over time only reinforcing this point. This same perspective exposes the strengths and vulnerabilities of church and state in the very act of setting up this saint's multiple expositions. The idea of practice also allows us to recognize that ritual performs on two levels: it simultaneously acts as a site for politics – a 'dense transfer point of power' in the words of Foucault[31] – and the symbolization of power.[32] Not only does Xavier's ritualization serve as a site for actual struggles between members of church, state, and public, but this saint ideally represents the power of church and state – jointly and separately – to its colonial subjects. Practice allows us to get at the production of the 'local' through Xavier's displays – specifically, the ways in which ritual makes the local less ephemeral by producing, maintaining and representing its materiality and discursivity, as well as extending it beyond the time and space of ritual itself.

Lastly, in the way that practice focuses our attention on ritual as a process, it is important to recognize the constituting role of the 'publics' (and counter-publics) in setting the limits of ritual activity,[33] and by extension colonial and missionary authority. Church and state officials may sanction the boundaries of the public (based on categories such as religion, nationality, gender, caste, class) that is allowed to attend Xavier's ritualization, but it is this same public that defines the success and failure of a particular set of ritual practices by their participation, actions, and engagement with this saint-in-the-making.[34] I record the transformation of the public that attends Xavier's ritualizations over a four-hundred-year period from a largely Catholic Portuguese one to a more diverse one which includes pilgrims (Catholic, Hindu, and Muslim) as well as male and female participants (including children), and, finally, to a diverse international secular public (Portuguese, Goan, European, Indian, African) that is in attendance.

I also track the changing composition of the public that attends Xavier's expositions by way of looking at the presence (and marked absence) of miracles of healing and conversions to Catholicism at these different ritual moments. Examining who experiences them, and when, reveals yet another layer of the public's increasing diversity. It is members of this same public who witness and produce written accounts of Xavier's ritualization, which in turn are circulated among an ever-widening reading and listening public (Jesuit, Portuguese, Papal, Catholic, Hindu, Goan, Indian, European, African, etc.) and which also contribute to the ritual process long after the event is over. It is at these various levels of understanding that ritual practice is one of the key analytics employed throughout this study.

I look for moments of both 'continuity' and 'rupture' within the space of ritual. At one level, the book showcases the repeated harnessing of Xavier's corpse as ritual's centrepiece at five distinct moments (1554, 1624, 1782, 1859, 1952). To this end, I examine closely the set of practices that comprise each ritual event, suggesting that many of them are carried over from one display to another, their signification sometimes assured and even empowered in the act of repetition. At another level, I show how new practices continue to be incorporated within the space of ritual, evidencing an alteration in Xavier's miraculous powers, the changing historical context, and the shifting agendas of church, state, and public. Sometimes the new context is so dramatically different that the signification of an older ritual practice is transformed in the process of being enacted at a later moment. Thus, by setting up each ritual moment in comparison to the ones that preceded it as well as indexing the next set of ritual practices, I am able to trace aspects of stability and change not only in ritual activity but also more importantly in colonial and missionary practices.

I view the space of ritual as simultaneously a practical and a discursive field.[35] At the same time that I chart Xavier's ritualization at a macro level, each chapter also pays attention to the micro details of the five sets of ritual practices. Focusing on the finer points of ritual allows me to capture the richness and distinctiveness of each public display of Xavier's corpse as it was organized, witnessed, and recorded at a particular moment and is imbricated in the institutions and structures of everyday life under Portuguese colonial rule. I first attend to the 'balance' of church and state[36] evidenced in ritual activity, bringing in the larger political, economic, and religious context in order to situate it as a 'historical event' accessible through a unique set of archival sources that are produced out of and indexical of that period, wherein certain colonial and missionary actors take on specified roles and organize certain ritual practices.

Next I develop a discourse that is being produced and circulated in conjunction with each of Xavier's ritualizations, a discourse that over time is increasingly detached from the physical condition of his corpse as its decomposition becomes increasingly more visible to Jesuit missionaries, colonial officials, and members of Goa's public alike. Each discourse – *incorruption* (1554), *canonization* (1624), *secularization* (1782), *resurrection* (1859), and *commemoration* (1952) – not only reveals the image of Xavier that is being (ideally) represented in the act of his public display but intimates the materialities and motivations of church and state undergirding ritual activity at that particular historical moment, and exposes the different types of 'miraculous' powers (religious, political, spiritual) assigned to Xavier in the space of ritual. This set of discourses is employed as an overarching structure for the organization (and titles) of the individual chapters. In 1554, Xavier's powers are rooted in the physicality of his 'incorrupt' corpse; by 1624, his saintly powers (following his canonization) have already shifted to his travelling body parts as relics; in 1782, his powers are no longer manifest in his corporeality, but rather through more secular titles, vestments, and his baton of command; in 1859 his waning miraculous powers have been resurrected, spreading by contagion from Xavier to other colonial bodies, animate and inanimate. Finally, by 1952 Xavier's powers are no longer rooted in his corpse – the miracle declared 'over' – but in (commemorating) his biography and memory. In this book, I trace the physical presence of a person and corpse to the memory of that same person and corpse.

Lastly, I access each of Xavier's five public displays through the eyes of at least one witness, these testimonies affording us the opportunity to view ritual as simultaneously an 'ethnographic act': in his ability to enter the world of ritual activity and record his impressions on paper, each eyewitness provides us with an invaluable and extremely rich account of a unique set of ritual practices. These attentive details in turn reveal the intricacies of colonial and missionary processes and practices at a particular moment in time.[37] First, he (always a 'he' unfortunately in these cases) typically reveals the various accoutrements associated with each event surrounding Xavier's corpse: candles, flowers, incense, gold, silver, keys, caskets, lights, etc. Second, it is largely through the eyes of our witness that I am able to access the composition of the increasingly diverse public (Catholic, Hindu, Portuguese, Indo-Portuguese, Goan, Indian, international) that attends the festivities surrounding Xavier, and that increasingly sets the limits of ritual activity and, by extension, colonial and missionary power. Third, he tends to reveal to us the kinds of devotional, and/or religious practices that members of the public engage in – for example, touching, kissing, crying, relic worship, healings, and conversions to Catholicism – practices sometimes but not always sanctioned by church and state officials that take place at the feet of Xavier's corpse during ritual activity, and which sometimes reconfigure ritual in the process.[38] In addition, our eyewitness exposes the different kinds of technologies (old and new) that are harnessed to strengthen the authority and endurance of a decaying saint (for example, the printing press, telegram, railway, photography, and radio are all employed at various historical moments). Throughout my ritual analysis, I argue that the various accoutrements, publics, devotional and religious practices, and technologies are all signs of changing times, relationships, and investments in Xavier. The ethnographic space of ritual activity also functions as a site to chart multiple (colonial) encounters, not only between colonial officers and missionary priests, but also between Catholicism and Hinduism, 'Portugueseness' and 'Goanness', differing publics and personalities, and, finally, the world as imagined and lived.[39]

One of the aims of this book is to revitalize ritual studies, suggesting that it is a powerful tool that lends itself to rich analyses that lie at the intersection of anthropology and history.[40] Precisely because one of the deepest forms of knowing is through doing, ritual helps us to get at the elusive category of 'experience' that both historians and anthropologists are invested in understanding.[41] Instead of denying its utility, realizing the (Western) genealogy of the concept 'ritual', including its epistemological underpinnings and the transformation of its meaning over time, should help us to employ it effectively in a variety of settings.[42]

Dead body politics

In viewing Xavier's corpse as a site for 'dead body politics', a term adopted from the anthropologist Katherine Verdery,[43] I am contributing to a larger body of works wholly concerned with looking at the ways in which illustrious figures of history have been immortalized in death, the 'political lives' of their dead bodies taking on a cult force all their own.[44] At the same time, this project is distinct in its examination of a Catholic saint (as opposed to a strictly secular state figure) as simultaneously a political, religious, and spiritual leader in death, and in its historical analysis over the *longue durée*.

I chart the parallel declines of a saint and a state in order to understand the complexities and subtleties of both processes, including their points of contact. One way in which I do this is to set up a mode of relationality between saint and state, demonstrating that the changing condition of Xavier's corpse over time maps on to the changing condition of the Estado da Índia throughout the endurance of both.[45] Here I rely on an extraordinary set of medical forensic reports that were issued by colonial officials in conjunction with each of Xavier's five public displays and that document in remarkable detail (as a form of diagnosis) the actual physical condition of his corpse at five historical moments. These medical examinations record Xavier's changing physical state: incorruption (1554), amputations (1624), desiccation (1782), shrinking stature (1859), and his body in parts (1952). On the one hand, that these corporeal examinations were alternately performed by Jesuits, colonial officials, archbishops, and trained medical experts suggests that as a genre and practice these report sit at the discursive crossroads of politics, religion, and science, which, in turn, reinforces their historical and historiographical value as an unusual set of source materials. On the other, that the details of these remarkable autopsy reports reveal a history of changing (medical) techniques, terminology, and treatments surrounding a saint's corpse that is deemed less and less 'miraculous' suggests a history of changing scientific conceptions of the human body – a body that is increasingly poked and prodded over time such that only in 1952 is the medical miracle of his corpse declared to be 'over' – that is, precisely (or conveniently) when the 'end' of the Portuguese India is in sight.

Thus, in a parallel move, I argue that Xavier's corporeal state during each of his ritual displays serves as window (or mirror) on to the increasingly precarious position of the Estado da Índia at each of these same moments.[46] The continual (and almost obsessive) documentation by state officials of the changing condition of Xavier's corpse through this series of medical examinations suggests a heightened level of anxiety over this saint's corpse (including its very real physical decline), and, by (metaphoric) extension, the demise of their own colonial rule. Given the intimate ties between saint and state such that colonial officials in Goa sought their salvation in Xavier's continued 'miraculousness' as a form of messianism, it makes sense that both started to exhibit the same corporeal qualities, replicating each other throughout history. Thus, one of my central arguments is that these medical forensic reports can potentially be 'read' for their diagnostic insights into the (changing) nature of Portuguese colonial state power.

Pushing further the mode of relationality between saint and state affords the opportunity to see that in 1554 both were 'incorrupt' – that is, both colonial bodies exhibited qualities of strength and endurance. By 1624 both saint and state were suffering from 'amputations': while Xavier's right arm and internal organs had been turned into relics, the Estado da Índia was rapidly losing parts of its Asian empire (Cochin, Malacca, the Moluccas) to the Dutch. By 1782 both saint and state were 'desiccated'; at the same time that Xavier's corpse was literally drying up from the inside, the colonial state was experiencing profound internal problems. By 1859 both saint and state were 'shrinking': that is, both colonial bodies had become physically smaller in size, the former owing to the ravages of time, the latter owing to the repeated incursions of various enemies of state. Finally, in 1952, both saint and state were 'in parts': while Xavier's head was now physically severed from his torso, Goa, now considered an 'overseas province', was in the process of breaking off from Portugal's colonial hold. These corporeal details not only act as evidence of the representational labour that Xavier's corpse performs over time in the space of ritual but also suggest the forensic capabilities (and absurdities) of such brutal physical reminders and remains. As his decay became more and more visible – the natural decomposition of Xavier's corpse always constraining his ideal representation in ritual – not only to church and state but also to members of the public, those in charge (both colonial and religious officials) resort to a variety of measures to cover up the increasingly fragile conditions of saint and state in the space of ritual, including restricting access or proximity to Xavier's corpse during his days of public display. This fascinating (hi)story of corporeal management – one where Xavier is regally dressed, propped up, and encased in glass – is equally one of mismanagement: one where Xavier's body is poorly placed, temporarily lost, hidden from view, or frequently neglected. Lastly, to suggest that Xavier's corpse operates by way of relationality is to reinforce the point that Goa's fate was increasingly intertwined with Xavier's in the face of both their physical declines. In other words, this book tells the remarkable story of a decomposing saint and state over a four-hundred-year period.

Another way in which I chart the parallel declines of a saint and a state, including their points of contact, is to explore the metonymic quality of Xavier's corpse. On one level, his relics always stand in for his personhood and corpse: in the process of being transferred to various sites (in Europe, India, and Asia), they imbue their new locations with his 'saintly' and 'miraculous' powers. On another level, Xavier's corpse (including his many relics) represents the entire Portuguese empire in Asia. I trace the multiple histories of Xavier's various body parts and personal effects as they travelled to other metropolitan, colonial, and missionary sites over a five-hundred-year period, in the process revealing yet another layer of the story of a dynamic Portuguese empire that increasingly turns to the 'spiritual' to authorize its own colonial rule. Xaverian relics and realia (including pieces of skin, vestments, and objects he touched in life) were often sent to those sites where Portuguese colonial governmentality was fading in the hopes of improving the position of the Society of Jesus or the Estado da Índia (or both), or gifted to important visiting dignitaries in the hopes of renewing and/or maintaining political and economic ties. As the 'miraculous' powers of Xavier (as they were rooted in the corpse itself) steadily diminished over time, they were increasingly transferred to other colonial bodies – Portuguese and native, Catholic and Hindu – as well as to commodities – souvenirs such as stamps, images, miniatures, and reliquaries[47] – in the space of ritual, which, by way of their direct contact with Xavier's corpse, allowed them to metonymically index the power of saint and state, long after ritual activity was over.

Lastly, this book explores how Catholic saint veneration comes to operate within a colonial context, in particular over an extended period of time.[48] As a religious practice rooted in early Christianity, one that became increasingly less popular in Europe after the twelfth century, when image devotion steadily began to take over relic worship,[49] I trace the manner by which it was adopted and adapted to accommodate the shifting agendas of the Society of Jesus and the Estado da Índia during a much later time frame (sixteenth to twentieth century). Thus, on one level, the importation of this European religious practice to Goa suggests the ability of the colonies to act as spaces where older (and often outdated) practices get revived in conjunction with new settings.[50] On another level, that the practice of Catholic saint veneration was used to simultaneously promote the power, religiosity, and spiritualism of Portuguese India, including the ability of Xavier's corpse to incite miraculous healings and conversions to Catholicism, suggests the manner by which the space of ritual acts as a site for exploring changing perceptions of 'faith' by church, state, and public over a four-hundred-year period.[51]

Historical anthropology: historicizing ritual, anthropologizing colonialism

This book is about the relationship between a colonial state, a religious order, a saint's corpse, and a public, and the *production* of this relationship through ritual at five distinct historical moments. My perspective is one that combines historical and anthropological methods and theories, contributing to an expanding field called 'historical anthropology'[52] that is continually (re)defining itself in relation to new sets of questions, differing contexts and concepts, and changing world orders.[53] Such an interdisciplinary approach allows me to 'historicize' ritual, typically an ahistorical non-Western category in anthropology, tracing the subtleties of its transformation over four hundred years to 'anthropologize' colonialism, typically a form of rule viewed through the lens of history.

This project was shaped by and indebted to a critical engagement in an ethnography of the archives, for according to Nicholas Dirks, the archive itself very often reflects 'the forms and formations of colonial epistemology in ways that have been misrecognized by the historians and anthropologists alike'.[54] In other words, much work is still required to better understand the archive as reflecting state categories, ideologies, and practices; this book is one small contribution to this line of thought. I also employ Shahid Amin's idea of 'historical fieldwork'[55] wherein historical and ethnographic analyses are set up as mutually constituting methodologies. It was through archival research that I was able to single out the five ritual moments – in large part thanks to the availability of certain 'historical' sources and the 'ethnographic' richness of these same materials – that have become the foci for this study. The kinds of sources that I located in the archives pertaining to Xavier also helped me to formulate the kinds of ethnographic questions that I asked while conducting fieldwork. It was through knowing the colonial history of Xavier's public displays (1554–1961) that I was able to ask relevant questions of persons who knew much about Xavier, as well as trace Xaverian rumours, collect materials located outside government archives, and interview members of Goa's contemporary public, including individuals who had attended Xavier's expositions that had taken place in the second half of the twentieth century (1952, 1961, 1964, 1974, 1984, 1994), some of whom continue to be influenced by Xavier through a variety of attachments, both imaginary and real. I also looked at the ways that this saint's biography in life and death is part of Goa's (and India's) postcolonial discourse on Xavier. Exploring the nature of Xavier's role within Goa's current landscape – including the retelling of archival events in the present – tells us something about his defining role during Goa's Portuguese past, and enduring legacy. Even as my ethnographic interviews are less represented in the book, all of my conversations with Goans today made me think more carefully about how to write a history of the present.

Yet another way in which I combine history and anthropology is through my chronological ordering of Xavier's history of display, where each ritual moment is set up in relation to those preceding and following. Again, I look at each set of ritual practices as alternately a historical 'event' – traceable through archival sources – and an ethnographic 'act' – traceable through eyewitness testimonies. For each ritual moment, I rely on a set of source materials ('as primary as they are secondary' to borrow a phrase from Filipa Lowndes Vicente)[56] that are available to access the event itself. These include: Jesuit biographies (1554), European travelogues (1624), Portuguese royal decrees and private Jesuit exchanges (1782), a state-commissioned book dedicated to Xavier and his expositions (1859), and, finally, a commemorative manual centred on Xavier (1952). I discuss each set of source materials as a genre with certain conventions and particular histories of invention, but I explore the production of a certain type of source material as a distinct social practice that is indexical of the time period in which it was produced. Not only do these sources access ritual activity but they tell us, by the nature of the type of source material available for each event, about the kinds of Xaverian investments made by members of the Society of Jesus and the Estado da Índia at that particular historical moment, particularly the balance of church and state ideologies and practices.[57] In addition, the shift in type of source materials is also suggestive of other kinds of historical shifts – political, economic, and religious. Finally, each chapter reflects the different tenors and vocabularies of the various archival sources I employ and stage in conversation at five distinct historical moments. In other words, I constantly 'read' my archival sources through an ethnographic lens, as cultural productions with their own systems of thought and representation.[58]

For each set of displays, I locate at the very least one eyewitness account. These testimonies afford us a window on to the elaborateness of ritual activity, with its many 'ethnographic' details recorded for a multi-tiered (seeing, reading, and listening) public. In 1554 I rely on the accounts of several different Portuguese Jesuit biographers of Xavier; in 1624 it is two European travellers, one a visiting (Portuguese) Jesuit, the other an Italian nobleman; in 1782 it is a visiting Superior of the Oratorians, the congregation of secular clergymen put in charge of managing the Church of Bom Jesus after the expulsion of the Jesuits from Goa in 1759; in 1859 it is a Papal-appointed Vicar Apostolic and returning Jesuit from Bombay; and, lastly, in 1952, I rely on the accounts of numerous international journalists who were specially invited to attend the festivities surrounding Goa's patron saint. Not only does each eyewitness record and represent ritual activity for a larger audience but the type of witness at each event sheds light on the form of ritual itself as well as how church and state wanted Xavier's ritualization to be (ideally) represented and for whom, at a specific moment in time. Finally, that the witness is increasingly over time an 'outsider' to Goan colonial society suggests both the slow transformation of Xavier's ritualization from a local to a global phenomenon and a concomitant expanding and diverse public.

For this kind of project – one that covers a four-hundred-year period – I have had to write a limited history. For each chapter of the book I rely largely on additional secondary sources to give an 'impulse' for each ritual moment, which in turn supplements our understanding of each of Xavier's five public displays as simultaneously a historical event and an ethnographic act. The issue of context – how much is enough, how much is too much – is a complex one for studies such as this one that bridge the gap between history and anthropology. However, what I have attempted for each chapter is to provide a sketch of Goa's changing political and economic landscape, enough to give the reader a sense of how each set of ritual practices is embedded in a larger set of ideologies and practices, including discussions of specific institutions that are directly related to ritual activity. I also engage to a limited extent in debates of historiography and expand the body of materials under analysis to include hagiographical sources. At another level, I view my study as an episodic history: it is about different moments or eras wherein each set of rituals echoes and is echoed in the other rituals; that is, instead of interrupting one another, they illuminate each other.

Lastly, I contribute to the field of historical anthropology by suggesting that Xavier's corpse operates as an archive in two senses.[59] First, his corpse is a literal archive in the way that it is marked physically; the details of his damages, amputations, relic productions, and general decay both identify and authenticate him as well as reveal the incredible story of a saint's deification in death. Second, Xavier's corpse operates at the centre of an archive around which a corpus of materials was produced, circulated, and organized by members of the Society of Jesus and the Estado da Índia.[60] Out of the repeated ritualization of his corpse was fashioned a series of discrete events and a distinct body of historical (and hagiographical) sources documenting and preserving these same events. Thus, it is through treating Xavier's image and corpse as a historical object worthy of critical analysis,[61] and as revealing the changing nature of Portuguese colonial state and Jesuit missionary formations, that I am able to create a distinctly Xaverian archives, in the process telling the story of the intimate ties between a state and a saint over five centuries.

Notes

All translations from Portuguese and Spanish are mine unless otherwise noted.

1 *The Oxford American Desk Dictionary and Thesaurus*, 2nd edn (New York: Berkeley Books, 2001), p. 705.

2 Dipesh Chakrabarty, 'Postcoloniality and the Artifice of History: Who Speaks for "Indian" Pasts?' *Representations*, No. 37 (Winter 1992), p. 21.

3 The idea of 'decline' is much disputed within Indo-Portuguese historiography. See Sanjay Subrahmanyam and Luís Félipe Thomaz, 'Evolution of Empire: The Portuguese in the Indian Ocean during the Sixteenth Century', in *The Political Economy of Merchant Empires*, James Tracy, ed. (New York: Cambridge University Press, 1991); Luís Félipe Thomaz, *De Cueta a Timor* (Lisboa: Difel, 1994); Glenn Ames, *Renascent Empire? The House of Braganza and the Quest for Stability in Portuguese Monsoon Asia, c.1640–1683* (Amsterdam: University of Amsterdam Press, 2000); Yi Liu, 'Clergy, Nobility and Crown in Decadência' *História* [online] (2005), Volume 24, No. 1: 167–90; Karen Barkey makes a compelling case for the Ottomans, suggesting that a focus on decline obscures the way the state adapts and adjusts over time. See her *Empire of Difference: The Ottomans in Comparative Example* (Cambridge: Cambridge University Press, 2008).

4 Following the historian Walter Mignolo, rather than write about a lineal succession of periods, it is helpful to think in terms of the co-existence of historical 'clusters', which in turns involves emphasizing the 'darker' aspects of a particular moment or era. See his *The Darker Side of the Renaissance: Literacy, Territoriality, and Colonization* (Ann Arbor, MI: University of Michigan Press, 1995), pp. 3–5.

5 Thomas Hansen and Finn Stepputat (eds), 'Introduction', to *States of Imagination: Ethnographic Explorations of the Postcolonial State* (Durham, NC: Duke University Press, 2001), pp. 1–38.

6 Ibid., p. 5.

7 Arjun Appadurai, *Modernity at Large: Cultural Dimensions of Globalization* (Minneapolis: University of Minnesota Press, 1996), pp. 180–1. Appadurai suggests that we cannot take the production of a locality as ephemeral; rather, it requires regular and hard work; specific activities such as ritual help to produce and maintain a place's materiality and discursivity as well localize its duration and extension.

8 It is important to recognize the ideological inseparability of church and state specific to the Portuguese 'civilizing process'. Here it is useful to take Vicente Rafael's point that 'Catholicism provided Spain's colonial enterprise with its ideological frame; it also embedded the structure of colonial rule within the practice of religious conversion' and apply it to the Portuguese case. See his *Contracting Colonialism: Translation and Christian Conversion in Tagalog Society Under Early Spanish Rule* (Durham, NC: Duke University Press, 1993), p. 17.

9 See Georg Schurhammer, S.J., *Francis Xavier: His Life, His Times*, tr. M. Joseph Costelloe, Volumes I–IV (Roma: The Jesuit Historical Institute, 1977); A. Mathias Mundadan, *History of Christianity in India*, Volume 1 (Bangalore: Theological Publications in India, 1983); Stephen Neill, *A History of Christianity in India, the*

Beginnings to AD 1707 (Cambridge: Cambridge University Press, 1984).

10 See António Manuel Hespanha, *As Vésperas do Leviathan* (Lisboa: Almedina, 1994); Catarina Madeira Santos, *Goa É A Chave de Toda a Índia Perfil Político da Capital do Estado Da Índia* (Lisboa: Comissão Nacional para as Comemorações dos Descobrimentos Portugueses, 1999).

11 Ann Stoler and Fred Cooper (eds), *Tensions of Empire* (Berkeley: University of California Press, 1997).

12 See Boaventura de Sousa Santos, 'Between Prospero and Caliban: Colonialism, Post-colonialism, and Inter-Identity', *Luso-Brazilian Review*, Volume 39, No. 2, Special Issue, *Portuguese Cultural Studies* (Winter 2002), pp. 9–43; Luís Madureira, 'Tropical Sex Fantasies and the Ambassador's Other Death: The Difference in Portuguese Colonialism', *Cultural Critique*, No. 28 (Autumn 1994), pp. 149–73.

13 The Portuguese often get left out of the historical narrative of colonial and postcolonial India precisely because current-day nationalisms dictate our subjects of history. Thus, 'Goa' as a subject of history problematizes the very foundation upon which the postcolonial Indian nation-state was built, and provides an alternative and complementary history of (colonial) India to that of the British colonizing experience.

14 Charles Boxer, *The Portuguese Seaborne Empire, 1415–1825* (New York: Alfred Knopf, 1969); Niels Steensgard, *The Asian Trade Revolution of the Seventeenth Century: The East India Companies and the Decline of the Caravan Trade* (Chicago: University of Chicago Press, 1974); K.N. Chaudhuri, *Trade and Civilization in the Indian Ocean* (New York: Cambridge University Press, 1985); Ashin Das Gupta and M.N. Pearson (eds), *India and the Indian Ocean: 1500–1800* (Calcutta: Oxford University Press, 1987); M.N. Pearson, *The Portuguese in India*, Volume 1(The *New Cambridge History of India Series*) (Cambridge: Cambridge University Press, 1987); Celsa Pinto, *Trade and Finance in Portuguese India: A Study of the Portuguese Country Trade, 1770–1840* (New Delhi: Concept Publishing Company, 1994).

15 See B.H. Baden-Powell, *The Land Systems of British India*, 3 Volumes (Oxford: Clarendon Press, 1892); Eric Stokes, *The English Utilitarians and India* (Oxford: Oxford University Press, 1959); Ranajit Guha, *A Rule of Property for Bengal* (Durham, NC: Duke University Press, 1966); R. Frykenburg (ed.), *Land Control and Social Structure in Indian Society* (Madison: University of Wisconsin Press, 1969); Burton Stein, *The Making of Agrarian Policy in British India, 1770–1900* (Delhi: Oxford University Press, 1992); Bernard Cohn, *Colonialism and Its Forms of Knowledge* (Princeton: Princeton University Press, 1996); Nicholas B. Dirks, *The Hollow Crown: Ethnohistory of an Indian Kingdom*, 2nd edn (Ann Arbor, MI: University of Michigan Press, 1993).

16 Anthony Disney, 'The Portuguese Empire in India, 1550–1650, Some Suggestions for a Less Seaborne, More Landbound Approach to Its Socio-Economic History', in *Indo-Portuguese History, Sources and Problems*, J. Correia-Afonso, ed. (Delhi: Oxford University Press, 1991); M.N. Pearson (ed.), *Coastal Western India* (New Delhi: Concept Publishing Company, 1981).

17 See B.S. Shastry (ed.), *Goan Society Through the Ages* (New Delhi: Asian Publication Series, 1987); Teotónio de Souza (ed.), *Goa Through the Ages Volume II. An Economic History* (New Delhi: Concept Publishing Company, 1987); Teotónio de Souza (ed.), *Essays in Goan History* (New Delhi: Concept Publishing Company, 1989); B.S. Shastry (ed.), *Socioeconomic Aspects of Portuguese Colonialism in Goa: 19th and 20th Century* (Belgaum: Yarball Offset Printers, 1990); P.P. Shirodkar (ed.), *Goa: Cultural Trends* (Panaji: Casa Packmaster, 1998); Pratima Kamat, *Farar Far: Local Resistance to Colonial Hegemony in Goa, 1510–1912* (Panaji, Goa: Institute Menezes Bragança, 1999).

18 The historian Sanjay Subrahmanyam has been at the forefront of 'indigenizing' maritime studies by exposing the role of the Portuguese in relation to pre-existing Indian trade networks. See his 'Commerce and State Power in Eighteenth Century India: Some Reflections', *South Asia Research*, Volume 8, No. 2 (1988); *Improvising Empire, Portuguese Trade and Settlement in the Bay of Bengal, 1500–1700*

(Delhi: Oxford University Press, 1990); *The Portuguese Empire in Asia, 1500–1700* (New York: Longman Publishing, 1993); *The Career and Legend of Vasco da Gama* (Cambridge: Cambridge University Press, 1997); (ed.), *Sinners and Saints: The Successors of Vasco da Gama* (Delhi: Oxford University Press, 1998); *Explorations in Connected History: Mughals and Franks* (Delhi: Oxford University Press, 2005).

19 See A.K. Priolkar, *The Goa Inquisition* (Bombay: A.K. Priolkar, 1961); Teotónio de Souza (ed.), *Jesuits in India: In Historical Perspective* (Macau: Instituto Cultural de Macau, 1992); Teotónio de Souza (ed.), *Discoveries, Missionary Expansion and Asian Cultures* (New Delhi: Concept Publishing Company, 1994); Charles Borges, *The Economics of the Goa Jesuits, 1542–1759, An Explanation of Their Rise and Fall* (New Delhi: Concept Publishing Company, 1994); Dauril Alden, *The Making of an Enterprise, The* Society of Jesus *in Portugal, Its Empire and Beyond, 1540–1750* (Stanford: Stanford University Press, 1996); Rowena Robinson, *Conversion, Continuity and Change: Lived Christianity in Southern Goa* (New Delhi: Sage Publications, 1998); Ines G. Županov, *Disputed Mission: Jesuit Experiments and Brahmanical Knowledge in Seventeenth-century India* (New Delhi: Oxford University Press, 1999); María Cristina Osswald, *Jesuit Art in Goa between 1542 and 1655: From Modo Nostro to Modo Goano* (PhD thesis, Instituto Universitário Europeu, Florence, 2003); Ananya Chakravarti, *The Empire of Apostles: Jesuits in Brazil and India* (Unpublished PhD, University of Chicago, 2012).

20 The historian Rowena Robinson made this same point during the 'Goa and Portugal: History and Development' Conference, Xavier Centre of Historical Research, Porvorim, Goa, 6–9 September 1999.

21 Rosa Maria Perez, *The Tulsi and the Cross: Anthropology and the Colonial Encounter in Goa* (New Delhi: Orient Blackswan, 2012), p. 21.

22 See, for example, Maria de Jesus Mártires Lopes, *Goa Setecentista: Tradição e Modernidade (1750–1800)* (Lisboa: Centro de Estudos dos Povos e Culturas de Expressão Portuguesa Universidade Católica Portuguesa, 1996); Timothy Coates, *Convicts and Orphans: Forced and State-Sponsored Colonizers in the Portuguese Empire, 1550–1755* (Stanford: Stanford University Press, 2001). Cristiana Bastos, 'Race, Medicine and the Late Portuguese Empire: The Role of Goan Colonial Physicians', *Journal of Romance Studies*, Volume 5, No. 1 (2005), 23–35; Rochelle Pinto, *Between Empires: Print and Politics in Goa* (Oxford: Oxford University Press, 2007); Arun Saldanha, *Psychedelic White: Goa Trance and the Viscosity of Race* (Minneapolis:University of Minnesota Press, 2007); Ângela Barreto Xavier, *A Invenção de Goa* (Lisboa: Imprensa de Ciências Sociais, 2008); Timothy Walker, 'The Early Modern Globalization of Indian Medicine: Portuguese Dissemination of Drugs and Healing Techniques from South Asia on Four Continents, 1670–1830', *Portuguese Literary and Cultural Studies*, No. 19 (2010); Claudia Pereira, 'The Gawada of Goa: A Debate on Status', *Oriente*, No. 6 (2003), pp. 74–85; Nandini Chaturvedula, *Imperial Excess: Corruption and Decadence in Portuguese India (1660–1706)* (Unpublished PhD, Columbia University, 2010); Jason Keith Fernandes, *Citizenship Experiences of the Goan Catholics* (Unpublished PhD, ISCTE–Instituto Universitário de Lisboa, 2013); Rosa Maria Perez, *The Tulsi and the Cross*. Filipa L. Vicente, *Other Orientalisms: India Between Florence and Bombay, 1860–1900* (New Delhi: Orient Blackswan, 2012).

23 Emile Durkheim, *Elementary Forms of the Religious Life* (New York: The Free Press, 1912); Max Weber, *The Sociology of Religion*, tr. Ephraim Fischoff (New York: Beacon Press, 1963 [1922]).

24 In much the same way that 'culture' has become an overdetermined concept in anthropology. See Jack Goody, 'Against Ritual: Loosely Structured Thoughts on a Loosely Defined Topic', in *Secular Ritual*, S. Moore and B. Myeroff, eds (Amsterdam: Van Gorcum and Company, 1977). Goody makes the assertion that the more we try to define it, the less we understand it.

25 See Victor Turner, *The Ritual Process: Structure and Anti-Structure* (Harmondsworth: Penguin Books, 1974); Max Gluckman, *Order and Rebellion in Tribal Africa* (London: Cohen and West, 1963); Max Gluckman, *Politics, Law and Ritual in*

Tribal Society (Oxford: Basil Blackwell, 1965); Peter Stallybrass and Allon White, *The Politics and Poetics of Transgression* (London: Methuen & Co., 1986); M.M. Bakhtin, *Rabelais and His World*, tr. H. Iswolsky (Bloomington: Indiana University Press, 1984).

26 See Stanley Tambiah, 'The Magical Power of Words', *Man*, Volume 3, No. 2 (June 1968): 175–208; Edmund Leach, *Culture and Communication* (Cambridge: Cambridge University Press, 1976); Victor Turner, *Dramas, Fields and Metaphors: Symbolic Action in Human Society* (Ithaca, NY: Cornell University Press, 1974); Michel Foucault, *Discipline and Punish: The Birth of the Prison*, tr. Alan Sheridan (New York: Vintage, 1979); David Cannadine and Simon Price (eds), *Rituals of Royality: Power and Ceremonial in Traditional Societies* (Cambridge: Cambridge University Press, 1987); Webb Keane, *Signs of Recognition, Powers and Hazards of Representation in an Indonesian Society* (Berkeley: University of California Press, 1997).

27 See Victor Turner, *Forest of Symbols: Aspects of Ndembu Ritual* (Ithaca, NY: Cornell University Press, 1967); Mary Douglas, *Natural Symbols* (New York: Random House, 1973); Michel Foucault, *Discipline and Punish*.

28 See John Pemberton, *On the Subject of 'Java'* (Ithaca, NY: Cornell University Press, 1994). I follow Pemberton in looking at Xavier's ritualizations as highly political events precisely because they are treated as and written about in patently ritualistic terms (like Java's political elections for Pemberton).

29 Here I suggest that the Estado da Índia increasingly relied on messianism as a means of salvation and explanation for their continued survival in Goa; it increasingly started to defend its empire in terms of its spiritual values, looking for its salvation in the 'miraculous' which would go along with their idea of being given a God-given right to maintain its hold in India. I suggest that Xavier was the (almost) perfect object for this focus on the 'miraculous'. See G.D. Winius, 'Millenarianism and Empire, Portuguese Asian Decline and the "Crise de Conscience" of the Missionaries', *Itinerario*, Volume XI, No. 2 (1987), pp. 37–51.

30 Pierre Bourdieu, *Outline of a Theory of Practice*, tr. Richard Nice (Cambridge: Cambridge University Press, 1977). For a practice-oriented guidebook for analysing ritual, see Catherine Bell, *Ritual Theory, Ritual Practice* (New York: Oxford University Press, 1992).

31 M. Foucault, *The Birth of the Clinic*, tr. A.M. Sheridan (New York: Vintage Books, 1994), p. xix.

32 The distinction between ritual as the symbolization of power and politics itself is an important distinction in ritual studies, and it has lent itself to more powerful analyses of ritual as altering society, not merely reflecting symbolically those continuities or disjunctures present in a given society. At the same time, the power of symbols cannot go unrecognized in the communicative aspects of ritual, that is, their efficacy in conveying sentiments, power structures, etc. See Catherine Bell, *Ritual Theory, Ritual Practice*, p. 170.

33 See Michael Warner, *Publics and Counterpublics* (New York: Zone Books, 2005); Miri Rubin, *Corpus Christi: The Eucharist in Late Medieval Culture* (New York: Cambridge University Press, 1991); Richard Trexler, *Public Life in Renaissance Florence* (Ithaca, NY: Cornell University Press, 1980); Edward Muir, *Civic Ritual in Renaissance Venice* (Princeton: Princeton University Press, 1981); Paula Sanders, *Ritual, Politics and the City in Fatimid Cairo* (Albany: SUNY Press, 1994).

34 As Foucault states, 'the exercise of power is not violence; nor is it consent which implicitly, is renewable. It is a total structure of actions brought to bear on possible actions; it incites, induces, seduces, it makes it easier or more difficult; in the extreme it constrains or forbids absolutely; it is nevertheless always a way of acting upon an acting subject or acting subjects by virtue of their acting or being capable of action. A set of actions upon other actions'. See his 'The Subject and Power', in *Michel Foucault: Beyond Structuralism and Hermeneutics*, eds Hubert L. Dreyfus and Paul Rabinow, 2nd edn (Chicago: University of Chicago Press, 1983), p. 220.

35 Nicholas B. Dirks, 'Ritual and Resistance: Subversion as Social Fact', in *Contesting*

Power: Resistance and Everyday Social Relations in South Asia, eds D. Haynes and G. Prakash (Berkeley: University of California Press, 1991).

36 I adopt the idea of exploring the shifting 'balance' of church and state from the Jesuit historian Charles Borges. See his 'Religious Orders and Estado da India in Goa: A Balancing Act', in *Goa's External Relations*, ed. P.P. Shirodkar (Panjim: Dr Wolfgang de Silva Marg, 1992), p. 29.

37 Here I take up Mary Louise Pratt's conception of 'contact zones' as spaces of colonial encounters wherein 'autoethnographic expression' takes place and which are important for 'unraveling the histories of imperial subjugation and resistance as seen from the site of their occurrence'. See her *Imperial Eyes* (London: Routledge, 1992), p. 9.

38 It is important to remember, as Vicente Rafael shows in his study of Spanish missionaries in the Philippines and the role of language (mis)translations and religious conversions, outward signs of devotion are not necessarily indicative of inner religious faith. See his *Contracting Colonialism*, pp. 136–7.

39 As Clifford Geertz suggests, the efficacy of rituals lies in the fact that it is through them that the world as lived and as imagined is fused. See his *The Interpretation of Cultures* (New York: Basic Books, 1973), pp. 112–13.

40 Here I suggest that the topic of colonial displays (in India) lies at this intersection of disciplines. See Bernard Cohn, 'Representing Authority in Victorian India', in his *An Anthropologist Among the Historians and Other Essays* (Delhi: Oxford University Press, 1987), pp. 632–79. Filipa L. Vicente is one of the few scholars looking comparatively at Portuguese and British colonial displays in India from both a historical and an ethnographic perspective. See her 'Exposições coloniais na Índia Portuguesa e na Índia Britânica (séculos XIX e XX)', *Oriente*. No. 8 (April 2004), pp. 70–88.

41 Historians such as Joan Scott have written extensively on the category of 'experience'. See her seminal piece, 'The Evidence of Experience', in *Questions of Evidence: Proof, Practice and Persuasion Across the Discipline*, eds James Chandler, Arnold Davidson, and Harry Harootunian (Chicago: University of Chicago Press, 1994). Anthropologists such as Victor Turner have dedicated themselves to understanding ritual as rooted in 'experience'. See his *The Ritual Process: Structure and Anti-Structure*. It is also important to emphasize that, following the anthropologist Talal Asad, 'we must recognize that ritual practices are disciplines taught and learned as well as created and experienced in conditions of power'. See his *Genealogies of Religion: Discipline and Reasons of Power in Christianity and Islam* (Baltimore: Johns Hopkins University Press, 1993), p. 9.

42 Following Talal Asad, it is important to recognize that the modern perspective on ritual as symbolic activity is itself historically shaped: its transformation in meaning from 'how to do something' to 'the symbolic meaning of what is done' is linked to modern Western assumptions about the self and the state. See his 'Toward a Genealogy of the Concept of Ritual', in *Genealogies of Religion*, pp. 55–79.

43 Katherine Verdery, *The Political Lives of Lives of Dead Bodies: Reburial and Post-Socialist Change* (New York: Columbia University Press, 1999), p. 3.

44 For example, the bodies of such state leaders as Eva Perón, Che Guevara, Benito Mussolini, and Lenin, among others, have endured political lives in death, all of which have been studied. For example, see Tomás Eloy Martínez, *Santa Evita*, tr. Helen Lane (Barcelona: Seix Barral, 1995); Nina Tumarkin, *Lenin Lives!: The Lenin Cult in Soviet Russia* (Cambridge, MA: Harvard University Press, 1997); John Foot, 'The Dead Duce', *History Today*, Volume 49, Issue 8 (August 1999).

45 As Catherine Bell asserts, 'it is important to recognize that the body is the foremost of all metaphors for a society's perception and organization of itself'. See her *Ritual Theory, Ritual Practice*, p. 95.

46 Following Shahid Amin, I look at a singular event, and analyse it both for its eventfulness and for its metaphorical qualities, that is, its ability to gather significance outside the time frame of the event itself. It is in this sense a 'double movement'. See his *Event, Metaphor, Memory: Chauri Chaura, 1922–1992* (Berkeley: University of California Press, 1995).

47 Susan Stewart discusses how souvenirs serve to authenticate the experience of the viewer, serving as a trace of that experience. The souvenir 'moves history into private time'. See her *On Longing, Narratives of the Miniature, the Gigantic, the Souvenir, the Collection* (Durham, NC: Duke University Press, 1993), pp. 134–8.

48 For the only example comparable with Xavier that looks at the changing image of a Christian figure across five centuries and within a colonial context, see D.A. Brading, *Mexican Phoenix, Our Lady of Guadalupe: Image and Tradition Across Five Centuries* (Cambridge: Cambridge University Press, 2001).

49 Patrick Geary, *Furta Sacra: Thefts of Relics in the Central Middle Ages* (Princeton: Princeton University Press, 1978); Peter R. Brown, *The Cult of Saints: Its Rise and Function in Latin Christianity* (Chicago: University of Chicago Press, 1981); Stephen Wilson (ed.), *Saints and Their Cults: Studies in Religious Sociology, Folklore and History* (Cambridge: Cambridge University Press, 1983).

50 As Ann Stoler and Fred Cooper suggest, this is a common trait of metropole–colony relations. See *Tensions of Empire: Colonial Cultures in a Bourgeois World*, pp. 7–11.

51 I understand 'faith' as being something that is understood less as purely religious faith, but, rather, following Talal Asad, as the product of the interplay of different epistemologies of faith. See his *Genealogies of Religion*, p. 23.

52 The field of historical anthropology is indebted to the pioneering work of Bernard Cohn. See his *An Anthropologist Among the Historians and Other Essays* (Delhi: Oxford University Press, 1987). For a set of more recent approaches to historical anthropology, see also Brian Axel (ed.), *From the Margins, Historical Anthropology and Its Futures* (Durham, NC: Duke University Press, 2002).

53 Historical anthropologists Jean and John Comaroff pose the question, how do we write an ethnography of the historical imagination? The answer lies, according to the authors, in a 'historical anthropology' that is dedicated to exploring the processes that make and transform particular worlds, that understands social life as simultaneously ordered and disorderly, and explores consciousness, representation, historical agency, social practice, domination and resistance, global and local social orders, and, finally, the politics and culture of colonialism. See their joint publication, *Ethnography and the Historical Imagination* (Boulder: Westview Press, 1992), p. 4.

54 Nicholas Dirks, 'The Crimes of Colonialism. Anthropology and the Textualization of India', in *Colonial Subjects: Essays on the Practical History of Anthropology*, eds P. Pels and O. Salemink (Ann Arbor, MI: University of Michigan Press, 1999), p. 175.

55 Shahid Amin, *Event, Metaphor, Memory*, pp. 14–16.

56 Filipa L. Vicente, *Other Orientalisms*, p. 35.

57 Here I follow Walter Mignolo, who looks at genres of source materials as revealing much about political, social, and economic practices of that time period. See his *The Darker Side of the Renaissance: Literacy, Territoriality, and Colonization*, p. 173.

58 Antoinette Burton, *Dwelling in the Archive. Women Writing House, Home, and History in Late Colonial India* (Delhi: Oxford University Press, 2003), p. 27.

59 For historical approaches to reading archives more creatively, see Natalie Davis, *Fiction in the Archives* (Stanford: Stanford University Press, 1987), and Carlo Ginzburg, *The Cheese and the Worms* (Baltimore: Johns Hopkins University Press, 1982). Jacques Derrida, *Archive Fever: A Freudian Impression*, tr. Eric Prenowitz (Chicago: University of Chicago Press, 1996). This is also a recently expanding topic in the field of historical anthropology. See Nicholas Dirks, 'Annals of the Archive: Ethnographic Notes on the Sources of History', in *From the Margins: Historical Anthropology and its Futures*, ed. Brian Keith Axel, pp. 47–65; Ann Stoler, *Along the Archival Grain: Epistemic Anxieties and Colonial Common Sense* (Princeton: NJ: Princeton University Press, 2009); Carolyn Hamilton, Verne Harris, Jane Taylor, Michele Pickover, Graeme Reid and Razia Saleh (eds), *Refiguring the Archive* (Cape Town: David Philip; Dordrecht, Netherlands: Kluwer Academic Publishers, 2002).

60 Michel-Rolph Trouillot emphasizes the power of archives to 'condition the possibility of existence of historical statements'. See his *Silencing the Past: Power and the Production of History* (Boston: Beacon Press, 1995), p. 5.

61 There is a small but growing corpus of studies focused exclusively on Xavier's image and corpse, to which I hope this book contributes. See Filipa L. Vicente, 'A exposição do corpo sagrado de S. Francisco Xavier e as exposições industriais e agrícolas em Goa', *Oriente* (Dezembro 2002): 55–66; and her 'Exposições coloniais na Índia Portuguesa e na Índia Britânica (séculos XIX e XX)'; and a special issue of *Oriente* (Dezembro 2005) dedicated to the topic of Xavier on the quincentenary of his birth, multiple authors).

CHAPTER TWO

Incorruption (1554)

> And now land was close at hand, the land so many others had longed to reach, that lay between the Ganges, sprung from the earthly paradise, and the Indus. Take courage, my brave men, who have set your hearts on the Victor's palm. You have arrived: the land of wealth abounding lies before you. – Luís de Camões, 1572[1]

In 1553 Luís de Camões, the Portuguese poet and soon to be author of *The Lusiads* – the epic story immortalizing the voyage of Vasco da Gama to India in 1498 – set sail for India. That same year, the corpse of the Jesuit priest Francis Xavier was disinterred from his grave by several members of his religious order on the deserted island of Sancian (off the coast of China) where he had died only three months earlier. His body was found to be 'incorrupt'[2] – meaning that his flesh had not decomposed – and was put on the next westward-bound Portuguese ship, stopping briefly in Malacca and arriving in Goa on 16 March 1554, where he was honoured in a small reception. The Viceroy led the procession that carried Xavier's decorated corpse to the prestigious Jesuit College of St Paul – his new home – and a diverse public, including numerous Jesuit priests and colonial officials, members of the Portuguese nobility, as well as several Catholic and non-Catholic 'native' Goans, was on hand to witness Xavier's many miracles, particularly his lack of decomposition and the sweet smell emanating from his corpse.

In this chapter I develop a discourse of incorruptibility as applied to both saint and state in the midst of an era of Portuguese political and economic expansion in which the Society of Jesus was defining and securing its position in Goa while operating under the patronage of the Estado da Índia. This discourse emerged not only in relation to Xavier's corpse; rather, I argue that its production and circulation had everything to do with representing the material successes of church and state overseas. In the same way that the publication of Camões's tome (1572) – based on ten years of living in Portuguese Asia in the period following Xavier's death – simultaneously narrates the epic voyage of Vasco da Gama to India and boasts the superiority of Portuguese navigation during a period when their maritime technologies exceeded those of many other European powers, the story of Xavier's multiple ritualizations in death (Sancian, Malacca, Goa) as it was recorded by his Jesuit biographers (1579–1701) boasts the potential of both Catholic sainthood and Portuguese statehood in Asia. By investing themselves in the 'incorruptness' of Xavier's corpse, church and state officials reveal much about themselves and their relations to each other, and to various 'Portuguese' and 'native' publics located in Sancian, Malacca, and Goa during the mid-sixteenth century. The trope of incorruption thus works as a mode of representation for the claims of a burgeoning colonial state. Lastly, the reception of Xavier's corpse in 1554 in Goa both initiated his 'canonization process' (1556–7, 1610–22) – this was the next step in 'authenticating' Xavier's incorruptibility (as well as that of the state) – and provided a precedent for future ritualizations of this missionary-turned-saint.

Xavier: 'His Life, His Times', 1506–52[3]

> The expression Estado da Índia in the 16th century did not mean a geographically defined space but a collection of territories, establishments, goods, people, and collective interests directed by the Portuguese Crown in the Indian Ocean and adjacent seas or rivers from the Cape of Good Hope to Japan. – Luís Filipe Thomaz, 1985[4]

In order to understand Xavier's multiple journeys in death and the subsequent drive for his canonization on the part of church and state officials based in Portuguese India in the second half of the sixteenth century – including the role of Jesuit biographies in producing and circulating this information in both metropole and colony – it is necessary first to provide the contours of this Jesuit missionary's 'life and times'. Here I adapt what the historian Sanjay Subrahmanyam calls a 'biographical approach' to writing the social history of early modern Portuguese Asia.[5] By emphasizing both the life and the death of various historical actors, I expand the notion of biography to suggest that what happens in *death* is just as telling as what happens in *life*. I also discuss parallel biographies, not only to connect Xavier's 'life and times' to other historical actors but to offer the necessary contextual backdrop for making sense of Xavier's various 'translations' in death in later sections.[6]

Figure 3 Souvenir of the Exposition of 1952 of the body of St Francis Xavier

In the same year – 1506 – that Francisco de Jassu y Javier was born into Basque nobility in Navarre, Spain,[7] the future second Governor of Portuguese India, a captain by the name of Affonso de Albuquerque, following in the footsteps of Vasco da Gama ('a man in search of pepper')[8] arrived on the western coast of India to establish a more permanent Portuguese foothold on Indian soil.[9] What made Albuquerque distinct from his predecessor, Viceroy D. Francisco de Almeida (1505–9), a man who had followed a 'strictly commercial policy',[10] was the fact that he sought to give the Portuguese empire a more 'land-based character.'[11] He, alongside a coalition of neighbouring (Hindu) forces from Vijayanagara,[12] successfully (re)captured 'Goa' – at that point a thriving port and commercial emporium ruled by the Muslim state of Bijapur[13] – on 25 November 1510, not insignificantly St Catherine's Day.[14]

Thus, it was Albuquerque, a man with 'an eye for everything political and strategic', who laid the foundations for a Portuguese empire in Asia.[15] During his tenure as Governor (1509–15) he put into practice several plans that not only permanently shaped the landscape of Goa but had long-term consequences for Portuguese colonial rule. First, he 'conquered and administered directly the strategic points and bases of eastern commerce',[16] eventually establishing Portuguese settlements in Malacca (1511) and Hormuz (1515), which operated alongside the expanding bases of Cochin and Goa.[17] The Estado da Índia was now beginning to take on its distinctive character described at the outset of this section by the historian L. Thomaz.[18] Second, Goa's second Viceroy 'built fortresses in lands he could not administer directly' and 'made vassals [out of] many indigenous chiefs', an effective political strategy that kept Portugal's enemies in check by creating formidable alliances.[19] Third, he colonized Goa, using his talents as a 'town planner and architect'[20] to create a municipal government using that of Lisbon as a model, establish schools and a hospital, and build a church dedicated to St Catherine, to whom he owed his overseas success.[21] Finally, this governor of Goa adopted the unusual policy of promoting the formation of a uniquely Indo-Portuguese Goan race – a group that came to be labelled the *casados* (married ones) – through miscegenation.[22] Specifically, he forcibly wedded Portuguese sailors with indigenous Muslim women with the aim of 'fusing the two civilizations',[23] a plan that was clearly undertaken for both political and economic reasons.[24]

Even though Albuquerque died in the year 1515 – his successor already chosen[25] – thus ending his successful reign as Governor, his colonial legacy would be felt by subsequent generations of *casados*. Shortly thereafter, his remains were buried in the Church of Our Lady of the Mount in Goa; they would be quietly 'translated' to Portugal in 1565.[26] Thus, owing in large part to the many successes of Albuquerque on land and at sea, King Emmanuel of Portugal, on 1 March 1518, proclaimed Goa to be a 'royal city, never to be severed from the Portuguese Crown'.[27]

Just as Albuquerque on his journey to India had been accompanied by three Dominican missionaries, so too was each annual fleet of ships that left Lisbon for India. Here it is important to extend Vicente Rafael's argument regarding the Spanish Philippines – that of the intimate relation of colonial rule to Catholic missionary practice and ideology – to the Portuguese case.[28] Earlier, in the year 1500, Pope Alexander VI had given the king of Portugal the privilege to found 'twelve convents and missionary centers in the discovered lands' in order to encourage and expand the propagation of the Catholic faith overseas.[29] The Franciscans, with concessions from the king which included land grants and money, led the way by establishing the first monastery and church in Goa in 1518. On 12 January 1522 one Franciscan priest submitted a report to the king of Cochin on the state of religious affairs in Goa, suggesting that all the Hindu temples of Goa be destroyed and 'in their stead, churches with saints [be] erected'.[30] Despite this request, and several others that followed in the coming years to curb the privileges of native Hindus under Portuguese dominion, they would continue to be protected under an ordinance passed in Goa in 1526 by the newly appointed King John III of Portugal (1521–57),[31] which assured not only their social organization but their freedom of religious expression. The Franciscans would have to await several additional measures, including the arrival of Francis Xavier, to see their religious mission fully implemented.

Meanwhile, the years 1524–5 witnessed Francis Xavier's arrival in Paris to attend the College of St Barbara (1525),[32] the death of the famed voyager Vasco da Gama during his short-lived term in office as Viceroy of Portuguese India (4–24 December 1524),[33] and the birth in Lisbon (1524) of Luís de Camões, the man who would immortalize the voyage of his distant kinsman. By the year 1530 the Portuguese had solidified their position of dominance in the Indian Ocean trade,[34] and Goa outrivalled Cochin as a thriving Portuguese colonial city such that it replaced the latter as the centre and new capital of the Estado da Índia.[35] Correspondingly, in 1534, the same year that the Portuguese also solidified their hold in Bassein, itself a convenient source of unlimited amounts of limestone for creating monumental buildings in a tropical climate, Goa acquired the status of a Diocese – including the establishment of the post of the Pae dos Cristãos (Father of the Christians) to oversee the management of any new converts to the Catholic fold. That same year saw Xavier take his formal vows at Montmartre.

The year 1541 witnessed Francis Xavier – now a member of the newly established religious order, the Society of Jesus initiated under his friend, fellow Basque and spiritual mentor, Ignatius de Loyola – in Lisbon preparing for his overseas mission. The year also saw the institutionalization of the Portuguese Inquisition and the declaration that Christianity was now the 'official religion' in Portuguese Goa, this latter change due in large part to the early successes of the Franciscan missionaries in bringing entire Hindu *gancares* (villages) into the Catholic fold. Two ecclesiastical organizations – funded largely by profits from a lucrative maritime trade[36] – were established to help propagate the Catholic faith in Goa specifically. While the 'Rigour of Mercy' promoted the destruction of Hindu temples and the subsequent acquisition of their lands and attachment to existing churches,[37] thus largely reversing the 1526 ordinance that had previously protected the religious freedoms of the native Hindus of Goa,[38] the 'Confraternity of Holy Faith' rendered help to poor Christians, sought preferences for these 'new converts' in government postings, and oversaw the upkeep of all churches in the area.[39] At the same time, additional churches and chapels were rapidly erected on the sites of these former Hindu temples in a sustained effort to promote continued attachments on the part of these so-called 'pagans' to their former places of worship.[40] Thus, in the period between 1510 and 1541, in the years following Albuquerque's conquest of Goa and its subsequent rapid buildup as a centre both of state administration and ecclesiastical activity, this port had been slowly transformed into a 'Christian city', a fact that deeply impressed Francis Xavier when he arrived on India's coast on 6 May 1542 to initiate the Society of Jesus, describing it thus:

> After four months and more we reached India, Goa (I mean), a city entirely of Christians, a most remarkable thing – a thing to be seen … It has a monastery, a very fine Cathedral with many canons, and many other churches. There is reason for giving many thanks to God our Lord on seeing how the name of Christ is flourishing so well in such distant lands among so many infidels.[41]

The stage had been set for the arrival of Xavier wherein the 'real work of his life, his missionary labours, his enterprise', began.[42]

Xavier spent the next ten years (1542–52) in the service of the Jesuit order. Expanding on what the Franciscans and Vicar General Miguel Vaz had already set up, Xavier transformed Goa into an even larger base of Catholic operations. He took up the administration of the recently established Seminary of the Holy Faith[43] (becoming its first Provincial head in 1549) and removed any profligate priests, thus improving the requisite standards for entrance into this institution of higher learning; reformed the practices of wayward Portuguese Christians living in Goa and its environs; promoted a campaign of 'mass baptisms'; requested a Holy Inquisition for Goa;[44] and lastly, regularized the practice of producing and circulating letters between Jesuits stationed overseas and their Superiors in Europe, a point I expand on in a subsequent section.[45] In the coming years the church in Goa only grew more militant: in 1545 all (Hindu) Brahmans were expelled from Goa with any remaining Hindu temples destroyed in the process.[46] By 1548 the Dominicans had entered the 'competition for souls'[47] and a high-profile (Hindu) conversion to Catholicism was celebrated with 'great éclat' in the streets of Goa,[48] a city whose population was now estimated at forty thousand persons.[49]

Just as the Estado da Índia was not defined by Goa alone, neither was Xavier's missionary effort directed only at this one Portuguese territory. Specifically, during this same time frame, while the Portuguese acquired the lucrative port of Diu (1547),[50] and Viceroy Dom João de Castro (1545–48) both signed a formal treaty of friendship with the Vijayanagara dynasty[51] and temporarily ceased hostilities with the Bijapurs,[52] Xavier too expanded the Jesuit mission beyond Goa's limits. Overall, his 'evangelical campaign' took him three times to the Fishery, Malabar, and Travancore coasts, twice to Bassein and Ceylon, five times to Malacca, and once to Amboina, the Moluccas, Japan, and, finally, the outskirts of China, where he would die awaiting permission to establish a Jesuit mission.[53] Thus, on the one hand, Xavier acted as an agent of the Estado da Índia by dedicating himself to setting up Jesuit missions in those places where the Portuguese had already established outposts, simultaneously strengthening the power of both church and state in the process. On the other, this 'man of God' acted as agent of the church by dedicating his efforts to establishing an even larger Jesuit umbrella organization that operated indirectly outside the confines of the colonial state, with Goa as its centre.[54]

It was during the last years of Xavier's life – as he attempted to enter China to expand the Jesuit mission – that the Estado da Índia experienced its first moment of crisis, largely an 'internal' as opposed to an 'external' one, owing to its rapid over-expansion and limited resources.[55] By the year 1550 the 'urge for general reform' was felt by almost everyone in both Lisbon and Goa, such that alternative plans that moved further afield from Albuquerque's grand vision were debated.[56] Two years later, in the midst of these larger concerns regarding the future shape of the Portuguese colonial state in Asia, Xavier was dead, his 'life and times' coming to a close only ten years after he had begun his mission. In the coming years, the Portuguese would survive, despite both a series of external setbacks and advances that would take place, the timeliness of Xavier's death and the miracle of his incorruptible corpse most conveniently lending itself to the sustenance, reshaping, and strengthening of its empire and its own representation as 'incorruptible'.

The cult of saints and relic translations: from Europe to Asia

> Far thinking churchmen looked beyond mortal efforts to supernatural defenders, and in importing saints hoped to find a solution to their society's ills – Patrick Geary, 1978[57]

Before turning to the topic of Xavier and the particulars of his journey to sainthood in Portuguese Asia, it is necessary to briefly situate the cult of saints, including the practice of transferring and venerating a potential saint's remains within a larger (European) Catholic framework. Specifically, Xavier's story is prefigured by a larger history that directly shapes the investments of church and state in his sainthood in sixteenth-century Portuguese Asia. However, as will become evident in the following analysis, missionaries and state officials also modified these same religious practices to fit a specific colonial context.

The European Catholic practice of relic 'translation', the name assigned to the movement of a potential saint's relics (whole corpse or part), was integral to promoting the 'cult of saints', a practice that has its origins in the cult of martyrs in Christian Rome.[58] Patrick Geary describes relic translation as a 'ritual kidnapping', wherein a relic was perceived as a 'living saint' and successfully passed from one community to another.[59] As a religious practice that reached its height during the Middle Ages (ninth to eleventh centuries), a potential saint's relic (usually a body part) was logically assigned 'saintly' attributes when moved to a new context, providing both a defence for its movement and a local 'vernacular' significance. Moreover, Geary suggests that relic translations typically exhibit certain qualities: the search for the relic often takes place in secret and at night, its authenticity is often an issue, it is 'miraculous' upon discovery, is often not appreciated in its original context (sometimes the saint wills its removal by exhibiting signs), is sometimes difficult to move, and, finally, is typically honoured in a joyful reception upon arriving at its new context, giving this site new signification in the process,[60] qualities that also emerge in the case of Xavier.

The 'cult of saints' was greatly transformed during 'the Age of Faith' (eleventh to thirteenth centuries) during which the church – 'monumental' now in terms not only of its great cathedrals but its centralized power – began to monitor the traffic in (potential) saints' relics.[61] The development of religious orders as powerful pan-European political institutions that invested in 'propagating new cults' from their own ranks,[62] and the formalization of the canonization process under the Roman papacy, also contributed to its evolution. These historical transformations, according to Stephen Wilson, 'reflected the progress of a certain channeling of sanctity into specialized ecclesiastical institutions'.[63] Moreover, the value of the saint himself was typically increased in the narration of the relic 'translation',[64] hence the regularized practice of recording a saint's story in death by those close to him or her. Lastly, the story of a saint's relic translation is also a story of a people's symbolic value system who 'assimilate him into their own history' by venerating his remains.[65] Accordingly, 'any change in the nature, force, or direction of its cult had to come entirely from the society itself'.[66]

Stories of relic translations reveal as much about the changing social, economic, and political values of the people who choose to venerate a particular saint at a certain historical moment as they do about the 'cult of the saint' in question. I emphasize for the purposes of this chapter that it was a peculiar proto-early modern development in Europe that made possible the expansive role of a potential saint's relics in promoting church and state, a practice that was also adopted and adapted in the early modern period to fit particular agendas – here those of the Society of Jesus and the Estado da Índia – and specific colonial spaces – here that of Portuguese Asia – once its potential in Europe had been realized.[67] Yet we will also come to see that the movement of Xavier, part and parcel as it is of a longer history of relic transfers as evidenced above, signifies a uniquely distinct history and practice by the nature of its colonial setting over the *longue durée*.

Jesuits, biographies, and the journey to sainthood

> The written voyages were scarcely less important in the transformation of Europe and the rest of the world than were the actual ones – Richard Helgerson, 1992[68]

Jesuit biographies of Xavier, written in the sixteenth and seventeenth centuries in the aftermath of his death, circulated in multiple colonies and metropoles, and contributed, as the historian Ines Županov has emphasized,[69] to the making of a particular saint and cult following. In this section, I discuss the multiple dimensions of these Jesuit biographies – as a social practice, genre, and historical source material – which undergird my larger analysis of Xavier's actual and written voyage in death, and introduce the authors whose works I rely on for my ritual analysis.

It was Xavier himself who had initiated the social practice of writing letters from the missionary field of India.[70] Several of his letters were published in Paris during his lifetime (1545),[71] and these aroused much curiosity in Xavier himself as a personality. More importantly, these (published) letters also kept alive the Jesuit mission in the eyes of an elite European and Jesuit reading public, thus preserving and ensuring the growth of the Society of Jesus in the process.[72] These letters served as an impetus and became the basis for producing the first set of biographies of the man who had firmly established the Society of Jesus in Goa. They were to be circulated for a two-tiered reading public (noblemen and clergy) located now both in Europe and the expanding Portuguese colonies.[73] Moreover, for many of these Jesuits, recording Xavier's life story was considered the 'mission' in itself.[74]

The majority of the Jesuit authors whose accounts I rely on – all Portuguese, with the exception of one – were writing in the late sixteenth century and early seventeenth century, that is, in the period in which the canonization of Xavier was 'in process' (1556–1622).[75] While these men held a variety of positions within the Jesuit Order and were either in Europe or stationed throughout Asia in various missionary capacities, some of the early biographers knew Xavier personally or were witness to some of the actual events which took place on Xavier's remarkable journey in death from China to India. Their unique placement, on the one hand, provided an incentive to produce biographies of Xavier and, on the other, offered credibility to some of the stories circulating about Xavier's 'incorruptible corpse'. Later biographers of the saint-in-the-making knew nothing of him from personal experience, but were compelled to record his biography in both life and death for obvious reasons,[76] the foremost being to promote Xavier's canonization and index the many successes of the Jesuit mission in Asia.

As a genre, these Jesuit biographies exhibit certain identifiable characteristics, only some of which I highlight here. First, these biographies all operate within one larger discursive field concerning the drive for Xavier's canonization. While each author may rely on different strategies or emphasize different historical details to make a case for Xavier's sainthood, they are complementary testimonies in so far as they concretize and reveal Xavier's potential sainthood-in-the-making. Second, not only did these Jesuit authors rely on their own impressions of and experiences in the missionary field, but they were also dependent on each other's biographies of Xavier to produce their own – some going as far as to cite their predecessors – that is, the 'dialogic' nature of these biographies is commonplace.[77] Thus, for some writers it was acceptable to adopt wholesale the textual version of others, whereas at other times this group of Jesuits dispute and debate the 'accuracy' of various details. Third, differences of style occur in the narration of Xavier's story of sainthood, particularly between those written in the period immediately following his death – when sainthood was still very much a premature idea – and during the period when his canonization drive was well under way, when sainthood was a more concrete possibility. Here I suggest the evolving nature of the genre from biographies wholly dedicated to Xavier to larger histories of the Society of Jesus, in which it was no longer about isolating Xavier's successes but rather about attaching him to the larger glories of the Jesuits in light of his impending canonization.

As a set of source materials, these biographies are situated between 'history and hagiography',[78] a point that, I argue, does not detract from their historical value, but rather adds to it, in so far as they provide a perspective on a topic that would not be included in more narrowly defined historical sources of this same period. On the one hand, these texts are hagiographical to the extent that they are wholly concerned with Xavier, the Jesuits, and a larger Catholic 'spiritual' conquest in Portuguese Asia. Moreover, they typically report only the most positive outcomes, tend to neglect time and chronology, and remain anchored to particular sites.[79] On the other hand, these Jesuit biographies are historical to the extent that they are connected to real persons, places, and events that took place during the sixteenth century. There is a 'territorial dimension' to these Jesuit biographies that is invaluable for both historical and historiographical reasons.[80] Thus, sometimes despite and because of their hagiographical slant, they tell us something about the structure and structuring of church and state, their mutual constitution in specific sites under Portuguese dominion, changing (Portuguese Catholic) ideas of sanctity and sainthood, and finally, the diversity of native and Catholic publics located in various colonial outposts during the sixteenth century.

The parallel (and intersecting) life histories of the various Jesuit biographers whose writings I rely on for my ritual analysis evidence the workings of the Jesuit mission and the Estado da Índia during the late sixteenth and early seventeenth centuries. They also suggest the arc of possibilities and challenges of location and writing for a group of itinerant Jesuits, and their differing investments and engagements with Portuguese colonial practices. Here I briefly introduce the authors whose writings I rely on for my ritual analysis. Manuel Teixeira, a Portuguese Jesuit who knew Xavier in life and witnessed the receptions of his corpse in Malacca in 1553 and Goa in 1554, as well as his medical examination in 1556, was the first to produce an 'official' biography of Xavier, completed in 1579 from Goa and sent directly to Rome in 1581.[81] Fernão Mendes Pinto was alternately a (Portuguese) slave, soldier, pirate, merchant, doctor, and ambassador, prior to becoming a Jesuit priest.[82] Like Teixeira before him, Pinto knew Xavier in life and witnessed the reception of his corpse in Goa in 1554 upon which he had a 'mystical conversion', joining the Society of Jesus after donating a large portion of his fortune.[83] While his 'unofficial' biography of Xavier is woven into the story of his own travels, it was written between the years 1569 and 1578 from Portugal, but from the perspective of a now-disillusioned Jesuit. The third Jesuit to record Xavier's story in life and death was Italian-born Alessandro Valignano, who, unlike his predecessors, was not witness to the multiple events surrounding Xavier's corpse in the aftermath of his death. He arrived in Goa only in 1574 to take up the position of Visitor of the Society of Jesus; his 'official' biography of Xavier was modelled closely on that of

Teixeira and completed in the year 1588.[84]

The next three Jesuit texts evidence a shift from these early biographies dedicated exclusively to Xavier. Not only were these authors the product of a different era – the seventeenth century – during which Xavier's canonization was well under way and almost nearing completion, but now Xavier's journey to sainthood was being incorporated into larger commissioned histories of the Society of Jesus, to varying degrees. João de Lucena was a Portuguese Jesuit who, unlike the other biographers whose work I discuss, never left Lisbon to visit the overseas mission. He completed his biography of Xavier in the year 1599; it was published the following year.[85] The fifth Jesuit to undertake such an endeavour was Sebastiam Gonçalves who, having arrived in Goa in 1593 from Lisbon to take up a position as a Supervisor within the Jesuit order, was commissioned in 1604 to write a history of the Society of Jesus, one that necessarily included Xavier's life-story. Using Lucena's recently published text (1600) as the basis for producing his own, he completed Part I – consisting of five books dedicated exclusively to Xavier – in 1614,[86] the same year that, interestingly, he witnessed the cutting off of Xavier's right arm as part of his canonization proceedings. The last Jesuit biography that is included in my larger analysis of Xavier's journey to sainthood is that of Francisco de Sousa, a Brazilian-born Portuguese Jesuit, who was stationed in Goa in the latter half of the seventeeth century. Even though his history of the Society of Jesus is largely indebted to the writings of Gonçalves,[87] his published work (1710) also differed from that of his Jesuit predecessors in that it was written after Xavier achieved sainthood.[88]

Thus, following Helgerson, whose quotation I relied on at the outset of this section, I trace Xavier's 'actual' and 'written' voyage to sainthood in this chapter. This set of Jesuit biographies allows me to explore this would-be saint's multiple 'translations' in death – from his initial burial in Sancian in 1552 to his brief interment in Malacca in 1553, to his arrival in Goa in 1554 – by addressing those hagiographical and historical processes by which the corpse of Xavier was deemed 'incorruptible' by church and state officials operating in each of the above sites. The incorruptible state of Xavier's body will by extension reveal the incorruptibility of church and state to varying degrees in Sancian, Malacca, and Goa during the mid-sixteenth century. Moreover, these biographies function by way of their production and circulation: in the continual reshaping and retelling of Xavier's remarkable 'story' in death, they operated as both a powerful Catholic sermon and a history lesson on the topic of Xavier, the Jesuits, and the Estado da Índia for a sixteenth/seventeenth-century European and Jesuit reading public located in both metropole and colony(s).

Of saint and state: developing a discourse of incorruptibility (1552–54)

> Xavier's holy presence in Asia ... was particularly propitious to the Portuguese. His 'apostolic' journeys sanctified not only the newly acquired territories through the foundation of religious institutions, improvement of social mores and Christianization, but also the vessels on which he traveled and the sea passages he plowed through. Whatever he *touched* became a mark on the map of Portuguese possession, even if it proved to be a temporary one.[89]

As suggested by the historian Ines Županov in the above epigraph, Xavier's apostolic journeys, not only in life but also in death, were directly connected to the mapping of a Portuguese empire in Asia. However, as will become evident, the 'making of a Portuguese saint out of a Spanish missionary' was 'not without problems'.[90] In the following section I trace the development of a discourse of incorruptibility on the part of colonial officials and Jesuit missionaries operating in three different locations within Portuguese Asia – Sancian, Malacca, and Goa – in the mid-sixteenth century, suggesting that Xavier's various relic translations in death were used to promote both his sainthood and his (Portuguese) statehood at each of these colonial outposts that he also visited in life. But in spite of attempts to transform each of the above sites – not only through Xavier's biographical ties but also through physical contact with his corpse – into thriving colonial bases connected to a larger empire centred at Goa, his travels in death simultaneously expose the strengths and vulnerabilities of church and state in Portuguese Asia.

I will also argue that these witnesses, by enforcing a cult of Xavier through repeated ritual practice, attempt to stabilize and standardize the identity of his corpse as defying deterioration in death both despite – in the case of Sancian and Malacca – and because of – in the case of Goa – his repeatedly new surroundings. In the end, the place most connected to Xavier's biography in life – Goa, the site where Xavier first initiated the Jesuit mission ten years earlier – will be determined to be the most suitable destination for his (future) ritualization. Thus, throughout his journey to sainthood, from the initial translation of his corpse from his burial spot on the island of Sancian (1552) to his second burial in Malacca (1553), and to his final translation to Goa (1554), Xavier exhibits numerous material signs of (in)corruptibility not only to church and state officials but also to various Catholic and 'native' publics located at each of the above sites, which in turn provides a rich portrait of the Society of Jesus and the Estado da Índia in sixteenth-century Portuguese Asia.

Sancian (1552)

> Portuguese trade reached far beyond the country's Indian possessions. Thus, for instance, for nearly three decades [1518–1548] ... they maintained an illicit trade along the Checkiang and Fukien coasts, using temporary basis in Kwantung. That is how St Francis Xavier found his last resting place in Shanchuan tao, one of the Portuguese smugglers' base[s]. – T.R. de Souza, 1988[91]

According to his many Jesuit biographers, Francis Xavier died during the night between 2 and 3 December in the year 1552 on the island of Sancian,[92] after awaiting (for two-and-a-half months) news about entering China to start up a Jesuit mission.[93] In this section I trace how his journey to sainthood was first initiated from this site in the aftermath of his death by the few available eyewitnesses – including several Jesuits, Portuguese traders and settlers, and one member of Sancian's 'native' Chinese public. My approach is thematic, summarizing the central defining characteristics of his first translation as recorded by Jesuit biographers of this saint-in-the-making. Xavier's corpse exhibits numerous signs of incorruptibility upon his first disinterment, three months after his initial burial. However, his corporeal state does not spread by way of contagion on to this burgeoning Portuguese colonial outpost (excepting the waters surrounding it) despite his biographical attachments to this place which, in turn, reveal Xavier's ill-treatment in death, expose the weaknesses of church and state activity in Sancian, and explain why his companions were compelled to translate his sacred remains to a more suitable site, the discursive power of his incorruptibility conveniently expanded in the process of travel.

Xavier is first accorded the status of a martyr and given a proper Christian burial by those present in Sancian.[94] Not only did he have his eyes fixed on the crucifix in his hands at the moment that he 'surrendered his soul completely to God' but his death was 'deeply regretted and mourned by everyone there', writes the Jesuit biographer Fernão Mendes Pinto.[95] Alessandro Valignano informs us that it was António, Xavier's Chinese interpreter and servant, a converted native who 'loved him so much', who first reported his death to the men onboard an unnamed Portuguese ship anchored in the harbour of Sancian.[96] Meanwhile, several of Xavier's 'devoted ones' immediately left the ship to assist in his burial.[97] João Lucena reports that despite the 'grace and vivacity of his [Xavier's] features, his composure [was] more of someone who was resting'.[98] Upon viewing him, several Portuguese settlers of Sancian 'cried as he was deceased'.[99]

Next his corpse – dressed with his priestly vestments – was placed inside a 'fitted box', a Chinese 'custom' that Valignano, Italian himself by birth, reflects on as paralleling death practices 'in Italy and other parts of Europe'.[100] He also reports that inside this coffin was placed fresh lime 'so that his flesh would be consumed more quickly'.[101] Francisco de Souza tells us that his coffin was then carried by the same devoted António who was assisted only by two 'mulattos' since many of the Portuguese settlers chose to remain inside their huts owing to the 'great cold that prevailed that day', to a place where a grave had already been dug.[102] Sebastiam Gonçalves informs us that 'they buried him in a hillock, at the foot of a cross, placing many stones at the head so that if a Jesuit were to pass by he would know the place of the grave'.[103] Lastly, this same Jesuit biographer reports that, on the day of Xavier's death, a religious image of a crucified Christ located in the castle in Navarra, Spain, where he had been born stopped sweating, a practice that had regularly occurred during the ten years of Xavier's overseas missionary activities; instead, on this auspicious day and on every Friday thereafter, the image began to issue drops of blood to 'signify the greatest works he suffered',[104] yet another marker of Xavier's martyrdom, miraculousness and biographical ties, in life and death.

Second, Xavier's corpse exhibits certain qualities of incorruptness at the time of his disinterment three months after his initial burial on Sancian. Despite the use of lime as an agent of decomposition which acts to 'clean' his bones of their flesh, his body defies deterioration in death, signifying once again his saintliness. The Jesuit biographer Manuel Teixeira informs us that it was on 17 February of the following year (1553) that the ship of Diogo Pereira – a wealthy Portuguese merchant and personal friend of Xavier's – stopped off in Sancian as part of its continuing journey to Malacca, the *Santa Cruz* being the same ship that Francisco Xavier himself had earlier travelled in to reach Sancian.[105] It is the same António of earlier accounts who informed Pereira of Xavier's death and the location of his burial, who, in turn, appointed a 'trusted' Portuguese sailor from his ship to examine the condition of Xavier's corpse.[106] Upon opening his coffin, he found it 'whole and healthy, like when they buried him, being near three months that he was buried, without any bad smell but that of the lime'.[107] Mendes Pinto tells us not only that Xavier's corpse was without any signs of deterioration but that 'not even the shroud and the cassock he wore were found to have any spots or blemishes, for both were as clean and white as if they had just been washed'.[108] Just as his incorruptness had spread to his priestly vestments, so too did they both emit 'a very pleasant smell that all found comforting', according to Valignano.[109] De Souza goes so far as to describe the smell as 'surpassing in sweetness the combined aroma of the most fragrant flowers',[110] proof once again of his saintliness.

Third, Xavier's sanctity is reinforced through the practice of producing and distributing relics. While Gonçalves informs us that, upon further examination of his corpse, his insides were determined to be 'full of juice and blood',[111] Francisco de Souza describes how Diogo Pereira requested that 'a slice of flesh about one finger's length [be] cut off of Xavier's left knee so as to determine if he exhibited additional signs of incorruptibility, a jet of fresh blood gushing at once from the wound, as though the flesh had been that of a living man'.[112] This confirmed Pereira's suspicions, which he proceeded to label as yet another 'mark of the incorruption of [his] sacred body'.[113] Moreover, the production and circulation of relics were not restricted to his corpse. This same Jesuit biographer informs us that a large piece of his cassock was also divided into relics and distributed among the Portuguese settlers present,[114] a practice that was not uncommon with a potential saint's relics.

Fourth, his companions were compelled to initiate his translation from this site by the fact that Xavier was not fully appreciated in Sancian – by both the place and its public.[115] Specifically, it was because of the limits of Portuguese statehood – Sancian was less a colonial outpost than a temporary safe haven and smugglers' den for commercial traffic – that enforced the need for his translation. While Mendes Pinto attests to the limited 'local conditions' for Xavier's proper burial,[116] Valignano characterizes Sancian as 'deserted and uncultivated', a 'place of heathens' that he passed by during his own travels in Portuguese Asia.[117] Meanwhile, Lucena describes the 'poor huts' that the scant numbers of Portuguese 'settlers' inhabited,[118] and de Souza informs us of the constant cold and fierce winds that regularly envelope Sancian, and that Xavier also experienced during his last days, thus contributing to his untimely death.[119] All of these factors functioned only to reinforce Sancian's unsuitability as a colonial outpost.[120] Mendes Pinto describes how many of these same Portuguese settlers, upon their first viewing of Xavier's incorrupt corpse, 'smote themselves repeatedly for their past error' in not attending to Xavier's initial burial owing to the extreme cold of that now momentous day.[121] Similarly, De Souza informs us that 'the sight of such a marvel … moved some to a transport of spiritual fervour, others to repentance for having forsaken the saint in his last illness'.[122] Lastly, Gonçalves points out that the burial of Xavier took place at the foot of the one (and only) cross planted by the Portuguese on this island, and was overseen by a 'native' as opposed to a group of Portuguese Christians.[123]

That Sancian was devoid of certain minimal traits required of a colonial outpost – sustained church and state activity and a defined Portuguese public – compelled his companions, in particular Xavier's trusted friend Diogo Pereira, to remove his sacred remains from this barren island, and its undeserving inhabitants. Moreover, the fact that, despite his poor treatment in life and death on Sancian, Xavier exhibited these numerous signs of his incorruptness made his sanctity appear even more marked.

Xavier's translation from Sancian was not only a ritualized activity: his corpse emitted additional signs sanctioning his continued travels in death. Lucena describes how Xavier's corpse was returned to his coffin – 'without removing the lime' – and then taken in procession on the shoulders of several Portuguese settlers where it was transferred to Pereira's ship, the *Santa Cruz*.[124] Gonçalves informs us that in Xavier's open grave, these same men 'interred afterwards a Portuguese, hoping in divine charity that he would receive his soul in the heavens by the intercession of the sacred father', and upon which a newly arrived Jesuit priest by the name of Father Melchior performed a Mass in the spirit of Xavier's life.[125] Francisco de Souza informs us that 'after the loading', as the *Santa Cruz* cast off from Sancian, destined for Malacca, the typhoons, 'so terrible and so frequent in those latitudes, seemed to have subsided, for the time at least, to allow safe passage to such a sacred cargo'.[126] That Xavier's incorruptness in death failed to sanctify the territory of Sancian itself seemed to echo his failure to enter China to start up a Jesuit mission. Once again, his biography in life is intimately connected to his biography in death. However, that a small degree of Xavier's miraculousness rubs off on to the waters surrounding Sancian which carry his sacred corpse – ensuring his safe voyage in the process – not only emphasizes the 'seaborne' character of the Portuguese empire in Asia during the sixteenth century, including its unsurpassed naval superiority at this time, but suggests that Xavier did not leave this biographical site completely untouched in either life and death,[127] and that his Jesuit and Portuguese protectors were justified in 'translating' Xavier's sacred remains from Sancian, their hopes pinned on Malacca at this point for sustaining and perhaps even expanding his incorruptness in death.

Thus far, I have thematized Xavier's initial burial and translation from Sancian as reported by his various Jesuit biographers, suggesting the initial development of a discourse of incorruptibility on the part of his Jesuit and Portuguese companions that incorporates certain corporeal traits (a pleasant smell, a wholeness, a lack of decomposition, and spurting blood), the production and distribution of relics (of corpse and cloth) and new sites (the waters surrounding Sancian but not the island itself), and which travel alongside his corpse. At the same time that the details of his translation promote his sainthood, they also expose the weaknesses of Portuguese statehood and underline the reasons for his removal from this particular site. In subsequent sections I will go on to show how a discourse in incorruptibility of saint and state continue to develop in relation to different sites located in Portuguese Asia.

Malacca (1553)

> At the end of the 16th century, Melaka was a quite different city from the one of Albuquerque's days. It was now a Portuguese stronghold in an increasingly hostile environment, a political, military, economic, and religious centre ... it was the privileged crossroads of trade routes, and checkpoint of men and merchandise.[128]

In this section we continue on the path of Xavier's journey to sainthood, stopping off in Malacca (or Melaka as it was also called) to examine the reception of his corpse, his five-month interment here, and, finally, his translation from this Portuguese colonial outpost. Once again, my approach is thematic, summarizing the central defining characteristics of his experiences and the ritualization of his body in Malacca as recorded by Jesuit biographers of this saint-in-the-making. Xavier's corpse will continue to exhibit numerous signs of his incorruptibility – both replicating many of those witnessed in Sancian and producing and circulating additional markers – in his new location. Here, more so than in the case of Sancian, Xavier's saintliness spreads by way of contagion precisely, I argue, because Malacca is a stronger and more developed colonial outpost, while Xavier's stronger biographical attachments to this site also played a role. However, in the end Xavier's poor treatment during his interment at this site exposes the vulnerabilities of church, state, and public, and eventually prompts his removal from Malacca. His companions are compelled once again, just as they had been earlier, to translate his corpse to a new setting (in this case Goa), the discursive power of incorruptibility once again expanded in the act of travel.

First, in the month-long journey from Sancian to Malacca – arriving here on 22 March 1553[129] – Xavier's corpse saves the ship from destruction and sanctifies the waters surrounding Malacca, thus justifying his translation from Sancian in the process. Manuel Teixeira, a witness to the event itself, reports that the *Santa Cruz* was 'saved from another ship that had been in front, because the body had come in that ship'.[130] Moreover, Mendes Pinto notes the arrival of his corpse in Malacca as marking his return 'nine months and twenty-two days' since he had first set off for his mission in China,[131] from this place. It had been Xavier who had initiated the Jesuit order in Malacca in 1548 and had been bequeathed a church by the acting governor to promote the city's religiosity. Xavier's corpse thus travels, in reverse, the circuit of his life story.

Second, Xavier's incorrupt corpse is honourably received in Malacca, his reception transformed into a ceremonious event that inscribes him with meaning in this new context – a typical trait of saint's relics – and incites various acts of religious devotion among Malacca's public. Teixeira informs us that 'by the great devotion that everyone had in him and with great happiness, they were determined to receive him with the most solemnity they could', especially Diogo Pereira, for it was he, Xavier's 'special devotee and friend', now turned 'ambassador', whose ship had transported his corpse to Malacca. It was also this same friend who had ordered a 'great quantity of wax' (candles) to be made and the city to be decorated in preparation for his reception.[132] Pereira's biographical attachments to both Xavier and Malacca are also qualified by the biographer Gonçalves, who points out that Xavier had earlier helped cure Pereira's young son through contact with a relic of St Thomas that he carried on his person.[133] Once again, the connection between the biographies of Xavier and Thomas affirms this missionary's exemplary life and ongoing ties with his predecessor. Valignano adds that it was this same loyal friend of Xavier's who 'paid the necessary expenses', and that it was 'in such a manner that all the principals of Malacca went to receive him in a procession with many candles and tapers burning, all of the city converging with much devotion and reverence to see that sacred corpse'.[134] Lucena informs us that this same public also 'kissed' and 'touch[ed] beads [of rosaries] to his coffin',[135] the power of contagion operating once again. Teixeira reports that this 'large multitude of people' converged on Xavier 'for devotion and for the concept that everyone had of that sacred father, and because of his fame that had already run throughout the city, of when he came whole and incorrupt'.[136] Thus, it was not only his biographical ties to this site but also the news of the miraculous state of his corpse that led Malacca's public to honour Xavier in death through the special lighting of the city with candles – thus provoking a religious atmosphere – and the seeing, touching, and kissing of his coffin.

Third, Xavier's corpse exhibits certain qualities (old and new) of incorruptness during his procession through the streets of Malacca, sanctifying both place and public in the process. Teixeira informs us that Xavier's procession is led by the Vicar of Malacca, who first confirms the continuing 'wholeness and freshness' of his corpse before giving 'thanks to our Master', and initiating the solemnities.[137] This procession also includes 'various clergy' (no doubt including Teixeira but otherwise devoid of any other Jesuits), Diogo Pereira, and the 'people of the city'.[138] It is during his movement through the streets of Malacca that Xavier performs his first miracle of healing through the power of touch. Our Jesuit eyewitness describes how 'a man [came] who was very sick in the chest, and that after having touched the body of the Father and entrusting himself to him, he remained healthy', a detail echoed in Lucena's account.[139] In addition, Teixeira reports that 'since the time that he arrived there, the sacred body had stopped the plague that had been going on in that city, [and] which had killed many people', a point echoed by various other Jesuit biographers.[140] That Xavier maintains his incorruption, miraculously heals a member of Malacca's public, and stops a pre-existing plague not only affirms his expanding powers of contagion in death but sanctifies his location in this colonial outpost.

Next Xavier's corpse arrives at a designated church in Malacca, wherein he is interred for a second time in a simple grave. According to our eyewitness Teixeira, the procession first stops at 'Our Lady of the Mount' – 'the church of the Jesuits' which had been granted to this religious order during Xavier's residence in Malacca.[141] Mendes Pinto informs us that it was this same chapel where Xavier 'had always made his home in Malacca'.[142] Moreover, it was 'with deep pain and grief on the part of all'[143] that Xavier was buried here, Gonçalves also pointing out that it was a 'Portuguese' who delivered the body.[144] Both of these details suggest once again the respect accorded Xavier as well as the remorse of Malacca's people, more so than in the case of Sancian's limited public, where a Chinese 'native' carried the body to his grave. Valignano reports that they 'took him out of the coffin conforming to the custom of the Portuguese by putting only a pillow under his head and covering the face with a cloth',[145] inside a grave located 'at the entrance to the sacristy', according to De Souza,[146] and before performing the 'appropriate funeral rites', according to Gonçalves.[147] While Lucena tells us that this same pillow was made of 'silk', de Souza reveals that Xavier's corpse was also 'simply wrapped in a shroud',[148] before he was put into the ground.

Fifth, Xavier's corpse exhibits additional (familiar) signs of incorruptibility upon the opening of his grave by several newly arrived Jesuits, five months after his interment at Our Lady of the Mount,[149] signs that incite additional acts of religious devotion and relic production, reinforce his continued sanctity in death, and reveal the increased involvement of the Jesuits in determining his journey to sainthood. Teixeira tells us that it was Juan de Beira, a Portuguese Jesuit who, with several companions, stopped off in Malacca desirous – 'in the extreme' – to see what had been described to him as the incorrupt corpse of his 'special friend' to whom he was much devoted.[150] Lucena informs us that this group of Jesuits 'secretly opened the hole at night' – again, circumstances reminiscent of European translations – upon which they saw the 'towel which covered his face', and the 'pillow upon which was the head' – both of which had 'passed red blood',[151] a sure sign of his continuing sanctity. In addition, his corpse was found to be 'as entire, fresh and fragrant as it was before being interred there', and his vestments were found to be 'perfectly intact' according to De Souza.[152] Valignano tells us that his incorruption was complete despite the 'fresh lime with its fire' and the 'earth with its humidity', a detail that suggests that lime had been employed once again just as had been the case in Sancian.[153] Gonçalves informs us that his preservation incited additional acts of religious devotion, Beira and his Jesuit companions 'kiss[ing] his sacred hand and feet [and] showering them with tears of devotion'.[154] Xavier's outer vestment, its preservation a sign of its relic status, was then removed by Father Melchior Nunes – one of the Jesuits who had accompanied Beira to Xavier's gravesite – and eventually carried to Japan.[155] Once again, the translation of Xavier's relics reinforces his biographical ties in life and death to both places and persons, in the process spreading his saintliness to additional sites.

But this same group of Jesuits determines that Xavier is not fully appreciated in Malacca, owing to damage evident on his corpse upon his second disinterment. This damage exposes the vulnerabilities of church, state, and public, and compels Xavier's translation from Malacca. De Souza informs us of Xavier's improper treatment during his interment by those 'Portuguese' put in charge, a point echoed by Gonçalves as well. Not only was the grave that was dug 'too short' to fit his corpse, but he was forced down into it; a 'recoiling' of the neck, 'deep cuts' in the neck and on the face, and a 'slight bruising' of the top of the nose were all bodily traits evidenced by Beira and his companions upon opening his grave.[156] Moreover, Xavier's simple burial – devoid of a coffin – is now viewed critically in light of the damage, De Souza affirming that it was a 'custom [existing] among the poorer classes', and Valignano going so far as to call it 'an act of disgrace'.[157]

Here Xavier's poor treatment has everything to do the vulnerabilities of church, state, and public in Malacca at this time. That there was no sizeable contingency of Jesuits – Teixeira inexplicably not accounted for – located in Malacca to preside over his interment, Beira and his companions only arriving one month later, is a point affirmed by Xavier's many Jesuit biographers.[158] This, in turn, suggests not only that Xavier's burial in Malacca lacked religiosity, but that there were no members of his own order there to sanction the interment of their founding father, or to promote his biographical ties to this site and ensure his proper burial. Moreover, Gonçalves alludes to the reason behind the fact that there were no Jesuits residing in Malacca, despite their ownership of Our Lady of the Mount, suggesting that earlier tensions with Malacca's acting governor, Dom Alvaro de Athaide, had led to his disapproval of the Jesuits such that they had consequently left the city as a result; in fact it had been Xavier himself who urged them to do so.[159] The governor's marked absence during the burial of Xavier's corpse – he had remained at a window observing his procession through the streets rather than partaking in them according to Gonçalves[160] – suggests that Xavier's burial had occurred without a proper 'balance' of church and state actors, as had been the case in Sancian.

That Malacca had been in the midst of a plague at the time of the arrival of Xavier's corpse suggests both a lack of hygiene in Malacca and the weaknesses of state officials to prevent its spread on to other Portuguese and native bodies. Finally, the lack of an organized Jesuit and colonial state presence in Malacca also points to the general disregard for colonial polices and religious practice among Malacca's public (both Portuguese and native) such that there were no Jesuits to preside over daily communions and conversions, Malacca's residents no doubt engaging instead in forms of trade. De Souza informs us that it was 'at that sight, [that] the authors of the secret exhumation judged it improper to hide anew, under the earth, such a treasure so neglected and so little appreciated',[161] a rationale also typically used in promoting European relic translations. In other words, Beira and his companions felt compelled to translate Xavier's corpse to a 'more decent place' – in this case Goa, the centre of the Portuguese empire in Asia – where he would be fully appreciated by church, state, and public.[162]

Xavier's translation from Malacca to Goa, just as had been the case in Sancian, is transformed into a ritualized event in which he is carried in procession to an awaiting ship accompanied by two of the above Jesuits. Teixeira tells us that on 15 August 1553 it was Juan de Beira who 'ordered a coffin to be made, in which the father put him, decently, and ordered that it be guarded in the house with much reverence, and leaving for the Moluccas, he left one of his fellow Jesuits in charge of overseeing the movement and management of Xavier's corpse to India, ensuring that it would be properly placed in the College of St Paul in Goa'.[163] Our eyewitness affirms not only that Xavier's journey was to be overseen by a Jesuit, thus suggesting that the same mistake would not be made as had occurred during his interment in Malacca, but that the new home for Xavier's corpse was a Jesuit institution in Goa. Also, that Beira himself was destined for the Moluccas suggests the larger Jesuit enterprise wherein members constantly travelled between colonial posts, helping to establish them in the process.

Valignano informs us that it was the same Diogo Pereira mentioned earlier who covered the costs of this commissioned coffin: it was 'very well made, covered with damask inside, and covered on the outside with a cloth of brocade'.[164] Next, according to de Souza, 'the holy body was laid [inside the coffin], pending its embarking for India, at the next monsoon'. It was during this waiting period that Xavier performed a miracle, thus sanctioning once again his translation from Malacca. De Souza writes: 'the interval of waiting lasted eighteen days, and a wax taper, which was lit by the side of the coffin and which could in the ordinary course of things have lasted at most ten hours, continued to burn all those eighteen days, and the wax that flowed from it weighed much more than the taper itself'.[165] Gonçalves informs us that this 'truly miraculous' event was witnessed by, at the very least, Diogo Pereira and Juan de Beira, two men who, significantly, had biographical ties to Xavier in life, and the cousin of Pereira, who later testified to its occurrence on oath in Portugal as part of Xavier's canonization process.[166]

Next Xavier's corpse is carried in procession, the month now being September (1553) and nearing the coming of the monsoon season,[167] towards the shores of Malacca, 'accompanied by many noblemen [where] he was placed on a sloop [small boat] that was already waiting, beautifully adorned with luxurious carpeting and a silk awning, on which he was taken to a ship belonging to a certain Lopo de Noronha, who was about to depart for India, and transferred aboard', according to the Jesuit biographer Mendes Pinto.[168] The emphasis on noblemen – including the status of Noronha himself – indexes Xavier's increased status in Malacca, compared to his earlier transport from Sancian on a Portuguese merchant's ship. Not only was the ship itself, and the berth reserved for Xavier's corpse, richly decorated but, during his translation, he was always surrounded by 'many smells and perfumes',[169] a detail that suggests that Xavier's corporeal fragrance was supplemented with artificial ones to ensure his 'odour of sanctity', a sure sign of his saintliness, during his journey. The biographers Lucena and Valignano give us additional information on the two Jesuits who, in the end, were selected by Beira to safeguard and sanction Xavier's journey to Goa, the first being Manuel de Tavora, one of the Jesuits who had accompanied Beira to Malacca and the second being Pedro de Alcáçova, a Jesuit who had only recently arrived from Japan, where he had been overseeing the Jesuit mission there, and who had been requested by a Portuguese colonial state official to 'do some business in India' on his behalf,[170] details that affirm Xavier's biographical ties to persons and places as well as the fact that Jesuits were often employed as agents of the state.

Lastly, Xavier performs additional miracles on the voyage to Goa, thus sanctioning the larger Portuguese 'seaborne' empire, his translation from Malacca, and his continued travels in death to additional colonial outposts, including brief stopovers in Ceylon and Cochin. Through these travels a discourse of incorruptibility expands, to include additional places and publics, mapping the Portuguese colonial empire and marking it with sanctity. Both Valignano and Teixeira attest to the fact that Xavier liberated the ship through his intercession from numerous 'certain dangers and shipwrecks'[171] caused by 'large storms on the journey',[172] the ship's (Jesuit) passengers 'invoking the name of Father Francis to keep them free and safe'.[173] Gonçalves informs us that, precisely when the ship was in danger, the candles and perfumes surrounding his corpse blazed even brighter and smelled even stronger, ritual details suggestive of the ability of his corpse to emit efficacious signs at critical moments, thus ensuring his public of their safeguarded journey.[174]

Teixeira reports that the ship first made a brief stopover in Ceylon (now Sri Lanka), this temporary stay giving credibility to the future rumour that, unbeknownst to his Portuguese and Jesuit protectors, Xavier's corpse was, in fact, switched with that of a Buddhist monk.[175] Next the ship carrying Xavier passed by Cochin – the former capital of the Estado da Índia, and the site where Vasco da Gama had in fact first landed, thus entangling their biographies (in life and death) once again – where, according to Lucena, he was 'also visited, and venerated with great contest, and devotion', by its public, which included Father Francisco Perez, Superior of the Jesuit residence there. Perez proceeded to open his coffin and observe him 'without any corruption',[176] this latter detail suggestive of Xavier's continued powers and the inroads that the Society of Jesus had made on Indian soil, as compared to the sites of his previous translations in Sancian and Malacca.

In this section I have explored a series of themes to characterize Xavier's translation to Malacca, his five-month interment here, and his continuing journey in death, relying on the same set of Jesuit biographies that earlier provided a window on to Xavier's experiences in Sancian. The discourse of incorruptibility recounted in these Jesuit biographies incorporates additional places, publics, and practices as it travels alongside Xavier's corpse. While this missionary's corpse exhibits many of the same signs of incorruptibility first evidenced in Sancian – a lack of decomposition, a fragrance, the spurting of blood, relic production and circulation – Xavier also incites new acts of devotion: the lighting of tapers, a richly decorated coffin, kissing, touching, and the shedding of tears. His stay in Malacca also reflects the availability of material goods in this centre of trade – silk, tapestries, perfumes, candles, and carpeting – and the greater wealth of Malacca as a Portuguese outpost in comparison to Sancian. Xavier performs additional miracles – curing a man of his sickness and ridding the city of a plague – and affirms his biographical ties to this site through such men as Pereira and Beira, precisely again because Malacca is a more developed colonial outpost than Sancian.

In the end, all of these signs work to sanctify Xavier's location here as well as the space of Malacca and its residents. However, Xavier's ill-treatment in death such that his body is damaged during his interment simultaneously exposes the vulnerabilities of church, state, and public in this colonial outpost. The Jesuits stationed in Malacca now take on a larger role in determining his journey to sainthood, and compel his translation from this colonial outpost to a more suitable site directly tied to his biography in life. Once again, as was the case in Sancian, that Xavier maintains his incorruption *in spite of* his location makes him that much more saintly.

Goa (1554)

> Goa under the Portuguese was always more than itself, more than simply a port city. It was the focus of their entire seaborne empire, its prosperity in the 16th century ... mark[ed] fluctuations in Portuguese fortunes in all Asia rather than any change in Goa and its hinterland.[177]

I continue on the path of Xavier's journey to sainthood. He arrived in Goa during the month of March 1554, the site of his last translation in death. His ceremonious reception in Goa will reveal the expanding role of the Jesuits in organizing the set of ritual activities surrounding his corpse and the reasons underlying his final interment in this colonial outpost, also the centre of the Portuguese empire in Asia, as reinforced above by the historian Michael Pearson. Once again, my approach is thematic, summarizing the central defining characteristics of his experiences in Goa as recorded by the same set of Jesuit biographers of this saint-in-the-making, and which includes several eyewitness accounts. Xavier's corpse continues to exhibit numerous signs of his incorruptibility – both replicating many of those witnessed at the sites of his earlier translations (Sancian and Malacca) and producing and circulating additional signs – in his new location. However, in the case of Goa, Xavier no longer emits signs *in spite of* his location. Here, to a stronger degree than in Malacca, Xavier's saintliness does spread by way of contagion both because Goa is a developed centre of colonial and missionary activity, and because of his even stronger biographical attachments to this site. Unlike in Sancian and Malacca, where his corpse was poorly treated, Xavier is fully appreciated in Goa. The reception of Xavier in Goa also exposes the strengths of church, state, and public and suggests the reasons why his travels in death ended at this location. However, in choosing to retain and maintain him at this site, Portuguese colonial officials and Jesuit missionaries did not let go of the discursive power of his incorruptibility; rather, as will become evident in a subsequent section, they immediately focused (two years after his arrival) on 'authenticating' it, finding new ways to propagate the incorruptibility of both saint and state in the process.

First, Xavier is given a private Jesuit reception, both prior to and in preparation for his celebrated arrival in Goa, a detail which suggests the expanding role of the Jesuits in defining Xavier's journey to sainthood. While Valignano informs us that the ship bearing the corpse of Xavier – the ship of a man called Lopo de Noronha – stopped off at the port of Batecala, only '23 or 24 leagues from Goa',[178] Teixeira describes how Xavier was honourably received at this site before performing additional miracles of healing – this time directed at women during childbirth[179] – while awaiting directions from the Jesuits of Goa.[180] Next, according to Gonçalves, the Vice Provincial of the College of St Paul – a Jesuit-owned institution in which Xavier's corpse would eventually be interred – with the permission of Goa's Viceroy, Dom Affonso de Noronha – a man who had known Xavier personally – organized a skiff to receive the corpse of Xavier in Batecala and transfer him to Goa's harbour.[181] Teixeira informs us that he personally accompanied the Vice Provincial Melchior Nunes, alongside two other Jesuit brothers and four or five boys of the Goa orphanage, 'who sang very well, in order to celebrate the body when they arrived at it'.[182] Upon locating Lopo de Noronha's ship three or four days later and viewing Xavier's corpse, they 'kissed the tomb, and embraced it with many tears, sentiments and devotion', while the captain of the ship adorned the ship with 'flags' and 'streamers', and 'fed the artillery' in preparation for his translation to Goa.[183] The physical transfer of his corpse was thus accompanied by much 'festivity' and 'rejoicing' and included the singing of 'hymns' and 'psalms' on the part of the orphans and the releasing of 'all' the artillery on the part of the ship.[184]

Next the Vice Provincial, again accompanied by our eyewitness biographer, Teixeira, and bearing the corpse of Xavier, arrived at 'Our Lady of the Presentation', a church 'within view of the city of Goa', in which they 'lay open the body' for a small Jesuit reception which lasted the duration of the night and which included a more thorough examination of the condition of his corpse.[185] Nunes also sends ahead two Jesuit priests to forewarn both the Jesuits of Goa and the Viceroy of both Xavier's impending arrival and state of incorruptness, while Noronha takes it upon himself to organize Xavier's reception at the docks the following day, the Jesuits staying up all night to adorn the College of St Paul in preparation for his interment.[186]

Second, upon its arrival in Goa on 16 March 1554 – during Holy Week[187] – Xavier's corpse is honourably received by a diverse group – including members of this city's well-developed triad of church, state, and public – thus initiating the translation process whereby he will be ascribed with new meaning relative to his new context. Lucena tells us that in preparation 'there were already six boats of Portuguese [men] with white torches in their hands and their young servants with tapers behind [them], after which one could see twelve or thirteen other ones, with up to thirty people with the same lights that they were making a beautiful view of light on the water'.[188] Teixeira gives us his account from inside the skiff as he approaches Goa's harbour, describing not only how Father Melchior Nunes immediately went forward to receive the same Diogo Pereira who had travelled with Xavier since Sancian, and had arrived separately in Goa in time for his reception, but also the manner by which all the bells of Goa's churches were rung 'by order of the Viceroy', in order to signify Xavier's arrival as an 'important person', and the crowding of 'so many people around us' who were invested in 'touching the tomb, and even the boat in which the father came'.[189]

De Souza informs us that this crowd also included a 'great number of sick ones' who were carried in the 'arms of strangers' and a group of natives 'who were throwing themselves on the ground, widening their arms in the style of invoking and praising the Saint',[190] this latter detail perhaps suggestive of the natives' prior contact with Xavier in life as well as their own distinctive religious practices. Mendes Pinto, a second eyewitness alongside Teixeira, provides us with an unforgettable description of Xavier's reception at Goa's pier. It is one where the Viceroy waits 'in full state with footmen bearing silver maces accompanied by all the nobility of India', the brothers of the Society of Jesus are in 'great number', and an 'enormous crowd' gathers with 'tears and sobs widespread', and includes a 'group of orphaned children'.[191] Together, the accounts written by Pinto, Lucena, Teixeira, and De Souza represent Xavier's arrival as a richly decorated religious affair – involving bells, cannons, silver maces, priestly vestments, tapers, brocade cloths, and a crucifix – and the whole city turned out, including not only the Viceroy – who had only the night before organized the festivities – but numerous Jesuit priests stationed here, Goa's nobility, a group of orphaned children and slaves, and even members of Goa's Christian and native publics. The various segments of Portuguese India (church, state, and public) are all represented during his reception, a contrast to the Malacca celebrations, where a certain state official and a Jesuit contingency were notably missing. In addition, Xavier's biographical ties (to place and people) are affirmed through the presence of such figures as Viceroy Noronha, Diogo Pereira, Manuel Teixeira, and Mendes Pinto, four very different men who knew Xavier at different moments and in various capacities and locations during his lifetime. Lastly, the scale and success of his reception (compared to the one staged in Malacca) index the power of the Viceroy as the representative of the colonial state to organize such a momentous event at such short notice.

In Goa, Xavier's corpse continues to exhibit characteristic traits of its incorruptness. It is carried in elaborate procession inside a newly built coffin – one with gold embroidery and fringes[192] – through the decorated streets of Goa, just as had been the case for Malacca, sanctifying both place and public as well as his translation to this new setting. However, in contrast to the site of Xavier's second translation, Goa already had a rich history of processions, both religious – including the regularized activity of carrying a relic (a piece of hair) of the Virgin Mary through the streets of Goa[193] – and stately – including the one staged in 1547 to celebrate the Portuguese victory in establishing the colonial outpost of Diu.[194] The local history of processions suggests both Goa's further development as a colonial outpost and the extent of church and state power there (as compared to Sancian and Malacca). Thus, the procession of Xavier's corpse through the streets of Goa was encompassed by a larger set of familiar practices that preceded and thus helped shape its form. It is our witness Teixeira who leaves us with a rich account of the carefully ordered structure of the procession ordered by the Viceroy, and in which he participated.[195] Teixeira's description indexes not only a prior history of 'solemn' processions in India wherein orphaned children of the Jesuit college typically wear 'garlands of roses' on their heads and carry 'palm branches' in their hands – details that also suggest an adaptation on the part of the Portuguese to an Indian setting – but also the fact that certain funereal practices were often carried over between colonial outposts within Portuguese Asia: the use of two incense burners to exude smells on to Xavier's corpse featured on the ship from Malacca as well. This same eyewitness also asserts the religiosity of the procession such that the Viceroy and Goa's public are preceded by the various religious figureheads and organizations of the city – again, all carrying their identifying flags and wearing their costumes.[196] The Jesuits of course are given the prestigious honour of carrying Xavier's corpse through the streets of Goa. However, these various church officials are also counter-balanced by the presence of the Viceroy – the representative figure of the state – who is followed by Goa's 'honourable' public. In the same way that Xavier was initially received by numerous members of Goan society, the procession itself is representative of the larger Portuguese colonial structure in Goa, the legacy of Albuquerque's Indo-Portuguese race – the *casados* – felt in the diversity of the public.

Our second eyewitness takes up where Teixeira leaves us, providing additional glimpses of the direction that this procession took. Mendes Pinto reveals not only that all the streets of Goa were decorated in honour of Xavier with 'carpets and silken hangings', but that the procession first passed through the city gates, then continued on to Goa's main street before finally stopping at the Jesuit College of St Paul, the designated site of his interment.[197] It is likely that Xavier's corpse was purposely carried throughout the city in order to sanctify it in the process. This same eyewitness also takes note of additional members of Goa's public who were present during the procession, but were restricted in their participation. He informs us that while the 'native heathens and Moors reportedly stuck their fingers in their mouths to show how deeply amazed they were, as was their custom' as the procession passed by, the windows overlooking the main streets of Goa were 'filled and crowded with the wives and daughters of all the noblemen'.[198] The presence of these two groups suggests, on the one hand, the expanded diversity of the public on hand to witness the solemnities of 1554 as well as their delegation to the sidelines of the procession owing to their inferior status within the Portuguese colonial order and, on the other, their crucial role in reproducing a hierarchical Portuguese colonial society. Lucena informs us these same streets were also 'glowing with lights, smelling sweetly of perfumes and filled with the best fleets of India', a detail that marks Goa as the centre of a larger seaborne empire as well as its ritualized transformation during Xavier's procession.[199] Finally, De Souza details how Xavier performed various miracles during his procession: not only did his corpse exude a 'most pleasing fragrance' that no doubt rivalled the smells already exuded by the city, but he 'gave health suddenly to the blind ones, crippled ones, lepers and others inflicted with various illnesses'.[200] These finer points suggest Xavier's continuing display of signs of incorruptness in death similar to those he exhibited earlier in Sancian and Malacca. Together, the accounts of Teixeira, Pinto, Lucena, and de Souza reveal not only the balancing of church and state, including the defining roles of the Viceroy and the Jesuits of Goa, but also Goa's riches, its organization, and the diversity of Goa's attendant public such that it now incorporates men, women, and children, and Christians and natives, Xavier's sanctity rubbing off on to place and public in such a manner as to confirm his translation to this new setting.

Following his procession, Xavier's corpse is placed, just as had been the case in Malacca, inside a Jesuit institution, only this time there are numerous Jesuits in residence to sanction and bless his translation, including Vice Provincial Melchior Nunes, who had earlier taken part in organizing his reception in Goa. While Teixeira informs us that the prestigious Jesuit College of St Paul was the chosen site for his interment – Xavier's biographical ties to this institution no doubt playing a role in its designation[201] – Valignano tells us that both the college and church had been painted white on this occasion – despite it being Holy Week – in order that everyone should receive Xavier with 'festivity' and 'happiness' rather than 'mourning'.[202] Once again, it is our eyewitness Mendes Pinto who provides a rich account of not only how the church was decorated with 'brocade frontals on all the altars, lamps, candlesticks [and] silver crosses' but also the details of Xavier's ceremonious placing 'next to the high altar on the Gospel side', and accompanied by a 'solemn mass', a 'beautiful chorus', and 'many musical instruments befitting the solemnity of such an important festivity'.[203] Together, these details are suggestive of the religiosity – imbued through objects, practices, and the presence of multiple religious orders – that accompanied Xavier's placement inside the College of St Paul in Goa. Moreover, these signs of reverence are in direct contrast to Xavier's ill-treatment in Sancian and Malacca.

Owing to the public's overwhelming desire to see his incorrupt corpse, Xavier was then subject to a three-day display – to an estimated crowd of six thousand persons[204] – prior to his interment. This ritualized event was unique to Goa (as compared to Sancian and Malacca) and included numerous religious acts of devotion and the production of additional miracles of healing and (unauthorized) relics. Both eyewitness biographers first explain how the idea of a public reception came about, its planning largely under the charge of the Jesuits. Teixeira recalls how the Jesuits had requested the Viceroy to leave the college 'with the other nobility' after the completion of the Mass, thinking that his absence would dissipate the large crowds gathered inside the college; instead, members of the public surged forward, desirous to 'kiss the feet' and 'touch [his] five toes', two religious acts of devotion characteristic of relic veneration which also echo what had happened in Malacca.[205] Meanwhile, Mendes Pinto recalls how 'the crush and press of the crowd were such that the grilles of the chapel, despite the fact that they were sturdy, were broken into many pieces'.[206] It is members of the Society of Jesus who decide to postpone his viewing until later in the afternoon,[207] while the role of the Jesuits in taking charge of Xavier's corpse and public reception continues, a point echoed as well by other Jesuit biographers.

De Souza informs us that, during this time that the public was barred from viewing Xavier, the Jesuits arranged the corpse of Xavier, 'with the face and hands open and the feet barefoot in order to be seen by the people'.[208] However, during his reception – which was scheduled to last three days and nights, ending on 18 March 1554 to coincide with Palm Sunday – and owing to the small size of the chapel, it was 'necessary to raise the body [i.e. stand him up] three times for the view of everyone in the proper manner'. His reception also included various acts of devotion – the singing of hymns, the performance of a Catholic Mass on the part of the Jesuits, the touching and kissing of his corpse, and 'infinite tears from those present'.[209] Teixeira informs us that, during his public reception, Xavier performed additional miracles of healing similar to those performed at other sites of his translation. One man's sight is completely restored after touching his blinded eyes to Xavier's corpse, while a woman is cured through the power of prayer alone, her illness disabling her from earlier taking part in Xavier's reception, despite her desire to do so.[210] Valignano informs us that, during this same reception, many members of the public were not satisfied just to see, touch, and kiss Xavier's corpse: rather many were desirous to 'take from him some relics' – a devotional practice that had been allowed in both Sancian and Malacca but was 'not granted' in Goa.[211]

This desire to obtain relics and its refusal on the part of those in charge suggests both the increasing value and fragility ascribed to his corpse as it travelled from site to site and the fact that the Jesuits had such an important role in Goa, specifically in sanctioning any and all activities centred on Xavier, a point confirmed by Melchior Nunes himself.[212] However, as De Souza points out, one member of Portuguese India's public – a woman of nobility in fact – managed to obtain a relic of Xavier. Doña Isabel de Carom[213] 'bit off with her teeth the small toe [of the right foot], from which blood ran to the astonishment of all those present',[214] this pious act (and infamous story) serving as proof of Xavier's continuing incorruptibility in death, its retelling a popular practice in coming centuries. Lucena informs us that at the close of the reception, that is, on the night between the third and the fourth day, Xavier was 'placed inside a coffin of a vaulted archway that opened next to the altar that was part of the Gospel [of the Jesuit college of St Paul]', even though the public's desire to 'see, praise, and confess in their infinite bond with the Lord' had not been satiated. Xavier's translation to Goa was now complete.

Xavier's full appreciation in Goa – as is evident in the rituals surrounding his translation – exposes the strengths of church, state, and public, affirms his biographical ties to this site, and explains why his sacred remains in the months following his interment were not translated to yet another colonial outpost, as in the previous cases of Sancian and Malacca. That Xavier stayed in Goa, in turn, acts to consolidate Goa's status as the centre of Portuguese Asia. Thus, throughout the various activities surrounding his corpse – his Jesuit reception, his initial arrival, procession, three-day display inside the College of St Paul, and interment – Xavier is treated with multiple signs of respect characteristic of European relic translations, which together suggest that he was meaningfully (and thus successfully) incorporated into this Indo-Portuguese community in a manner distinct from his past translations. First, Goa in 1554 is marked by the presence of a strong head of state, a presence notably absent in both Sancian and Malacca. That is, Viceroy Affonso de Noronha, unlike Governor Athaide of Malacca, both takes charge of and participates in the various activities centred on Xavier's corpse. Moreover, the various objects (both religious and not, including but not limited to rich tapestries, silk hangings, vestments, incense burners, wax, tapers, bells, candlesticks, musical instruments, silver, etc.) that are incorporated into the Goa celebrations reinforce its position as a centre of Portuguese trade. Second, Goa is characterized by a developed church infrastructure, one that includes Jesuits, Franciscans, and various religious institutions (churches, chapels, orphanages, colleges, etc.), incites numerous acts of religious devotion among its public (including kissing, touching, shedding tears, singing hymns, performing Masses), is adapted to an Indian setting (native participation is encouraged, alongside the wearing of rose garlands and the carrying of palm branches), and operates under the umbrella of the Estado da Índia, with the Viceroy being given a prominent position alongside the Jesuits throughout the festivities.

That the Jesuits preside over and ensure Xavier's proper interment (including their organization of a private reception restricted to members of their own religious order, his three-day public display, and his burial) also suggests their increasing investment in labelling Xavier as one of their own, and marks the beginnings of a separate Jesuit public attendant to his corpse. Xavier had, after all, initiated the Society of Jesus from Goa only twelve years earlier; his biographical attachments to Goa parallel the Jesuits' own development as a religious order. Thus, there is a balancing of church and state that is evidenced throughout Xavier's translation to Goa, a balancing markedly absent during his first and second translations in Sancian and Malacca respectively. Third, Goa is characterized by a diverse public, one that evidences both Albuquerque's legacy and the policies of religious conversion such that it includes men and women (of Indian, Portuguese, and mixed descent), children and orphans, Christians and natives, and promotes the Catholic faith throughout the celebrations. Goan colonial society is not only racialized, classed, and gendered, but it evidences both its Portugueseness and its Indianness simultaneously. Fourth, Goa, more so than Sancian and Malacca, is defined by Xavier's numerous biographical ties to institutions and individuals located here (including of course the Jesuits, but also the College of St Paul, Viceroy Noronha, eyewitnesses Teixeira and Mendes Pinto, and merchant Diogo Pereira). Lastly, that Xavier's corpse continues to exhibit numerous signs of incorruptibility (including a wholeness, a fragrance, and a freshness in his ability to spurt blood, as well as miracles of healing) throughout his interment, signs that spread by contagion on to Goa the space, reinforces his emplacement in this location and strengthens Goa's centrifugal power. Thus, despite such a long journey, Xavier had arrived at a site where his value finally matched his location. In other words, Goa in 1554 was the one colonial outpost in Portuguese Asia deemed incorrupt enough to maintain his sacred remains; Xavier had finally found a suitable home. Moreover, Xavier's translation to Goa – specifically his three-day display – marks the beginning of his repeated ritualization throughout the duration of Portuguese colonial rule in India, a subject taken up in later chapters of the book.

Thus far, I have attempted to trace the development of a discourse of incorruptibility that travels alongside Xavier's corpse from Sancian to Malacca to Goa, incorporating new places, publics and (ritual) practices along the way. At each site I have explored the details of his relic translation and the workings of church, state, and public, suggesting that they are intimately connected in so far as they reveal the parallel drives for sainthood and statehood in mid-sixteenth-century Portuguese Asia as well as the many problems encountered along the way. That Xavier himself had earlier visited each of these sites connects his apostolic journeys in death to those in life and reveals his defining role (both in life and death) in the early mapping of a Portuguese empire in Asia. That Xavier's corpse exhibits certain qualities of incorruptness not only sanctifies Sancian, Malacca, and Goa to varying degrees but marks these colonial outposts as integral to his fashioning as a saint of Asia in that they stabilize (and thus concretize) his miraculous identity over a sixteen-month period, sometimes in spite of his location. That Xavier is only fully appreciated in Goa exposes the vulnerabilities of church and state in Sancian and Malacca, and compels his translation to this centre of colonial and missionary activity, a site not coincidentally where he had the strongest biographical attachments. That a set of Jesuit biographers, including several eyewitnesses, sought to record his journey to sainthood not only reveals the territorialness of the Portuguese 'seaborne' empire in the early modern period but also speaks to an increasing investment in Xavier as representative of their own history in Portuguese Asia. The reproduction of his remarkable story for a larger reading public (both Jesuit and Europe) located within and beyond Asia affirmed the ties between metropole and or colonies, and suggests that both the 'actual' and 'written' journey mattered at a time when Xavier's canonization process was under way, the subject of the final section of this chapter.

Xavier's canonization process (1556–1616): authenticating incorruptibility

> His [Xavier's] name was famous all over India and everybody knew him, wherever he worked, as the Holy Father, and when towards the end of 1548 the news spread in Goa that he had been killed at Cape Comorin, his friends declared, even though his body should cost them 30,000 *cruzados* to get him canonized, they would have to obtain it ... the rumors about the death of the father were unfounded this time. But, when five years later the news reached Goa again that Master Francis had died, it proved to be true – Georg Schurhammer, 1923.[215]

As is evident from the above quotation, church and state officials located in Portuguese Asia had first proposed the idea of Xavier's canonization after the circulation of a (false) rumour that he had died as early as 1548, an event which no doubt foreshadowed their (increased) investment in his canonization in the aftermath of his actual death in 1552. In this section, I briefly examine the two phases of Xavier's canonization process (1556–7, 1610–22), which were initiated from Goa in the aftermath of his interment there. Now that Jesuit missionaries and Portuguese colonial officials had succeeded in developing a discourse of incorruptibility associated with his corpse, they were invested in authenticating it alongside their own power in Portuguese Asia.

Two years after Xavier's reception in Goa – as news of its success had spread to Europe – plans were made to formally initiate Xavier's canonization process. In a letter written to his newly appointed Viceroy of Goa, Dom Pedro Mascarenhas (1554–5) – a man who had known Xavier in life – King John III of Portugal outlines the basic requirements of canonization, requesting also that the Viceroy personally oversee the proceedings. He writes:

> Lisbon, 28th of March, 1556. Viceroy, my friend. The life and marvellous actions of Francis Xavier are so very admirable that their publication should necessarily result in the glory of our God. I order you, for this reason, that you listen to the testimonies in all the parts where he was, that you proceed to organize an inquiry into all the prodigious acts of that extraordinary man, about all the superhuman deeds that he performed, about all the wonders that God performed through his ministry or his orations, that occurred during his life and after his death. Please send me these authentic acts in their original. Please write all the facts and all the inquiries, day by day, with their dates, registered by

the public. This inquiry should be done in the most appropriate style, that everything is known about this man, the particulars of his life, his actions, the habits of Francis Xavier, the countries which he visited, in good conscience and under the faith of a vow, the questions should be formed and responded to. Please send me a remittance, signed with your signature and the auditor general, three copies of which sent by three different ways. With this I am very obliged to you. Viceroy, my friend, I send you much health. I, the king.[216]

Here the Portuguese king is duly concerned about authenticating Xavier's incorruptibility by establishing an evidentiary proceeding to oversee the collection of information on this potential saint-in-the-making. Not only should an inquiry be set up to examine the 'life and times' of Xavier – including the locations he visited, his actions and habits, etc. – but it should also review the many miraculous acts performed by this 'extraordinary man', witnesses from various publics located in Portuguese Asia deposing their testimonies under oath to this effect. Moreover, the findings of the commission must be sent via three different routes, thus ensuring their safe passage and arrival in Lisbon, before being forwarded to Rome for final papal approval. Lastly, that it is the Viceroy, the literal head of the Estado da Índia, who is put in charge of organizing this Jesuit missionary's canonization drive speaks to the mutual investment of church and state in Xavier as a representative figure of their joint power.

As Pedro Mascarenhas had died in office in the interim, it was Goa's next Viceroy, Francisco Barreto (1555–58), who was put in charge of executing the king's 'royal command'. Barreto formally initiated the canonization proceedings by requesting his personal physician, a man who interestingly had met the potential saint in life, having arrived in Goa on the same ship as Xavier in 1542, to examine his corpse; the expertise of a trained medical physician was required to duly authenticate Xavier's incorruptibility, since this same act had only been cursorily performed by the Jesuits upon his reception in Goa in 1554. Cosmas de Saraiva, attached to the prestigious Royal Hospital of Goa – an institution started by Governor Albuquerque himself – directed the autopsy of Xavier's corpse, which took place on 18 November 1556.[217] Here I reproduce the details of Saraiva's autopsy report:

I, Doctor Cosmas Saraiva, physician to the Viceroy, have been to examine the body of Father Master, brought to the city of Goa. I felt and pressed all the members of the body with my finger, but paid special attention to the abdominal region and made certain that the intestines were in their natural position. There had been no embalming of any kind nor had any artificial preservative agents been used. I observed a wound in the left side near the heart and asked two of the [Jesuit] Society who were with me to put their fingers into it. When they withdrew them they were covered with blood which I smelt and found to be absolutely untainted. The limbs and other parts of the body were entire and clothed in their flesh in such a way that, according to the laws of medicine, they could not possibly have been so preserved by any natural or artificial means, seeing that Father Francis had been dead for a year and a half and buried for a year. I affirm on oath that what I have written above is the truth. Doctor Cosmas de Saraiva. At Goa, 18 November 1556.[218]

Saraiva's medical report reads like an official autopsy report, one which more or less certifies the incorruptibility of Xavier – specifically, in his various body parts – in death. He pokes and prods Xavier's corpse in order to medically attest to the facts: that 'various members' and limbs of his body are 'entire and clothed in their flesh', and in their 'natural position', this latter detail suggestive of perhaps a concern with ensuring that his corpse was not tampered with during his many travels in death. This doctor also notes that fresh blood is evident, blood that does not smell bad, suggesting that it is not 'tainted', a sure sign of his decomposition. This bodily emission on the part of Xavier is a familiar one, as it came up earlier during the receptions of his corpse in Sancian, Malacca and Goa, respectively. However, this time, blood acts as medical proof for Xavier's incorruptibility, simultaneously making plausible his earlier emissions at these previous locations. Lastly, Saraiva states with certainty that Xavier's corpse was neither embalmed nor submitted to 'artificial preservative agents', relying on the 'laws of medicine' to argue for his own expertise in the matter at hand, and stating that what he writes is the 'truth' and affirmed 'on oath', details which together authenticate the incorruptibility of Xavier's corpse, four years after his death.

However, Saraiva's report alone would prove to be insufficient for authenticating Xavier's incorruptibility. Only two weeks later, on 1 December 1556, Xavier's corpse was submitted to yet another, more detailed autopsy, only this time the person presiding over the examination was a man by the name of Ambrósio Ribeiro, the Vicar General of Goa, who was also a trained medical doctor. I reproduce the details of his report in its entirety.

I, Dr. Ambrósio Ribeiro ... certify under oath of my office ... that we went to inspect the body. At 9 or 10 o'clock we opened the coffin which was in the main chapel of St. Paul's and saw the body at leisure; I felt it with my own hands from the feet up the knees and almost all the other parts of the body. I certify that in all these parts the flesh was entire, covered with its natural skin and humidity without any corruption. On the left leg a little above the knee on the exterior there is a little cut or wound, a finger in length, which looked like a hit [all in one stroke].

> All round the wound there oozed out a streak of blood gone black. And much above on the left side near the heart there is a small hole which looked like a hit [wound]. Through it I inserted my fingers as deep as I could and found it hollow. Only inside I felt some small bits which seemed to me like pieces of intestines dried up owing to the long time the body lay in the grave. But I smelt no corruption although I put my face quite close to the body. The head rested on a small Chinese damask pillow, leaving on it below the neck something like a stain of blood similar to that on the leg, faded in colour and turned black. I directed the notary to draw up a report stating the way I had examined the body. He did so and I sign it with my own hand on 1 December 1556. (And I, Jorge Gomez, the notary, made it.). Doctor Ambrósio Ribeiro.[219]

Like Saraiva before him, Ribeiro attests to that which is visibly apparent to him, drawing on his own medical expertise to support his findings. He views the body 'with leisure', confirming the entirety, colour, and texture of the flesh on various different body parts and noting that these parts are 'covered with its natural skin and humidity without any corruption'. Nor does Xavier's corpse smell bad, a statement he made after putting his face 'quite close the body', interestingly, a detail noted by our first medical expert as well. In other words, like Saraiva before him, Ribeiro authenticates 'on oath' Xavier's lack of decomposition.

However, at the same time, Ribeiro's medical report is markedly different from that of his predecessor. First, Ribeiro attests to the 'drying up' of Xavier's corpse in three different locations, in contrast to Saraiva's earlier report. For example, fresh blood had flowed freely from a wound near Xavier's heart for Saraiva, while it is 'hollow' and containing 'small bits which seemed to me like pieces of intestines dried up' for Ribeiro, a detail which suggests the latter's more cautious approach to examining Xavier's corpse as well as his more reserved judgement on Xavier's incorruptibility.

Second, there is an increased level of detail evidenced in Ribeiro's report as compared to Saraiva's, and this authenticates Xavier's corpse. For example, he reports on the condition of Xavier's left leg, discovering a wound one finger in length, wherein 'all round the wound there oozed out a streak of blood gone black', a detail that – if one reviews the history of Xavier's travels in death – indexes the first piece of flesh removed at Sancian by Diogo Pereira, which in turn was transformed into a sacred relic. This same doctor also makes a note of a 'stain of blood similar to that on the leg, faded in colour and turned black' which he found on the 'Chinese damask pillow' upon which Xavier's head rested, two details that index the manner by which he was buried in Malacca, including his improper treatment there. The inclusion of these identifying corporeal markers in Ribeiro's report not only provides a history to his incorruptibility but authenticates the corpse on the table as that of Xavier, all notable points missing in Saraiva's report.

Third, Ribeiro performed his autopsy of Xavier without a Jesuit contingency by his side, and in stark contrast to Saraiva, who was assisted by not one but three Jesuits who separately attested to his findings, a discrepancy that perhaps suggests that their presence had earlier 'tainted' Saraiva's medical expertise. In other words, a second more 'objective' examination was perhaps required, one less swayed by the agenda of the Jesuits, a religious order bent on proving Xavier's incorruptibility at all costs, a point borne out by the quotations at the outset of this section. That Ribeiro is accompanied by a 'notary' – his presence notably missing in Saraiva's account – also suggests the latter's heightened investment in authenticating Xavier's incorruptibility according to the standards outlined by King John III. Thus, another level of analysis, one that looks beyond the content of the reports themselves to examine more closely the production of two autopsy reports by Saraiva and Ribeiro, respectively, and the discrepancies between them, produced within a two-week span, is to address the larger politics of the canonization process, of which these medical examinations were one small part. In the end, however, and in spite of their differences of degree and emphasis, both reports operate within a larger discursive field of authenticating Xavier's incorruptibility in death.

Between November 1556 and May 1557[220] – the opening and closing months of this first phase of Xavier's canonization process – a commission was organized to collect, investigate, and record depositions from eyewitnesses attached to the biography of Xavier (in both life and death) currently located within Portuguese Asia. That many of these eyewitnesses – members of church, state, and public – were solicited from the same route that Xavier's corpse had travelled less than two years earlier suggests both the significance of these places in Xavier's journey to sainthood and their defining role in authenticating his incorruptibility. In Malacca alone, six witnesses deposed their testimonies on the 'miracles and virtues of Father Francis' between 24 November 1556 and May 1557, whereas in Goa, thirty-six eyewitness testimonies deposed theirs between 18 November 1556 and 10 January 1557.[221] Additional 'ocular' testimonies were collected in Cochin – thirteen in total – between 8 and 27 January 1556 and in Bassein – eight in total – between 10 December 1556 and 6 January 1557.[222] Together, this first set of depositions, alongside the medical reports of Saraiva and Ribeiro, were sent to Lisbon for examination prior to their arrival in Rome for papal review.[223]

During this same time frame, the Portuguese also commissioned the first official biographies of the Estado da Índia, by João de Barros and Diogo do Couto, contemporaries of Luís de Camões[224] – who was also stationed in Goa at this time – to chronicle the colonial state's prodigious ascendancy in Portuguese Asia throughout the first half of the sixteenth century. That the Portuguese kingdom was subsumed under the Spanish empire by the year 1580 – ironically the same year that Camões, Portugal's first 'nationalist' poet, died in Lisbon a pauper eight years after the publication of his triumphant ode to Portuguese exploration[225] – indexes the internal problems that it was experiencing during this time such that Xavier's canonization would be delayed as a direct result. These political problems would yield a turn to greater spiritualism, not only in Portugal but in the colonies, which would enhance Xavier's value as a symbol of messianic power.[226]

Whereas colonial officials harnessed Xavier's corpse to solidify state control in Portuguese Asia, church officials located in Goa harnessed Xavier's biography to promote a 'religious revival' in the aftermath of his death and reception.[227] Earlier, in 1556, the printing press had been installed in this centre of missionary activity. Not surprisingly, the first piece of material published and distributed under the direction of the Jesuits was the *Doutrina Christa* written by Xavier himself as part of his missionary labours, its publication also furthering his canonization drive.[228] In 1558 Goa acquired the position of an Archdiocese, Xavier's missionary travels in life and death no doubt contributing to this outpost's elevated status as the centre of religious activity in Portuguese Asia as well as the shaping of its territorial jurisdiction to include the newly established bishoprics of Cochin and Malacca.[229] In 1560 church officials implemented the Goa Inquisition, an institution that Xavier himself had personally requested in 1546, the very public *auto da fé* modelled on the highly successful Inquisitions of Spain and Portugal.[230] In the wake of the Inquisition, Goa experienced a virulent anti-Hindu campaign wherein native temples were targeted for destruction and all Brahmins removed.[231] In addition, starting in 1567, the newly established Archdiocese of Goa set up a series of Provincial Councils to better oversee the management and care of Catholic religious instruction and conversion, which was now under the purview of not only the Jesuits but also additional religious orders established at Goa, specifically the Franciscans, and, after 1572, the Augustinians.[232] Lastly, in 1586, the Jesuits of Goa sought to build a separate church dedicated exclusively to Xavier; in light of his impending canonization the College of St Paul was deemed not honourable enough.[233]

The second phase of Xavier's canonization process took place between 1610 and 1616.[234] Again, owing to larger circumstances –

including the premature death of King John III in 1557, the joining of the Spanish and Portuguese kingdoms in 1580, and in 1588 the development of the Sacred Congregation of Rites which had, reviewing Xavier's case only in 1612, determined that his first phase had omitted many key eyewitness testimonies – a second commission was set up to authenticate the incorruptibility of Xavier's corpse one last time. First, in 1610, Xavier's corpse was removed from the College of St Paul and translated to the newly completed Church of Bom Jesus which had been built especially to house him. Second, a wider range of eyewitnesses attached to the biography of Xavier – this time, from both Portuguese Asia and Europe – deposed their testimonies, including many Jesuits who had been overlooked the first time around. In Europe alone, a total of seventy-nine witnesses deposed their testimonies.[235] In Portuguese Asia, a total of 221 witnesses deposed their testimonies, including fifty-six from Goa, Daman, and Thana in 1615, twenty-seven from Malacca in 1616, and 138 from Cochin, the Fishery Coast, Manar, Travancore, and Quilon in 1616.[236] While a smaller number of 'ocular' witnesses were available sixty-five years after the death of Xavier, this set of testimonies involved a more diverse and representative group from church, state, and public, including a large number of Jesuits, and even one Hindu.[237]

Third, upon the request of Pope Paul V, who was desirous of a Xaverian relic for the Vatican in light of his impending canonization, the Jesuits of Goa were assigned the honour of amputating Xavier's right arm (below the elbow), the right arm chosen because it had supposedly been the one used in conferring baptisms.[238] The arm itself was to be handled with reverent care and sent to the Holy City accompanied by the above eyewitness testimonies; this was the final act in authenticating Xavier's incorruptibility and completing his canonization process. The Jesuit Reverend General Claude Aquaviva took charge of the medical procedure which took place 'at night' and 'in secret' on 3 November 1614, in the presence of four Jesuits, again practices typical of European Catholic relic translations.[239] That Xavier's amputated arm, in the year 1615, was put on the same Lisbon-bound ship as Gonçalves's finished manuscript is more than mere coincidence: it suggests the importance of both the actual and the written journey, the material as well as the discursive in making a case for Xavier's sainthood.[240] Finally, a second amputation of the rest of Xavier's arm (including the shoulder blade) took place on 12 April 1619;[241] additional relics were to be made and distributed to numerous Jesuit colleges located at sites travelled to by Xavier in life and death – Japan, Malacca, Cochin, and Macao.[242] This last corporeal act served to both reiterate Xavier's biographical mapping of the colonies and spread his corporeal powers beyond Goa's borders to other sites within Portuguese Asia. In other words, the distribution of Xaverian relics, with Goa at the centre maintaining the wholeness of his corpse, iconically represented the Portuguese Asian empire itself during this time frame.

On 25 October 1619, Pope Paul V issued, at the request of the Society of Jesus, the Brief of Beatification, allowing Francis Xavier to be styled 'Blessed', and the Jesuits to publicly praise God for him in the Liturgy (Office and Mass) everywhere in their churches, and in all the 'kingdoms' of the East Indies.[243] On 12 March 1622, Pope Gregory XV canonized Francis Xavier on the basis of the 'holiness of his life, the sincerity of his faith and the number and greatness of his miracles', all three of which had been 'clearly proven'.[244] However, it was left to Gregory's successor, Urban VIII to issue the customary 'Decree of Canonization', which he did on 6 August 1623.[245] The mutually constituting practices of Portuguese colonial officials and Jesuit priests had finally succeeded in transforming Francis Xavier, a missionary of Spanish origin, into a saint of Portuguese Asia.

Conclusion

The body in parts is not always the body in pieces.[246]

This chapter has traced the actual and written journey to sainthood of Francis Xavier, from his death and initial interment on the island of Sancian to his translation to Malacca, to the celebrations surrounding the arrival of his body in Goa, and lastly to his process of canonization. Throughout my analysis of this ritualized and ritualizing process I have relied on a set of Jesuit biographies as historical source material, particularly since these texts attest to the remarkable development and authentication of a discourse of incorruptibility attached to Xavier's corpse. I have also attended to the larger historical context in which Xavier's travels in both life and death were embedded, relying on additional source materials to affirm the importance of his biographical attachments – to persons, publics, and places – in determining the path of those travels, and to suggest that the physical body indexes the social body such that the story of this saint-in-the-making is simultaneously that of a state (and church) in-the-making.

I have explored a series of colonial and missionary practices at varying moments and sites, their ad hoc management and containment of Xavier's body evidencing a mutually reciprocal relationship, one not without problems at this early modern stage of development, in which the Jesuits worked under the patronage of the Estado da Índia, both harnessing Xavier's 'exemplary' life and 'saintly' death to promote a state of incorruptibility at each of the three above burgeoning colonial outposts. However, Xavier's corpse was not fully appreciated in either Sancian or Malacca. It was only when his corpse was translated to the centre of the Portuguese empire in Asia that he was finally and fully appreciated; Goa could now be recognized as a (potential) site for his future ritualizations.

The period between Xavier's death in 1552 and his canonization in 1622 can also be characterized as one in which Xavier's corpse was handled in an odd assortment of ways by church and state officials alike: he was interred three times and disinterred twice, alternately treated poorly and with respect; he exuded a wholeness, freshness, and fragrant smell, spurted blood, was subject to numerous act of religious devotion and relic productions, medical examinations and amputations, and by the end was missing a toe and an arm. However, these corporeal details are not without significance; rather, they intimate the connections between the European practice of translating a saint's relics and Portuguese colonial state-building processes in sixteenth-century Asia.

Notes

1 Luís Camões, *The Lusiads*, tr. William Atkinson (New York: Penguin, 1952), Canto VII, Stanza I, p. 161.

2 'Incorruptible: that cannot be corrupted, esp. by bribery, that cannot decay; everlasting, moral, noble, upright, righteous, pure, upstanding; lasting enduring.' *The Oxford American Desk Dictionary and Thesaurus*, 2nd edn (New York: Berkeley Books, 2001), p. 415.

3 See Georg Schurhammer, S.J., *Francis Xavier: His Life, His Times*, tr. M Joseph Costelloe, Volumes I–IV (Roma: The Jesuit Historical Institute, 1977).

4 Thomaz quoted in Maria Augusta Lima Cruz, 'Notes on Portuguese Relations with Vijayanagara, 1500–1565', in *Sinners and Saints: The Successors of Vasco da Gama*, ed. Sanjay Subrahmanyam (New Delhi: Oxford University Press, 1998), p. 13.

5 Sanjay Subrahmanyam, 'Introduction: The Portuguese and Early Modern Asia', in his *Sinners and Saints: The Successors of Vasco da Gama*, p. 9.

6 Here I am indebted to the exhaustive and innovative work of Donald Lach for looking at reverse processes during the early modern period; not only how Europeans viewed Asia but how Asia, in turn, influenced Western culture. See his *Asia in the Making of Europe*, Volume I (Chicago: University of Chicago Press, 1994).

7 Many biographers of Xavier assign 1497 as his date of birth so as to link his provident birth with the year that Vasco da Gama set sail for India, but 1506 (7 April) is accepted by most biographers.

8 On da Gama and the pepper trade see Dauril Alden, *The Making of an Enterprise, The* Society of Jesus *in Portugal, Its Empire and Beyond, 1540–1750* (Stanford: Stanford University Press, 1996), Chapter 3, p. 41.

9 In 1507, Albuquerque had tried to conquer Ormuz, at the entrance of the Persian Gulf, since Aden, Ormuz, and Malacca were the three principal keys to Eastern trade. See A. da Silva Rego, *Portuguese Colonisation in the 16th Century: A Study of the Royal Ordinances* (Johannesburg: Witwatersrand University Press, 1959), p. 34.

10 Even though he tends to be overshadowed historically by Albuquerque, Almeida

should be given credit for firmly establishing a Portuguese maritime and commercial empire in the Indian ocean. He initiated a system of *cartazes* (safe conducts) whereby other traders had to obtain permission, paying a tax in effect to pass through the Indian ocean. See Carmo Azevedo, 'The Casados', in *Goan Society Through the Ages*, ed. B.S. Shastry (New Delhi: Asian Publishing Services, 1987), p. 106.

11 T.R. de Souza, 'The Portuguese in Asia and Their Church Patronage', in *Western Colonialism in Asia and Christianity*, ed. M.D. David (Bombay: Himalaya Publishing House, 1988), p. 13.

12 Vijayanagar was a south Indian dynasty whose dealings with the Portuguese were generally peaceful at this time. Part of Albuquerque's strategy was to make alliances with Hindus to solidify attacks on Muslims. See Maria Augusta Lima Cruz, 'Notes on Portuguese Relations with Vijayanagara, 1500–1565', *Santa Barbara Portuguese Studies*, Volume II (1995), pp. 13–14.

13 See Boies Penrose, *Goa–Rainha do Oriente, Goa–Queen of the East* (Lisboa: Commissão Ultramarina, 1960), p. 39.

14 On this same day, Albuquerque ordered that all Muslims found inside the city should be killed, and set about building fortresses in and around Goa, thus establishing the foundations of a Portuguese empire on a solid basis. See Bailon de Sá, 'The Genesis of Portuguese Discoveries and Their Influence on Indian Culture', in *Discoveries, Missionary Expansion and Asian Cultures*, ed. Teotónio de Souza (New Delhi: Concept Publishing Company, 1994), p. 70.

15 The historian Panikkar quoted in Carmo Azevedo, 'The Casados', p. 106. For additional details on Albuquerque's insights, see Stephen Neill, *A History of Christianity in India, The Beginnings to AD 1707* (Cambridge: Cambridge University Press, 1984), Chapter 5, p. 94.

16 Carmo Azevedo, 'The Casados', p. 107.

17 T.R. de Souza, 'The Portuguese in Asia and Their Church Patronage', p. 13.

18 Herein the Portuguese were wholly concerned with maintaining their naval superiority over the Indian Ocean to safeguard the passage of trade items such as the spices of Asia, slaves of West Africa, and sugar, tobacco, and gold of Brazil. See Charles Boxer, *Four Centuries of Portuguese Expansion, 1415–1825; A Succinct Survey* (Berkeley: University of California Press, 1969), p. 63.

19 See Carmo Azevedo, 'The Casados', p. 107.

20 Boies Penrose, *Goa–Rainha do Oriente*, p. 40.

21 See Carmo Azevedo, 'The Casados', p. 107. See Boies Penrose, *Goa–Rainha do Oriente*, p. 40. See also Bailon de Sá, 'The Genesis of Portuguese Discoveries and Their Influence on Indian Culture', p. 70.

22 Carmo Azevedo suggests that the *casados* must be regarded as 'effective agents to cultural impenetration. See his 'The Casados', p. 107.

23 Ibid.

24 Carmo Azevedo, 'The Casados', pp. 108–11. The *casados*, in time, came to occupy a high status position in society, and were generally more loyal to the Catholic religion than to the king of Portugal.

25 His successor was Lopo Soares de Albergaria: September 1515 to 1518. See A. da Silva Rego, *Portuguese Colonisation in the 16th Century*, p. 40.

26 See Joseph de Barros, 'Discoveries and Martyrs of Missionary Expansion in the East', in *Discoveries, Missionary Expansion and Asian Cultures*, ed. Teotónio de Souza (New Delhi: Concept Publishing Company, 1994), p. 88.

27 A. da Silva Rego, *Portuguese Colonisation in the 16th Century*, p. 54.

28 Vicente L. Rafael, *Contracting Colonialism: Translation and Christian Conversion in Tagalog Society Under Early Spanish Rule* (Durham, NC: Duke University Press, 1993), p. 17.

29 Joseph de Barros, 'Discoveries and Martyrs of Missionary Expansion in the East', p. 87. Papal Bull dated 26 March 1500.

30 This priest's letter was reproduced in A.K. Priolkar, *The Goa Inquisition* (Bombay: Bombay University Press, 1961), Chapter 6, pp. 66–7.

31 King John III is regarded as one of the most influential kings in the history of Portuguese colonization. See A. da Silva Rego, *Portuguese Colonisation in the 16th Century*, p. 59.

32 P. Rayanna, S.J., *St Francis Xavier and His Shrine*, p. 9.

33 Da Gama died unexpectedly on 24 December, in Cochin on the battlefield. His bones were initially buried there with honours in the chapel of the monastery of Santo António. Eventually his remains were exhumed by his son in 1538 and taken back to the family properties at Vidigueira, Portugal. See Sanjay Subrahmanyam, *The Career and Legend of Vasco da Gama* (New Delhi: Cambridge University Press, 1997), p. 11.

34 Stephen Neill, *A History of Christianity in India, The Beginnings to AD 1707*, Chapter 5, p. 98.

35 Boies Penrose, *Goa–Rainha do Oriente*, p. 39.

36 K.S. Mathew, 'Church Economics in 16th Century Goa', in *Goa: Cultural Trends*, ed. P.P. Shirodkar (Panaji: Casa Packmaster, 1998), p. 125.

37 P.P. Shirodkar, 'Socio-Cultural Life in Goa During the 16th Century', in *Goa and Portugal: Their Cultural Links*, eds C. Borges and Helmut Feldmann (New Delhi: Concept Publishing Company, 1997), pp. 30–1.

38 P.P. Shirodkar 'Evangelization and Its Harsh Realities in Portuguese India', p. 80.

39 P.P. Shirodkar, 'Socio-Cultural Life in Goa During the 16th Century', p. 30.

40 P.P. Shirodkar 'Evangelization and Its Harsh Realities in Portuguese India', p. 80.

41 Xavier quoted in P. Rayanna, S.J., *St Francis Xavier and His Shrine*, p. 66. This excerpt is from the second of many letters that Xavier wrote from the missionary field, dated 20 September 1542.

42 Ibid., p. 89.

43 P.D. Xavier, 'The Church and Society in 16th Century Goa', p. 103.

44 From a letter dated the year 1546. The Inquisition was implemented in Goa only in 1560, eight years after Xavier's death. It is estimated that Xavier converted approximately thirty thousand persons as opposed to the hagiographical number of one million attributed to him. For more details on his conversion methods, see Georg Schurhammer, 'Historical Research into the Life of Francis Xavier in the 16th C', *Revista de Historia*, No. 47–48 (July–December 1923) (Lisboa: Empresa Litteraria Fluminens), pp. 195–6.

45 Letter writing was a practice that both he and Ignatius promoted amongst the Jesuits. His letters were first published in Paris in 1545, arousing much interest in both Xavier himself and the practice of writing missionary letters 'from the field'. See Georg Schurhammer, 'Historical Research into the Life of Francis Xavier in the 16th C', p. 193. These documented 'eyewitness accounts' transformed the missions, making them alive in the eyes of their European readers. See also John Correia-Afonso, *Jesuit Letters and Indian History, 1542–1773*, 2nd edn (Bombay: Oxford University Press, 1969).

46 See P.D. Xavier, 'The Church and Society in 16th Century Goa', p. 102.

47 They raised their own church and college in the city of Goa. The Recollect Franciscans would follow in 1566, then the Augustinians in 1572, and the Discalced Carmelites in 1607. See P.D. Xavier, 'The Church and Society in 16th Century Goa', p. 103.

48 A.K. Priolkar provides the details of this high profile conversion of a Hindu by the name of Loqu, who supposedly ranked second among the Hindu leaders of Goa. See his *The Goa Inquisition*, p. 72.

49 P.P. Shirodkar, 'Socio-Cultural Life in Goa during the 16th Century', p. 32.

50 Boies Penrose, *Goa–Rainha do Oriente*, p. 39.

51 See Maria Augusta Lima Cruz, 'Notes on Portuguese Relations With Vijayanagara, 1500–1565', p. 26.

52 See Sanjay Subrahmanyam, 'Palavras do Idalção: Un Encontro Curioso em Bijapur no Ano de 1561', *Cadernos do Noroeste*, Volume 15, Nos 1–2 (2001), p. 516.

53 Dauril Alden, *The Making of an Enterprise*, Chapter 3, p. 43.

54 Ibid.

55 Paulo Jorge Sousa Pinto, 'Purse and Sword: D. Henrique Bendahara and Portuguese Melaka in the Late 16th Century', *Santa Barbara Portuguese Studies*, Volume II (1995), pp. 77–8.
56 Paulo Jorge Sousa Pinto, 'Purse and Sword', p. 78.
57 Patrick Geary, *Furta Sacra* (Princeton: Princeton University Press, 1978), p. 18.
58 See Stephen Wilson's 'Introduction' to *Saints and Their Cults: Studies in Religious Sociology, Folklore and History*, ed. Stephen Wilson (Cambridge: Cambridge University Press, 1983).
59 See Patrick Geary, *Furta Sacra*, pp. 10–12.
60 Patrick Geary, *Furta Sacra*, p. 12.
61 See John Bowen, *Religions in Practice: An Approach to the Anthropology of Religion*, 2nd edn (Boston: Allyn and Bacon, 2002), pp. 151–2.
62 Ibid., p. 151.
63 Ibid., p. 5.
64 Patrick Geary, *Furta Sacra*, pp. 9–10.
65 Ibid., p. 7.
66 Ibid.
67 The only colonial parallel to the veneration of Xavier is that of the Our Lady of Guadalupe in Mexico. See Stafford Poole, *Our Lady of Guadalupe: The Origins and Sources of a Mexican National Symbol, 1531–1797* (Tucson: University of Arizona Pres, 1995). Also see D.A. Brading, *Mexican Phoenix, Our Lady of Guadalupe: Image and Tradition Across Five Centuries* (Cambridge: Cambridge University Press, 2001).
68 Richard Helgerson, 'Camões, Hakluyt, and the Voyages of Two Nations', in *Colonialism and Culture*, ed. N. Dirks (Ann Arbor, MI: University of Michigan Press, 1992), p. 27.
69 Ines Županov, 'The Prophetic and the Miraculous', p. 136.
70 See John Correia-Afonso, *Jesuit Letters and Indian History*, pp. 1–8.
71 See Georg Schurhammer, 'Historical Research into the Life of Francis Xavier in the 16th C', p. 193.
72 By 1583 selections from the annual letters were printed for the first time, including many of Xavier's writings. See John Correia-Afonso, *Jesuit Letters and Indian History*, Chapter 1, p. 6.
73 Ines Županov, 'The Prophetic and the Miraculous', p. 136.
74 Ibid.
75 With the exception of Francisco de Souza, whose biography of Xavier was published in 1708.
76 'Lives of saints' were promoted by ecclesiasticals in Europe throughout the Christian era in order to humanize the life of Christ, that is, saints functioned to exemplify and demythologize the characteristics of Christ; as a result the laity could more readily identify with him. See Stephen Wilson, *Saints and their Cults: Studies in Religious Sociology, Folklore and History*, pp. 5–6.
77 M.M. Bakhtin, *The Dialogic Imagination: Four Essays*, ed. M. Holquist, tr. C. Emerson and M. Holquist (Austin: University of Texas Press, 1981).
78 Patrick Geary, *Furta Sacra*, p. 9.
79 Ines Županov, 'The Prophetic and the Miraculous', p. 136, 154.
80 Ibid., p. 155.
81 Manuel Teixeira, S.J., 'Vita S. Francisci', reproduced in *Monumenta Xaveriana*, Tomus Secundus (Matriti: Typis Gabrielis Lopez del Horno, 1912). It was completed in 1579 and sent directly in 1581 to Rome, where it was circulated among the papacy. The original of his text, written in Portuguese, is now lost. One extant copy in Spanish translation is available and was produced in 1590; it was first published in 1912 in *Monumenta Xaveriana*.
82 Pinto is a colourful figure, and his life story well known. His life and times also parallel those of Xavier. He was born in 1510, at a time when Albuquerque had conquered Goa. He was in Asia between 1537 and 1558 and first met Xavier in Japan, prior to becoming a Jesuit, giving him funds to erect a church there. See Rebecca

Catz's introduction to Fernão Mendes Pinto, *The Travels of Mendes Pinto*, ed., tr. Rebecca Catz (Chicago: University of Chicago Press, 1989) , pp. xxv–xxxi, 22–34.

83 According to Rebecca Catz, Fernão Mendes Pinto, *The Travels of Mendes Pinto*, pp. xxv–xxxi.

84 Alessandro Valignano's text was not published in full until 1944, but circulated in manuscript form in the years after its completion in 1588. His original title was: *Historia del Principio y Progresso de la Companhia de Jesus en las Índias Orientales (1542–1564)*. It is reproduced as Alessandro Valignano, S.J., 'Vita S. Francisci' in *Monumenta Xaveriana*, Tomus Primus (Matriti: Typis Augustini Avrial, 1899–1900).

85 João de Lucena, *Historia Da Vida do Padre S. Francisco de Xavier, e do que Fizeram na Índia Os Mais Religiosos da Companhia de Jesu* (Lisboa: Noa Oficina de António Gomes, 1600).

86 Sebastiam Gonçalves, S.J., *Primeira Parte da Historia dos Religiosos da Companhia de Jesus e do que fizeram com a divina graça na conversão dos infieis a nossa sancta fee Catholica nos reynos e provincias da Índia Oriental* (1616), Volume I, ed. Joseph Wicki, S.J. (Coimbra: Atlantida, 1957).

87 According to John Correia-Afonso, *Jesuit Letters and Indian History*, Chapter 11, p. 121.

88 Francisco de Souza, S.J., *Oriente Conquistado a Jesu Christo pelos Padres da Companhia de Jesus, da Provincia de Goa* (Lisboa: Valentim Da Costa Deslandes, 1710).

89 Ines Županov, 'The Prophetic and the Miraculous', p. 149. Emphasis mine. Here I extend the power of Xavier's touch, applying it to both his journeys in life and death.

90 Ibid., pp. 136–7.

91 T.R. de Souza, 'The Portuguese in Asia and Their Church Patronage', p. 14. According to Schurhammer, Sancian had been uncultivated and uninhabited until 1523, the second year of the emperor Chia Chang, when some families began to settle there because of the overcrowding of the mainland. See Georg Schurhammer, S.J., *Francis Xavier: His Life, His Times*, Volume IV, Chapter VII, p. 620, n. 1. The historian Lea Williams points out that after 1523 the Chinese banned all trade with the Portuguese. That is why Portuguese merchants resorted to smuggling and piracy. See Lea E. Williams, 'Inauspicious Ambience: The Historical Setting of Early Luso-Chinese Contacts', in *Indo-Portuguese History: Old Issues, New Questions*, ed. Teotónio de Souza (New Delhi: Concept Publishing Company, 1985), p. 37.

92 The day (Friday, Saturday, Sunday) and the date of his death (2 December or 3 December) are a topic of much debate. See Moreno de Souza's unpublished article, 'When Did Francis Die?' sent to *The Examiner* (1994). Most historians of Portuguese Asia call it Sancian; it was also called Sao João (St John), the Portuguese name given to the island. All variations are derived from the Chinese Shan-chuan tao. See Lea E. Williams, 'Inauspicious Ambience', in *Indo-Portuguese History: Old Issues, New Questions*, ed. Teotónio de Souza (New Delhi: Concept Publishing Company, 1985), p. 37.

93 For additional details on Xavier's death, see Georg Schurhammer, S.J., *Francis Xavier: His Life, His Times*, Volume IV, Chapter VII, pp. 620, 640–3.

94 That he died for his missionary cause is one of the first revealers of sainthood; a Christian burial is a sign of the respect accorded in death to a martyr. See Pierre Delooz, 'Towards a Social Study of Canonized Sainthood in the Catholic Church', in *Saints and Their Cults: Studies in Religious Sociology, Folklore and History*, ed. Stephen Wilson (Cambridge: Cambridge University Press, 1983) pp. 202–12.

95 Fernão Mendes Pinto, *The Travels of Mendes Pinto*, Chapter 215, pp. 497–8.

96 Alessandro Valignano, S.J., 'Vita S. Francisci', pp. 194–7.

97 Ibid.

98 João de Lucena, *Historia Da Vida do Padre S. Francisco de Xavier*, pp. 399–405.

99 Ibid.

100 Alessandro Valignano, S.J., 'Vita S. Francisci', Chapter 30, pp. 194–7.
101 Ibid. It was thought that lime would act as an agent of decomposition, a common practice adopted to rid bones of their flesh. However, Maurice Collins provides an alternative theory for this lack of decomposition, suggesting that the particular lime used was of such a 'quality or strength' that it instead acted as a preservative. See Sebastião Manrique, *The Land of the Great Image: Being the Experiences of Friar Manrique in Arakan*, ed. Maurice Collins (New Delhi: Asian Educational Services, 1995), p. 38.
102 Francisco de Souza, S.J., translated and quoted in John Castets, S.J., 'The Miracle of the Body of St Francis Xavier', *Indian Catholic Truth Society*, No. 113 (1925), pp. 3–9.
103 S. Gonçalves, S.J., *Primeira Parte da Historia dos Religiosos da Companhia de Jesus*, pp. 418–22.
104 Ibid., pp. 422–5.
105 Manuel Teixeira, S.J., 'Vita S. Francisci', pp. 898–900.
106 Ibid.
107 Ibid.
108 Fernão Mendes Pinto, *The Travels of Mendes Pinto*, pp. 498, 499.
109 Alessandro Valignano, S.J., 'Vita S. Francisci', pp. 194–7. This 'odour of sanctity', as it was called, was not uncommon to European saintly bodies. Importing this belief to Asia served as yet another revealer of sainthood.
110 Francisco de Souza, S.J., in John Castets, S.J., 'The Miracle of the Body of St Francis Xavier', pp. 3–9.
111 S. Gonçalves, S.J., *Primeira Parte da Historia dos Religiosos da Companhia de Jesus*, pp. 418–22.
112 Francisco de Souza, S.J., in John Castets, S.J., 'The Miracle of the Body of St Francis Xavier', pp. 3–9.
113 Ibid.
114 Ibid.
115 Characteristic of a saint's relics is that they will be moved if not placed in the appropriate surroundings.
116 Fernão Mendes Pinto, *The Travels of Mendes Pinto*, pp. 498–9.
117 Alessandro Valignano, S.J., 'Vita S. Francisci', pp. 194–7.
118 João de Lucena, *Historia Da Vida do Padre S. Francisco de Xavier*, pp. 399–405.
119 Francisco de Souza, S.J., in John Castets, S.J., 'The Miracle of the Body of St Francis Xavier', pp. 3–9.
120 This also had to do with Malacca's governor Dom Alvaro de Athaide. It was from Malacca that Xavier left to enter China; it was this same Governor who had thwarted his efforts to set up a Jesuit mission in China. See Francisco Correia Afonso, *The Spirit of Xavier* (Bangalore: Good Shepherd Convent Press, 1922), pp. 128–32.
121 Fernão Mendes Pinto, *The Travels of Mendes Pinto*, pp. 498, 499.
122 Francisco de Souza, S.J., in John Castets, S.J., 'The Miracle of the Body of St Francis Xavier', pp. 3–9.
123 S. Gonçalves, S.J., *Primeira Parte da Historia dos Religiosos da Companhia de Jesus*, pp. 418–22. Despite his conversion, he was still not considered Christian enough to define Xavier's burial as Christian.
124 João de Lucena, *Historia Da Vida do Padre S. Francisco de Xavier*, pp. 399–405.
125 S. Gonçalves, S.J., *Primeira Parte da Historia Dos Religiosos da Companhia de Jesus*, pp. 418–22.
126 Francisco de Souza, S.J., *Oriente Conquistado*, pp. 680–4. While some Jesuits such as Teixeira and Lucena assert that he was already destined for Goa, others such as Valignano and De Souza argue that at this time his corpse was destined only for Malacca.
127 Sancian's links to Xavier would not be completely forgotten. In subsequent years, passing ships would fire artillery in view of the island to honour Xavier. See J.M.S. Daurignac, *Historia de São Francisco de Xavier, Da Companhia de Jesus, Apostolo*

das Índias e do Japão, Protector do Oriente, 3rd edn (Goa: No Publisher Listed, 1880), pp. 210–11.

128 Paulo Jorge Sousa Pinto, 'Purse and Sword', p. 75.

129 All of Xavier's Jesuit biographers record this as the date of his arrival, except for Mendes Pinto, who incorrectly reports his date of arrival as 17 March.

130 Manuel Teixeira, S.J., 'Vita S. Francisci', pp. 898, 900. He recorded his account from Cochin in 1554.

131 Fernão Mendes Pinto, *The Travels of Mendes Pinto*, pp. 498, 499.

132 Manuel Teixeira, S.J., 'Vita S. Francisci', pp. 899, 900.

133 S. Gonçalves cited in Ines Županov, 'The Prophetic and the Miraculous', p. 151.

134 Alessandro Valignano, S.J., 'Vita S. Francisci', pp. 194–7.

135 João de Lucena, *Historia Da Vida do Padre S. Francisco de Xavier*, pp. 399–405.

136 Manuel Teixeira, S.J., 'Vita S. Francisci', pp. 899, 900.

137 Ibid.

138 Ibid.

139 Ibid. See also João de Lucena, *Historia Da Vida do Padre S. Francisco de Xavier*, pp. 399–405.

140 Ibid.

141 Ibid.

142 Fernão Mendes Pinto, *The Travels of Mendes Pinto*, pp. 498–9.

143 Ibid.

144 S. Gonçalves, S.J., *Primeira Parte da Historia dos Religiosos da Companhia de Jesus*, pp. 418–22.

145 Alessandro Valignano, S.J., 'Vita S. Francisci', pp. 194–7. This practice compares to the Chinese custom of putting Xavier in a fitted box, as was done in Sancian.

146 Francisco de Souza, S.J., *Oriente Conquistado*, pp. 680–4.

147 S. Gonçalves, S.J., *Primeira Parte da Historia dos Religiosos da Companhia de Jesus*, pp. 418–22.

148 Francisco de Souza, S.J., *Oriente Conquistado*, pp. 680–4.

149 According to the majority of his Jesuit biographers, Xavier's corpse remained in the ground from 23 March to 15 August.

150 Manuel Teixeira, S.J., 'Vita S. Francisci', pp. 900–9.

151 João de Lucena, *Historia Da Vida do Padre S. Francisco de Xavier*, pp. 399–405.

152 Francisco de Souza, S.J., *Oriente Conquistado*, pp. 680–4.

153 Alessandro Valignano, S.J., 'Vita S. Francisci', pp. 194–7.

154 S. Gonçalves, S.J., *Primeira Parte da Historia dos Religiosos da Companhia de Jesus*, pp. 422–5. According to John Castets, the sacredness of Xavier's right hand lies in the fact that he had used this hand to confer baptisms. See his article 'The Miracle of the Body of St Francis Xavier', p. 6.

155 S. Gonçalves, S.J., *Primeira Parte da Historia Dos Religiosos da Companhia de Jesus*, pp. 422–5.

156 Francisco de Souza, S.J., *Oriente Conquistado*, pp. 680–4.

157 Alessandro Valignano, S.J., 'Vita S. Francisci', pp 194–7.

158 Ibid. Also see João de Lucena, *Historia Da Vida do Padre S. Francisco de Xavier*, pp. 399–405.

159 S. Gonçalves, S.J., *Primeira Parte da Historia dos Religiosos da Companhia de Jesus*, pp. 418–22.

160 Ibid.

161 Francisco de Souza, S.J., *Oriente Conquistado*, pp. 680–4

162 Ibid.

163 Manuel Teixeira, S.J., 'Vita S. Francisci', pp. 900–9.

164 Alessandro Valignano, S.J., 'Vita S. Francisci', pp. 194–7.

165 Ibid.

166 S. Gonçalves, S.J., *Primeira Parte da Historia dos Religiosos da Companhia de Jesus*, pp. 422–5.

167 Francisco de Souza, S.J., *Oriente Conquistado*, pp. 680–4.

168 Fernão Mendes Pinto, *The Travels of Mendes Pinto*, pp. 498–9.

169 Manuel Teixeira, S.J., 'Vita S. Francisci', pp. 900–9.
170 João de Lucena, *Historia Da Vida do Padre S. Francisco de Xavier*, pp. 399–405.
171 Alessandro Valignano, S.J., 'Vita S. Francisci', pp. 194–7.
172 Manuel Teixeira, S.J., 'Vita S. Francisci', pp. 900–9.
173 Alessandro Valignano, S.J., 'Vita S. Francisci', pp. 194–7.
174 S. Gonçalves, S.J., *Primeira Parte da Historia dos Religiosos da Companhia de Jesus*, pp. 422–5.
175 This rumour suggests that Xavier's body was thrown into the ocean upon its arrival in Sri Lanka. His body was then replaced by that of a Buddhist monk as a way of ridiculing the Portuguese, who would then unknowingly continue to worship a Buddhist in Goa. See John Holt, *Buddha in the Crown, Avalokitesvara in the Buddhist Traditions of Sri Lanka* (New York: Oxford University Press, 1991), Chapter 4, p. 236, endnote no. 9.
176 João de Lucena, *Historia Da Vida do Padre S. Francisco de Xavier*, pp. 399–405.
177 Michael Pearson, 'The Port City of Goa: Policy and Practice in the 16th C', in his *Coastal Western India*, XCHR Studies, Series No. 2 (New Delhi: Concept Publishing Company, 1981), p. 74.
178 Alessandro Valignano, S.J., 'Vita S. Francisci', pp. 194–7.
179 Manuel Teixeira, S.J., 'Vita S. Francisci', pp. 900–9.
180 Ibid.
181 S. Gonçalves, S.J., *Primeira Parte da Historia dos Religiosos da Companhia de Jesus*, pp. 422–5.
182 Manuel Teixeira, S.J., 'Vita S. Francisci', pp. 900–9.
183 Ibid.
184 Ibid.
185 Manuel Teixeira, S.J., 'Vita S. Francisci', pp. 900–9.
186 Ibid.
187 Engelbert Jorissen identifies this week as Passion Week. He notes that the Jesuits were anxious to have him arrive before Easter so as to ensure his religiosity. See his '16 March 1554, Reflections of a Mid-Sixteenth Century Scene in Goa', in *Goa and Portugal, Their Cultural Links*, ed. Charles Borges and Helmut Feldmann (New Delhi: Concept Publishing Company, 1997), p. 235.
188 João de Lucena, *Historia Da Vida do Padre S. Francisco de Xavier*, pp. 405–7.
189 Manuel Teixeira, S.J., 'Vita S. Francisci', pp. 906–9.
190 Francisco de Souza, S.J., *Oriente Conquistado*, p. 683.
191 Fernão Mendes Pinto, *The Travels of Mendes Pinto*, Chapter 218, p. 501.
192 Ibid., pp. 498–9.
193 See Charles Borges, 'Some Popular Religious Expressions in 16th Century Catholic Goa', in *Souvenir of the Laying of the Foundation of the Extension to the Holy Family Church, 8th September, 1991* (Porvorim, Goa, manuscript).
194 Michael Pearson, 'The Crowd in Portuguese India', in his *Coastal Western India*, XCHR Studies, Series No. 2 (New Delhi: Concept Publishing Company, 1981), pp. 42–3.
195 Manuel Teixeira, S.J., 'Vita S. Francisci', pp. 906–9.
196 Ibid.
197 Fernão Mendes Pinto, *The Travels of Mendes Pinto*, Chapter 218, p. 501.
198 Ibid.
199 João de Lucena, *Historia Da Vida do Padre S. Francisco de Xavier*, pp. 405–7.
200 Francisco de Souza, S.J., *Oriente Conquistado*, p. 683.
201 Manuel Teixeira, S.J., 'Vita S. Francisci', pp. 906–9.
202 Alessandro Valignano, S.J., 'Vita S. Francisci', pp. 197–9.
203 Fernão Mendes Pinto, *The Travels of Mendes Pinto*, Chapter 218, p. 501.
204 Engelbert Jorissen, '16 March 1554, Reflections of a Mid-Sixteenth Century Scene in Goa', p. 235.
205 Manuel Teixeira, S.J., 'Vita S. Francisci', pp. 906–9.
206 Fernão Mendes Pinto, *The Travels of Mendes Pinto*, Chapter 218, p. 501.
207 Ibid.

208 Francisco de Souza, S.J., *Oriente Conquistado*, p. 683.
209 Ibid., pp. 680–4.
210 Manuel Teixeira, S.J., 'Vita S. Francisci', pp. 906–9.
211 Alessandro Valignano, S.J., 'Vita S. Francisci', pp. 197–9.
212 Nunes quoted in Francisco Correia Afonso, *The Spirit of Xavier*, p. 132.
213 For additional biographical details, see Rocha Martins, *O Apostolo das Índias, S. Francisco Xavier* (Lisboa: Agencia Geral das Colonias, 1942), pp. 445–6. It is unlikely that this story is true as she was not even alive then; her father was the Augsburg merchant Ferdinand Cron who came to India only in the 1580s. It is the details of this fantastical story (and its retelling) that are significant here.
214 Francisco de Souza, S.J., *Oriente Conquistado*, p. 683.
215 Georg Schurhammer, 'Historical Research into the Life of Francis Xavier in the 16th C', pp. 195–6.
216 Letter reproduced in J.M.S. Daurignac, *S. Francisco Xavier, Apóstolo das Índias*, 6th edn (Braga: Livraria Apostolado da Imprensa, 1880), p. 471.
217 This date thus marks the beginning of the canonization process, for the Commission was set up on that same day. There is some debate as to whether these medical examinations took place in 1556, or earlier in 1554. P. Rayanna suggests that they probably took place in November 1556. See his *St Francis Xavier and His Shrine*, pp. 152–3.
218 Cosmas Saraiva quoted in P. Rayanna, S.J., *St Francis Xavier and His Shrine*, p. 151.
219 Ibid., p. 150.
220 P. Rayanna, S.J., *St Francis Xavier and His Shrine*, pp. 228–30, Schurhammer calls this the 'informative process', one part of canonization process. See his *Francis Xavier: His Life, His Times*, Volume II, Appendix II, p. 678.
221 Georg Schurhammer, S.J., *Francis Xavier: His Life, His Times*, Volume II, Appendix II, p. 678.
222 Ibid. The term 'ocular' is adopted from P. Rayanna, S.J., *St Francis Xavier and His Shrine*, p. 238.
223 P. Rayanna, S.J., *St Francis Xavier and His Shrine*, pp. 228–30.
224 After Camões's five-year banishment to Macao, he returned to Goa. Between 1561 and 1567 he continued working on *The Lusiads* and other poems. He was surrounded by a group of intellectuals, including Garcia de Orta, the famed botanist, and the chroniclers Gaspar Correa and Diogo do Couto. See Boies Penrose, *Goa–Rainha do Oriente*, p. 49.
225 Ibid., pp. 49–51.
226 Dauril Alden, *The Making of an Enterprise*, Chapter 4, p. 92. The 1580s and 1590s saw the beginnings of a movement called Sebastianism. Even though the mutilated body of the young late king (killed during a failed campaign in Morocco in which Camões also took part and lost an eye) had been returned to Lisbon in 1582, many in Portugal believed that the corpse was not his. They were convinced that he was still in captivity somewhere or in hiding, and that he would return to liberate the Portuguese kingdom from the Spanish yoke. Also see G.D. Winius, 'Millenarianism and Empire, Portuguese Asian Decline and the "Crise de Conscience" of the Missionaries', *Itinerario*, Volume XI, No. 2 (1987), pp. 37–51.
227 See Sebastião Manrique, *The Land of the Great Image*, p. 160.
228 With the establishment of the printing press by the Jesuits in Goa on 6 September 1556, it was his treatise, the *Doutrina Christa*, which was the first book chosen to be printed in all of India in 1557. The *Doutrina Christa* was a small booklet used for imparting religious instruction and was distributed between 1557 and 1561. See A.K. Priolkar, *The Printing Press in India, Its Beginnings and Early Development* (Bombay: Marathi Samshodhana Mandala, 1958), pp. 2–15.
229 T.R. de Souza, 'The Portuguese in Asia and Their Church Patronage', p. 14.
230 José da Fonseca, *An Historical and Archaeological Sketch of the City of Goa* (Delhi: Asian Educational Services, 1986 [1878]), p. 218.
231 See António de Noronha, 'Desolação dos gentios depois da destruição dos pagodes', in *A Índia Portuguesa*, Volume Segundo, ed. Menezes Bragança (Goa: Imprensa

Nacional, 1923), Chapter 5, pp. 237–8.

232 See J.H. da Cunha Rivara, *Archivo Portuguez-Oriental*, Fasciculo 4, Parte 2 (New Delhi: Asian Educational Services, 1992).

233 This new church was the Professed House and Church of Bom Jesus. See P. Rayanna, S.J., *St Francis Xavier and His Shrine*, pp. 162–8.

234 See Georg Schurhammer, S.J., *Francis Xavier: His Life, His Times*, Volume II, Appendix II, p. 679. On the concurrent drive for his canonization in Europe, see Dauril Alden, *The Making of an Enterprise*, Chapter 24, p. 641. Interestingly, during the seventeenth century, the missions' Procurator of the Eastern provinces in Lisbon spent as much as 23.4 per cent of its resources to promote the canonization of Francis Xavier.

235 See Georg Schurhammer, S.J., *Francis Xavier: His Life, His Times*, Volume II, Appendix II, p. 679.

236 Ibid.

237 P. Rayanna states that twice as many witnesses were interviewed this time around from different ranks, classes and professions, such as pilots, captains, merchants, nobles, priests, Jesuits, and even a Hindu. See his *St. Francis Xavier and His Shrine*, p. 238.

238 John Castets, S.J., 'The Miracle of the Body of St Francis Xavier', p. 14.

239 Ibid.

240 Ines Županov, 'The Prophetic and the Miraculous', p 155.

241 P. Rayanna, S.J., *St Francis Xavier and His Shrine*, p. 239.

242 See Newman Fernandes, 'The Body of St Francis Xavier', *Renovação*, No. 22 (16–30 November 1994), p. 424.

243 P. Rayanna, S.J., *St Francis Xavier and His Shrine*, p. 239.

244 Ibid. No doubt the Jesuit biographies played a role in proving his case. Xavier was canonized along with Ignatius Loyola (1491–1556), Isidore of Madrid (1080–1130), Philip Neri (1515–95), and Teresa of Avila (1515–82). None of these other saints was subjected to the kinds of translations, ritualizations, and medical examinations that Xavier experienced in death.

245 Ibid.

246 David Hillman and Carla Mazzio, 'Introduction' to *The Body in Parts: Fantasies of Corporeality in Early Modern Europe*, eds David Hillman and Carla Mazzio (New York: Routledge, 1997), p. xi.

CHAPTER THREE

Canonization (1624)

Introduction

We paid a Visit to the Domo of Bon Jesu, the Church an admirable Piece, the Repository of St. Xaverius, the Indian Apostle, where is a famous Tomb in Honour of him, who first spread the Gospel as far as China, and sealed it with his Martyrdom, near Two Hundred Years ago, leaving his Body a Miraculous Relick of his better part, it still retaining its vivid Colour and Freshness, and therefore exposed once a Year to publick view, on the Vespers of his Festival. – John Fryer, 1676[1]

I take it [the body of Saint Francis Xavier] to be a pretty Piece of Wax-work that serves to gull the People of their Money, for many visit with great Veneration, and leave something at its Shrine for the Maintenance of Candles and Olive Oyl, that continually burn before it: And a Priest attends weekly to shave his Head and Beard; but none but that Priest has the Honour to come within the Iron Rails that are placed about the Corps, four or five Yards distant from it. Now if any should question the Truth of *Xavier's* Story of *Goa*, they would be branded with the odious Name of an obstinate incredulous Heretick, and perhaps fall in the Hands of a convincing Inquisition. – Alexander Hamilton, 1692[2]

In 1624 the Estado da Índia staged a reception to honour Francis Xavier's recent canonization, a celebration that was markedly different from the small reception held in 1554 to honour the successful transfer of his 'incorrupt' corpse in Goa from Sancian via Malacca. It was on 12 March 1622 that Xavier had been officially declared a saint by Pope Gregory XV and celebrations in papal Rome, Lisbon, Madrid, and Spanish Mexico took place shortly thereafter[3] to recognize the contributions of a missionary who had both converted so many 'idolaters' to the Roman Catholic faith through his alternative methods and requested a Holy Inquisition for Portuguese India. Given that they received the news only approximately eighteen months later,[4] church

Figure 4 Souvenir da Exposicao de 1922, 1931, 1932

and state officials in Goa postponed the veneration of their saint until they could properly organize an event befitting his newly acquired status. Invested in this Catholic celebration were not only the primary organizers of the event, the Society of Jesus, the religious order that had also organized Xavier's earlier reception in 1554, but also the Estado da Índia – the financiers of the event – for whom Xavier's canonization represented the power of their 'civilizing mission', and a diverse Indo-Portuguese public, for whom the 'incorrupt' body of the saint was already an object of veneration.

On 10 February 1624 Xavier's canonization celebration commenced with 'great public rejoicing and brilliant festivities'.[5] The people of Goa – *fidalgos* (noblemen), priests, *casados* (married ones), colonial officials, and 'natives' – all joined together to formally ritualize their newly canonized saint. It was a lavish affair: not only was Xavier's corpse clothed in the finest European dress, placed in an Italian coffin, and ceremoniously moved from the College of St Paul to his new home, the recently built Baroque-style Church of Bom Jesus where he still lies today, but parades, dances, Portuguese Renaissance music, dramas, and liturgical services were all central to the royal pageantry.

This momentous 'translation of body'[6] also took place before a large and varied group of visitors, one that included Sebastião Barreto, a travelling Portuguese Jesuit who quietly observed from the sidelines, and Pietro Della Valle, an Italian nobleman who dressed up in Roman costume and participated in its multiple acts. The written accounts of these two European travellers become the basis for my analysis of the spectacle of Xavier's canonization as a set of distinct and meaningful ritual practices which are also indexical of certain missionary and colonial rationalities on the part of the Society of Jesus and Estado da Índia in 1624.

In this chapter I develop a discourse and materality of Goa Dourada by situating within a larger historical context not only the eyewitness testimonies of Barreto and Della Valle but those of a multitude of European travellers, including the disparate accounts of John Fryer and Alexander Hamilton quoted at the outset of this chapter, who flocked to Portuguese India, often described as a 'Rome in India'[7] throughout the seventeenth century. Embedded in this set of travelogues are a wide range of responses by European travellers – prior to, during, and after Xavier's canonization festivities – to an image of 'Golden Goa' that was perpetuated by the Estado da Índia precisely because it was experiencing its own demise on land and at sea at the hands of the British, the Dutch, and the Marathas after a period of unremitting success in building a high-profile empire in Asia. Not coincidentally, it was also during the seventeeth century that an inordinate number of travellers stopped off in Goa – Xavier's 'miraculous' corpse a recently featured attraction – as part of a larger 'India' tour, each recording the details of his travels for a European (reading) public. Thus, given Xavier's historical ties to Goa, and the location of his corpse in this (once) thriving centre of ecclesiastical and colonial state activity, one of the many ways in which Portuguese colonial officials and Jesuit missionaries reinforced Goa's 'goldenness' to subjects, residents, and travellers alike was through the staging of an elaborate celebration to mark Xavier's newly acquired status as a saint of India.[8]

In exploring the spectacle of Xavier's canonization, I focus on how the space of ritual epitomizes the gold of Goa, both literally and figuratively. Here I suggest that, on the one hand, ritual provides an arena in which colonial and Jesuit officials promote their respective and collective strengths through the success of Xavier's canonization. On the other hand, because of the colonial state's increasingly evident decline, ritual simultaneously serves as a point of distraction; it contradicts the day-to-day dealings of a steadily weakening Portuguese colonial economy, and helps to renew not only 'communitas'[9] but rather different epistemologies of 'faith' between church, state, and public.[10]

This spectacle turns the focus away from this saint's corporeality towards his accoutrements in much the same manner that Goa itself has been 'dressed up' for this special occasion in 1624.

Travel writing as genre, social practice, and historical source

> In the fifteenth century the number of European visitors to India was few and their evidence scanty, both as regards value and amount; in the sixteenth the number was far larger, and their evidence proportionately more valuable, though the monopolising policy of the Portuguese, who, while by their discoveries stimulating the curiosity of Europe, strove to repress its power of satisfying it, tended to discourage Indian travel in all but their own countrymen. *But in the seventeenth century, when it became evident that India was not to be for ever a private domain of Portugal, the tide set full and strong, and, one after another, men landed at Surat, or Goa, or some other convenient port, and set forth on their travels ... They came, they saw, and though conquest was reserved for a later era, at least they wrote.*[11]

While this chapter is mostly about ritual, it is also about representation and the practice of travel in the seventeenth century. I discuss not only the travel of people and ideas from metropole to colony but reflections on one colony by travellers from several (competing) metropoles, travellers with a variety of linguistically and culturally diverse backgrounds who relied on their senses to remember and record their experiences.

For all these travellers the act of travel and the act of writing are inseparable; it is in these dual and sometimes simultaneous acts that 'differences' between guests and hosts and between colonizer and colonized are constituted and reinforced as colonial rationalities for various reading publics located in multiple metropoles.[12] The 'dialogism' of these travel accounts no doubt influenced their writing and reception in that travellers very often read others' accounts prior to, during and after the act of travel at the same time that audiences very often read a multitude of travelogues focused on one place such as 'Golden Goa'.[13]

In *Imperial Eyes*, Mary Louise Pratt argues that travellers are always less than 'innocent bystanders'.[14] While European travellers more often than not implicitly supported colonial agendas, they also often betrayed the 'aspirations of economic expansion and empire'[15] in that their observations often critiqued the same political and economic processes that made their travel possible in the first place. Pratt's perspective emphasizes how subjects are constituted in and by their relations to each other through the act of travel. Her point is crucial for understanding how travellers like Pietro Della Valle and Sebastião Barreto viewed Goa through the lens of their own linguistic and cultural affiliations at the same time that they were fundamentally shaped by their travel experiences, getting caught up in Xavier's canonization festivities and recording their most minute details for a reading public located elsewhere.[16] Furthermore, Pratt's idea of 'contact zone' also takes into account the experiences of a wide variety of additional travellers to Goa outside the space of ritual – in this case, mostly noblemen, but also priests, doctors, lawyers, traders, and jewellers – and their linguistic and cultural backgrounds – Italian, English, Scottish, French, Dutch, and German – who interacted with an Indo-Portuguese public, sometimes even with each other, in a colonial space such as Goa, and whose daily observations constantly shaped their representations. Lastly, Pratt argues that 'particular corpuses of travel accounts [are] connected with particular historical transitions',[17] a point that echoes the historian Oaten's statement quoted at the outset of this section. That there is an abundance of travel writings on Goa during the seventeenth century is precisely because of the geopolitics of imperial expansion during this time frame, which levelled the colonial playing field so to speak, with individual travellers witness to the waxing and waning of the Estado da Índia.[18]

Johannes Fabian, in *Out of Our Minds*, argues that European travellers, often 'out of their minds' owing to the ravages of travel,[19] rationalized certain subjects often also 'out of their minds', which in turn helped lay the foundation for certain colonial rationalities.[20] Identifying what specific travellers sought to 'rationalize' from such an 'altered perspective' in their writings helps us to trace the genealogies of future colonial rationales, particularly since these same European travellers often proved that imperialism was more often than not 'weaker' than the image it projected of itself to its visitors.[21] Not surprisingly, then, in the case of those travellers to Goa during the seventeenth century, many of whom were suffering from a variety of bodily ailments as evidenced in their detailed biographies, the Portuguese are a continued popular object of curiosity – depicted often as 'less rational' in their travel writings. Such representations, circulating beyond Goa itself, inadvertently helped set the stage for the convergence of additional imperial powers on to the Indian scene.

Lastly, I argue that this set of travelogues is invaluable because they evidence 'Golden Goa' in both its materiality and discursivity and are available for roughly the entire span of the seventeenth century, thus constituting by far the most valuable historical source for analysing the Estado da Índia during this tumultuous period.[22] While Oaten earlier suggested that these travelogues reveal changing political circumstances, the historian Teotónio de Souza argues that they also highlight certain particularities of Goan society. He writes:

> Unlike the tourists of our days, the Europeans who visited Goa in the seventeenth century were not attracted by the idyllic beauty of the Goan villages; by and large they restricted their movements and observations to the city walls. This was probably owing to the Government policy of checking the free movement of foreigners, particularly Europeans other than Portuguese, as well as by the difficulties of communication, both of language and of transport. However, what they describe at length, namely life in the city of Goa, they do most vividly, enabling us to flesh out the dry bones of archival records ... Fortunately, there exist accounts by European travellers who visited Goa, at more or less regular intervals, during the entire span of the seventeenth century ... The picture of growing misery and unrest in the city and of an aristocracy straining to cover it up with a show of extravagance is what strikes us in the[se] accounts. These travellers belong to different walks of life and their varying interests led them to observe life in the city of Goa from different perspectives.[23]

These travel accounts, then, 'constitute valuable evidence for reconstructing the past of Goa'[24] and are especially useful 'by adding descriptions of urban life to the missionary portrayals of the rural life'.[25]

I now briefly introduce the two groups of travellers whose eyewitness testimonies I rely on for my ritual analysis. P. Sebastião Barreto was a Portuguese Jesuit priest who attended the canonization festivities, and whose description was included in the annual letter to the General of the Society of Jesus on 15 December 1624.[26] Even though there is no biographical information available on this visiting Jesuit priest, it is plausible to suggest that Barreto was more than likely a *fidalgo* (nobleman) who had been stationed in Goa for some time prior to the canonization festivities, given the depth of knowledge of Goan society evident in his testimony.[27] Barreto's text is the product both of his own experience as an eyewitness and his reading of the *Traça da Pompa Triunfal* (hereafter the *Traça*)[28] – he references it twice as an authoritative source:[29] an anonymously authored pamphlet which reproduces a description of the festivities and was printed by the Jesuit College of St Paul in Goa in 1624.[30]

In contrast, Pietro Della Valle, an Italian traveller to India, wrote down his eyewitness account of Xavier's canonization festivities in the form of a letter on his way home to Rome, dated 4 November 1624.[31] During the twenty months he spent in Goa (arriving on 10 February 1623), he wrote eight letters to his friends in Naples, a practice not uncommon among European travellers; his description of the canonization festivities is included in the last letter. In characterizing Della Valle's travel writing style, his biographer George Hull describes him as alternating between being 'pompous and verbose' and 'fresh, perceptive and entertaining'.[32] While several of Della Valle's letters were published during his lifetime, the bulk of his letters, eighteen in total, were published posthumously in Italy by his sons, the exact date unknown.[33]

As a (ritual) counterpoint to the testimonies of Barreto and Della Valle, I rely on the accounts of a second group of travellers who were not witness to the spectacle of Xavier's canonization. Instead, their testimonies contextualize the former event within a larger body of representations of Goa during the seventeenth century, thus allowing us to 'read' the two key texts (of Barreto and Della Valle) more effectively. These travellers who visited Portuguese India, very often as one stop in a larger 'Eastern' tour, recorded the vicissitudes of colonial life in Portuguese India. This group[34] included not only John Fryer, an English surgeon in the employ of the East India Company (1676), and Alexander Hamilton, a Calvinist Scottish captain and free-trader who visited Goa twice (1692 and 1704),[35] but also the Dutchmen John Huyghen Van Linschoten (1583–88) and Phillip Baldeus (1672), Frenchmen François Pyrard de Laval (1608–10), Jean-Baptiste Tavernier (1641 and 1648), M. de Thevenot (1666) and Abbé Carré (1672),[36] German traveller John Albert Mandelslo (1639),[37] and finally Italian doctors Niccolao Manucci (1666)[38] and Gemelli Careri (1695). Together, these travel accounts span more than a century (1583 to 1704), and record a period in which 'Golden Goa' was undergoing historical transformations not only having to do with multiple colonial investments in the Indian subcontinent.

Xavier's canonization festivities of 1624: notes on a ritual

> For just as it becomes a preacher of the Gospel to appear mean and poor when such an appearance is conducive to the greater glory of God and to the salvation of souls, so does it become the preacher with his ornaments and splendidness, when this is thought necessary for the praise and glory of God and for the welfare of souls. – Roberto Nobili, Jesuit priest, c. 1613[39]

Sebastião Barreto and Pietro Della Valle: (eye)witness testimonies

The seeds of the festival that was organized in 1624 to celebrate the canonization of St Francis Xavier had been planted earlier in the form of a small-scale public ceremony recognizing the arrival of this missionary's 'incorrupt' body in Goa in 1554, its success no doubt influencing the Estado da Índia's decision to stage yet another festival, only on a much grander scale now befitting a saint. Relying on the eyewitness testimonies of Sebastião Barreto and Pietro Della Valle for 'reading' this event, I identify, on the one hand, certain ritual components in each of their texts, historicizing them as colonial and missionary practices. On the other hand, Xavier's canonization festivities open up a space for exploring this colonial centre's transformation into a spectacle of 'Golden Goa', the interplay of 'balancing' church and state investments, and, finally, the participation of a developing '(Catholic) Portuguese' and 'native' public. My analysis will also intimate the power of ritual to interpolate its participants. That these lavish celebrations purposely remove any attention from the material condition of Xavier's corpse – instead, his newly designed and richly decorated baroque casket takes on the role of ritual's centrepiece – will mirror the character of the Estado da Índia in 1624.

First I reproduce Sebastião Barreto's account of the spectacle of Xavier's canonization which was recorded on 15 December 1624, eleven months after the festivities took place. He writes:

> The canonization festivities of Our Saint and Patriarch Ignacio and Saint Francis Xavier began on 21 January with great applause and expectation from all of the Court. There were distinguished marches of devotion in the form of five pyramids which, with much co-operation were co-ordinated so as to move through the five most public squares of all of the city, first the yard [in front of] of the Archway of the Viceroys, the second in front of the See Cathedral, the third in front of the Church of Bom Jesus; the last two pyramids placed themselves in front of the Old and New College of St. Paul.
>
> The work of art – the procession of pyramids – was a lot to see and consider. The tops [of the pyramids] reached the highest roofs of the buildings. On these pyramids there were many emblems, designs, expressions, rich art work, the major part of the oil paintings were gilded with a lot of gold and silver and other works worthy of such costs. They marched from the Mount of New St Paul through the steep streets on foot without any misfortune. They were accompanied by troops of cavalry of various nations and all were gallant accompaniments those who were the best were from the Santa Fe Seminary and the best students of Goa; and being all of the same age and type, the parents of these students did not lose sight of the fact that the jewels, gold, silks, and expenses would help their children's cause and intention. There were three squadrons, which represented Asia, Africa and Europe.
>
> In between there were floats with music, dances with all kinds of instruments, tea music, sonnets and everything else to express thanks and devotion to the saints. This can also be seen in the *Tratado* [the *Traça*] which says the same. And for the reason that it was not possible

to accompany the cavalry, those who desired to serve the saints – the students then entered who, until then were outside, helping the soldiers, brothers, and parents – all of them together, reinforcing the weight of the festive pomp of the show, and making such a show that it was quite noisy, thus making one doubt which part of the show was more successful. In the city a third of the gentlemen and captains displayed the grandeur and success they deserved.

In the most sacred feasts, which the Church pays for, I cannot speak of. Rather, in the kind of solemnities in front of me, the presence of the Viceroy [D. Francisco da Gama]of the court, Bishop of Cochin and Archbishop of Goa [D. Frei Sebastião de S. Pedro], clergy, Inquisitioners, religious – with the co-ordination of all types of musical instruments – they seem as if they cannot desire or hope for more; and in one of the streets, in which this city has captains and sentinel, one hears prayers and songs of grace and feasts, bulls, lights and other signs of celebration.

The tragedy [drama] which was staged lasted four days, and was dedicated to St Francis for good reason. There was present, as always, the Count Viceroy with all the gentlemen, citizens, the judges, the Chancellor and Attorney General, the Town Council, and the captains. All of the windows were filled with people, underneath on the streets, were the palanquins [a type of carriage], they were not allowed in places that were not approved. Likewise, the idolaters and Moors had recourse to derive pleasure from those windows which never inverted [opened fully]. There was the most serious work of art, the spectators each time more numerous, the marches were very distinguished and devoted to fate, which caused much happiness; there were also tears of devotion. One felt the grace of the Saint in the next lifetime, not losing disgrace nor losing sight of where the gold and pearls were so many and worth so much.

At the end of the festivities there was a procession so sumptuous in quantity one can see that its description dominates the Extract [the *Traça*]. Positioned at the back of the procession, they walked towards the tomb of the saint. Carried on the shoulders of the Jesuits was the sarcophagus [coffin] of the Patriarch, Saint Francis Xavier. It weighed seven *aroubas* in silver. It exhibited fine workmanship in embedded stone. The work of art, which cost 6000 *pardãos*, was covered with illustrations, miracles, and points in the life of the saint. The banner that was given to the city had on it in gold the figure of the saint, who is recognized as the patron saint of Goa, some of the *fidalgos* took the costs which excluded the differences between them, to the Father Visitador, P. Andre Palmeiro SJ. The pomp was so grand and varied, the procession going from Old St Paul's to the Casa Professa, being a one mile walk, for where the procession passed, there was little space for walking, and the coaches, the wooden frameworks to carry statues in processions, horses, vessels, too many dances, they were all started from the Old College of St Paul. The most pleasing view would be this one: at this end of the streets would be the lanes, crossroads, stores, windows, yards, public squares, all full of many people. One hopes that His Excellency [the Viceroy] enjoys all the pomp and pageantry, he will retire in front of the See Cathedral with the Bishop Governor and many gentlemen to see the vessel of the Church [the procession], floats of glory and other inventions of sorts, that the Viceroy ordered it to stop so as to give each the advantage to see it from his point of view. There occurred at the end of this ceremony at noon, on the vespers [on the Eve] of his saint's day, a ceremony that was very different from what occurs in other parts of the world, where he is celebrated, feasted, and adored.[40]

Next I reproduce Pietro Della Valle's eyewitness account for the reader, which was circulated by way of a letter written ten months after the spectacle of Xavier's canonization. He writes:

HOME TO ITALY

From Goa, 4 November 1624

My last letter I sent by the ship which departed from Goa for Portugal on 1 February, and was the only ship of that kingdom sent here this year. The bells were rung in Goa that day,[41] and there were great rejoicings, particularly in the churches of the Society of Jesus, of the Augustinians, of the Dominicans and Franciscans, upon news being brought of many martyrs. Many of the religious in those Orders had been lately martyred in Japan; among the Jesuits three Italian, namely, Fr Carlo Spinola, a Genovese of high quality; Fr Eamillo Coastanzo, a Calabrese, or rather a Neapolitan, of a family whose estate is in Calabria; and Fr Pietro Paolo, also a Neapolitan, if I am not mistaken.

On 10 February, to begin the solemnities for the canonization of St Francis Xavier, the Jesuits sung vespers in the church of the Professed House of the *Gesù*. At night, they arranged for a sortie on horseback, with lights, of numerous young students, not collegians but those living out, all appearing in emulation dressed up richly and gallantly, following behind a standard with the effigies of saints portrayed on it.

On the eleventh, there was sung a solemn Mass, in the church of the Gesù [Church of Bom Jesus], with a sermon given by the visitor, Fr Andrea Palmeiro, at which the Viceroy was present. In the late evening, on a huge stage which had been built on the square outside the church for the representation, many days running, of the life of St Francis Xavier, they caused a squadron of young men disguised as peasants to dance I don't know how many elegant ballets with music. On 12 February, in the presence of the Viceroy and of all the nobility and people of the city (for whose convenience scaffolds and seats were erected in the piazza and round about the theatre, both for men and women) the first act of the above mentioned play, or tragedy, as they said, of the life of St Francis Xavier was performed.

This tragedy was a truly formidable extravaganza, staged and recited by more than three hundred people, all lavishly dressed, with many jewels, many items of music, and most elegant dances, as well as various contrivances of chariots, ships, galleys, pageants, heavens, hells, mountains and clouds; and I shall write down no more, since I have the printed programme by me.[42] On 13 February, the Viceroy being indisposed, the festivity was suspended, and nothing was done. But in the three days which followed, with two acts a day, the whole tragedy was recited; it comprised not only the life but also the death, the transportation of the saint's body to Goa, the ascent to heaven, and finally also the canonization of St Francis Xavier. On the seventeenth, Mass was sung in the new college of St Paul, with the sermon being preached by the Italian, Fr Flaminio Calo, on the beatification of the blessed Luigi Gonzaga, also a priest of the Society of Jesus.

In the evening the Portuguese men passed through the streets all dressed up and accompanied by chariots and music; whereupon from the house of Signor António Baraccio, about twelve or more of us, all friends, came forth, all clothed in the same livery. This I had carefully had made according to my fancy in the fashion of Roman warriors of old, just as the emperors of old used to be depicted: the colours were carnation and pink and we wore different emblems on the breast, everyone following his own taste. In the night this looked excellent, and was the best and strongest group of the whole masquerade.

On 18 February, the morning solemn Mass was sung, and a sermon was preached on the canonization of the saints in old St Paul's. Then late in the day, after lists and a quintain and a ring had been prepared in front of the church of the Gesù, many gaily attired Portuguese appeared on the scene to career against one and the other, vastly entertaining the ladies, who stood there looking at them from the balconies and platforms. After this, they went on to do the same in the street of San Paolo Vecchio [Old College of St Paul], where it is customary to gallop with horses, and where, too, many ladies stood watching from the windows. On 19 February in the morning, a most solemn procession made its way from San Paolo Vecchio as far as the Gesù, after winding through the main streets of the city; and this procession exceeded all the rest in its number of chariots, ships and other contraptions full of people, all representing different things: and also in good music, accompanied with many dances on foot and a variety of other pretty diversions. At the rear of the procession walked many priests wearing capes and bearing the body of St Francis Xavier, enclosed in a rich and splendid silver coffin, under a canopy also of silver, utterly lovely, with the saint's own effigy behind. Next in the procession was borne a large standard with the images of the saints, also carried by some of the fathers. And after that appeared all the crosses of the parishes of Salcette, and just one band of Franciscan friars, but no one from the other religious orders, because they refused to join in the Jesuits' processions seeing that the Jesuits would not join theirs. The ceremonies of the canonization finished with this procession, which ended about noon.[43]

Juxtaposing these two richly detailed accounts provides complementary and contrasting images of Xavier's canonization festivities, which, in turn, can be analysed for their ritual components. Methodologically, I will focus on those ritual practices that are central to both accounts, tracing the material and discursive strategies underlying the Estado da Índia's showcasing of 'Golden Goa' through these celebrations honouring Xavier. I look at the varying degrees of investment in certain ritual practices on the part of each of these authors, suggesting that what is paid attention to in one travel account and less so in another does not signify its lessened ritual significance but rather the differing perspectives of each eyewitness, their respective positions with regard to church and state practices, and, lastly, the experience and power of ritual to impress its individual participants in distinct ways. The testimonies of additional European travellers to Goa during the seventeenth century, impressions made outside the confines of ritual, will reinforce and sometimes disrupt the Estado da Índia's image of Goa Dourada perpetuated in the space of ritual in 1624. Their accounts then contextualize those of Barreto and Della Valle within a larger body of representations of 'Golden Goa' during the seventeenth century.

Goa as Spectacle

> [Seventeenth-century Goan society was] rough, violent and extravagant, all characteristics of a frontier society, which indeed it was. – Michael Pearson, 1981[44]

In this section I trace the development of a discourse of Goa Dourada ('Golden Goa'), before discussing its representation in the space of Xavier's ritualization in 1624. Historian Caroline Ifeka explores the history of the (seemingly timeless) image of Goa Dourada by locating its materiality in Portugal's seafaring roots and its moments of colonial contact. The idea of Goa's goldenness first gained its discursive weight through the act of travel starting in the late fifteenth century. That which was initially in need of rationalization or glorification for the Portuguese was their position both within Europe and overseas. According to Ifeka, this discourse was first perpetuated by Portuguese travellers who arrived in India hoping to realize their full potential. She writes,

> Goa Dourada is a remarkably resilient ideology transplanted on to Indian soil by a southern European civilisation struggling for long against the Moors and an interventionalist Castille [*sic*, Spain] and perhaps in consequence becoming deeply imbued with an idealistic, sometimes bucolic romanticism, tempered by a certain quiet stoicism.[45]

Internal political and religious conflicts within Portugal, its controversial position vis-à-vis Spain and the rest of Europe, and its seafaring history all contributed to a search for 'pastoral simplicity'.[46] The famed voyage to India by the explorer Vasco da Gama in 1498 had quickly become immortalized in the epic poem of Luís de Camões, *The Lusiads*. Its publication helped to promote a vision of 'Golden Goa' throughout Europe after 1572.[47] For the Portuguese, Goa increasingly became the chosen 'other' place – in contradistinction to their homeland – where power, prosperity, and piety reigned perpetually. Thus, it must be underscored that a discourse of Goa Dourada initially grew out of a particular set of Portuguese historical successes, but also instabilities, anxieties, and contradictions, which in turn, by the seventeenth century, were visibly apparent to many European travellers visiting Portuguese India.

Ifeka notes that an image of Goa Dourada was evidenced materially as well. The epithet also refers to the gold which adorns the many 'altars, pulpits, and images of cathedrals in Old Goa and churches in Ilhas and Bardez (two Catholic regions in Goa) that the conquerors built in rapid succession, wonderstruck worshippers gazing at them in awe'.[48] Thus, the goldenness of Goa became its 'trademark',[49] it was placed upon such sites as the marketplace and the house, and produced a 'plural society where continuity, not change, consensus, not conflict, became the dominant worldview'.[50] Portuguese 'dominance', a 'dominance without hegemony' – to apply Ranajit Guha's famous description of the British in the nineteenth century to the Portuguese in the seventeenth century[51] – in Goa was typically made to seem primordial and the past and present seamlessly joined.[52]

In the ritual analysis that follows, I argue that two individual travellers are directly inflected by the power of Goa Dourada precisely because they get caught up in the 'spectacle' of Xavier's canonization celebration. That they viewed Goa in its full ritual glory in 1624 is indexical of what the Estado da Índia sought to publicly display and their relative success in doing so.[53] More importantly, Xavier's canonization festival belied what in fact was taking place both internal and external to Goa, and which seriously undermined the power of the Estado da Índia throughout the seventeenth century. First, Portugal was under Spanish Hapsburg rule (1580–1640)[54] at the time of the canonization of St Francis Xavier, who, in turn, was a Basque Spaniard himself. Thus, a Spanish missionary's 'incorrupt' corpse was being ritually marked as that of a Portuguese saint in Goa, a representation that was 'not without problems',[55] even though, as will become evident, Xavier's canonization did mark a huge success for the now thriving Society of Jesus. Second, at the same time that the Vatican maintained the right arm of this Jesuit priest in a reliquary in Rome as proof of its investment in both Xavier and Goa, it had created, beginning in 1622 – significantly, the same year as Xavier's canonization – the *Propaganda Fide*, an initiative for promoting its own religious orders to function outside the purview of the colonial state because of what it saw as serious neglect on the part of the Portuguese in properly propagating the Catholic faith overseas.[56] Third, Portugal was experiencing a population shortage throughout the seventeenth century, its dwindling resources becoming increasingly more depleted,[57] a fact reinforced by several factors: a series of epidemics that took place during this period,[58] the widespread 'corruption' that was commonly practised by both church and state officials in the colonies,[59] and, finally, the lavishness of Xavier's canonization festivities in 1624 which drained the colonial treasury.

Fourth, alongside the increasing competitiveness of the Jesuits,[60] the Estado da Índia was suffering at the hands of its Asian enemies,[61] including a serious blow from the Safavid Persians who, working alongside the British, took Hurmuz from the Portuguese in 1622.[62] The Portuguese also experienced numerous attacks at the hands of the nearby Marathas throughout the seventeenth century. Their invasion of 1683 would seriously undermine Portuguese state control in the eyes of their many Asian neighbours.[63] Lastly, many 'tensions of empire' were visible; the Dutch and the British were threatening Portuguese power, both at sea and on land.[64] Not only were the Portuguese rapidly losing their position of naval supremacy as a result of numerous Dutch incursions – their ninth blockade of Goa's port in 1640 was by far the most consequential for the Portuguese[65] – but Portugal's attempt to align itself with the British as an added protection against the Dutch had also not been completely successful.[66] The highly competitive British East India Company (1600) would only continue to expand its powers in India in coming centuries, steadily encroaching upon the Portuguese in the process.

Together, these historical conditions shaped the Estado da Índia's slow turn inwards, particularly after 1640,[67] since it could not adequately confront all these threats, both internal and external, without spreading its power, population, and resources too thinly. Involution also involved establishing Goa as a pillar of strength in the midst of a declining Asian empire, particularly since the Portuguese, and in many cases the Jesuits also, would eventually lose Malacca in 1643, (coastal) Ceylon in 1658, and Cochin in 1663 to the Dutch.[68] Promoting Xavier's role as a saint of India in 1624 through the staging of a set of elaborate festivities was thus very much part of this process of fortifying Goa, both politically and spiritually.[69]

Xavier's canonization celebration first represents 'Golden Goa's' materiality[70] on stage by constructing a spectacle of the city. Employing a variety of ritual components, 'Golden Goa' as a place is imbued with a set of characteristics that clearly identify it as a thriving (European and Catholic) colonial city that has the ability to hold processions.[71] In 1624, not only does it have 'five main squares' and 'lanes, streets, and crossroads, and piazzas' but it maintains many houses with roofs, and 'windows, balconies, yards', according to its two key eyewitnesses.[72] Both Barreto and Della Valle also identify several of its religious buildings: St Paul's (both Old and New) College and the newly built Church of Bom Jesus dedicated to housing Xavier's sacred corpse.[73] Barreto interestingly suggests his familiarity with the layout of the city; he identifies additional sites such as the Arches of the Viceroy and the See Cathedral.[74] This Jesuit also qualifies Goa as operating under the larger umbrella of Portugal's colonial empire in Asia and Africa. For Della Valle, Goa is marked through its European architecture, rather than by specific historic sites. In the end, the abundance of churches and learning institutions pointed out by both visitors represent 'Golden Goa' as characteristically European and Catholic to a reading public situated most likely elsewhere, traits that, as will become evident, were simultaneously supported and criticized by various other travellers to Goa during the seventeenth century.

An element of theatricality also lends itself to dressing up Goa in a manner befitting Xavier.[75] Thus, despite initially being poor patrons of (European) music and dance, the Portuguese organizers employ both during the many performances, dramas, and processions that make up this saint's canonization festivities.[76] On the one hand, our visiting Jesuit notes that there are daily floats with 'music, dances with all kinds of instruments, tea music, [and] sonnets', which are used to 'express thanks and devotion to the saints'. Certain types of liturgical music and dance – often sombre in tone – promote the Catholic religiosity of the festivities. Interestingly, it was Xavier himself who first took musical instruments as gifts to Japan in 1550,[77] a historical detail that reinforces the biographical importance of music during Xavier's canonization festivities. On the other hand, our travelling Italian nobleman notes that 'a squadron of young men disguised as peasants danced I don't know how many elegant ballets with music' as part of a staged drama. Similarly, he points out that while many Portuguese men 'all dressed up' passed through the streets of Goa, accompanied by music, a different type of music is reserved for the 'singing of vespers'.

Both travellers also focus their attention on the 'drama' or 'tragedy' that is staged over a period of four consecutive days to illustrate the life, death, and canonization of Xavier. While Barreto points out that the drama, a typical Jesuit pedagogical tool,[78] is 'dedicated to St. Francis Xavier for good reason', Della Valle emphasizes that the tragedy is a 'truly formidable extravaganza, staged and recited by more than three hundred people, lavishly dressed, with many jewels, many items of music, and most elegant dances'. Thus, both authors' testimonies evidence a rich Catholic Portuguese musical and dance tradition, even as Della Valle perhaps highlights its showiness during public celebrations such as this one. Lastly, their accounts demonstrate ritual's ability (including the power of the visual and the auditory) to interpolate its participants such that Goa's 'goldenness' – as it is manifested in music and dance – is recorded for a larger public.

The two authors point to many additional visual markers that contribute to the richness of the canonization festivities. Barreto describes the casket of St Francis Xavier as covered with 'illustrations, miracles, and points in the life of the saint'. Meanwhile, Della Valle is fascinated with the various props that are part of the drama and present in the final procession. The visiting nobleman takes note of the 'chariots, ships, galleys, heavens, hells, mountains and clouds' that are used to convey the history of the life and death of St Francis Xavier. These ritual items are iconographically significant in that they connect our saint to the larger histories and successes of the Society of Jesus and the Estado da Índia and convey them to an attendant public.

The two visitors promote the material gold of Goa in their respective accounts, reinforcing the idea that the theatre of ritual and the marketplace are not in fact 'worlds apart'.[79] Barreto first describes the five pyramids staged by the Jesuits to promote their missions in Asia, Africa, and Europe, as 'works of art'. Specific details – their 'emblems, designs, the gold and silver and other works worthy of such costs' – make them so. This visiting Jesuit also mentions the casket of St Francis Xavier, describing it too as a 'work of art' that 'weighed seven *aroubas* in silver', 'exhibited fine workmanship', and that 'cost 6000 *pardãos*'.[80] Lastly, he points to the use of a flag during the final procession which includes 'the figure of the saint in gold'. Barreto's repeated attention to gold as a material commodity as it is evidenced in the space of ritual is significant given that Goa's foundation was built on the discovery and trade of gold, and its churches were literally filled with this same gold. Barreto's attention to the abundance of gold also takes on a more figurative role for ritual's public by promoting a seamless discourse of Goa Dourada. Interestingly, Della Valle's focus is on the use of silver, a ritual detail that continues to support Goa's goldenness in its commodity value. He mentions the silver detailing on the casket of St Francis Xavier, noting that his 'rich and splendid silver coffin' is 'under a canopy also of silver, utterly lovely'. Here Della Valle seems struck with awe – his expression 'utterly lovely' reinforcing once again the power of ritual to invoke unexpected emotions in its participants. Thus, when juxtaposed, the accounts of Barreto and Della Valle reveal the multiple ways in which Goa is transformed into a spectacle in 1624, the visual and the auditory components in ritual functioning to convey sentiments[81] that are both political and personal, educate an expanding public, and finally, propagate agendas of both church and state, all ongoing themes of this chapter.

> If you have seen Goa, you needn't go to Lisbon. – Seventeenth-century Portuguese proverb[82]

The 'goldenness' of Goa does not escape the eyes and ears of additional travellers during the seventeenth century who witnessed Portuguese India outside the confines of ritual. The Frenchman Thevenot (1666) provides a general overview of this colonial capital. He writes:

> This Town hath good Walls, with Towers and great Guns, and the Isle itself is Walled round, with Gates towards the Land, to hinder the Slaves from running away, which they do not fear (towards the Sea) because all the little Isles and Peninsules that are there, belong to the *Portuguese*, and are full of their Subjects. This Isle is plentiful in Corn, Beasts and Fruit, and hath a great deal of good water. The City of *Goa* is the Capital of all those which the *Portuguese* are Masters of in the *Indies*. The Arch-Bishop, Vice-Roy and Inquisitor General, have their Residence there; and all the Governours and Ecclesiastick and secular Officers of the other Countries (subject to the *Portuguese* Nation in the *Indies*) depend on it ... It is a great Town, and full of fair Churches, lovely Convents, and Palaces well beautified; ... few Nations in the World were so rich in the *Indies as* the Portuguese were.[83]

In the same way that Barreto and Della Valle earlier focused on certain European characteristics to identify Goa's 'goldenness' during the spectacle of Xavier's canonization, so too does this French traveller point out Goa's worth, only viewed from outside the frame of ritual. Not only is it fortified with 'good' walls, towers, and 'great' guns, but it is also comprised of 'fair' churches, 'well beautified' palaces and 'lovely' convents. However, he also blames Goa's 'chief cause of ruin' on its 'excessive vanity'.[84]

The Dutch traveller Phillip Baldeus (1672) also visited the famed city of Goa. He writes:

> The city of Goa increasing every year in Riches and Traffik, increased also in Strength by the addition of serverl [*sic*] forts near the Waterside; this being the Capital City of the Portuguese of the Indies. Its Traffik was more considerable formerly than of late years, since by our blocking up the Bar of Goa they were not a little disturb'd by our Ships ... The great

> Street of Goa has many rich shops well-stor'd with Silks, Porcellain, and other precious Commodities, Drugstery Wares, Manufactories, &c. Some of these as well as fresh Provisions are sold every day in the Market-places, where you hear a Crier, or Auctioneer, to sell in publick all sorts of Goods, both moveable and unmoveable.[85]

Baldeus both records on paper the great Portuguese trade in 'precious commodities' that he witnesses in the streets and many shops of Goa and attributes its increased traffic to the role of his own countrymen, the Dutch. The observations made by (the Italian) Gemelli Careri (1695) are also revealing. He writes:

> Those that envy the Honour of the *Portugueses* ascribe their losses to their want of Zeal for Religion, and their not persisting long in the propagation of it; for they say that the Portugueses [*sic*] entering India with the Crucifix in one Hand and the Sword in the other, finding much Gold, they laid aside the Crucifix to fill their Pockets: and not being able to hold them up with one Hand they were grown so heavy, they dropp'd their Sword too. Being found in this Posture by those that came after, they were easily overcome. This is an excellent contrivance of ill Tongues; but the chief cause of their Ruin was their having made so many Conquests so far divided from one another.[86]

While Careri circulates a perception of the Portuguese as largely motivated by a greed for gold, he also suggests that it is jealousy (on the part of others) that motivates these same derogatory remarks.

The British doctor John Fryer (1676) takes a closer look at the city he describes as a 'Rome in India'.[87] He writes:

> The city of Goa looks well at a small distance, not being to be seen far by reason of the adjacent Hills and windings of the River; it is Ten Miles up the River, stands upon Seven Hills; every where Colleges, Churches, and glorious Structures; it has Gates to it, and a Wall; it is modelled but rudely, many Houses disgracing it with their Ruins, the Streets interfering most confusedly ... the Cathedral is not often excelled by ours at home for the bigness of the Pile; the Architecture but Plain, though very Neat; the Altar and side Chappels filled with Images of delicate Sculpture of our Blessed Saviour and the Virgin Mother, Gilded all over with Gold.[88]

At first glance, this traveller's attention to Goa's many 'glorious structures' as well as its many sculptures 'gilded all over with gold' promotes its perpetual state of goldenness, and from outside the space of ritual. However, he simultaneously denigrates Goa's image when he describes a wall as being 'modelled but rudely', houses as 'ruins', the streets as 'interfering most confusedly', and finally, the Cathedral as 'not excelled by ours at home'. Perhaps Fryer likens Goa to the city of Rome in order to highlight its double meaning for his European readers; like Rome, Goa had reached its zenith, but was now a city in decline, in an inevitable state of 'ruin' in comparison to its past glory. Fryer also visits Old Goa,[89] the site of Xavier's earlier canonization festivities, likening it to the position of 'mistress' to the nearby 'noisy' commercial centre of Goa. Not only does it relieve him to be among its 'rich inhabitants, groves, and gardens' – all European traits – but he also takes note of the fact that fewer drunken soldiers litter its streets, as opposed to the 'other' Goa.[90] By suggesting that Old Goa, the ecclesiastical capital of Portuguese India, is preferable to its commercial centre, Fryer sets it up as an inherently more idealized place for staging ritual activity.

Fryer's commentary reinforces my larger argument in this chapter that Goa is intentionally made a spectacle during the canonization festivities of St Francis Xavier for its esteemed guests. This last point is made stronger when one takes note of an observation made outside the space of ritual by our same visiting Italian nobleman during his visit to Goa in 1624. It is perhaps somewhat of an uncharacteristic remark given the laudatory nature of his comments made on the occasion of Xavier's canonization. Pietro Della Valle writes:

> I believe that there is no other country in the world where they have so many processions each year as in Goa; these are motivated by the number of religious orders in Goa, many more than the city needs; these orders have much authority and are very rich; the natives are idle and greedy for spectacles, undervaluing (scorning) other cities of more weight and certainly more profi ... [Goa] is a city confined by enemies, and the metropole of the king situated between barbarians that are always waging war.[91]

That Della Valle is less flattering and more critical of 'Golden Goa' from outside the confines of ritual – pointing to its over-reliance on processions, the excessive wealth and number of its religious men, the native greed for spectacles, and finally its numerous competing enemies – only reinforces the power of ritual to enthral its participants while covering up its daily realities. Particularly in light of the Estado da Índia's weakening economy throughout the seventeenth century and the encroachment of competing powers such as the Dutch, the English, and the Marathas on to the scene, it is plausible that 'Golden Goa' is constructed as an idealized place in 1624, in contradistinction to the many outward signs of decline noted by a number of travellers, including Thevenot, Baldeus, Fryer, and Careri. Thus, ritual affords a space where the Estado da Índia can perfectly display itself to its (two) visitors, who in turn, take the 'gold' of 'Golden Goa' at face value, reproducing it wholesale in their travel accounts which are then circulated in Europe, long after the event of ritual.[92] However, the accounts of this second group of travellers complement and complicate the idealized testimonies of the former, suggesting that 'Golden Goa' as a space is both resilient and diminished throughout the seventeenth century owing to a number of factors directly tied to the operations of church and state, points not lost even on Della Valle.

The Society of Jesus and the Estado da Índia, a balancing act[93]

> The religious orders closely aligned themselves with the administration of the Estado da Índia. The relationship was one of assistance, yet can be characterized as a love-hate one too. The religious [orders] seemed both a help to the Estado's expansion, as well as a threat to it.[94]

> The Canonization [of St Francis Xavier] marked a turning point for the Society of Jesus. It was an undisputed triumph, the end of a long road to acceptance; the Jesuits had entered the mainstream. In particular, the canonization was an investiture of the Society of Jesus as the greatest force in defending Counter-Reformation Catholicism and promoting it militantly to the 'pagan' sectors of the world, such as India.[95]

In this section, I briefly contextualize the history of the Society of Jesus in seventeenth-century Goa before I compare and contrast the eyewitness accounts of Sebastião Barreto and Pietro Della Valle, tracing their respective representations of the Jesuits during Xavier's canonization festivities in order to examine their seminal role in enacting this set of ritual practices. My analysis will point to the multiple aspects of Xavier's reception in which the Jesuits were involved. I then turn to descriptions by additional travellers to Goa who saw this religious order's operations in the quotidian, pushing these accounts up against each other so as to enrich and complicate our viewpoint of the Jesuits operating as a harmonious unit both internally and externally.

The Jesuits (1542) were one of the many religious orders – alongside the Franciscans (1518), Dominicans (1548), and Augustinians (1572) – who came to Goa under the patronage of the Portuguese in the sixteenth century.[96] With the initial financial support of the Portuguese Crown,[97] a vast network had been set up in which the Society of Jesus was divided into the Provinces of Goa, Malabar, and Japan (including China), Goa functioning as the ecclesiastical centre for all this religious activity.[98] The historian Charles Borges states that these various Jesuit institutions were places where 'men came to study and rest, to work and to move'.[99] The young priests who stopped off or remained in Goa were of differing European backgrounds, cultural rivalries even surfacing at times,[100] particularly between Portuguese and Spanish Jesuits.[101] A fine 'centralised set-up was at the heart of this religious order' according to Borges: priests wrote regularly to Rome – again, following a practice initiated by Xavier himself – and Visitors and briefs from their Superior-General 'kept matters and activities in check when needed'.[102] Furthermore, these men of God 'manned parishes alongside native clerics and other religious [orders], served in hospitals, taught in the seminaries, and converted where they could'.[103] In Goa itself, the Jesuits possessed the College of St Paul's (1542), the Church of Bom Jesus, also called the Professed House (1593),[104] the Novitiate of Chorão (1584), the Colleges of Rachol (1574) and Margão (1597), and eleven residences in the region of Salcette, Goa. They also administered the Royal Hospital at Goa (1579).[105] The Jesuits quietly and successfully attended to their missions under the umbrella of the Portuguese colonial state which, in turn, continued to support them both financially and ideologically.

However, starting in the seventeenth century, when the 'promised Crown subsidies' were 'either not forthcoming or inadequate',[106] the Jesuits exponentially increased their wealth through a variety of entrepreneurial activities. They initiated their own private fund-raising which included the buying, selling, and renting of plots of land, and the management of a flourishing palm-grove business. They also became landowners in Goa and moneylenders to colonial officials, often supplying the Estado da Índia with funds whenever the need arose.[107] However, according to Borges, 'their life-style and fund-raising [also] excited the passions and the envy of many'.[108] By 1624, the Jesuits had developed into the most powerful religious order operating in Goa, Xavier's canonization only proving their continued success and their favoured status with colonial officials, even as they increasingly became less dependent on them financially.[109]

I now turn to my two eyewitness accounts, looking at their (complementary and contradictory) representations of the Jesuits throughout the festivities centred on Xavier. Sebastião Barreto, a Jesuit who dialogically relies on the anonymous *Traça*, highlights the prestige of the Jesuits at the expense of the other religious orders operating in Goa. Barreto first describes the five pyramids which 'move[d] through the five most public parts of the city', three of which – the Old College of St Paul, the New College of St Paul, and the Church of Bom Jesus – were Jesuit-owned institutions. By suggesting that it is this one religious order that single-handedly created three of the five 'public' parts of the city, Barreto provides the Jesuits with a seminal role in first making 'Golden Goa' a possibility. Barreto also includes a description of three squadrons that are part of a procession of pyramids, squadrons that represent Asia, Africa, and Europe, the three continents where the Jesuits had the most successful missions. For Barreto, the 'best' students who accompany the troops of cavalry during the festivities are from the Santa Fe Seminary (the Old College of St Paul), the prestigious Jesuit-run institution mentioned above. Thus, not surprisingly, for this visiting Jesuit priest, the abundance of distinctive markers of Catholicism in Goa, including their ability to incite religious devotion in the space of ritual, are attributed largely to the Jesuits,[110] marking this religious order as one of the central forces behind the success of Goa Dourada in 1624.

Della Valle's description of the Jesuits complements Barreto's testimony by providing additional valuable ritual details. However, he also contributes a contrasting viewpoint of the role of the Jesuits during Xavier's canonization festivities. First, Della Valle reveals that the Jesuits were not the only religious order to have their own elevated figures such as Xavier in 1624. He writes, 'the bells were rung in Goa that day [1 February 1624], and there were great rejoicings, particularly in the churches of the Society of Jesus, the Augustinians, the Dominicans and Franciscans, upon news being brought of many martyrs', three of whom were of 'Italian' descent – a Genovese, a Calabrese, and a Neapolitan. He also notes the recent death of three 'Italian' Jesuits in Japan while one of the sermons held in the Church of Bom Jesus is led by an Italian Jesuit – Fr Flaminio Calo – who speaks on the beatification of yet another Italian Jesuit – Luigi Gonzaga. Della Valle's testimony reveals that the Jesuits who take part in this set of ritual practices are not only of Portuguese descent but include several Italian brothers, this traveller reinforcing once again his apparent interest in all things 'Italian'. In the end, Della Valle represents the Jesuits of Goa as a particularly pious religious order, including descriptions of them as 'singing vespers' and 'preaching sermons' throughout the canonization festivities. Della Valle also represents himself as a particularly pious Catholic, perhaps precisely because of his location so far from 'home'.[111]

In discussing the final procession of the corpse of St Francis from the College of St Paul to the Church of Bom Jesus, Della Valle singles out 'one band of Franciscan friars' that is located at the rear of the procession, the Franciscans being the oldest religious order operating in Goa, one founded by an 'Italian', Francisco de Assisi. The Italian author concludes that 'no one from the other religious orders' attended 'because they refused to join in the Jesuits' processions seeing that the Jesuits would not join theirs'. His statement reveals a tension between different religious orders, between Franciscans and Jesuits in particular, during ritual that is not evident in the testimony of Barreto, who, as a Jesuit himself, is perhaps more intent on recording their activities to the exclusion of other religious orders operating in Goa.[112]

Analysing the testimonies of Barreto and Della Valle in one discursive field reveals that each traveller emphasizes different aspects of the role of the Jesuits in turning Catholic 'faith' into a public spectacle. Thus, for the former, the amount of religious devotion displayed during Xavier's canonization festivities is largely reflective of the sustained efforts of the Jesuits, whereas, for the latter, the efforts of the Jesuits are generally contextualized within a larger Catholic structure, which includes additional orders involving both Portuguese and Italian brothers, and which is strengthened through the author's own piety. These perspectives, in turn, might have something to do with Barreto's position as a Portuguese Jesuit and Della Valle's position as a member of the Italian aristocracy. However, neither representation detracts from the resilience of Goa Dourada as it is manifested in the religious practices and institutions of the Jesuit order, or from the power of ritual to enthral its participants, in this case Barreto even more so than Della Valle.

> The Policy, as well as the Trade, of this place, is mostly devolved from private Persons or the Paulistins [Jesuits], wherefore this saying is in every Body's Mouth: The Franciscan takes care of my woman[wife]; the Jesuit takes care of my money – John Fryer, 1676.[113]

Travellers to Goa – like Fryer and even Della Valle – left behind a multitude of images of the Jesuits in their daily practices throughout the seventeenth century. These additional descriptions, in turn, supplement my characterization of the Society of Jesus during Xavier's canonization festivities by detailing their activities outside the realm of ritual.

The French traveller Thevenot (1666) notes the high visibility of the Jesuits in Goa, relative to other religious orders, by the very number of buildings they maintain. He writes that 'there are several Orders of Religious – both Men and Women There [in Goa], and the Jesuits alone have five publick Houses'.[114] John Albert Mandelslo (1639), was invited to attend a feast at the New College of St Paul, a centre of Jesuit learning where he estimates a house of 'a hundred and fifty fathers and at least as many scholars or students'.[115] After resting from the heat of the day, Mandelslo, alongside additional visitors, was 'taken into a hall where the "divertisement" of a ball had been arranged to entertain them, and which was danced by Indian children who had been baptized and instructed in the Roman Catholic faith'.[116] Similarly, the French traveller Pyrard de Laval (1609) is invited during his stay in Goa by the Jesuits to visit to the Professed House of the Bom Jesus – the very church dedicated to Xavier and the object of translation for his canonization festivities in 1624. He writes:

> It was richly built and all gilded within; it is not yet complete, but the work is proceeding day by day. I have seen there a cross of solid gold, which the company of Jesuit Fathers have had made for a present to the Pope: it was three feet in length, four fingers in width, and two in thicknes, and embellished with all manner of precious stones richly set: it was priced there at more than 100,000 crowns and was sent to His Holiness by the vessel on which I embarked on my return.[117]

Laval is also much impressed by the 'arched hallways' of the Bom Jesus, as well as the fact that the Viceroy has the 'pride of place at the meal' which includes 'fruit and bread' and which is served on 'dishes of porcelain', at the end of which is presented a 'musical show of florentines and tarts'.[118]

Meanwhile, the French traveller Tavernier (1648) gestures to the unlawful ways in which the Jesuits accrue their wealth, hinting at the fact that they involve themselves in business opportunities that lie outside their defined role as propagators of the Catholic faith. He reports that they do a 'brisk trade in rough diamonds',[119] a trade he is familiar with, being a jeweller himself. According to this French visitor to Goa, they disguise themselves as pilgrims to escape notice; he once met one of these disguised Jesuits, who was supposedly travelling on business for the Viceroy of Goa.[120]

He is also witness to rivalries between the Augustinians and the Jesuits. He writes:

> There are in Goa numbers of people connected with the Church ... The Augustins, who were the first comers in Goa, were well situated at the base of a small elevation, their church being on the main street with a handsome square in front. But the Jesuits, having built a house, begged the Augustins to sell them the elevated ground, which was then unoccupied, under pretext of wishing to make a garden for the recreation of their scholars; and, having at length purchased it, they built a splendid college, which shut out the convent of the Augustins, and prevented it from receiving any fresh air. They have had great disputes with one another over this matter, but the Jesuits have at length gained their case.[121]

Just as the Jesuits 'gained their case' against the Augustinians in this particular instance, the Jesuits also created the ideal arena – the canonization festivities of St Francis Xavier of 1624 – in which to represent their contributions to Goa's perpetual state of 'goldenness'. Thus the testimonies of these 'other' travellers highlight the role of the Jesuits in shaping Goan society outside the space of ritual, suggesting that they were alternately praised or maligned for their wealth and competitiveness which, in turn, has everything to do with internal and external rivalries between various members of the many religious orders operating in Goa during the seventeenth century.[122] Lastly, these supplementary travel accounts provide a glimpse of the workings of the church with respect to the state, suggesting that they are perhaps less perfectly 'balanced' in their daily practices than is evidenced during the canonization festivities.

> High appointments in the Portuguese empire were normally granted as favors, to suitably qualified and experienced candidates, and were in that sense patrimonia. The more profitable offices were naturally sought after ... The Viceroyalty of Goa in the 17th century was still one of the most lucrative of all, and large private fortunes continued to be made from it, despite the severe financial difficulties of the state, thus the crown picked carefully in choosing the Viceroy.[123]

In the last section I explored how the arena of ritual in 1624 served as an ideal space for the Jesuits to represent themselves, particularly since they could claim St Francis Xavier as one of their own. In my reading of various travelogues and in my detailing of its day-to-day functions as an organization, the Estado da Índia was often an absent presence; behind the success of the Jesuits in their missionary efforts lay the approval of the Portuguese colonial state, for Xavier's canonization festivities could not have taken place without its consent and financial support.[124] Thus, on the one hand, since certain ideological interests of the Jesuits in this period were often congruent with those of the Estado da Índia – it was a commitment to civilizing the 'native' population through active religious conversion that was shared by both – one must take care not to separate out too much the interests of the 'state' from those of the 'church'.[125] On the other hand, I argue that Xavier's reception, as a set of ritual practices, functions as a space where the interests of the Estado da Índia are perfectly imagined and exhibited – the Jesuits purportedly operating neatly underneath its umbrella – and are worthy of analysis for this very reason.

In this section, I discursively trace the elusive figure of the Viceroy as closely representative of the colonial state in the testimonies of Barreto and Della Valle. I suggest that his actions, when juxtaposed to those of the Jesuits, reinforce my larger argument that the Estado da Índia and the Society of Jesus were engaged in what historian Charles Borges calls a 'balancing act' during the ritual in 1624.[126] Once again, I rely on accounts of additional travellers to Goa to complicate our picture of the Viceroy in his day-to-day activities, suggesting that he was perhaps less able to articulate the power of Goa Dourada outside the confines of ritual practice.

The role of Viceroy of Portuguese India was particularly important both inside and outside the space of ritual given that he 'exercised an over-all supervision of the entire administrations of Portuguese India'.[127] The historian Anthony Disney provides an overview of his duties, suggesting that we cannot underestimate the arduous and crucial nature of his position. He writes:

> The central fiscal, judicial, naval and other administrative organs of the Estado da Índia, which were located at Goa, were under the viceroy's immediate supervision, and he participated regularly in their work. He took ultimate responsibility for the security, good government and financial viability of all the outlying captaincies and factories, and had the power to suspend and replace most of their officials. He was to a certain extent involved in the direct administration of Goa and the Goa territories, and watched over the activities of the various local administrative and corporate bodies, trying to adjudicate and curb their frequent and often protracted disputes. He was required to perfect the activities of the *Padroado* church and the clergy, to maintain the *Carreira da Índia* and to foster trade. Finally, he had to nurture as far as possible satisfactory relations with a vast range of rulers and peoples throughout monsoon Asia and eastern Africa. All these responsibilities required a wide grasp of complex political and military affairs, and familiarity with a mass of accumulated rules, procedures, and practices of the local bureaucracy.[128]

The all-important role of Viceroy required a person of varied skills – political, bureaucratic, and diplomatic. He was simultaneously assisted by a Secretary and advised by a Council of State and Senate.[129]

Sebastião Barreto's image of the Viceroy during Xavier's canonization festivities reinforces the centrality of his role. For this visiting Portuguese Jesuit, the Viceroy is present at all of the major events that together make up ritual. He also functions as the sponsor of this momentous 'Jesuit event'. Not only does the first procession of five pyramids appropriately stop in front of the Archway of the Viceroy but the final procession carrying the holy body of the saint stops – following the request of the Viceroy – in front of the See Cathedral where the Viceroy has conveniently retired with his retinue. Thus, the power of the Viceroy is ritually recognized in the movement of the processions, and in the landmarks that it stops in front of and pays tribute to. Nor is the Viceroy represented without his court by his side. The power of the colonial state is represented through the presence of an entourage – consisting of various advisers and including such government officials as Goa's Chancellor and Attorney General – following on the heels of the Viceroy. Barreto also points to the many soldiers, sentinels, and captains – all less visible but still crucial state actors – who participate on the sidelines of ritual. Lastly, this Jesuit visitor appeals to the Viceroy when he writes, 'One hopes that His Excellency enjoys the pageantry'. Thus, for Barreto, the Viceroy's role is that of sponsor and esteemed spectator to a largely Jesuit-organized event, the prestige afforded him in the space of ritual only reinforcing Goa's 'goldenness'.

Della Valle gives equal weight to the Viceroy's responsibilities during Xavier's reception.[130] While he accounts for his presence during the first act of the drama dedicated to St Xavier, Della Valle also reinforces, perhaps even more so, the elevated position of the Viceroy in ritual. He writes: 'On February 13, the Viceroy being indisposed, the festivity was suspended, and nothing was done'. Della Valle's testimony illuminates the role of the Viceroy as the singular authority to suspend and, by implication, to control ritual, a point that is reinforced by the fact that the colonial state covered most of the expenses for this celebration. Like Barreto, this Italian traveller also notes that the Viceroy is always represented alongside his court. However, his focus is on those members of the nobility of Goa, men not so different from himself. Lastly, our Italian traveller attests to the highly visible role of the Viceroy in the various liturgical functions that take place inside the Church of Bom Jesus, and in attending to the many visitors, like himself, who had the remarkable opportunity to see 'Golden Goa' during the festivities. Thus, for Della Valle, the Viceroy's participation is crucial to the staging and success of ritual.

The accounts of Barreto and Della Valle together speak to the power of the Estado da Índia to promote the gold of Goa through the figure of the Viceroy in the space of ritual. The colonial state, by sparing no cost, and displaying its material and discursive weight, largely succeeds in getting its participants caught up in the signification of ritual practice. Again, I point to the efficacy of ritual in achieving certain desired effects even as they are interpreted differently by our two eyewitnesses. For Barreto, a Portuguese Jesuit, the Viceroy is the sponsor of a Jesuit event, while for Della Valle, an Italian nobleman, the Viceroy's participation is integral to the festivities themselves. Together these travellers illuminate the role of the Viceroy as the literal and figurative head of the state during this moment of heightened ritual activity. In the following section I provide additional glimpses of the Viceroy, but in his everyday dealings, relying once again on the testimonies of those same travellers of earlier sections who encountered him outside the realm of ritual. Once again, their accounts also provide a window on to the waxing and waning resilience of Goa Dourada throughout the seventeenth century, suggesting that the Viceroy occasionally had a less flattering image outside the confines of ritual, a perspective which had everything to do with the amount and kind of power he wielded.

> This frequent change of Viceroys is displeasing to the Portuguese ... To illustrate which they tell a parable, how that one day there lay a poor man at the door of a church, his legs full of ulcers, and so covered with flies as was pitiful to behold; up came a neighbor who, thinking to do him a kindness, drove away the flies: whereat the poor patient was much vexed, saying that the flies he drove away already had their bellies full, and would not bite him more, whereas those that would come would be hungry and would sting him worse. So it is, they say, with the Viceroys, for the gorged depart and the hungry arrive. – Pyrard de Laval, 1609[131]

The testimonies of these other travellers to Goa provide multiple views on the Viceroy in his day-to-day dealings. The French traveller Tavernier (1648) describes the post of Viceroy as one of great wealth and prestige. He writes:

> The Viceroy alone does not trade, or if he does, it is under the name of another, and moreover, he has a sufficient income without it ... [It is] one of the most splendid posts in the world for a noble to be Viceroy of Goa, and there are few monarchs who are able to bestow governments worth so much as are those which depend upon this Viceroy.[132]

The German traveller Mandelslo (1639) suggests that the Viceroy's tenure was set at three years for specific reasons. His account also reveals the extra 'duties' of the Viceroy. He writes:

> He [the Viceroy] had about him a court of more than fifty gentlemen who gave him the same respect that was owing to the king in Europe. The Viceroy was changed about every three years: partly because the king thought it unsafe to allow a subject to hold such a dignity for long, and also because the King desired to distribute his patronage among a large number of his nobles so as to enable them to amass a fortune in short period. This was possible because the court of the Viceroy at Goa was maintained at the king's expenses and also because the disposal of all the revenues was left in his hands. Every year the Viceroy made an extensive tour over the territories under his control, and this brought him a large sum of money by way of presents from the neighbouring princes and from the governors and other subordinate officers.[133]

This German traveller's account reveals not only that the position of Viceroy was a highly coveted one amongst the Portuguese nobility but that in his official capacity he had the ability to amass vast amounts of wealth through the receiving of gifts from his 'neighbouring princes' and his 'subordinate officers'. Mandelslo's account reveals that a particular kind of 'corruption' was a state-sanctioned activity in seventeenth-century Goa, a characterization that suggests that the Viceroy's everyday activities were sometimes motivated by individual monetary pursuits. Here the Viceroy is characterized in a manner that is reminiscent of Pyrard de Laval's parable reproduced at the outset of this section. In the words of this French traveller, 'So it is with the Viceroys, the gorged depart, and the hungry arrive'.

Using the accounts of these 'other' European travellers as a counterpoint to the eyewitness testimonies of Barreto and Della Valle not only serves to fill out the coveted and prestigious position of Viceroy as the representative head of state but reveals his multiple duties, both inside and outside ritual. Thus, on the one hand, in the space of ritual, the gold of Goa is reified through the singular figure of the Viceroy. On the other, the fact that this man took personal advantage of the wealth of the Estado da Índia that was largely at his disposal – meaning his power largely went unchecked – serves to represent the Viceroy in perhaps a less noble light. Furthermore, given the fact that Xavier's canonization festivities were in fact so lavish, it is not insignificant that the acting Viceroy in 1624 was Francisco da Gama,[134] his high visibility during ritual suggesting both his own political and personal investment in promoting Goa Dourada and the legacy of his legendary great-grandfather Vasco da Gama.

Producing a 'Portuguese' and 'native' public

> A sense of Portuguese identity was stronger here [in Goa] than in the motherland. This sort of unity appeared most fully in conflictless situations, such as the more important religious processions and occasions of public rejoicing. Here all Portuguese could unite … and celebrate their common nationality, despite their location 10,000 miles and three months sailing distance from Portugal.[135]

In this section, I explore the attendance of a diverse 'Portuguese' public at Xavier's canonization festivities in 1624. However, before I explore the various sectors of Goan society as they are represented in the testimonies of Barreto and Della Valle, the discrete category of a 'Portuguese' public is historicized. Next I address the many 'European' markers of status that are associated with ritual's Portuguese participants, at the same time noting Barreto's representation of a 'native' public. I also look to clothing as a marker of status, suggesting that Della Valle pays particularly close attention to its power to signify multiple aspects of Goa's 'goldenness'. Lastly, I suggest that ritual helps produce an idealized public, one that clearly demarcates those who are labelled 'Portuguese' and those who are not, and includes spectators like Barreto and Della Valle. Ritual is simultaneously the product of its public.

Tracing the history of the Portuguese as a linguistic and cultural group is complicated by the colonial enterprise. Thus, the idea of a Portuguese public as a category in itself is fractured. 'Portugueseness' in the colonies was, starting in the sixteenth century, delineated according to degrees of blood; it was also always in a state of flux as a result. Thus, one realizes that being 'Portuguese' and, by implication, 'Catholic' was always being negotiated and contested in a place like Goa. According to the historian Teotónio de Souza, the population of Goa at the beginning of the seventeenth century was approximately 75,000 persons.[136] The number of households in the city and its immediate surroundings was approximately 5,000 with each household consisting of fifteen persons, including the many slaves imported from its African colonial outposts.[137] And of these city dwellers, 'not more than 1,500 were Portuguese (Catholics); the rest were native Christians, Hindus, and African slaves'.[138]

Goan social structure was extremely hierarchical since it was strictly organized along racialized lines.[139] At the top of Portuguese colonial society were the *reinois*; they were 'blue-blooded Portuguese nationals who came to India as high officials and occupied such positions as those of the Governors, Viceroys, Archbishops, and Bishops, Captains and Judges, and so on'.[140] Most did not settle in Goa for they often returned to Portugal upon the completion of their term in office. Nor was it encouraged for any members of this high-status group to intermarry with the local women, given the 'purity' of their Portuguese blood.[141] These *reinois* could be further distinguished between *fidalgos*, those of higher nobility, and *nobres*, those of lesser nobility. Below them were the *casados*, those Portuguese who 'married local women and settled down in Goa or elsewhere in a Portuguese colony'.[142] Marriage alliances eventually led to the creation of further divisions among the offspring of the *casados*, 'namely the *castiços* of pure Portuguese blood, whose parents were Portuguese men and women; and [the] *mestiços* of mixed blood born of Portuguese and Indian parentage or Portuguese and African parentage whose progeny was called *mulattos*'.[143] Outside the 'pale of the Portuguese society as such were the *naturais* or the 'natives' who were then further divided into the Christians[144] and non-Christians, the latter group being 'rendered to the status of a deprived class'.[145] African slaves maintained the lowest positions in the social organization of Goan society.[146] While 'racial tolerance' was the policy put forth in theory by both church and state officials, in practice, as is well known, 'a great deal of discrimination was indulged in',[147] including even within the space of ritual.

Barreto's view of the public, as was his view of the Jesuits and the Viceroy during the canonization festivities, is informed by a knowledge of Portuguese colonial society. He distinguishes between the various segments of the strictly 'Portuguese Catholic' population that is present in 1624, including those persons who were involved in the festivities outside of an official capacity – students, parents, brothers, the cavalry, guards, soldiers, *fidalgos*, and captains – at the same time noting the 'tears of devotion' on the part of many of these ritual participants. He also notes that the 'lanes, crossroads, stores, windows, yards, and public squares [are] all full of many people' who have harmoniously come together to celebrate the canonization of their patron saint. Barreto also distinguishes between those who maintain 'palanquins' – a clear marker of Europeanness[148] – and those who are barred from maintaining such a status symbol, the 'native' public, a group that is further broken down into categories of 'idolaters' and 'Moors',[149] and who are provided an 'inferior' view of the tragedy from the windows located above the square, windows that never fully open, and from where they 'derive their pleasure'. That a crowd of people (both Portuguese and native) clamours to Goa's public spaces to watch the festivities no doubt helps represent its state of 'goldenness'.[150]

Della Valle's observations of the 'Portuguese' public present at Xavier's canonization festivities are just as idealized but less historically informed as compared to Barreto's. He also omits any mention of a 'native' public in attendance. However, he must also be positioned as more of an 'outsider' to Goan society on this occasion.[151] Interestingly, Della Valle relies almost exclusively on dress as a marker of status;[152] it becomes a way to distinguish between the different segments of Portuguese colonial society, Goa's 'goldenness' promoted through the particular dress of its participants. Our traveller notes that on the same day of the preaching of a sermon 'many gaily attired Portuguese appeared on the scene, vastly entertaining the ladies' – a group notably missing from Barreto's description[153] – 'who stood there looking at them from the balconies and platforms'. He takes note of the 'numerous young students dressed up richly and gallantly' while more than 'three hundred people, all lavishly dressed' look on as the drama is staged. Similarly, in the evenings, the Portuguese men 'pass through the streets all dressed up'. Here the communicative power of dress cannot be underestimated in conveying occupations, religious affiliations, and hierarchies in public spaces, particularly for a visitor like Della Valle, who constantly draws attention to costume, including his own, as a marker of status even though he does not include specific sartorial details. Lastly, Della Valle's testimony reinforces the efficacy of ritual as an aesthetic and sensorial experience for all its participants, both Portuguese and 'native'.

Historical evidence offers instead an alternative role for Goa's 'natives' – both Hindu and Muslim – during Xavier's canonization festivities. Michael Pearson notes that non-Catholic participants were banned from all public religious activities, including Xavier's canonization celebration.[154] In light of this colonial legislation, the attendance of these 'natives' in 1624 is less about affirming the logic of ritual.[155]

Rather, in their position on the sidelines of ritual, these 'subaltern' groups can perhaps be interpreted as contesting ritual activity in a manner reminiscent of Bakhtin's discussion of the 'carnivalesque'.[156] In the end, their participation in Xavier's canonization festivities in 1624 not only fractures a coherent image of 'Golden Goa' but is historically, religiously, and politically significant.

> I have never seen men of wit so fine and polished as are these Indians: they have nothing barbarous or savage about them, as we are apt to suppose. They are unwilling indeed to adopt the manners and customs of the Portuguese: yet do they readily learn their manufactures and workmanship being all very curious and desirous of learning. In fact, the Portuguese take and learn more from them than they from the Portuguese; and they that come fresh to Goa are very simpletons till they have acquired the airs and grace of the Indies. – Pyrard de Laval, 1609[157]

Additional travellers such as Laval reveal that Goa's 'goldenness' as it is manifest in its 'Portuguese' public was in fact fading throughout this period, sometimes nothing more than a showy display such that, in a reverse process, it was often they who took and learned from their colonial Indian subjects. The French jeweller Tavernier (1648) provides a brief glimpse of the many Portuguese *fidalgos* (noblemen) who were highly visible during Xavier's canonization festivities. He writes,

> The Portuguese who go to India have no sooner passed the Cape of Good Hope than they all become *Fidalgos* or gentleman, and add Dom to the simple name of Pedro or Jeronimo which they carried when they embarked; this is the reason why they are commonly called in derision '*Fidalgos* of the Cape of Good Hope.'[158]

His remarks mirror those of his fellow countrymen Pyrard de Laval in that he too pokes fun at the Portuguese nobility living in Goa, suggesting that it is the very act of travel that allows them to acquire the 'airs and graces of the Indies', thus improving their status in the colony because of the flexibility it afforded as compared to the rigidity of categories of bloodlines in the metropole. A colonial space such as Goa even enables them in some sense to exaggerate their 'Portugueseness'.

Our same French traveller Laval (1609) also helps to contextualize the presence of women, specifically the wives of the Portuguese *fidalgos*, in public. He writes:

> The rich ladies of quality go but seldom to church, save on the great feast days, and then superbly attired in the Portuguese mode. Their gowns for the most part are of gold, silk, and silver brocade, enriched with pearls, gems, and jewels at the head, arms, hands, and waist. Over all they wear a veil of the finest crape in the world, reaching from the head to the foot. They never wear stockings, their pattens, or chapins, are open above, and

> cover only the soles of the feet; but they are all embroidered with gold and silver, hammered in thin plates which reach over the lower surface of the chapin, the upper part being covered with pearls and gems and the soles half a foot thick with cork.[159]

Laval's testimony speaks to not only the power of ritual to enthral its participants but also the important role of the wives of noblemen in promoting Goa's 'goldenness' through their elaborate dress. He also affords us a window on to the public spaces Portuguese women inhabited in Goan society during the seventeenth century. Their failure to attend minor social functions, excepting 'great' Catholic feast days, reinforces not only the relative seclusion of female nobility as per the norms of Portuguese colonial society but the importance of the canonization festivities of St Francis Xavier since their presence – 'on balconies and platforms' – was duly noted by Della Valle.[160] Ritualized Goa is 'fashioned' as a public space wherein the wives of these *fidalgos* openly showcase the fruits of Portuguese overseas trade. In addition, our French traveller's curious attention to dress mirrors that of Della Valle, reinforcing the power of European dress to convey markers of status to its many visitors.

At the same time, Laval provides a less flattering image of Goan women in their day-to-day activities. He writes,

> the women of Goa are exceedingly lewd, as the climate and the diet of the country inclines them so ... they are so amorous and so addicted to fleshy pleasures that when they find the smallest opportunity, they fail not to use it.[161]

These additional travellers to Goa also attest to a cohesive Goan 'native' public, a community that was noted as largely absent during the canonization festivities owing to the nature of Portuguese colonial legislation at this time. For example, the Dutch traveller Linschoten (1588) attests to the business acumen of Goa's Hindu population.[162] He writes:

> Heathenish Indians that dwell in Goa are verie rich merchants and traffique much, there is one streete that is full of shops by these heathenish Indians, that not only sell all kinds of silkes, sattins, damaskes, and curious works of velvet, silke, sattin, and much like, brought out of Portugall, which by means of their brokers they buy by the great and sell them againe by the peece or seller, wherein they are verie cunning, and naturally subtill.[163]

His detailing of such a thriving 'native' community not only emphasizes the economic and political power of this 'heathenish' group within Portuguese colonial society[164] but also points to their 'fine and polished wit' that Laval described earlier.

Lastly, I turn to a set of less flattering comments made by Della Valle outside the confines of ritual, and that targeted both the Portuguese and Goa's African slave population. He writes:

> The people is numerous, but the greatest part are slaves, a black and lewd generation, going naked for the most part, or else very ill clad, seeming to me rather a disparagement than an ornament to the City. Portugals there are not many; ... they have not much wealth, but are rather poor. Nevertheless, they live in outward appearance with splendor enough, which they may easily do both in regard of the plentifulness of the Country, and because they make a shew of all they have.[165]

Our Italian visitor's description suggests that there was a large but impoverished slave community in Goa at this time, even as they were noticeably absent during the days of ritual. He also emphasizes the 'showiness' of the Portuguese, a representation that echoes the accounts of these other travellers who also emphasize the ostentatiousness and exaggerated character of the Portuguese in their everyday encounters. All of these observations are supported by Pearson's thesis that 'frontier societies', of which Goa was one, were often characterized by a 'show of extravagance'.[166]

The combined testimonies of all these travellers to Goa also help to delineate the crucial role of the public in defining Xavier's canonization festivities. The historian Richard Trexler argues that such spaces as the 'street' and the 'town square' were essential for the formation of a public in the early modern period since they function 'as the place[s] of contact, the arena of competition, [and] the space[s] in which civic form was shaped, challenged, and reshaped'.[167] Thus, the staging of a celebration in 1624 on Goa's 'Rua Direita', the main artery of the city, and the processions that wound themselves through its streets, all contributed to the formation of a public that comprised mostly male and female 'Portuguese' but also included, significantly, a few 'native' participants who attended on the sidelines. Second, Trexler argues that 'formal public life ... articulated the changing order of things, and was part of that change',[168] a point pertinent to my own ritual analysis. Members of this same public affect colonial policy making and conversion practices inside as well as outside the space of ritual. Lastly, the overt display of wealth – again, a detail emphasized by both sets of travellers – on the part of Goa's 'Portuguese' public highlights Trexler's important point that 'the chance for better status could be found only in public',[169] ritual in 1624 no doubt affording a perfect opportunity to do so. In the end, Pearson's description of the canonization festivities of 1624 as an 'occasion for massive public rejoicing'[170] is well borne out through this reading of a variety of travellers' texts.

The (absent) body in ritual

Just as I began the chapter with the alternating descriptions of Xavier's corpse by travellers – in this case Fryer and Hamilton – who visited Goa outside the space of ritual, I end my analysis of his canonization festivities by examining the marked centrality of this saint's corpse in this set of ritual practices.[171] Specifically, it is his physical body – ritual's centrepiece – that is made a spectacle for public display in 1624. Here I argue that in their dual positions as travellers and ritual participants, Sebastião Barreto's and Pietro Della Valle's curious collective lack of attention to the condition of Xavier's corpse – markers of his 'incorruptness' or 'miraculousness' – is illuminating given the amount of lavish attention it receives by additional travellers to 'Golden Goa' throughout the duration of the seventeenth century as well as during the festivities that preceded and followed his canonization celebration, that is, in 1554 and 1782 respectively. I argue that this ritual omission evidences the import of Xavier's canonization (and ornate casket) in replacing his physical corpse as the main signifier of the larger successes of the Society of Jesus and the Estado da Índia in 1624.

In their emphasis on the visual and auditory aspects of ritual, these two European visitors record instead the elaborateness of the casket containing this saint's corpse which is carried in final procession to his new 'home', the Church of Bom Jesus. In my earlier discussion of 'Goa as spectacle', I showed how both authors focus their attention on the casket's materiality, its 'goldenness' taking centre stage in their respective descriptions. Thus, while Barreto labels Xavier's casket a 'work of art' of unsurpassed value, Della Valle recognizes its fine silver craftsmanship. Both authors also focus their attention on the biography of Xavier as it is represented on stage during his canonization festivities, Barreto noting the visual representation of 'miracles and points in the life of the saint' on his casket, and Della Valle emphasizing his life story as one of the themes of the staged tragedy, including the 'transportation of the saint's body to Goa'. Thus, in the same manner by which Goa is finely dressed through a variety of accoutrements for ritual activity, so too is Xavier's corpse, its physical condition escaping the attention of these two travellers precisely because they are caught up in the elaborateness of his casket and the details of his life story, perfect signifiers of Xavier's canonization and Goa's 'goldenness' in 1624.

> In a fine stately Church dedicated to St. *Paul* the Apostle, lies the Body of *St Francis Xavier* a *Portugueze* Apostle, and a *Jesuit* by Trade, who died in his Mission to *Japon* in the fifteenth Century; and, about fifty Years after, as a *Portugueze* Ship was going to, or coming from *China*, being near an Island on that Coast, called after St. *Juan* some Gentleman

> and Priests went ashore for Diversion, and accidentally found the Saint's body uncorrupted, and carried it Passenger to Goa, and there, with much Veneration and ecclesiastical Ceremony, it was deposited in an Isle of St. *Paul's* Church, where it lies still, and looks as fresh as a new Scalded Pig, but with the Loss of one Arm, for, when the Rumour of the Miracle reached *Rome*, the Sovereign Pontiff ordered his right Arm to be sent, that he might find out if there was any Imposture in it or no, or perhaps make him fadge in a *China Bonzee* into his Calendar, under the Name of a *Christian* Saint. Accordingly, his Arm was fairly cut off by the Shoulder, and sent to *Rome* to stand its Trial. When his Holiness had viewed it, he called for Pen, Ink, and Paper to be brought on a Table, and the Arm set near them. After a little Conjuration, in full View of the Sacred College, who were there present, and no Body else, the Saint's Hand took hold of the Pen, and dipt it in Ink, and fairly wrote Xavier. – Alexander Hamilton, 1692[172]

The accounts of a variety of additional travellers to Goa suggest that Xavier's corpse was increasingly an object of historical curiosity and medical scrutiny throughout the seventeenth century. Their perspectives, in turn, have the potential to enrich our understanding of its (absent) role in ritual in 1624. At the outset of this chapter, I illustrated how the British doctor Fryer (1676) labelled it a 'Miraculous Relick' – defying the natural process of decomposition – whereas the Scottish trader Hamilton (1692) viewed Xavier's physical state after death more suspiciously, calling it a 'pretty Piece of Wax-work', and in his more idealized version, quoted above, likened his flesh to that of a 'new scalded pig'.[173] Meanwhile, the German traveller Mandelslo (1639) attests to the 'sweet smell' emanating from Xavier's corpse,[174] and the Italian medical doctor Careri (1695) records the 'shrinking' stature of Xavier's corpse after being granted special permission to kiss it.[175] Together, all of these descriptions by additional European travellers afford a window on to the condition of Xavier's corpse throughout this time frame. Their testimonies suggest, on the one hand, that his physical body exhibits numerous signs of its 'saintliness' for its esteemed visitors and, on the other, that its 'incorruptible' state is declining (or as in the case of Hamilton, was never a reality) medical 'expertise' in at least two instances (for Fryer and Careri) playing a role in determining the veracity of its condition and monitoring its changing corporeal state. That the range of representations of Xavier's corpse by this set of travellers parallels the range of observations concerning Goa's 'goldenness' made outside the space of ritual is significant, reinforcing the indexical (metaphoric and metonymic) quality of Xavier's corpse, a continuing theme of this book.

Conclusion

The Dutch menace was the skeleton of every Goan feast.[176]

In the end, the gold of Goa as it was materially and discursively displayed in and through a set of ritual practices was witnessed by at least two European travellers whose representations would continue to circulate in multiple colonies and metropoles long after the year 1624. The disparate testimonies of additional visitors to Goa such as Hamilton and Fryer, travellers who were not witness to Xavier's canonization celebration but whose multiple impressions simultaneously enrich our understanding of ritual activity, are less at odds with each other if seen as produced out of the historical fissures that defined the Estado da Índia during the seventeenth century and which, I have argued, were purposely kept out of the idealized space of ritual activity. As John Fryer noted so astutely in 1676, 'the city still presented a noble appearance, and the inhabitants still made an attempt at display despite their increasing misery, but it was the "splendid outside" which had no real substance behind it'.[177] Thus, it is not coincidental that just as the Portuguese in Goa were experiencing their demise, slowly turning inward as a result, a variety of European travellers set sail for Goa as part of a larger 'India' tour, their testimonies preserving glimpses of Goa Dourada as it was intermittently fading away, in the process exposing its vulnerabilities for future colonial investments, particularly on the part of the Dutch and British.

My argument concerning the similarities and differences that are visible between authors – Barreto and Della Valle – and authorities – the Society of Jesus and the Estado da Índia – during these festivities is based on the idea that ritual is a site for multiple acts of 'encounter'. Thus, the 'balancing' of church and state evidenced in the space of ritual indexes the intersecting histories of a host of Portuguese colonial practices and Catholic missionary practices. As a result, I neither take 'church' and 'state' power to be absolute nor can I assign full intentionality to the Jesuits or the Viceroy as historical actors or as the principal organizers of Xavier's canonization festivities. Rather, each person or group's authority 'seems balanced or even undermined by the very different configurations of power characteristic of the other groups'.[178] Thus, in the case of the festivities of 1624, power is embodied, inscribed, and constrained in a multitude of ways, and viewed from a multiplicity of perspectives. Ritual practice reflects not only differences between 'Portugueseness' and 'Italianness' or between colonial officials and Jesuit priests. It also serves as an arena for competing discourses and materialities – between colonial powers such as the Portuguese and the Dutch; between Jesuits, Franciscans, and various other religious orders, between a 'Portuguese (Catholic)' public and a 'native' public, between men and women, between styles of dress as markers of status, between competing 'faiths' – political and religious – and, finally, between degrees of Goa Dourada. Lastly, I argue that ritual is very much about the social reproduction and circulation of sentiments, sensibilities, and subjectivities.[179] In the same manner that Barreto and Della Valle get caught up the richness of the festivities of 1624, so too did many, but perhaps not all, of its Indo-Portuguese participants. Colonial officials would hardly lose sight of this saint's mutability as a ritual centrepiece, particularly in 1782 after its expulsion of the Jesuits from Goa, the subject of my next chapter.

Notes

1 John Fryer, *A New Account of East India and Persia, Being Nine Years Travel, 1672–1681*, Volume 3, ed. William Crooke (New Delhi: Asian Educational Services, 1992), p. 12. Note that he approximates the death of Xavier to be 'near 200 years ago' (1476), which is inaccurate: the saint died in 1552.

2 Alexander Hamilton, *A New Account of the East Indies. Being the Observations and Remarks of Capt. Alexander Hamilton. From the year 1688–1723. Trading and Traveling by Sea and Land, to Most of the Countries and Islands of Commerce and Navigation, Between the Cape of Good Hope and the Island of Japan*, Volume 1 (New Delhi: Asian Educational Services, 1995), p. 252–4, emphasis his.

3 See Georg Schurhammer, 'Mejico Y Javier: Un Documento Inedito sobre Su Culto', in *Varia I* (Lisboa: Centro de Estudos Historicos Ultramarinhos, 1965), p. 549.

4 Owing to the monsoon season, there was approximately an 18-month to three-year lag time in communications between metropole and colony and vice versa. See Charles Boxer, *Portuguese India in the Mid-Seventeenth Century* (Delhi: Oxford University Press, 1980), p. 6.

5 As described by José da Fonseca, *An Historical and Archaeological Sketch of the City of Goa* (Delhi: Asian Educational Services, 1986 [1878]), p. 286.

6 Here 'translation' refers to the movement of the body of Xavier from the Jesuit St Paul's College to the Church of Bom Jesus; I follow up on my use of 'translation' in my previous chapter, where I discussed the transfer of Xavier's corpse from Sancian to Malacca and finally to Goa.

7 John Fryer, *A New Account of East Asia and Persia*, p. 26.

8 Part of building this empire in Asia was about transforming Xavier into a saint of *Asia*, the topic of my second chapter, whereas by 1624 the Portuguese were invested in turning Xavier into a saint of *India*.

9 Victor Turner, *Ritual Process* (Harmondsworth: Penguin Books, 1974).

10 I understand 'faith' as something that is less understood as religious faith, but rather, following Talal Asad, as being the product of the interplay of different epistemologies of faith. See Talal Asad, *Genealogies of Religion* (Baltimore: Johns Hopkins University Press, 1993).

11 E.F. Oaten, *European Travellers in India, During the Fifteenth, Sixteenth and Seventeenth Centuries, the Evidence Afforded by Them with Respect to Indian Social Institutions, and the Nature and Influence of Indian Governments* (New Delhi: Asian Educational Services, 1991 [1909]), p. 4. Emphasis mine.

12 See Michel Foucault, *The Order of Things: An Archaeology of the Human Sciences* (New York: Vintage Books, 1973).

13 The 'dialogism' of these texts, as outlined by Bakhtin, cannot be discounted in forming representations of the Other; in this case, my focus is on the Portuguese as Other; particularly since some of the very travellers whose testimonies I rely

on in this chapter reference the accounts of other travellers. See M.M. Bakhtin, *The Dialogic Imagination: Four Essays*, ed. M. Holquist, tr. C. Emerson and M. Holquist (Austin: University of Texas Press, 1981).

14 Mary Louise Pratt. *Imperial Eyes: Travel Writing and Transculturation* (London: Routledge, 1992), p. 3.

15 Ibid., p. 4.

16 Here I emphasize Pratt's idea of 'anti-conquest' by which she refers to 'the strategies of representation whereby European bourgeois subjects seek to secure their innocence in the same moment as they assert their European hegemony'. See Mary Louise Pratt, *Imperial Eyes*, p. 7.

17 Ibid.

18 It is important to note that very few accounts written by Portuguese travellers, outside an official capacity, exist for the seventeenth century. Thus, these other travellers' accounts are particularly important for reflecting the interests of competing metropoles during a crucial period in the Estado's history.

19 Johannes Fabian, *Out of Our Minds: Reason and Madness in the Exploration of Central Africa* (Berkeley: University of California Press, 2000), p. 3.

20 Ibid., p. 4.

21 Here I follow the work of Ann Stoler, who, along with Fred Cooper, has been at the forefront of exposing the strengths and vulnerabilities of empires, and emphasizing the important links between metrole and colony. See *Tensions of Empire*, eds Ann Stoler and Fred Cooper (Berkeley: University of California Press, 1997).

22 Most historians of Goa writing on this period attest to the significance of these travelogues as source materials. Also, historiographically, the seventeenth century marks the beginning of the end of the Estado da Índia's golden era.

23 Teotónio de Souza, 'Bibliographical Essay', in his *Medieval Goa: A Socio-Economic History* (New Delhi: Concept Publishing Co, 1979), pp. 194–5.

24 Ibid., p. 194.

25 Ibid.

26 This description of the festival is taken from the *Annua* of P. Sebastião Barreto, S.J., who wrote this description in Goa on 15 December 1624. Reproduced in Georg Schurhammer, 'Festas em Goa no Ano 1624', in *Varia I* (Roma: Institutum Historicum, 1965), pp. 493–7.

27 Background information on Barreto is unavailable. More than likely Barreto was the son of nobility, since it was common practice among this class rank for one son to enter the priesthood. Also, by the fact that his knowledge of and familiarity with Goa is evident in his testimony, Barreto might have been stationed in Goa for some time prior to witnessing Xavier's canonization festivities.

28 My focus is on Barreto and the influence of this authoritative source on his description. I will be relying on P. Rayanna's paraphrasing of the *Traça da Pompa Triunfal* which was included in a booklet printed by the press of the College of St Paul in 1624. See his *St Francis Xavier and His Shrine*, 2nd edn (Panjim, Goa: Imprimatur, 1982), p. 240. The *Traça* in its entirety is reproduced in Schurhammer's 'Festas em Goa no Ano 1624', *Varia I* (Roma: Institutum Historicum, 1965), pp. 496–7. According to Schurhammer, the original is lost, but a copy of it exists in the Rome Archives of the Society of Jesus, its full title: '*Traça* da pompa triunfal com que os padres da Companhia de Jesus celebram em Goa a canonização de S. Ignacio de Loyola seu fundador e patriarca, e de S. Francisco Xavier, Apostolo deste Oriente, no anno de 1624. Impresso no Collegio de S. Paulo de Goa da Companhia de Jesus. Ano 1624'(anonymous).

29 The *Traça* is referred to by Barreto as the most detailed description of the procession. Here the 'dialogism' of these two texts is evident, Barreto expanding on many points not included in the *Traça*. As will become evident, the *Traça* was written for the purpose of highlighting the success of the Jesuits not only in Goa, but throughout Europe, Asia, and Africa whereas Barreto's testimony more explicitly promotes the Jesuits in Goa.

30 The printing press came to India via the Jesuits in 1556 and was first set up in

Goa. It contributed much in the way of disseminating religious propaganda; it was Xavier's sermons that were first printed on this new press as well as the first (Jesuit) biographies of St Francis Xavier.

31 Pietro Della Valle, *The Pilgrim, The Travels of Pietro Della Valle*, ed., tr. George Bull (London: Hutchinson, 1989 [1652]), pp. 290–2. Pietro Della Valle (1586–1652).

32 Ibid., pp. xvii–xviii.

33 Ibid. The first English translation of his travels was published in 1664.

34 Here I identity linguistic and cultural background, year of travel to Goa, and profession when available. Because of the limited scope of the chapter, I do not provide additional background information even though for some (but not all) travellers their life stories are thoroughly sketched by their official biographers.

35 His virulent anti-Roman Catholicism permeates his travel account. It is significant that he visited Goa at a time when the Dutch were encroaching on Goa and (Dutch) Protestantism was being promoted in all the former Portuguese colonies lost to the Dutch.

36 Laval, a sailor by profession, had been living as a castaway on the Maldive Islands before arriving in Goa. Carré was reportedly a diplomatic carrier for Louis XIV. For additional biographical details on Laval and Carré, see Boise Penrose, *Goa–Rainha do Orient, Goa–Queen of the East* (Lisbon: Comissão Ultramarina, 1960).

37 Ibid. Mandelslo was a member of the Duke of Holstein's mission to Persia. It is significant that Mandelslo witnessed Goa during the powerful Dutch blockade of 1639, a blockade that seriously undermined Goa's economic strength.

38 He later wrote an in-depth history of the Mughals in India. It is more than likely that he visited the Mughal court of Shah Jahan.

39 The Jesuit priest Roberto Nobili quoted in Ines Županov, 'Aristocratic Analogies and Demotic Descriptions in the Seventeenth Century Madurai Mission', *Representations*, 41 (Winter 1993), p. 131.

40 This description of the festival is taken from the *Annua* of P. Sebastião Barreto, S.J., reproduced in G. Schurhammer's 'Festas em Goa no Ano 1624', pp. 493–7. Barreto references those other canonization celebrations of Xavier which took place in Europe prior to the festivities in Goa, as well as the fact that the celebrations in Goa also marked the canonization of Jesuit founder Ignacio de Loyola.

41 There exists a discrepancy with regard to the start date between authors: Barreto establishes the starting date as 21 January (1624) whereas according to Della Valle, the festivities commenced on 10 February (1624) and ended on February 19. According to the Jesuit historian Newman Fernandes, Della Valle's dating of the festivities is correct. See his *St Francis Xavier and Old Goa, An Historical Guide* (Panjim: Kolnia Publications, 1994), p. 37.

42 This programme that Della Valle refers to could be the *Traça*.

43 The full description of the festival was originally published in Italian several years after Della Valle's death in 1652 (exact date unknown) and translated into English in 1664 and 1892. The version that I rely on is from George Bull's translation *The Pilgrim, The Travels of Pietro Della Valle*, pp. 290–2.

44 Michael Pearson, 'The Crowd in Portuguese India', *in Coastal Western India*, XCHR Studies, Series No. 2 (New Delhi: Concept Publishing Company, 1981), p. 62.

45 Caroline Ifeka, 'The Image of Goa', in *Indo-Portuguese History, Old Issues, New Questions*, ed. Teotónio de Souza (New Delhi: Concept Publishing Company, 1985), p. 181. See also Pratima Kamat, *Farar Far: Local Resistance to Colonial Hegemony in Goa, 1510-1912* (Panaji, Goa: Institute Menezes Bragança, 1999).

46 Ibid.

47 Luís de Camões, *The Lusiads*, tr. William Atkinson (New York: Penguin, 1952). He is considered Portugal's first 'nationalist' poet.

48 Caroline Ifeka, 'The Image of Goa', p. 181. Ifeka juxtaposes Goa Dourada with the epithet of Goa Negra as perhaps more historically appropriate since it takes into account the 'colour of the labour force which dug up the gold and which helped build Old Goa's religious houses and places of worship'.

49 This trademark was also fashioned by a discourse of Goa as 'European', which I suggest is inseparable from its 'goldenness'.

50 Caroline Ifeka, 'The Image of Goa', p. 185.

51 Ranajit Guha, *Dominance Without Hegemony: History and Power in Colonial India* (Cambridge, MA: Harvard University Press, 1997).

52 According to historians, the closest thing to a golden era of Goa if in fact one existed was the period roughly between 1570 and 1600; by 1600 the bulk of its architectural monuments had been built with its reserves of gold, and its population was at a peak before decline fully set in by 1640. This is what makes observing Goa in 1624 so interesting – it is on the cusp of a state of golden-ness.

53 The expenses incurred by the canonization festivities were a financial drain on the colonial state's increasingly limited resources during this period, the irony being that, through their Herculean effort to promote the gold of Goa through Xavier's ritualization, the actual amount of gold in Goa was greatly reduced.

54 1580 marks the year that Spain (experiencing its own 'Golden Age') annexed Portugal. Even though Portugal wrestled control from Spain in 1640, this 'war of independence' was costly and lasted until 1668, acting as a further drain on its economy and thus contributing to its inward spiral. For more details, see Dauril Alden, *The Making of an Enterprise, The* Society of Jesus *in Portugal, Its Empire and Beyond, 1540–1750* (Stanford: Stanford University Press, 1996), p. 94.

55 See Ines Županov, 'The Prophetic and The Miraculous in Portuguese Asia: A Hagiographical View of Colonial Culture', *Santa Barbara Portuguese Studies*, Volume II (1995), p. 137.

56 See Fr Cosme José Costa, S.F.X., *A Missiological Conflict Between Padroado and Proaganda in the East* (Pilar, Goa: Pilar Publications, 1997), pp. 30–44.

57 One of the reasons for Portugal's downfall as an empire had to do with the fact that it was always trying to control far more territory than its own meagre resources and population could in fact support, a shortage that was felt acutely in Portuguese India starting in the seventeenth century. For more details, see Charles Boxer, *Portuguese India in the Mid-Seventeenth Century* (New Delhi: Oxford University Press, 1980), pp. 3–5.

58 There was a general lack of hygiene in Goa: the sewage disposal system was rudimentary, numerous epidemics (cholera, dysentery, and venereal disease) were commonplace, and the whole area was becoming increasingly malarial in the seventeenth century. Severe plagues were experienced in 1625 and 1640. See Boies Penrose, *Goa–Rainha do Oriente, Goa–Queen of the East* (Lisboa: Commissão Ultramarina, 1960), p. 104.

59 George Winius reinforces the widespread nature of corruption in the colonies, making a list of 24 common practices of corruption (abuses) in Portuguese India as witnessed by Diogo do Couto (1542–1616). See Diogo do Couto, *Black Legend of Portuguese India: Diogo do Couto, His Contemporaries and the Soldado Pratico. A Contribution to the Study of Political Corruption in the Empires of Early Modern Europe*, XCHR Studies, Series, No. 3 (New Delhi: Concept Publishing Company, 1982), p. 104. Michael Pearson, 'Corruption and Corsairs in Sixteenth Century Western India: A Functional Analysis', in his *Coastal Western India* (New Delhi: Concept Publishing Company, 1981). The cultural distinctiveness of 'corruption' as a widespread and state-sanctioned activity in the Portuguese colonial context is a topic that has just recently been taken up in more depth. For a fascinating and important new study on this topic, see Nandini Chaturvedula, *Imperial Excess: Corruption and Decadence in Portuguese India (1600-1706)* (Unpublished PhD, Columbia University, 2010).

60 Even as early as 1630, the state conducted an investigation into Jesuit finances, suggesting that it was already concerned with and perhaps threatened by their success. See Mira Mascarenhas, 'The Church in Eighteenth Century Goa', in *Essays in Goan History*, ed. Teotónio de Souza (New Delhi: Concept Publishing Co, 1989), pp. 82–3.

61 Including the neighbouring Bijapur dynasty and the Marathas. The Portuguese also attempted to use their good relations with the Mughals to help in their fight against the Dutch and British, playing one power off another by signing a peace treaty with them in 1615; these good relations lasted only until 1625. For additional details, see Stephen Neill, *A History of Christianity in India, The Beginnings to AD 1707* (Cambridge: Cambridge University Press, 1984), pp. 260–2.

62 Charles Boxer, *Portuguese India in the Mid-Seventeenth Century*, p. 3.

63 For more details on the numerous Maratha invasions of Goa which repeatedly weakened the Portuguese colonial state, see Sanjay Subrahmanyam, *The Portuguese Empire in Asia, 1500–1700* (New York: Longman Publishing, 1993).

64 For more details on Portugal's European rivals in India, see Michael Pearson, *The Portuguese in India* (Cambridge: Cambridge University Press, 1987). Also see Sanjay Subrahmanyam and Luís Filipe F. R. Thomaz, 'Evolution of Empire: The Portuguese in the Indian Ocean during the Sixteenth Century', in *The Political Economy of Merchant Empire*, ed. J. Tracey (Cambridge: Cambridge University Press, 1991), pp. 298–331.

65 The historian Charles Boxer argues that the Dutch victory in Asia can be reduced to three main reasons: superior economic resources, manpower, and sea power. See his *The Portuguese Seaborne Empire, 1415–1825* (New York: Alfred Knopf, 1969), p. 114.

66 See G. Scammel, 'England, Portugal and the Estado da Índia, c. 1500–1635', in *Seminario Internacional de Historia Indo-Portuguesa* (Lisbon: Instituto de Investigação Cientifica Tropical, 1985), p. 445.

67 According to historians of Portuguese India, 1640 marks the official 'beginning of the end' of Goa Dourada, a period marked by decline but as I argue one marked also by survival and dynamism. See Charles Boxer, *Portuguese India in the Mid-Seventeenth Century*, pp. 3–5, 14.

68 Ibid., p. 5, 34. I thank historian Sanjay Subrahmanyam for his insights on the involution of the Portuguese in India during this time frame.

69 In Chapter 2, I argued that in 1554 church and state were invested in making Xavier a saint of *Asia*. On the early messianism of the Portuguese, see also Luís Filipe F. R. Thomaz, 'Factions, Interests and Messianism: The Politics of Portuguese Expansion in the East, 1500–1521', *The Indian Economic and Social History Review*, Volume 28, No. 1 (1991), pp. 97–109. In 1624 church and state were more invested in turning Xavier into a saint of *India*, given the loss of the bulk of their Asian colonies, which in turn, mirrors their turn inward. See G.D. Winius, 'Millenarianism and Empire, Portuguese Asian Decline and the "Crise de Conscience" of the Missionaries', *Itinerario*, Volume XI, No. 2 (1987), pp. 37–51.

70 For the role of ritual in producing and maintaining a locality's materiality, see Arjun Appadurai, *Modernity at Large: Cultural Dimensions of Globalization* (Minneapolis: University of Minnesota Press, 1996), pp. 180–1.

71 J.H. da Cunha Rivara, 'Book 1 of the Letters that the King of Portugal Wrote to the city of Goa', *Archivo Portuguez-Oriental*, Fasciculo I, 2nd edn (Nova Goa: Imprensa Nacional, 1877), p. 86. A decree dated 16 February 1577 states 'the king says that the Viceroy with the Archbishop will determine the place in the city where the processions will take place'.

72 Again, I am referring to the eyewitness testimonies of Barreto and Della Valle reproduced in an earlier section. Hereafter, any statement in quotation marks is a direct reference from these accounts.

73 Briefly, the Old College of St Paul was completed in 1542. It rose to importance after Xavier himself chose to reside there in 1544. See José da Fonseca, *An Historical and Archaeological Sketch of the City of Goa* (Delhi: Asian Educational Services, 1986 [1878]), pp. 270–90. The celebrations of 1624 were in large part to ritually transport Xavier to his new 'home'.

74 Ibid. The Arches of the Vicery marked the entrance to Portuguese India, and were built in 1599 by Francisco da Gama, the Viceroy at the time and great-grandson of Vasco da Gama. The See Cathedral, the first religious institution in Goa, was built under the direction of the Goa's second Viceroy, Affonso de Albuquerque, starting in 1510.

75 Just as images of saints had to be properly attired, so too did Goa during ritual activity. Convening in 1585, the 3rd Provincial Council of Goa (decree No. 16) ordered that images of the saints be dressed very honestly (decently) and treated with care. Neither could they be ornate in any excessive manner nor could they be put to profane use. See J.H. da Cunha Rivara, *Archivo Portuguez-Oriental*, Fasciculo 4 (New Delhi: Asian Educational Services, 1992), p. 164.

76 See Victor Coelho's 'Connecting Histories: Portuguese Music in Renaissance Goa', in *Goa and Portugal: Their Cultural Links*, ed. C. Borges and H. Feldman (New Delhi: Concept Publishing Co, 1997) pp. 131–47.

77 Victor Coelho, 'Kapsberger's Apotheosis', in *Genre, Nationhood and Sexual Difference*, eds R. Dellamora and D. Fischlin (New York: Columbia University Press, 1997), p. 36.

78 Ibid., p. 28. Victor Coelho argues that drama was 'especially effective as a pedagogical tool in the Jesuit colleges [of Europe] through its representation of martyrdom and other biblical stories on stage, enhanced by special effects and all-embracing metaphors'.

79 Jean-Christophe Agnew, *Worlds Apart: The Market and the Theater in Anglo-American Thought, 1550–1750* (Cambridge: Cambridge University Press, 1986), p. x. Here the market and the theatre are mutually constituting, the theatre a laboratory for forging new social relations based on commodity relations.

80 Even though I cannot provide an exact value in today's market economy, it is a large sum of money.

81 Here sentiments are very much 'structures of feeling' as outlined by Raymond Williams. See his *Marxism and Literature* (New York: Oxford University Press, 1977), pp. 128–35.

82 John Albert Mandelslo is just one of the many travellers who refers to this proverb in his description of Goa. See his *Mandelslo's Travels in Western India (1638–9)*, ed. M.S. Commissariat (London: Oxford University Press, 1931), p. 63.

83 Monsieur de Thevenot quoted in G. Careri and M. de Thevenot, *Indian Travels of Thevenot and Careri: Being the Third Part of the Travels of M. De Thevenot into the Levant and the Third Part of the Voyage Round the World by Dr. John Francis Gemelli Careri*, ed. Surendranath Sen (New Delhi: National Archives of India, 1949), pp. 129–30. Goa is the name both of the region and the city.

84 Thevenot quoted in José Fonseca, *An Historical Sketch of Goa* (Delhi: Asian Educational Services, 1986 [1878]), p. 171.

85 Philip Baldeus, *A Description of the East India Coasts of Malabar and Cormandel with their Adjacent Kingdoms and Provinces, & of the Empire of Ceylon and of the Idolatry of the Pagans in the East Indies* (New Delhi: Asian Educational Services, 1996 [1672]), p. 608.

86 Gemelli Careri quoted in G. Careri and M. de Thevenot, *Indian Travels of Thevenot and Careri*, p. 198.

87 John Fryer, *A New Account of East India and Persia*, p. 26.

88 Ibid., p. 10.

89 Ibid., pp. 21–2.

90 Ibid.

91 Della Valle quoted in Menezes Bragança, *A Índia Portuguesa*, Volume 2 (Goa: Imprensa Nacional, 1923), p. 63. The author also points out that the French traveller Pyrard de Laval noticed the same thing, namely the excessive number of feasts and processions in Goa.

92 Returning to Ifeka's point, the image of 'Golden Goa' becomes a cyclical discourse wherein there is neither a singular author nor a singular reason for its perpetuation.

93 I adopt this subtitle from Charles Borges, 'Religious Orders and Estado da Índia in Goa: A Balancing Act', in *Goa's External Relations*, ed. P.P. Shirodkar (Panjim: Dr Wolfgang de Silva Marg printers, 1992), p. 29.

94 Ibid., p. 22.

95 Victor Coelho, 'Kapsberger's Apotheosis', p. 29.

96 These orders were followed by the Carmelites in 1607 and other minor orders. See

Dauril Alden, *The Making of an Enterprise*, p. 43. Also see Charles Borges, *The Economics of the Goa Jesuits, 1542–1759, An Explanation of Their Rise and Fall* (New Delhi: Concept Publishing Company, 1994).

97 The state itself was a major source of income for the church initially. By the time of Xavier's canonization festivities in 1624, the religious orders, in particular the Jesuits, were less dependent on state subsidies since they had developed their own methods independent of the state for funding their activities. For more details, see B.S. Shastry, 'Sources of Income and Items of Expenditure of the Church in Goa (c.1510–1800 AD): A Note', in *Goan Society Through the Ages*, ed. B.S. Shastry (New Delhi: Asian Publication Series, 1987), pp. 35–8.

98 Charles Borges, *The Economics of the Goa Jesuits*, pp. 18–19.

99 Ibid., p. 17.

100 Ibid. Most of these Jesuits came from Spain, France, Italy, and Portugal, i.e.southern Europe.

101 Charles Borges gives such weight to this Spanish/Portuguese rivalry that he concludes that the Jesuit mission to China failed for this very reason. See his *The Economics of the Goa Jesuits*, p. 31.

102 Ibid., p. 17.

103 Ibid.

104 Ibid., p. 23. Originally called the 'Casa de Jesus' (House of Jesus), the Jesuits later changed the church's name to the 'Bom Jesus' in the seventeenth century. In Portuguese Bom ('Good') Jesus refers to the Infant Jesus whose statue was added next to those of St Francis and St Ignatius. The name of the church was also derived from the name of the Jesuit organization, the Society of Jesus. This house was built for an explicit purpose: it was where 'the practice of the Institute could show itself'.

105 Ibid., pp. 18–19.

106 Ibid., p. 41.

107 Ibid. It was their entrepreneurial activities combined with their financial wizardry which proved their success. Interestingly, the Jesuits were also classified as the first multinational corporation. See Dauril Alden, 'The Society of Jesus as the Alleged First Multinational Firm', in his, *Making of an Enterprise*, Appendix B, pp. 668–9.

108 Charles Borges, *The Economics of the Goa Jesuits*, p. 41.

109 Ibid., p. 25. For example, a report by Jesuit António Simões in 1623 mentions that the Jesuits received by far the largest portion of state funds reserved for religious orders. See B.S. Shastry, 'Sources of Income and Items of Expenditure of the Church in Goa (c.1510-1800 AD): A Note', p. 39.

110 Devotion as a sign of religious faith needs to be explored more fully. As Vicente Rafael shows in his study of Spanish missionaries in the Philippines and the role of language (mis)translations in conversions, outward signs of devotion are not necessarily indicative of inner religious faith. See his *Contracting Colonialism: Translation and Christian Conversion in Tagalog Society Under Early Spanish Rule* (Durham, NC: Duke University Press, 1993), pp. 136–66.

111 His biographer also suggests his Catholic piety. One is reminded of Pratt's point concerning the assertion of innocence by travellers in the face of complicity, Della Valle doing so here by asserting his Catholic piety.

112 According to the historian Georg Schurhammer, the silver casket of Xavier was indeed carried by the 'brothers of St Francis of Assisi', which in turn supports Della Valle's viewpoint. See his 'Die Heiligsprechung Franz Xavers' in his *Varia I* (Lisboa: Centro de Estudos Historicos Ultramarinhos, 1965), p. 470, translation Marco Prieschl.

113 John Fryer, *A New Account*, p. 12. The Italian traveller Niccolao Manucci also attests to the wealth of the Jesuits, believing it to surpass the Crown in all Portuguese possessions in India. See Niccolao Manucci, *Storia do Mogor, or Mogul India, 1653–1708*, Volume III, ed., tr. William Irvine (Calcutta: Editions Indian, 1966), p. 265.

114 Monsieur de Thevenot quoted in Gemelli Careri and M. de Thevenot, *Indian Travels of Thevenot and Careri*, pp. 129–30.

115 John Albert Mandelslo, *Mandelslo's Travels in Western India (1638–9)*, p. 63.
116 Ibid., p. 64. Commissariat, his biographer, paraphrasing Mandelslo.
117 Pyrard de Laval quoted in John Albert Mandelslo, *Mandelslo's Travels in Western India*, Appendix B, p. 104. 'Pyrard de Laval on the Church of Bom Jesus'.
118 Pyrard de Laval paraphrased by the historian Charles Borges, *The Economics of the Goa Jesuits*, p. 32.
119 Charles Borges paraphrasing Tavernier in *The Economics of the Goa Jesuits*, p. 85.
120 Ibid.
121 Jean-Baptiste Tavernier, *Travels in India by Jean-Baptiste Tavernier*, Volume 1, ed. William Crooke (New Delhi: Munshiram Manoharlal Publishers Pvt Ltd, 1995), p. 159. Note that Tavernier is incorrect in stating that the Augustinians arrived prior to the Jesuits; rather, it was the opposite. According to historian Charles Borges, this was a particularly contentious rivalry. He notes that the Augustinians and Jesuits also fought over the issue of toilets (where to place them), causing much bad blood between them. In addition, the Jesuits had a bitter rivalry with the Dominicans that originated in Spain and spread to the colonies. See his *The Economics of the Goa Jesuits*, pp. 94–5.
122 Charles Borges, *The Economics of the Goa Jesuits*, p. 31.
123 Anthony Disney, 'The Viceroy Count of Linhares at Goa, 1629–1635', in *Seminario Internacional de Historia Indo-Portuguesa, 1978* (Lisboa: Instituto de Investigação Cientifica Tropical, 1985), p. 305.
124 By 4 February 1653, the king of Portugal had allotted 4000 *xerafins* for the city of Goa each year, this money going towards the payment of expenses for processions. See J.H. da Cunha Rivara, 'Livro dos Privilegios da Cidade de Goa', in *Arquivo Portuguez-Oriental*, Fasciculo 2 (Nova Goa: Imprensa Nacional, 1857), pp. 259–60.
125 Nor can 'state' and 'church' be understood as static categories, but rather as complex, historical, and dynamic bodies and constitutive of many different organs and individuals.
126 Again, Charles Borges describes their relationship as one that was characterized by both 'competition and cooperation'. See his 'Religious Orders and Estado da Índia in Goa: A Balancing Act', p. 22.
127 P.D. Xavier, *Goa: A Social History, 1510–1640* (Panji: Rajhauns Vitaran, 1993), p. 10.
128 Anthony Disney, 'The Viceroy Count of Linhares at Goa, 1629–1635', p. 307.
129 P.D. Xavier, *Goa: A Social History*, p. 10.
130 His outsider perspective (to a degree more than Barreto) is not necessarily a more 'secular' perspective considering that his piety shows through at different moments. Instead, I argue that his lack of affiliation with the Jesuits allows him to demarcate church and state more clearly.
131 Laval quoted in John Albert Mandelslo, *Mandelslo's Travels in Western India*, p. 76.
132 Jean-Baptiste Tavernier, *Travels in India by Jean-Baptiste Tavernier*, p. 153.
133 Commissariat paraphrasing Mandelslo's description of the Viceroy (Dom Pedro da Silva) at the time of Mandelslo's visit to Goa in 1639. See John Albert Mandelslo, *Mandelslo's Travels in Western India*, pp. 75–6.
134 Francisco da Gama (1565–1632) was fourth Count of Vidigueira, and twice Viceroy at Goa, from 1597 to 1600 and from 1622 to 1628. He was the great grandson of Vasco da Gama, thus belonging to one of the most important noble families of Portugal. For additional details, see Sanjay Subrahmanyam, 'The Viceroy as Assassin: The Portuguese, the Mughals and Deccan Politics, c. 1600', *Santa Barbara Studies*, Volume II (1995), pp. 165–6.
135 Michael Pearson, 'The Crowd', p. 43.
136 Teotónio de Souza, 'Urban Topography and Demography' in *Medieval Goa: A Socio-Economic History* (New Delhi: Concept Publishing Co., 1979), p. 115.
137 Ibid.
138 Ibid. According to a census of Goa ordered by the Viceroy Francisco da Gama – the same Viceroy in charge of Xavier's canonization festivities – in 1623, there were approximately sixty thousand native Christians, and nearly one hundred thousand non-Christians living in and around Goa. See Teotónio de Souza, 'Hindu Dominance

of Goan Economy', *Indica*, Volume 12, No. 1 (March 1975), p. 29. For additional estimates on the number of Portuguese women and children (mostly prostitutes and orphans) living in Goa, see Timothy Coates, 'State Sponsored Female Colonization in the Estado da Índia, ca. 1550–1750', *Santa Barbara Portuguese Studies*, Volume II (1995), p. 51.

139 The Portuguese were obsessed with blood as a sign of lineage. According to many historians, the Portuguese who initially came to Goa were often from the lower classes. Once in Goa, they often fabricated their lineage and maintained a tight hold on those newcomers to Goa so as to hold on to a social hierarchy that placed them at the top. For additional details, see Charles Boxer, *The Portuguese Seaborne Empire, 1415–1825*.

140 P.D. Xavier, *Goa: A Social History, 1510–1640*, pp. 29–30. He notes that many of these officials brought their wives with them.

141 Ibid. In the meantime, lower-status groups were at different historical moments encouraged to intermarry with local women, following the earlier example of the *casados*.

142 Ibid.

143 Ibid., pp. 31–2.

144 Ibid., p. 32. There has been a tendency to ignore the indigenous Christian population because of the nature of the Portuguese categories outlined above. See Kenneth MacPherson, 'A Secret People of South Asia: The Origins, Evolution and Role of the Luso-Indian Goan Community from the Sixteenth to Twentieth Centuries', *Itinerario*, Volume XI, No. 2 (1987), p. 74.

145 Ibid., p. 33. The majority of non-Christians were Hindus – a thriving community despite their lowly status in the colonial hierarchy. Also, a small minority in Goa were Muslims, most Muslims having left Goa for other parts of India in the immediate aftermath of Portugal's conquest of Goa in 1510.

146 Unfortunately, there has been little historical analysis on this sizeable group of men and women who were frequently transported between Goa and Brazil.

147 P.D. Xavier, *Goa: A Social History, 1510–1640*, p. 32.

148 A 'palanquin', according to Thevenot, is 'a kind of couch. [It] hangs by a long Pole ... in the bottom there are Mats and Cushions to lie or sit upon ... it requires four men to carry a Palanquin ... everyone adorns his Palanquin according to his humor'. Thevenot quoted in Gemelli Careri and M. de Thevenot, *Indian Travels of Thevenot and Careri*, p. 76.

149 'Idolaters' were those Hindus who refused to convert to Catholicism; all Muslims were labelled 'Moors', a carryover from Moorish Spain.

150 My earlier historical discussion suggests that the boundaries between the categories of 'Portuguese' and 'non-Portuguese' were in fact more fluid and were often contested in real life.

151 As a result, he does not grasp the complexities of Portuguese colonial society, neither its categories of varying degrees of 'Portugueseness' nor its 'native' public.

152 According to the historian Teofilo Ruiz, the role of clothing in early modern European festivities 'articulated very specific messages about the hierarchical nature of society'. See his 'Elite and Popular Culture in Late Fifteenth Century Castilian Festivals: The Case of Jaen', in *City and Spectacle in Medieval Europe*, eds B. Hanawalt and K. Ryerson (Minneapolis: University of Minnesota Press, 1994), p. 303. See also A. Weiner and J. Schneider, 'Introduction' to *Cloth and the Human Experience*, eds A. Weiner and J. Schneider (Washington: Smithsonian Institution Press, 1989), pp. 1–2.

153 Barreto makes no note of women as a category in itself, which is interesting given Della Valle's attention to the women present during the festivities.

154 Michael Pearson, 'The Crowd', p. 43. Pearson mistakes the date of the canonization festivities, stating it took place in 1642 rather than in 1624.

155 This would be reminiscent of an argument put forth by Stallybrass and White wherein order already prepares itself for disorder – it plans for the attendance of outsider groups such that their participation only reinforces the existing hierarchy.

See Peter Stallybrass and Allon White, *The Politics and Poetics of Transgression* (London: Methuen & Co., 1986).

156 See M. Bakhtin, *Rabelais and His World*, tr. H. Iswolsky (Bloomington: Indiana University Press, 1984).

157 Laval quoted in Gemelli Careri and M. de Thevenot, *Indian Travels of Thevenot and Careri*, p. xl.

158 Tavernier quoted in John Albert Mandelslo, *Mandelslo's Travels in Western India*, p. 77.

159 Laval quoted in John Albert Mandelslo, *Mandelslo's Travels in Western India*, pp. 78–9.

160 Fryer also attests to the fact that women were highly monitored by their husbands, especially when seen in public: 'To Ogle a Lady – If a Person of Quality – in a Balcony is revenged with a Blunderbuss'. John Fryer, *A New Account*, p. 26.

161 Laval quoted in Boise Penrose, *Goa–Rainha do Oriente, Goa–Queen of the Orient*, pp. 91–3. Other travellers have also commented on the salaciousness of the women of Goa.

162 Travellers such as Mandelslo, Careri, Hamilton, and even Della Valle (outside ritual) also point to this thriving community.

163 Linschoten quoted in Teotónio de Souza, 'Hindu Dominance of Goan Economy', p. 31.

164 See Michael Pearson, 'The Goa Rendas 1600–1700', from *Mare Luso-Indicum*, Tome II (Paris: Librairie Minard, 1973), pp. 61–73. More importantly, the economy of the Estado da Índia was dependent on the wealth of both Muslim and Hindu merchants who were involved in the circuit of trading goods such as pepper, and on Hindu peasants for their supply of rice.

165 Pietro Della Valle, *The Travels of Pietro Della Valle in India*, p. 156.

166 M.N. Pearson, 'The Crowd in Portuguese India', p. 62.

167 Richard Trexler, *Public Life in Renaissance Florence* (Ithaca, NY: Cornell University Press, 1980), p. 277.

168 Ibid., p. 214.

169 Ibid., p. 277. Again, following Trexler, I suggest that members of the Goan public sought out the festivities as an arena for display and competition; Portuguese men and women were very aware of the potential for improved (colonial) status during Xavier's canonization festivities.

170 Michael Pearson, 'The Crowd', p. 43.

171 Catherine Bell, *Ritual Theory, Ritual Practice*, p. 95. It is important to recognize that the body is the foremost of all metaphors for a society's perception and organization of itself.

172 Alexander Hamilton's view of the canonization process. See his *Goa, A New Account of the East Indies*, pp. 252–4.

173 These contrasting views of Xavier's incorruptibility on the part of Hamilton once again affirm my point that inconsistencies often existed within the testimony of one individual traveller, and not just across travel accounts.

174 John Albert Mandelslo, *Mandelslo's Travels in Western India*, p. 68.

175 See Gemelli Careri and M. de Thevenot, *Indian Travels of Thevenot and Careri*, p. 199. Careri was given special permission from the Provincial of the Jesuits based on a recommendation of the Viceroy, to be allowed to kiss the body of the saint, in order to take a *biretta* (religious cap) which he carried to the Conde de Alvor. See Francisco Xavier da Costa, *Exposição do Venerando Corpo de S. Francisco Xavier em 1931* (Nova Goa: Tip. A Voz de S. Francisco Xavier, 1935), p. 182.

176 As described by Leonard Blusse and George Winius, 'The Origin and Rhythm of Dutch Aggression against the Estado da Índia, 1601–1661', in *Indo-Portuguese History, Old Issues, New Questions*, ed. Teotónio de Souza (New Delhi: Concept Publishing Company, 1985), p. 73.

177 Antony Hutt paraphrasing Fryer. See his *Goa, A Traveller's Historical and Architectural Guide* (New Delhi: Scorpion Publishing United, 1988), p. 74.

178 Catherine Bell, *Ritual Theory, Ritual Practice*, p. 134.

179 Ibid.

CHAPTER FOUR

Secularization (1782)

Introduction

> Viceroys of India may come and go, but the Jesuit Fathers are always with us [in Goa]. – popular eighteenth-century saying[1]

> The persecution of the Society of Jesus was unleashed under the Marquis of Pombal, and this ended in the total suppression of the worthy society and the confiscation of their properties in favor of the state [in 1759]. It was in the wake of this relentless persecution that the ignoble calumny spread to the four corners of the earth that the Society, on withdrawing from Goa, had carried away the precious treasure of the relic of St Francis Xavier. To disprove the impious rumors, to soothe the embittered people, and comply with their spontaneous requests, the ecclesiastical and civic authorities felt obliged to promote the first public exposition of the relics from [the] 10th to 12th February 1782. – Father Caetano Cruz, Chairman for the Diocesan Committee for the Exposition of 1984[2]

While church and state had worked together in promoting a façade of Goa Dourada through the spectacle of St Francis Xavier's canonization in 1624, the context for and production of a set of ritual practices in 1782 was dramatically different. In this chapter, I explore the increasing 'secularization'[3] of Xavier as he becomes a symbol and agent of colonial state authority in the midst of escalated tensions between the Estado da Índia and the Society of Jesus, including parallel concerns over the physical deterioration of Xavier's corpse – its state of 'desiccation'[4] – and which culminates in the expulsion of this religious order from Goa in 1759. My analysis will suggest that, despite attempts by the Portuguese Crown to assert its monopoly over access to Xavier's corpse and image at the expense of the Jesuits, thus managing his (future) power of signification, the state's control of Xavier is never completely realized in the period leading up to and including the staging of the

'First Solemn Exposition' of St Francis Xavier in 1782. That is, in spite of the forced removal of the Jesuits twenty-three years earlier, their legacy unwittingly thrives in the space of ritual by way of rumours and the actions of certain individuals which undermine the state's sole claim to Xavier (and by extension Goa), a point borne out in the above popular saying regarding the defining role of the Society of Jesus in constituting Portuguese India. More generally, the Estado da Índia had underestimated the endurance of the very organization (including the power of the legacy of its founding member, Xavier himself) that had become the *subject* of such anxiety and the *object* of such scrutiny in their attempt to secularize both church and state.

In tracing the contours of multiple Xaverian investments in the period leading up to ritual in 1782, I look at two types of correspondence that circulated between colony and metropole and vice versa: royal (state) decrees and internal Jesuit exchanges, both those intended for private or limited audiences and those received by members of the wider public. I purposely stage these source materials in conversation in order to explore the role of official and unofficial (including rumour) documentation in serving and disrupting church and state doctrine. In many ways, these acts – the bequeathing of titles, money, and vestments, and directives against future openings of Xavier's casket – index differing anxieties (those levelled both at Xavier and by metaphoric extension on to themselves) on the part of certain members of the Society of Jesus and the Estado da Índia at a time when their respective agendas were perhaps most at odds. Those investments and anxieties outlined here (concerning saint and state), in turn, will anticipate future ones (and which in some sense find fuller form later) discussed in subsequent chapters.

In the aftermath of the Jesuit expulsion, ritual practice in 1782 takes on a distinct shape as compared to earlier celebrations wherein members of this religious order held prominent positions inside the space of ritual, and public debates over the authenticity and location of Xavier's corpse in Goa were noticeably absent. Here I rely on the testimony of a visiting Italian Oratorian by the name of Ansolani – the only extant eyewitness account – to explore the form and content of this three-day display (10–12 February) in light of these changing historical circumstances, and in terms of the enduring legacy of the Jesuits despite their physical absence from the space of ritual activity. That a medical report is issued in conjunction with these festivities – a testament to his body being both (more or less) intact, real and present in Goa, and one that promotes his ability to be displayed – shows that ritual in 1782 explicitly takes on a distinct burden of proof as compared to past displays of his corpse, which were wholly concerned

Figure 5 Souvenir of the Exposition of the body of St Francis Xavier at Goa in 1974–75

with proving his incorruptibility (1554) or marking his canonization (1624). By effectively overturning an earlier decree issued by Portugal's king (1755) barring the public display of his body, this autopsy report functions to authenticate not only Xavier's corpse as the 'real' one but, most importantly, the Portuguese, as opposed to the Jesuits, as the rightful heirs to this invaluable corpse. Thus, colonial officials are now invested in controlling Xavier – both guarding the real condition of his corpse and promoting his 'secularized' image – in the absence of the Jesuits.

Lastly, the staging of the first 'Solemn Exposition' functions as a public appeasement of sorts, an appeasement to circulating stories (as evidenced in the epigraph at the beginning of the chapter) which again suggest that the body of Xavier had been illicitly removed by the Jesuits in a defiant last act when they were suppressed by the state in 1759. Portuguese colonial officials viewed themselves as increasingly responsible to an inquiring and diverse public that, given this saint's historical ties to Goa and his past ritualizations, also had an increased investment in Xavier. I explore the expanding role of the participants in this 'exposition' – a term which by its very definition implies a public[5] – as constituting and constitutive of this set of ritual practices at a time when the colonial state was perhaps most acutely in need of one to defy the very real desiccation of saint and state in the midst of larger political and economic turmoil that marked both metropole and colony throughout the eighteenth century.

State decrees, Xaverian titles, and (Jesuit) keys to the casket

> All the ruin of this state can be blamed on the fault of commerce. – Viceroy João Saldanha de Gama, 1729[6]

It was during the late seventeenth century – a period in which the state faced multiple setbacks, both financial and political, while the Jesuits continued to gain in strength and number[7] – that the Estado da Índia first seized on the potential of St Francis Xavier as an exclusive agent of the state. At a time when perhaps it was most in need of 'divine intervention' to offset these so-called 'dark days',[8] which included a series of fiscal crises, an increase in unofficial commerce, and repeated attacks from both the Dutch and their neighbouring Marathas,[9] St Francis Xavier became a focal point for state investment, evidenced through the passing of legislation, the bequeathing of titles, and the promotion of old and new ritual acts centred on his corpse. In other words, the state increasingly regulated Xavier's image and ritualization to its own ends throughout the late seventeenth century (1681–99).

Initially, state requests were made to elevate Xavier's (political) status in and through public display by providing him with the proper (ritual) accoutrements. For example, António Pães de Sande, the acting Governor of Portuguese India who had in 1678 been cured of a grave illness by touching Xavier's *sobrepeliz* (outer garment),[10] wrote to the king of Portugal on 24 January 1681, asking him to increase the lighting of the city on the vespers of his feast day.[11] Additional examples of proposed legislation include the setting aside of 500 *xerafins* annually from the Treasury of the Estado da Índia to help reduce the costs of Xavier's annual feast day celebrations (1683),[12] the regular contribution of each incoming Viceroy to the growing expenses of the Church of Bom Jesus (1736),[13] and the (re)assigning of 3 December as Xavier's feast day (1694) in light of the resurgence of an earlier controversy concerning the date of his actual death.[14]

State decrees also included initiating new ceremonies surrounding Xavier's corpse and tomb. Throughout the second half of the 1600s, Goa had suffered a series of political setbacks at the hands of the neighbouring Marathas, an Indian dynasty led by the famed Shivaji, a man who had repeatedly been involved in minor skirmishes with both the Portuguese and the Mughals. By November 1683 the Marathas, under the direction of Shivaji's son and successor, Sambhaji, were heavily invested in taking over the centre of the Portuguese empire in India.[15] It was when defeat for the Portuguese was near at hand that Viceroy D. Francisco de Tavora appealed to the saint for his 'divine intercession', handing over his baton of command to him in the process.[16] As a result of his (Tavora's or Xavier's) success in staving off another invasion, a new ritual practice called the *posse*[17] was initiated, by which each newly appointed Viceroy or Governor, shortly after his arrival in Goa, received Xavier's blessing in the act of exchanging his staff of command, recognizing his power and protection and accepting his position as the saint's 'vassal' for the duration of his term.

One final piece of legislation consolidated Xavier's image as an agent of the state and asserted the continued role of the *Estado* in his ritualization. On 24 March 1699 St Francis Xavier was given the honorific title of 'Defender of the Orient' by royal decree, an action that linked his earlier success against the Marathas in Goa (1683) to his future intercession and protection of not just one colony but all those now under Portuguese dominion in the East.[18] King Dom Pedro II (1683–1706), in writing to his Viceroy, António Luís da Coutinho Cámara, states: 'with such a defender on your side, you have every reason not to fear the enemies of the state and to hope that the greatest dangers will only bring you the most glorious triumphs'.[19] The same king then sent a new staff of command, which was 'richly ornamented' and which bears an inscription to St Francis Xavier: 'Apostle and Defender of the East, recently come to the throne, 1699'.[20] It was this same staff of command that would be sanctioned for all future *posse* ceremonies.[21] Queen Maria Sophia of Portugal (1666–99) also sent a rich 'chasuble' – an outer vestment typically worn by priests – in which to dress the holy body of Xavier. It was embroidered with her own hands and bore the following inscription: 'The Queen of Portugal to her dear St Xavier'.[22] Lastly, in 1748, by special request from both the viceroy of Goa and the king of Portugal in an appeal to Pope Benedict XIV, Xavier was granted the title of 'Patron and Protector of the Indies' from the Cape of Good Hope to the kingdoms of China and Japan.[23]

Just as Portuguese colonial officials had their own set of investments in Xavier, so too did the religious order that considered him their founding father. Here I briefly detail certain investments in Xavier's ritualization on the part of the Jesuits stationed in Goa at the turn of the century, a time when, despite (and compared to) the financial difficulties of the Estado, they were considerably well off.[24] It was also during this same time frame that many Jesuits were beginning to fear the very real possibility of the 'desiccation' of Xavier's corpse.[25] In the years between 1681 and 1686, several prohibitions were issued by various Jesuit authorities against the public viewing of Xavier's corpse in an attempt to prevent his further corruption.[26] They also foresaw the very real possibility that 'the devotion of the people would cool down' as a result of his continued display.[27] Between 1703 and 1708 numerous (additional) pleas were written by different Jesuit officials, each requesting that his coffin be closed permanently in order to prevent any further desiccation of his body.[28] One of the first requests was made in 1703 by the Superior General Michael Angelo Tamborini, who ordered that the body of the saint be placed in a 'lead box' so that it could never be opened.[29] However, as an added measure, a lock was added to the case and three identical keys were issued; each key was then placed in the hands of a different Jesuit official who was head of a different institution located in and around the capital, in Old Goa, Bassein, and Rachol.[30] This act was not without controversy, going so far as to elicit a written plea, issued in 1708, by the acting Rector of the Professed House of Bom Jesus who desired a more radical prohibition against the viewing of Xavier's corpse.[31] It would take a royal decree issued by the king of Portugal to make official what the Rector had asked for, only forty-seven years too late, and after two additional openings of his corpse to state officials, in the years 1744 and 1751.[32]

In a letter dated 2 April 1755, the king of Portugal, Dom José I, writes:

> Conde de Alva, Viceroy, and Capt. General of the State of India, friend. I, the king, send you many greetings, much as I love you. It has been presented to me that there have been openings several times of the coffin in which is protected the corpse of St Francis Xavier, which has resulted in some damage, and that it [opening] is not prevented for the future, and it can cause much more [damage] to the importance of conserving the so venerable deposit ... Nor that any favour be accorded to any person whomsoever, neither a person of higher quality or elevated character and employment ... and it will be ordered to register this letter in the books of the Secretary of this State, and in those of the Senate of Goa, in order that always it is executed and observed without violation of my Royal determinations. Written in Lisbon, 2 April, 1755. King.[33]

Not only does the king finally address the very real concerns of the Jesuits – it almost appears as if he is responding point by point directly to De Souza's earlier request made in 1708 – but he uses his authority to override all state requests, fulfilling the Jesuit desire finally to put Xavier to rest.[34] Interestingly, the king went one step further by ordering that two copies of his letter be preserved, one in Lisbon in the hands of the Secretary of State, the other in the records of the Senate of Goa. This act ensurd not only that metropole and colony were in continued communication with each other, but also that in case one decree was somehow destroyed as a result of unforeseen circumstances – here the king's prescience is remarkable given that the Lisbon earthquake would take place seven months later on 1 Novembe 1755, on All Saints' Day[35] – another copy of his royal decree would still exist. This repeated practice of preserving decrees in archives highlights once again the Estado da Índia's growing sense of its historicity – its greatness in decline – as well as perhaps even a growing sense of its own demise in the near future.

Postponing ritual: expelling the Jesuits, secularizing the state (1759)

> No servant can be a slave to two masters: you cannot serve God and money – Matthew 6: 24[36]

In this third section of the chapter, I briefly outline the historical context under which members of the Society of Jesus were expelled from Goa, with long-term consequences for the secularization of saint and state. When Sebastião José de Carvalho e Melo, otherwise known as the Marquis de Pombal, became the acting Minister of War and Foreign Affairs under King Dom José I (1750–77),[37] he envisioned a different kind of government for Portugal, where commercial activity thrived without the burden of intolerant religious policies.[38] He had earlier been appointed as Portugal's Ambassador to London in 1738 and had been much impressed with the successful maritime economy of Great Britain, promoting it as a model to be reproduced at home.[39] In his official capacity as Minister, he had first made a name for himself with his effective handling of the Lisbon earthquake of 1755.[40] It was he who rebuilt the devastated city, establishing it once again as a thriving port at a time when Portugal was increasingly dependent on its Brazilian empire as a source of trade and profit.[41] It was in this context that Pombal, wielding much power and influence, both at home and abroad, chose to suppress the activities of the Society of Jesus in Portugal as well as its overseas colonies.[42] Using an attempt on the king's life on 3 September 1758, a threat supposedly masterminded by the Jesuits, as the explicit reason for their expulsion,[43] he proceeded with his plan to rid the state of the many 'ills' – economic, political, social, and religious – that he attributed solely to the work of the Jesuits.[44]

Thus, by 1759, the Society of Jesus had been forcibly removed from all its overseas territories, including Goa, its members either imprisoned indefinitely in the colonies or shipped off to Europe under Pombal's directives. As we saw in previous chapters, the Jesuits were as much a commercial enterprise as a religious institution, accumulating wealth through their role as moneylenders and landowners,[45] wealth that the colonial state could potentially seize and employ to buttress its failing economy. Pombal also suspended the Goa Inquisition (1774), viewing it as excessive and outdated,[46] promoting instead a policy of 'racial equality and tolerance' among religious orders and colonial officials. It was under his direction that the capital of the Estado da Índia was slowly shifted from a recently plague-infested Old Goa[47] – with Xavier's body remaining inside the Church of Bom Jesus – to the burgeoning new port city of Panjim (Nova Goa),[48] located ten kilometres away, the latter eventually replacing the former as the capital of Portuguese India (1843), a point I take up in the following chapter. Thus, not only did the second half of the eighteenth century mark a shift in the 'balancing' of church and state that had sustained, more or less, the Estado da Índia for so long but it correspondingly marked a shift in jurisdiction with regard to the 'incorrupt' corpse of St Francis Xavier. Now the body of this revered saint was placed under the auspices of the Portuguese Crown, with the Congregation of the Oratorians, an organization of 'secular' (non-ordered) clergymen[49] appointed to oversee his general care and management, while still responsible to the Archdiocese and Viceroy. It was to ratify this shift in responsibility concerning Xavier – thus gaining public recognition of it as well – and to disprove rumours of his secret 'translation'[50] by the Jesuits when they had been forced to leave Goa twenty-three years earlier that Xavier's corpse was deemed medically 'fit' for public display and the first 'Solemn Exposition'[51] of St Francis Xavier took place in Goa in 1782. However, despite all of Pombal's efforts to 'secularize' saint and state during the latter half of the eighteenth century, the Jesuits would continue to act as a spectre during the days of ritual.

Staging ritual: the 'solemn exposition' of 1782

Burdens of proof

When a group, even one with a united history, begins to fail in its objective, gossip and scandal accelerate the process of disintegration. – Max Gluckman, 1963[52]

In the last section of this chapter, I examine the staging of Xavier's first 'Solemn Exposition', an event which took place during a period of exclusive investments in and concerns with his corpse on the part of the Estado da Índia. As my analysis has suggested thus far, these 'saintly' preoccupations throughout the eighteenth century were not unrelated to the state's very real sense of anxiety concerning its own political and economic viability in the face of steady involution.[53] However, that Portugal and its colonies experienced a political and economic revival of sorts in the aftermath of Pombal's liberal policy-making also made the staging of a set of ritual practices in 1782 more feasible. Here I rely on state decrees as well as the eyewitness testimony of a visiting Oratorian – the congregation now in charge of managing the Church of Bom Jesus and Xavier himself – to 'expose' the details of this exposition. I will suggest that in 1782 ritual took on several interrelated burdens of proof, distinct from his past displays. Not only was the king's earlier decree barring his public display (1755) overturned by way of a medical examination, thus sanctioning his ritualization but this exposition took on a particular character because of several combined factors: the absence of the Jesuits, the desiccated condition of Xavier's corpse, and, finally, the power of rumour, which consistently questioned his authenticity and location in Goa.

Issuing a medical report: authenticating Xavier, refuting rumours

It was the newly appointed Superior of the Oratorians, again the congregation of secular priests chosen by Pombal to take over the care and management of Xavier's corpse, who pushed with renewed force for his public display. The historian J. Castets (1925) provides the circumstances under which the queen of Portugal finally agreed to a formal examination of his body by state officials on 4 March 1781. He writes:

> Queen Maria I, yielding to the entreaties made to her by the Superior of the Congregation of the Mission [the Oratorians] delegated at that time for the administration of the Bom Jesus, as well as to the prayers of many other ecclesiastics, considering the long time that had elapsed since the last display of the sacred body to the veneration of the public, gave orders to proceed, first of all, to a previous examination of the state of preservation of the sacred body, in order to decide whether it could 'in all decency and without inconvenience' be exposed to public veneration.[54]

Xavier's exposition would no doubt help solidify their own position in Goa, just as it had for the Jesuits in the past. However, the (above) concerns of the queen reinforce the power of the state to control the fate of the Jesuits as well as that of their beloved saint; just as this religious order had been removed from Goa by royal decree, so too could Xavier's display under the Oratorians be disavowed.

Relying on the same set of keys to open his casket, only now placed in the hands of state officials,[55] Xavier's medical examination was held on 1 January 1782, and was witnessed by the acting Governor and Captain General, the Archbishop, the Secretary of State, and several additional colonial officials.[56] Castets provides a summary of this autopsy report, recorded by Governor D. Frederico Guilherme de Sousa. He writes:

> The Governor General, in obedience to orders received from Her Majesty to examine the sacred body and see in what state it is, has caused the coffin in which the sacred body is deposited to be opened, and the body was found vested in sacerdotal vestments. The head is well preserved, with a small quantity of hair on the skull. The face with all its features was a sufficiently good colour, and covered with skin, except the right side, which has a small bruise. It had both the ears and all the visible teeth except one. The left arm and the hand were entirely covered with skin and of satisfactory colour, but the right arm was wanting, and tradition said it had been taken to Rome, at the time of the Jesuit Fathers. For the rest of the body, the intestines were wanting, as it was discovered by His Excellency by palpating the body under the vestments. The thighs were covered with a withered skin, the feet were equally covered with skin, through which the veins could be seen, and all the toes that remained had also their nails. One toe of the right foot was wanting, as it had been snatched away through devotion, by a devout person and was now in the house of the Intendente General, as that official attested it. Finally, all the undersigned have come to the conclusion that the body and the relics of the Saint are in such a state that they may be exposed to the public, to excite and increase the devotion of the faithful.[57]

This autopsy report carries with it several interrelated burdens of proof which both sanction by state decree Xavier's ritualization and set the conditions for his public display in 1782, again in the face of rumours suggesting that Xavier's corpse had been secretly removed from Goa by departing Jesuits. First, that this medical examination was performed only in the presence of a limited audience suggests a concern that colonial officials had with the desiccated condition of Xavier's corpse[58] – it might not, in fact, have been deemed satisfactorily 'fit for public display' had a qualified medical doctor been on hand during the proceedings. Second, it is left to certain colonial officials to prove Xavier's worthiness for ritualization, 'in all decency' as the queen puts it, a worthiness that requires striking a careful balance between a representation of his corpse as in a state of complete incorruptibility and one of 'covered bones' given the king's prior decree of 1755 on the deplorable state of Xavier's body. These same officials manage to strike a fine balance between two extremes: while his head is 'well preserved' and the face a 'sufficiently good colour', his intestines are found 'wanting' and his thighs covered with 'withered skin'. Thus, state officials manage to find in 1782 the appropriate language to deem Xavier 'fit enough' for public display while stopping short of declaring his corpse a miracle. Third, this saint's corpse is authenticated in the act of conducting this autopsy report. In detailing how Xavier's Jesuit past was inscribed in his various body parts, the state confirms Xavier's location in Goa as well as the fact that the corpse lying in Goa is in fact, and beyond a doubt, that of Xavier. Upon examination, he is found to be dressed in his sacerdotal vestments, a reminder of the gift from Portugal's queen in 1744, his right arm wanting, as 'tradition said that it had been taken to Rome in the time of the Jesuit fathers' – a direct reference to his canonization proceedings of 1622 – and one toe of the right foot wanting, 'as it had been snatched away in devotion': a reminder of the infamous story of Doña Isabel Carom which circulated long after Xavier's public display in 1554.

It is in the details of these distinctive corporeal markers that the body is made real, proving Xavier's existence in Goa and his authenticity, and by implication the authenticity of the Estado da Índia (as opposed to the Jesuits) as his rightful heir. Thus, in the face of historical upheavals concerning the removal of the Jesuits and persistent doubts concerning the location and condition of Xavier's corpse, the idea reinforced repeatedly throughout this autopsy report is that it is Xavier's body that is, in fact, being readied for ritual in Goa. Lastly, this examination sanctions Xavier's ritualization, reinforcing the queen's earlier decree that it must be performed 'without inconvenience' such that his public display will serve to 'excite and increase the devotion of the faithful'. In this time of political weakness, economic unpredictability, and the promotion of a policy of religious tolerance, devotion in its many forms (both religious and political) is perhaps just what the Estado da Índia needs most.

(Eye)witnessing ritual: themes on an event

With Xavier's medical exam providing the acceptable 'proof' for his ritualization to take place, plans for what was deemed a 'Solemn Exposition' of St Francis Xavier were instigated shortly thereafter by state and church officials in Goa. Nor was the choice of the title 'Solemn Exposition' by colonial officials insignificant, considering that this event was as much an 'explanation' of Xavier's location in the absence of the Jesuits as it was an 'exposure' of his corpse, as well as a state 'exhibition' requiring an attendant public. This ritual event was officially announced and inaugurated by a pastoral letter dated 15 January 1782, written by Archbishop D. Frey Manuel de Sá Catharina, the same official who had taken part in confirming Xavier's authenticity during his medical examination.[59] The dates for ritual were suggested for 10–12 February of the same year so as to provide plenty of time for the news to circulate amongst Goa's curious public.[60]

By all historical accounts, when Xavier's first 'Solemn Exposition' was staged on these prescribed dates, it was a 'grandiose' affair, its expenses covered by royal funds,[61] and attended by a large concourse of people, both 'Catholic' and 'native'.[62] The diverse public – estimated at forty thousand persons[63] – was reportedly barred from kissing (but not from seeing and thus venerating) his corpse by way of a 'glass casing' that was newly installed to prevent any 'indiscreet acts of devotion'.[64] Given the desiccated condition of Xavier's corpse, colonial officials most likely desired the public to be close enough to authenticate the corpse as undoubtedly his, but far enough away not to realize the actual material condition of his corpse. This last ritual detail both confirms the state's authority in deeming certain kinds of devotional acts appropriate (or not) given the circumstances in 1782 and the constituting role of the public in affirming the authenticity of Xavier's corpse, and thus the 'success' or 'failure' of the exposition amid circulating rumours that Xavier's body had earlier been 'whisked away' by the Jesuits.

Turning away from these general contours of the 'Solemn Exposition' of 1782, I now explore ritual's finer details through the eyes of a witness, his testimony elaborating many of these same themes. The Italian priest Ansolani, stationed in Goa at this time in his capacity as Superior of the Congregation of Oratorians, attended the festivities. His description, recorded on 21 March 1782, provides a window on to this set of ritual practices during a time when the state was invested in promoting Xavier's 'secularization' as well as its own. Ansolani writes:

> I am going to comply with my promise by giving you a faithful report of what happened at Goa, during the exposition of the body of St Francis

Xavier the Apostle of India. His Grace D. Fr. Manuel de Santa Catharina, of the Order of Barefooted Carmelites, Bishop of Cochin, and at the same time, Administrator of the Archbishopric of Goa, and the Governor of this city, considered it prudent to hold this exposition, in view of the persistent rumor, that the body of the saint had been robbed.

The body of this zealous missionary reposes in a handsome marble sepulchre, in the Church of Jesus in the vicinity of the three houses, which the Jesuits possessed here. Outside the sanctuary of this Church a platform was erected. It was covered with rich damask, purple in colour. Over this was placed an urn of glass, the upper portion of which was decorated with gilt ornaments. The platform was protected by a wooden railing.

After all these arrangements were made, Saturday the 9th of February was secretly selected as the date for the ceremony and during the night, soldiers were placed about the church. A little while after the Administrator with his staff, the Governor with his principal officers, the Judges, the Advocates, many *fidalgos* [noblemen] with their ladies, and a large number of Canons and Priests of Various Congregations entered the edifice.

In the first place, candles were distributed among more than fifty people and the procession marched through an inner door (as that of the church was closed), to the sepulchre. Mr. Catalani, a lay brother of the *Society of Jesus*, and an Engineer of these parts, by means of an improvised ladder, ascended the mausoleum, and with the eight keys, which the Archbishop, the Governor, and the other persons selected to guard this relic, keep with them, opened the sepulchre towards the feet, and in the presence of all the witnesses, drew out the coffin.

This coffin is two feet high, and eight feet long. Its cover is curved. It is closed with three keys and over the cover is placed a cloth worked in gold. The coffin was then taken in procession to the platform in the body of the church. The Bishop, the Governor, four of our missionaries [the Oratorians], and four other priests, took the body by their hands. I felt very much that I was deprived of this honour by an attack of erysipelas and a painful swelling in one of my thighs, but when the body was taken back to the mausoleum, I was well enough to become one of the bearers. After the coffin was deposited on the place destined for it, the cover was opened and a silk veil, which covered the body of the saint was now removed. This veil [will be] sent to the Queen of Portugal by the same vessel that [will] carry this letter of mine. There was seen the entire body. The feet and thighs are in a fair state of preservation, the cranium is covered with a dry skin, the general aspect of the face is so clear ... the left arm and hand are in sound condition, and repose on his breast.

The saint is in his sacerdotal vestments. Although these were [earlier] presented by the Queen of Portugal, wife of D. Pedro II, of the House of Saboya, they are almost as new; short is the stature of the saint, the feet are shrunk and of a dark colour probably owing to exposure and to his extensive travels, bare-footed. Of the right foot, two toes are missing,

> and the right arm is said to be in Rome. As soon as the veil was removed all those present kissed the body. They also touched the body, rosaries, crucifixes, and handkerchiefs. The coffin was then placed in a glass case. The *Te Deum* was sung, and the body was exposed for public veneration. During the first night the body was guarded by the Dominicans and by the soldiers selected for the vigil. On the following Sunday, the 10th of February, already at daybreak, great was the concourse of the people, which on every succeeding day showed a further increase in number. Although one of the panes of glasses was broken, in the crush, neither the attendant priests, nor the soldiers interfered with the regular flow of people around the body.
>
> In the vast multitude of the people could be noticed many gentiles [Hindus] who had come to see the body of the Holy Apostle of the Indies and among them, a neighboring Raja. This prince, through his interpreter, declared that he considered our religion the only true one. In spite of this affirmation there was not a single conversion.
>
> The clergy of the Order of the Observers passed the second night in the Church and the priests of S. Filipe Neri the third night. During these three days the Church of Bom Jesus was attended by different religious orders, who chanted the *Te Deum*, and assisted at the High Mass.
>
> On the third day was celebrated the Pontifical Mass. The Governor with his entire staff, the Magistrates and all the other officials were present in gala dress. After Mass, the Archbishop gave the Papal Blessing, and to the sound of a cannonade from all the fortresses, published the Plenary Indulgence.
>
> On the third day, the 13th of February, the crowd having greatly diminished, the doors of the church were easily closed. A few persons guarded the place, and during the night, the body was replaced in the mausoleum in the presence of the Archbishop and the Governor.
>
> Thus ended the Solemn Exposition of the body of St Francis Xavier of the Society of Jesus, the Apostle of the Indies. I presume that they will not frequently expose the body, because the body of the Saint is affected by the air, by the warmth of the lights, and by the heat of the throng of people, who are present at this ceremony.[65]

In his 'faithful report', Ansolani provides us with a invaluable eyewitness account of Xavier's first 'Solemn Exposition', suggesting first and foremost that it was the 'persistent rumor that the body of the saint had been robbed', which led the Estado da Índia to organize this particular set of ritual practices surrounding Xavier's corpse. Thus, much was at stake for the Portuguese in Goa in staging Xavier's exposition in 1782 precisely because of the absent presence of the Jesuits via the power of rumour, the desiccated condition of saint and state, and the constituting role of the public in setting the conditions for display.

In the following ritual analysis, I adopt a thematic approach. Curiously, in his position as a secular priest, Ansolani omits neither

Xavier's status as a Jesuit nor the historical contributions of this religious order to Goan society. Rather, he greatly admires the 'handsome marble sepulchre'[66] of this missionary who reposes in the Church of Jesus, one of three houses previously owned by the Jesuits, a detail that suggests a lack of animosity or competition between secular and religious-ordered priests operating in Goa. That is, despite state efforts to disassociate him from the Society of Jesus, Ansolani acknowledges Xavier's Jesuit past, going so far as to identify Xavier as a 'zealous' missionary, this latter detail perhaps the only indication of his own position as a secular priest and their distinct approach to missionizing as compared to that of the religious orders. In attending to Xavier's Jesuit past, this Italian priest delinks the fate of the Jesuits from that of their favourite saint – a detail which no doubt helps to dispel the circulating rumour that his corpse had earlier been 'robbed'. For Ansolani, even though the Jesuits may have been forced to leave Goa under less than fortunate circumstances, Xavier remains in Goa under the management of the Oratorians, the Congregation of which he is the head and to whom he more than likely addresses his account.

Our eyewitness provides us with the rich details of the preparations that went into readying Xavier's corpse for his public veneration which, relative to his past displays in Goa (in 1554 and 1624), takes place for the first time without the organization of the Society of Jesus. In charge of the festivities is the Governor alongside Goa's Archbishop, both taking on visible roles just as they had during Xavier's medical examination. Second, in the public square facing the former Jesuit church inside of which lies Xavier's corpse, several tasks are performed: a platform is erected, one that is covered in a 'rich damask' cloth, 'purple in colour'; then an 'urn of glass' is placed on top, one which is decorated with 'gilt ornaments'; lastly a 'wooden railing' is erected for added protection. Third, soldiers are installed inside the Church of Bom Jesus during the first night of his opening, no doubt to guard what is deposited inside. All of these ritual details signify the value assigned to Xavier's corpse, the amount (and cost) of the preparations that went into organizing ritual activity,[67] and the state's heightened sense of anxiety over exposing his body to Goa's public in the midst of concerns over his fragility and location.

Ansolani also informs us that Xavier's casket was initially opened for a select few members of church, state, and public. The participants at this 'ceremony' include not only the Archbishop and the Governor but judges, advocates, *fidalgos* (noblemen) and their ladies – Portuguese India's most notable citizens – as well as the Administrator of the Church of Bom Jesus, his staff, and numerous canons and priests of various congregations, and finally himself. These ritual details affirm the privileged status assigned to both the Oratorians and Ansolani – as its head – during the festivities and their role in taking over the ritual activities normally prescribed to the Jesuits; they also intimate that only certain (elite and Catholic) members of Goa's colonial structure were invited to 'witness' this momentous opening of Xavier's casket. That candles are distributed 'among more than fifty people' provides an estimate of the size of this carefully selected public. Next, this same group of participants move in 'procession' with their lit candles to Xavier's sepulchre, entering by way of an 'inner door', since the regular entrance is normally closed at this time of night. Lastly, a 'lay brother' of the Society of Jesus, an 'engineer' by training – his involvement a reminder of the previous owners of the Church of Bom Jesus and the current status of the Jesuits in Goa[68] –'ascends Xavier's mausoleum' by way of a ladder, and, using the eight keys supplied to him by those 'selected to guard this relic', he draws out Xavier's coffin. That this task is performed 'in the presence of all the witnesses' suggests the constituting role of this elite public during ritual activity; that is, their participation is required to affirm the state's ability to both take care of and guard Xavier's corpse in the face of circulating rumours that question their capabilities.

Ansolani pays much attention to Xavier's coffin during its transfer (outside), ritual details which simultaneously suggest his own sense of curiosity and involvement in the proceedings. Not only does he take note of the coffin's dimensions, the fact that its cover is 'curved', and that a cloth 'worked in gold' is placed on top but he confirms the state's continued practice of relying on three sets of keys to open his coffin in the aftermath of the Jesuit expulsion. That this Italian priest is assigned a position during the transfer of Xavier's coffin to the specially erected platform located outside the Church of Bom Jesus suggests once again his own prominent status throughout the festivities. However, that an attack of 'erysipelas' and 'a painful swelling' in his thigh 'deprived him of this honour' suggests his disappointment, a disappointment made up only by the fact that he was later 'well enough' to take part – as a 'bearer' – in returning Xavier's coffin to his mausoleum. Ansolani also notes that Xavier's coffin is 'taken in procession' in the 'hands' of the Archbishop, the Governor, four of 'our missionaries', and four 'other' priests, this detail confirming once again the prominent positions of these heads of state as well as the effective replacement of the Jesuits with this secular clergy in order to present a respectable balance of church and state in the space of ritual. Lastly, Xavier's coffin is 'deposited on the place destined for it', a fate used to determine his veneration by members of church, state, and public.

Our eyewitness also provides us with the details of the brief ceremony that takes place for this select group of participants on the eve of his public exposition. First, the cover of Xavier's casket is opened before the 'silk veil' covering his corpse is removed. Next, 'all those present' proceed to 'kiss' the body as well as touch various (religious) items – rosaries, crucifixes, and handkerchiefs – to this same corpse, his saintly powers spreading by way of contagion on to these personalized objects. In a final act, the coffin is placed in a glass case in preparation for his public veneration starting the next day, and the Latin 'Te Deum' is sung, a ritual marker that closes his semi-private viewing. Here I suggest that this opening ceremony serves as a dress rehearsal of sorts, on the one hand, pacifying Goa's most influential members of church, state, and public, and on the other, ensuring that the final performance – Xavier's public 'exposition'– will be flawless. Lastly, Ansolani tells us that the same 'silk veil' which presently covers Xavier's body will soon be sent to the queen of Portugal as a relic – again, its direct contact with Xavier's corpse imbuing it with his saintly powers. That it is this same queen – Doña Maria I – who had earlier donated new vestments for Xavier suggests the various circuits of relics and confirms the continual production and circulation of (new types of) Xaverian relics precisely because of his desiccation. That this same precious relic would be placed on the same Lisbon-bound vessel carrying Ansolani's eyewitness account of the festivities of 1782 offers evidence of the value of both material objects and confirms the likelihood that this Oratorian recorded his testimony for a larger European reading public.

Just as Ansolani focuses his attention on the saint's coffin, he is equally fascinated with recording the condition of his corpse before it is encased in glass; these ritual details suggest once again his morbid curiosity and intended audience. On the one hand, Ansolani notes that the feet and thighs are in a 'fair state of preservation', his cranium is 'covered with dry skin', the 'general aspect of the face is so clear', and his 'left arm and hand are in sound condition' – corporeal details that affirm once again Xavier's 'fitness' for public display. On the other hand, the priest informs us that Xavier is 'short' in stature, that 'two' (and not one) toes are missing from his right foot, and that his feet are 'shrunken' and of a 'dark colour' owing to 'exposure and his extensive travels, barefooted'. These additional corporeal details not only index Xavier's biography in life and death, and represent his body as neither completely corrupted nor completely miraculous, but also intimate the constrained positions of the Governor and Archbishop during his prior autopsy such that they purposely omitted these particulars from their formal report in order to sanction his public display. Lastly, this priest's account serves, in a manner similar to this saint's medical examination, to authenticate without a doubt that the corpse exposed in front of him is in fact that of Xavier. He informs us that the right arm is 'said to be in Rome' – a reminder of Xavier's canonization process – and that he is found dressed in his 'sacerdotal vestments', which, despite the fact that they were bequeathed to Xavier 'by the wife of Dom Pedro II, king of Portugal' many years earlier, are 'almost as new' – ritual details that affirm Xavier's authenticity through his dress and bodily markers.

This eyewitness account affords us a valuable window on to Xavier's three-day public 'exposition',[69] Ansolani first detailing for us the added security measures that were implemented during this period of heightened activity. Again, Xavier's corpse is encased in glass throughout the festivities, colonial officials now forbidding the general public from 'touching' and 'kissing' him, a practice earlier sanctioned exclusively for members of Goa's elite public. This ritual detail suggests both a real concern on the part of colonial officials with the fragile condition of Xavier's corpse such that they desire to prevent any further damages during his exhibition, and a distinction between kinds of publics in attendance at Xavier's exposition, those with full and those with limited access. In addition, soldiers and priests (both ordered and secular) take turns standing guard over the saint's body each night of the festivities; in light of circulating rumours that Xavier's corpse had been removed unlawfully, this detail affirms the state's sense of (in)security, its added precautionary measures, and the filling in of Jesuit duties by other religious men to restore the balance of church and state required of ritual activity.

Our visiting priest highlights the constituting role of Goa's large public during Xavier's exposition. Ansolani informs us that on the first day of the event – Sunday 10 February – starting at 'daybreak', there was a great 'concourse of people, which on every succeeding day showed a further increase'. Moreover, no one – neither priest nor soldier who had been put in charge of guarding Xavier's corpse – is allowed to interrupt, despite the damage to his glass casing during 'the crush', the 'regular flow of people around the body'. It is only on the third day, 12 February, the crowd having 'greatly diminished', that colonial officials decided to 'close the doors' of the church.[70] These details both affirm the public's investment in venerating Xavier's corpse and enforce their role in defining ritual practice such that they dictate the duration of the display and engage in devotional practices normally not sanctioned by the state. In other words, the Estado da Índia could not stage a successful exposition if it did not have a public desirous of venerating Xavier's corpse.

The Italian priest's account also affords a window on to the religiosity of Xavier's exposition, affirming that the Catholic faith is represented and promoted through a variety of ritual activities and persons throughout ritual's duration. Not only does Ansolani attend a High Mass but he witnesses 'Papal blessings', 'plenary indulgences', and devotional chanting. Ansolani also notices the 'gala dress' of the Governor, his staff, and additional colonial officers during the performance of the Pontifical Mass on the third and final day of the festivities, dress here a marker of their prominence and the respect accorded religious ceremonies. In addition, numerous priests are always on hand to assist the Archbishop during these religious performances, our eyewitness noting the presence of clergymen representing the Dominican order, the Congregation of St Filipe Neri, and the Order of the Observantes. Not only do these religious men stand guard over Xavier's corpse during the three nights of his public exposure but they assist in chanting the 'Te Deum' and performing the High Mass. Thus, in the absence of the Jesuits, these other priests (both ordered and secular) are called upon by state officials to perform duties and share responsibilities (a trait perhaps found lacking in the Jesuits) proving their religious efficacy by upholding the Catholic faith throughout the days and nights of the exposition.

At the same time, Ansolani attests to the diversity of Goa's public that participates in Xavier's ritualization in 1782. The 'vast multitude of people' includes not only Catholics but also 'many gentiles' (Hindus) who 'had come to see the body of the Holy Apostle of the Indies', the inclusion of Xavier's title in his narrative reinforcing Xavier's historical role and wider appeal beyond Goa for the priest's intended audience. Ansolani also singles out the participation of a 'neighboring Raja [Hindu prince]', his attendance alongside other 'gentiles' reinforcing Portugal's policy of religious tolerance implemented directly under Pombal, the Estado da Índia's ongoing diplomatic ties with neighbouring Hindu kingdoms, and the distinctiveness of ritual practice in 1782 relative to Xavier's past displays in 1554 and 1624 wherein the previous publics were predominantly Catholic. It is this same visiting Hindu prince who declares 'through his interpreter' that Catholicism is the 'only true' religion, a detail that suggests the power of ritual to enthral its participants in spite of cultural and language barriers. That 'there was not a single conversion' in spite of the prince's 'affirmation' suggests this Hindu leader's (religious and political) authority among his own people, reinforces the increasing secularization of saint and state such that respect for religious difference is explicitly accorded a space during ritual by Portuguese colonial officials, and, finally, intimates the limitation of Xavier's powers, as well as those of the Estado da

Índia in 1782 – that is, the desiccation of saint and state – relative to earlier ritual moments. Thus, it is a diverse public that joins together in venerating Xavier's corpse during his first 'Solemn Exposition'; both Catholics and Hindus located within and beyond Goa's borders are encouraged to take part, which in turn serves to reaffirm the resilience of a colonial state to adopt and adapt to the needs of its public during a general period of political and economic instability.

Ansolani also attends to the closing of Xavier's exposition, representing it as a relatively simple affair. He notes that on this last day the Church of Bom Jesus is carefully 'guarded', Xavier's translation taking place 'at night' after the church doors have been 'closed' to the public. Once again, it is the dual figures of the Governor and Archbishop who preside over the return of Xavier's corpse to his mausoleum, a ritual detail that reinforces the careful balance of church and state represented and practised throughout the three days of Xavier's exposition. The details of the closing ceremony are indexical of what the Estado da Índia desires to prove in the larger space of ritual: its efficacy in restoring political, economic, and religious order in Goa in the face of many historical upheavals during the eighteenth century, including but not restricted to the expulsion of the Jesuits.

Ansolani ends his account by initiating his own rumour concerning Xavier: he 'presumes' that in the future colonial officials will not frequently expose him, 'because the body of the Saint is affected by the air, by the warmth of the lights, and by the heat of the throng of people who are present at this ceremony'. In providing an explanation for his slow decomposition over time, Ansolani shows that his frequent displays have inadvertently caused permanent damage to his corpse; hence the now 'desiccated' state more than two hundred years after this missionary's death. I suggest that the circulation of this new rumour (of a corpse restricted from public view) via Ansolani's account will only add to Xavier's value in the act of denying public access to him. It is entirely plausible that in the future Goa's public will be even more desirous to venerate the corpse of their favourite saint as a result, as will the priest's European and Oratorian reading public be even more desirous for additional news concerning Xavier.

Thus what Ansolani offers us is a perspective on ritual that is grounded in 'faith': faith in his own perspective to record what he sees, faith in the Catholic religiosity of the event, faith in Xavier's past as a Jesuit missionary, faith in the Oratorians to appropriately take over the duties of the expelled Jesuits, faith in the diversity and strength of Goa's public, and, finally, faith in the renewed power of the Estado da Índia in 1782 to assert a balance of church and state. Nor is the crucial role of Xavier – despite his desiccated condition – in harnessing state power and garnering public support forgotten in the midst of shouldering this particular set of burdens of proof: he is treated in a manner befitting a saint throughout the entire ritual process.

Conclusion

This chapter has been wholly concerned with exploring ritual in the face of the Estado da Índia's increasing 'secularization' of Xavier, a state investment that is very much related to its own attempts to re-define its political and economic character during the eighteenth century and that includes the purging of all excesses from Goa, including the Society of Jesus. Here 'secularization' is not about making Xavier into a non-religious, anti-Catholic figure, but rather about reconfiguring him into an agent of a more 'secularized' state. I have relied on state decrees as well as Jesuit exchanges as my source materials, and explored the role of official and unofficial documentation in serving and disrupting church and state doctrine, as well as in circulating within, among and between church and state officials and hierarchies. In many ways, these acts of communication – the bequeathing of titles, money, and vestments, and the various prohibitions against opening his casket – all suggest an ongoing series of Xaverian investments and anxieties. I have also argued that a new set of discursive and material strategies concerning Xavier's desiccation were steadily adopted by the Estado da Índia in an attempt to harness his saintly powers to its own agenda.

This chapter has explored a variety of themes in the hope of complicating ritual practice. I have sought to understand how burdens of proof, circuits of knowledge, and material and discursive strategies of investment are all part of the ongoing secularization of saint and state. I have relied on state decrees and Jesuit communications, rumours and facts, medical examinations and eyewitness testimonies to address different relations – between church and state, the Jesuits and the Estado da Índia, and between metropole and colony – during the eighteenth century, a period fraught with change. Finally, I have explored the nature of colonial saint veneration in 1782: I have elaborated on glass casings, veiled coverings, and sacerdotal vestments, touching and kissing, royalty and relic worship, and finally, exposures and expositions.

Despite the success of Xavier's first 'Solemn Exposition' in 1782, the Estado da Índia continued to experience very real setbacks in the overlapping realms of politics, economics, and religion. Interestingly, by 1793 the Estado da Índia had regularized by state decree, once again, the *posse* ceremony surrounding Xavier, thus ensuring at the very least his continuing role as an agent of a state facing an increasingly uncertain future. However, by this time the Portuguese in Goa had already experienced their first rebellion by native clergymen – the Pinto Conspiracy of 1787[71] – and were embroiled in additional conflicts not entirely outside the inseparable realms of politics, economics, and religion, including one involving neighbouring Mysore's ruler, Tipu Sultan, who was bent on taking over Goa but who died before such an attack could be realized.[72] Nor could the Estado da Índia continue to ignore the history and expanding presence of their British colonial counterparts in South Asia, an imperial power that had steadily gained a foothold in India throughout the eighteenth century.[73] These very real concerns would be evidenced in the space of ritual in 1859, the topic of my next chapter.

Notes

1 Saying reproduced in Charles Boxer, *Portuguese India in the Mid-Seventeenth Century* (Delhi: Oxford University Press, 1980), p. 19.

2 Fr Caetano Cruz, 'History of the Expositions', *The Herald* (21 November 1984), p. 4.

3 I am using 'secularization' in a particular way – to imply not that Xavier was transformed into an-anti-religious, anti-Catholic figure but rather that he was actively disassociated from the Jesuits, the religious order that he had initiated in Goa in 1542 (thus becoming a 'secular' priest, one without affiliation to a particular order) and simultaneously transformed into an agent of the colonial state.

4 Desiccate: 'dry out (especially food for preservation)'. *The Oxford American Desk Dictionary and Thesaurus*, 2nd edn (New York: Berkeley Books, 2001), p. 208.

5 Exposition: 'large public exhibition'. In *The Oxford American Desk Dictionary and Thesaurus*, p. 279.

6 De Gama quoted in Menezes Bragança, *A Índia Portuguesa*, Volume II (Goa: Imprensa Nacional, 1923), p. 68. Sanjay Subrahmanyam characterizes the eighteenth century as a period of 'growing commercialization of the state and state power' (both colonial and Indian state power), a point I develop in relation to the Estado da Índia by looking at policy reforms instigated under Pombal. See Sanjay Subrahmanyam, 'Commerce and State Power in Eighteenth Century India: Some Reflections', *South Asia Research*, Volume 8, No. 2 (November 1988), pp. 97–110.

7 This time frame marks the apogee of the Jesuits in Goa. See Charles Borges, *The Economics of the Goa Jesuits, 1542–1759, An Explanation of Their Rise and Fall* (New Delhi: Concept Publishing Company, 1994), pp. 46–7.

8 Celsa Pinto, *Goa: Images and Perceptions: Studies in Goan History* (Goa: Prabhakar Bhide, 1996), p. 1. These 'dark days' refer to both this historical period and the lack of historiography on Goa during this period which has been characterized by the historians as one of 'decline and decay', but without complete stagnation. For a revised history, one which suggests that this time frame can also be characterized as one of innovation and dynamic change, see Glenn J. Ames, *Renascent Empire?: The House of Braganza and the Quest for Stability in Portuguese Monsoon Asia, ca. 1640–1683* (Amsterdam: University of Amsterdam Press, 2000).

9 For setting up this larger historical context, see Celsa Pinto, Chapter 1, in *Trade and Finance in Portuguese India: A Study of the Portuguese Country Trade, 1770–1840* (New Delhi: Concept Publishing Company, 1994).

10 Francisco Xavier da Costa, 'Private Opening', in *Exposição do Venerando Corpo de S. Francisco Xavier em 1931* (Nova Goa: Tip. A Voz de S. Francisco Xavier, 1935), p. 182.

11 Felippe Neri Xavier, *Resumo Historico da Maravilhosa Vida, Conversões, e Milagres de S. Francisco Xavier, Apostolo, Defensor, e Patrono das Índias*, 2nd edn (Nova Goa: Imprensa Nacional, 1861), p. 316 (Livro das Moncões 45, fl. 197).

12 King Pedro II's decree reproduced in Felippe Neri Xavier, *Resumo Historico*, pp.

317–18 (Liv. de Registo de Alv. Reães, No. 8, p. 27 v).

13 The Viceroy contributed, starting in April, 150 *ashrafis* (Rs 615) annually. The state also increased its annual contributions to the Church of Bom Jesus, and included a steady increase in expenditures. See B.S. Shastry, 'Sources of Income and Items of Expenditure of the Church in Goa (c.1510–1800 AD): A Note', in *Goan Society Through the Ages*, ed. B.S. Shastry (New Delhi: Asian Publication Series, 1987), pp. 38–9.

14 See Felippe Neri Xavier, *Resumo Historico*, p. 21 (Summary of Livro de Moncões 58, fl. 348).

15 Dauril Alden, 'Chapter 7' in *The Making of an Enterprise, The* Society of Jesus *in Portugal, Its Empire and Beyond, 1540–1750* (Stanford: Stanford University Press, 1996), pp. 197–202.

16 John Castets, 'The Miracle of the Body of St Francis Xavier', *Indian Catholic Truth Society*, No. 13 (1925), pp. 16–18. It is unclear whether it was in panic (when the Maratha troops were already knocking at the doors of Goa) or in gratitude (after their withdrawal) that the Count handed over his baton of command to the saint.

17 P. Rayanna, *St Francis Xavier and His Shrine*, 2nd edn (Panjim: Imprimatur, 1982), p. 247.

18 *Boletim da Filmoteca*, No. 30/1: 'Carta regia para o Vice-Rei da India', Lisboa, 24 de Marco de 1699. 'Inform him [the Viceroy] that desiring to prove his thanks and particular devotion to St Francis Xavier, I have resolved to declare him "Defensor de Oriente"'.

19 John Castets, 'The Miracle of the Body', pp. 18–19 (Monções 63, fl. 109).

20 Ibid.

21 Ibid., pp. 16–19.

22 Ibid. There is a historical debate over who donated these new vestments with a border of royal arms, with some arguing that it was not Queen Maria Sophia, but rather her successor D. Maria Francisca Isabel de Saboia, who in fact offered the vestments for Xavier. See Francisco de Simas Alves de Azevedo, 'O Brasão de Armas bordado na Casula de St Francis Xavier', *Hidalguia*, No. 16 (Madrid: May–June, 1956), p. 398.

23 Rayanna, St F*rancis Xavier and His Shrine*, p. 244.

24 According to Charles Borges, the wealth of the Jesuits during the late seventeenth century was produced largely through their roles as loan-givers, slave employers and landowners, their wealth even surpassing that of the Crown. Also the Jesuits assisted the state financially during the war with the Marathas (1654–1759) to rebuild the city of Goa. See his *The Economics of the Goa Jesuits*, pp. 46–7, 86. For more details on the nature of the activities of the Jesuits as moneylenders, see Dauril Alden, *The Making of an Enterprise*, Chapter 22, pp. 552–67, and Appendix B, pp. 668–9.

25 'Desiccation' is the word used by various Jesuits in describing the condition of Xavier's corpse at this time. See Newman Fernandes, *St Francis Xavier and Old Goa, An Historical Guide* (Panjim: Koinia Publications, 1994), p. 31.

26 Ibid.

27 Ibid.

28 Ibid.

29 Francisco Rodrigues, 'St Francis Xavier: Duas Exposições de Seu Corpo em 1744 and 1751', *Revista de Historia*, No. 47–8 (Lisboa: Empresa Literaria Fluminense, July–December 1923), p. 181.

30 Carmo Azevedo, 'A Miracle no More', p. 13.

31 John Castets, 'The Miracle of the Body', p. 20.

32 Francisco Rodrigues, 'St Francis Xavier: Duas Exposições', p. 180.

33 Felippe Neri Xavier, *Resumo Historico*, p. 336 (Liv. das Monções 128, fl. 621).

34 The king went so far as to pass a decree in 1757 stating that any Senate members with keys to Xavier's casket must hand them over to the appropriate Jesuit official. See Viriato A.C.B. de Albuquerque, *O Senado de Goa: Memoria Historico Archeologica* (Nova Goa: Imprensa Nacional, 1909), p. 322.

35 The Lisbon earthquake which took place on 1 November 1755 (All Saints' Day) destroyed the commercial heart of Lisbon, killing thousands in the process. It was the 'most shattering natural phenomenon to disturb Europe's peace of mind in the eighteenth century', writes historian David Birmingham. See his *Concise History of Portugal* (Cambridge: Cambridge University Press, 1993), p. 73.

36 Quoted in Dauril Alden, Chapter 24, in *The Making of an Enterprise*, p. 614.

37 Sebastião José de Carvalho e Mello, the Marquis de Pombal (1699–1782), has been described alternately as a 'great figure of Enlightened Absolutism' and a 'half-baked philosopher and full blown tyrant'. For additional details on his life and times, see Kenneth Maxwell, *Pombal: Paradox of the Enlightenment* (Cambridge: Cambridge University Press, 1995), pp. 1–3.

38 See B.S. Shastry, 'Marques de Pombal and the Jesuits of Goa', in *Jesuits in India: In Historical Perspective*, ed. Teotónio de Souza (Macau: Instituto Cultural de Macau, 1992), p. 52.

39 Charles Borges, *The Economics of the Goa Jesuits*, p. 125.

40 For additional biographical details on Pombal and his rise to power in the wake of rebuilding Lisbon, see David Birmingham, Chapter 3, in *Concise History of Portugal*, pp. 65–95.

41 For more details on the role of Brazil in sustaining Portugal's economy, see Dauril Alden, Chapter 23, in *The Making of an Enterprise*, pp. 597–603. The 'Second Portuguese empire' of the eighteenth century – the one based in Brazil – was less glorious than the first in Asia but more profitable, resting on the plantations and mines of golden Brazil and supporting the Goa empire. For additional details on this 'second' empire, see Gervase Clarence-Smith, *The Third Portuguese Empire, 1825–1975, A Study in Economic Imperialism* (Manchester: Manchester University Press, 1978), pp. 1–3.

42 See Charles Borges, *The Economics of the Goa Jesuits*, p. 126.

43 Ibid.

44 Ibid., pp. 126–7.

45 Dauril Alden, *The Making of an Enterprise*, Chapter 22, pp. 552–67, Appendix B, pp. 668–9.

46 The Inquisition of Goa was abolished by King Dom José in 1774 on the suggestion of Pombal, and of the Grand Inquisitor Cardinal Cunha. It was reinstated by his daughter and successor Queen D. Maria I in 1778 for another five years. It was not completely dismantled until 10 October 1812, under D. João VI, by the Viceroy D. Bernardo José Maria da Silva Lorena, 5th Count of Sarzedas (1807–16). See Jorge de Abreu Noronha, 'A New Dimension to the Inquisition', *Goa Today* (December 1994), p. 31. For additional details on the history of the Inquisition, see A.K. Priolkar, *The Goa Inquisition* (Bombay: Bombay University Press, 1961).

47 See José da Fonseca, *An Historical and Archaeological Sketch of the City of Goa* (Delhi: Asian Educational Services, 1986 [1878]), p. 174.

48 Ibid., p. 186.

49 The Oratorians had been instituted the same year as the Jesuits (1540) in Europe under the direction of St Philip Neri, an organization that spread through Italy, France, Spain, and Portugal. The Oratorians was made up of secular, non-ordered priests, who took vows of chastity and simplicity. They were also the largest organization of secular clergy in Goa. They were chosen by Pombal because of their liberal ideologies – evidenced by the fact that they had encouraged the entry of native clergy at a time when other religious orders, particular the Jesuits, had discriminated against native clergy, barring them from all but the lowest ranks. See Maria de Jesus dos Mártires Lopes, 'Teaching Methods in Goa (1750–1800)', in *Discoveries, Missionary Expansion and Asian Cultures*, ed. Teotónio de Souza (New Delhi: Concept Publishing Company, 1994), p. 172.

50 Carmo Azevedo, 'A Miracle No More', *Goa Today* (November 1984), p. 14. Another circulating rumour suggested that the Jesuits, as a last act of resistance, had replaced Xavier's corpse with the embalmed body of a young native Goan canon by the name of António Gomes. For additional details on the second rumour, see the unpub-

lished manuscript of Vincent Correia Afonso entitled 'Xavier in Kunkolistan', pp. 14–16 (Xavier Centre for Historical Research, Porvorim, Goa).

51 The name 'Solemn Exposition' was first given to this festival of 1782 by Portuguese colonial officials.

52 Max Gluckman, 'Gossip and Scandal', *Current Anthropology*, Volume 4, No. 3 (June 1963), p. 314. One of the themes of this chapter is the power of rumour as a force of history, and as a historical source that allows access to state processes as well as conditions of the 'local'.

53 For insightful overviews of the Portuguese overseas empire during the late eighteenth century – a period historiographically underdeveloped – see A.J.R. Russell-Wood, *The Portuguese Empire, 1415–1808: A World on the Move* (Baltimore: Johns Hopkins University Press, 1998) and Maria de Jesus Mártires Lopes, *Goa Setecentista: Tradição e Modernidade (1750–1800)* (Lisboa: Centro de Estudos dos Povos e Culturas de Expressão Portuguesa Universidade Católica Portuguesa, 1996).

54 John Castets, 'The Miracle of the Body', pp. 24–5 (Moncões do Reino 162, fl. 103, dated 4 March 1781).

55 Ibid., p. 24 (Moncões de Reino 138, fl. 640).

56 The Secretary of State, Dr Feliciano Ramos, recorded the minutes of the meeting: 'Summary of the opening of the tomb of St Francis Xavier that took place on 1 January 1782', *Boletim do Governo*, No. 80 (14 December 1859).

57 John Castets, 'The Miracle of the Body', pp. 24–5 (Moncões do Reino, 162, fl. 105).

58 Ibid., p. 30. John Castets proposes an additional explanation for why Xavier's corpse was severely desiccated in 1782, suggesting that, some time between 1759/1765 and 1782, damages were caused, when his coffin (with the corpse inside) fell from a considerable height and rebounded once it hit the floor.

59 Newman Fernandes, *St Francis Xavier and Old Goa*, p. 41.

60 Ibid.

61 Ibid. Fernandes describes the event as 'grandiose'. Francisco Xavier da Costa confirms that the expenditures for this particular exposition were covered by the royal exchequer. See also Francisco Xavier da Costa, *Exposições do Venerando Corpo de St Francis Xavier em 1900–1910–1922* (Nova Goa: Tip. Bragança & Co., 1924), p. 108.

62 Ibid.

63 Ibid. C. Nazareth also supplies an estimate of forty thousand persons, see his *Mitras Lusitanas no Oriente, Catalogos dos Prelados da Egreja Metropolitana e Primacial de Goa e das Dioceses Suffraganeas com A Recopilação das Ordenancas por elles Emittadas, e Summario dos Factos Notaveis da Historia Ecclesiastica de Goa*, 2nd edn (Lisboa: Imprensa Nacional, 1897), pp. 320–1. See also Francisco Xavier da Costa, *Exposições do Venerando Corpo*, pp. 105–6.

64 Francisco Xavier da Costa, *Exposições do Venerando Corpo*, pp. 105–6.

65 Ansolani's account (no first name supplied) is reproduced in Alex A. Pais, *A Pilgrim's Guide to the Shrine of St Francis Xavier at Goa* (Mangalore: KM Book Press, 1922), pp. 80–5. His account was also reproduced for a Goan reading public, but almost one hundred years after the event itself. See John Godinho, 'The Exposition in 1782', *Boletim do Governo*, No. 94 (1863). No additional biographical details on Ansolani are available.

66 In 1688, the then Procurator of the Goa Province, Fr Francisco Sarmento, 'carried and offered to the Duke in Florence [the Grand Duke of Tuscany, Cosmas III (1670–1723)] a cushion on which the head of the holy body of St Francis Xavier had been resting [for] some time'. Upon receiving this precious relic, the Duke had been 'moved to order a splendid tomb in fine Italian inlaid marble' for Xavier. This mausoleum, completed ten years later in 1698, was reportedly the work of a famous Florentine sculptor by the name of Giovanni Batista Foggini. It was then packed in pieces in sixty-five boxes and sent directly to Goa, accompanied by two artists, one of whom, Placido Francisco Ramponi, kept a diary of his voyage as well as the details of his craftsmanship; it took him approximately three weeks (14 October to 8 November 1698) to assemble the tomb. See P. Rayanna, *St Francis Xavier and His*

Shrine, pp. 192–5. For additional information on Ramponi, as well as excerpts from his diary, see Carlos de Azevedo, 'Um Artista Italiano em Goa', *Review Garcia de Orta*, Numero Especial (1956), p. 277.

67 Vincent Correia Afonso proposes an alternate theory, that the exposition in 1782 was staged in order to fill the coffers of the Royal Treasury with the monetary donations made by members of Goa's public. See his 'Xavier in Kunkolistan', pp. 14–16.

68 There were still some Jesuits remaining in Goa: those who had been saved from imprisonment because of their lowly status within the order were not deemed enemies of the state. Some were even allowed to stay in the Church of Bom Jesus, as prisoners, and in order to assist the Oratorians in the day-to-day affairs of running the church. See Charles Borges, *The Economics of the Goa Jesuits*, p. 135.

69 This three-day display took place between 10–12 February. Here Ansolani gets his dates wrong, labelling the third day of the exposition as 13 February.

70 Casimiro Christavão de Nazareth suggests otherwise, stating that 'many were forced to turn back because they didn't arrive on time', See his *Mitras Lusitanas no Oriente*, p. 320.

71 The Pinto rebellion of 1787, much like the mutiny of 1857 for the British in India, made the Portuguese in India realize most acutely their own vulnerabilities, since it was also the first veritable war of independence that they experienced. For a more thorough understanding of this conspiracy and its implications for Portuguese colonial rule, see Joaquim Heliodoro da Cunha Rivara, *Goa and the Revolt of 1787*, ed. Charles Borges, tr. Renato da Cunha Soares (New Delhi: Concept Publishing Company, 1996).

72 See Celsa Pinto, *Goa: Images and Perceptions*, p. 3.

73 The British went so far as to occupy Goa between 1799 and 1815; this was aimed at denying France a foothold in coastal western India in light of the French revolution of 1789. For additional details, see P.P. Shirodkar, 'British Occupation of Goa (1799–1815)', *Researches in Indo-Portuguese History*, Volume 1 (Jaipur: Publication Scheme, 1998), pp. 229–58.

CHAPTER FIVE

Resurrection (1859)

Introduction

Nothing remains of this city [Old Goa] but the sacred, the profane is entirely banished. – Denis L. Cottineau de Kloguen, French priest and visitor, 1827[1]

Old Goa has few charms when seen by the light of day. The places usually visited are the See Primacial [Cathedral], the nunnery of Santa Monaca, and the churches of St Francis, St. Caetano, and Bom Jesus. The latter contains the magnificent tomb of St Francis Xavier. His saintship, however, is no longer displayed to reverential gazers in mummy or 'scalded pig' form. Altogether we reckoned about thirty buildings. Many of them were falling to ruins, and others were being, or had been, partially demolished. The extraordinary amount of havoc committed during the last thirty years, is owing partly to the poverty of the Portuguese. Like the modern Romans, they found it cheaper to carry away cut stone, than to quarry it; but unlike the inhabitants of the Eternal City, they have now no grand object in preserving the ruins. At Panjim, we were informed that even the woodwork that decorates some of the churches, had been put up for sale ... Yet in spite of these disenchanting details, a feeling not unallied to awe creeps over one when wandering down the deserted aisles, or through the crowdless cloisters. In a cathedral large enough for a first-rate city in Europe, some twenty or thirty native Christians may be seen at their devotions, and in monasteries built for hundreds of monks, a single priest is often the only occupant. The few human beings that meet the eye, increase rather than diminish the dismal effect of the scene; as sepulchral looking as the spectacle around them, their pallid countenances, and emaciated forms seem so many incarnations of the curse of desolation which still hovers over the ruins of Old Goa. – Richard Burton, Captain, British Army, 1847[2]

Ritual practice in 1859 continued the Portuguese pattern of staging 'Solemn Expositions' that had been initiated in 1782 amidst public rumours that Xavier's corpse had been removed by members of the Society of Jesus when they were expelled from Goa in 1759. However, seventy-seven years later, ritual was no longer about securing this saint's location in Goa – the keys to his casket that had been so carefully guarded throughout the eighteenth century first by the Jesuits and then by colonial officials were now inexplicably lost and the 'management' of his corpse less a concern for the Estado da Índia, which was now experiencing even more acutely its own precarious position in Goa. In this chapter I explore the ritual dimensions of the 'Second Solemn Exposition' of 1859 that was staged in the face of a ruinous state that was increasingly uncertain about the longevity of its colonial rule given the dominating presence of the British in India, and their slow but steady encroachment upon this Portuguese colony throughout the nineteenth century. Thus, in 1859, the Portuguese turned once again to Xavier's public display, relying on his corpse as its ritual centrepiece and using ritual's official documentation in the governmental press as an ideal space to represent the richness of their role in Goa – past, present, and future – to a wider and more diverse audience than on previous occasions. This ritualized moment marks a discursive and material shift from past celebrations, state officials now capitalizing on newly emergent technologies of industrialization and communication developed in the nineteenth century to publicize their patron saint more widely, including outside the strict confines of Portuguese India. They also distributed Xaverian relics and advertised stories of miracles and acts of conversion in order to memorialize what they, with the help of their 'Defender and Apostle of the East', had produced in Goa: a model Portuguese Catholic colony, despite the vicissitudes of history.

My larger thematic approach to analysing this set of ritual practices is one of developing a discourse of 'resurrection' in relation to saint and state. I focus on the manner by which Old Goa is 'resurrected', both physically and ideologically; its successful and simultaneous representation as a 'civilized' colony and protected space of (Catholic) religiosity being one of the driving concerns of this exposition. Interestingly, what is being promoted in 1859 through the now 'secularized' figure of Xavier is an open form of Catholicism as a colonial strength, one that is tolerant of categories of 'difference', be it religion, caste, class, or nation. It is this same 'sacredness' that our French visitor to Goa Cottineau de Kloguen attests to at the outset of this chapter. Meanwhile, Xavier and Old Goa are continually guarded by military officials during the month-long exposition because of a heightened state of affairs on the wider Indian subcontinent, including the Mutiny (1857) which had taken place on British Indian soil two years earlier.

Figure 6 Souvenir of the Exposition of the body of St Francis Xavier at Goa in 1974–75

Just as I have done in previous chapters, I turn to an eyewitness perspective to provide the rich details of ritual in 1859. Alexis Canoz, a visiting Vicar Apostolic and returning Jesuit from Bombay, gives us a first-hand account of his royal tour of this now antiquated ecclesiastical centre – the majority of Goa's population having abandoned Old Goa for the newly built Panjim (Nova Goa) after 1843 – and Xavier's 'Second Solemn Exposition', which was officially staged from 3 December 1859 to 1 January 1860. Xavier's corpse had earlier been deemed 'corrupted' but arguably 'fit' for public veneration in order to 'augment the devotion of the people' by way of a medical examination prior to his public display; however, this time around, there is a real concern with his 'shrinking' stature, a concern that, as will become evident, parallels the position of the Estado da Índia in 1859.

In this chapter my ritual analysis is dependent on a specific source material that was very much the product of a new discourse of 'scientific' history that emerged in the nineteenth century as part of the project of modernity. Felippe Neri Xavier, a prominent Goan Catholic and Director of Goa's National Press, was specially appointed to produce a state-commissioned book dedicated to recording all of the ritual's details in 1859 for Goa's visiting (and reading) public. I suggest that this type of colonial state-commissioned book (and compiled by an indigenous author, no less) could have been imagined only at a particular historical moment when certain new technologies and epistemologies were emerging as central to Portuguese colonial governmentality. By distributing copies of this state-commissioned book during ritual itself, members of the diverse attendant public not only owned an official history of Xavier but also became part of that celebrated history, both Goans (Catholic and Hindu) and Catholics (Goan and Indian) linked as distinct communities across the Indian subcontinent via print capitalism in the face of a dominant British India. In the end, Neri's ritual manual serves as a testament to the mutually constituting roles of saint and state in resurrecting each other in 1859.

To return to the impressions of Sir Richard Burton on Goa that I quoted at the outset of this chapter, I suggest that it is not coincidental that the very things that he saw as the downfall of the Portuguese in India – Catholic religious conversion and racial miscegenation – are the very colonial strengths celebrated by the Portuguese during the 'Second Solemn Exposition' of 1859. Thus, Burton's comments not only illuminate the nature of British investments in Goa during the second half of the nineteenth century but also contextualize Portuguese investments in ritual within this larger historical frame. While the British were interested in learning from what they considered to be the mistakes of their colonial predecessors (Goa itself simultaneously a 'symbol of a great imperial project' and an 'object lesson in poor management'),[3] the Portuguese were preoccupied with representing on stage what they had gloriously achieved in Goa with the help of their favoured saint, and that which would remain their legacy for all of India to see in the face of an increasingly uncertain future.

Shifting capitals, shifting corpses: regulating ritual in turbulent times (1799–1857)

During the first half of the nineteenth century there was a continuing concern on the part of the Estado da Índia to regulate all religious festivities in Goa – including those centred on the corpse of St Francis Xavier – in the hope of establishing a semblance of order during what were considered to be turbulent times. For example, in one such decree, which was issued in November 1840,[4] colonial officials determine that owing to insufficient funds all religious festivities will be transferred from the charge of the Municipal Chamber to the more distant Bishop of the See Primacy, which included Goa at this time. It is now in the hands of a religious official, rather than an organ of the state, which will ensure that any excessive spending will be reduced but without sacrificing the 'pomp' and 'solemnity' of such festivities.

A second decree, written less than one year later, in August 1841, expresses a concern with the location of Xavier's corpse and mausoleum.[5] Curiously, in this decree the queen of Portugal cautions against what can only be considered an unusual request from the Governor General of Goa to move the precious corpse of St Francis Xavier from Old Goa to the newly built city of Nova Goa after its completion in 1843, on the site of an older village, Panjim. Instead, the queen argues that the body of Goa's patron saint will be best protected if it remains where it had originally been placed, and so long as it is not in imminent danger. Interestingly, in making her case, she relies on Xavier's historical and religious significance and the state's providence over religious practices to suggest that the body of Xavier should remain where it is – in the church of Bom Jesus, Xavier's 'home'. Only in a last instance, that is, if Xavier's corpse faced possible irreparable damage without recourse to public funds, should it be moved. Thus, even though the capital of Portuguese India had been shifted, its patron saint would not follow suit, remaining in Old Goa, where he had historically lain in state.

Together, these two pieces of legislation point to my larger argument in this chapter concerning the Estado da Índia's increasing reliance on ritual (and its regulation of religiosity) in the face of a ruinous state. I also mention these various exchanges between metropole and colony concerning the regulation of ritual activity in the period leading up to Xavier's display in 1859 to suggest that one way to establish the setting for this set of ritual practices is to contextualize both why such a request was made in the first place on the part of the acting Governor General in 1841 and the reasons for its rejection on the part of the Portuguese queen. In this section, I argue this appeal to continue the 'secularization' of Xavier – by moving his corpse to secular Panjim – is less remarkable if understood within the context of the precarious political, economic, and religious conditions under which the Portuguese ruled Goa during the nineteenth century. In the previous chapter I left the reader with a distinct image of ritual practice in 1782 wherein the Estado da Índia sought to provide proof for Xavier's location in Goa in the 'absent presence' of the Jesuits and sought wider public recognition of Xavier by appealing to this saint's 'secular' qualities. I also suggested that, prior to the turn of the nineteenth century, the Portuguese would have to contend not only with their first native insurrection but also with the domination of the British in India; all these historical threads I take up more explicitly in this chapter, as they help characterize the political and economic instabilities faced by the Portuguese prior to staging ritual in 1859, thus giving shape to ritual itself.

Throughout the nineteenth century, not only did the Estado da Índia continue to operate in a state of decline that had started in the mid-seventeenth century with the steady incursions of the Dutch and English but it was now experiencing the profound political and economic consequences of such a long-term downward spiralling effect. With the overlapping of multiple colonial investments in India starting in the eighteenth century, French imperial interests had quickly turned towards Goa in the wake of Napoleon's recent rise to power and his plan to take over Europe, not excluding Portugal.[6] Since the French were now considered overt 'enemies' of the Portuguese, the latter called upon the British as their 'intimate and old friend' for additional protection, an 'ancient alliance' that had earlier been solidified through marriage in 1662.[7] Not only did the British seize the opportunity to protect their old ally, supposedly with their best interests in mind,[8] but they in effect made Portugal into a British dependency by occupying Goa from 1799 to 1813,[9] an occupancy that, as this chapter will suggest, had long-term unforeseen consequences, many of which will take form during ritual in 1859.[10] Great Britain's glib offer to buy Goa in 1839 for half a million pounds was – not surprisingly – immediately and firmly rejected by the Portuguese.[11]

It was also during this same period that the Portuguese suffered numerous setbacks having to do with frequent native insurrections and the colonial loss of Brazil. These followed on the heels of the Pinto rebellion in 1787, which, although minor in scale and largely unsuccessful,[12] sowed the seeds for multiple criticisms of the Portuguese government in Goa.[13] In addition, a series of Rane Revolts throughout the nineteenth century proved to have far more serious consequences than initially considered.[14] The loss of Brazil as a colony in 1822 and Portugal's denial of this reality for three years only enforced the political and economic instability felt by those in charge in Portuguese India.[15] Together, these numerous internal and external threats having to do with other colonial agendas on Indian soil turned Goa into a heightened military state throughout the nineteenth century.[16] It was now necessary to station numerous regiments at various posts throughout Portuguese India for added protection, levy higher taxes on its citizens in hopes of improving its stagnating economy, and, finally, establish regularized colonial budgets.[17] Lastly, as part of this same initiative to create a more defensive Goa, the fortification of Panjim – again, a project initiated under Pombal – as the official state capital was completed in 1843, but not without a significant drain on the colonial treasury, and the exploitation of many of its colonial subjects.[18]

Throughout these numerous incidents in which Portuguese colonial state-building suffered continual setbacks such that the empire, just like Xavier himself, was now 'shrinking' in size, the Estado da Índia could not fail to recognize the 'permanent settlement' of the British in India,[19] their own political and economic dependence on them as a 'client state',[20] and the resulting transformations in Goan society, despite their earlier and unsuccessful attempt to stave off any British encroachments in Goa.[21] While Pombal's free trade policies had temporarily injected capital into a flailing colonial economy during the late eighteenth century, by the turn of the next century it was only his liberal reforms that outlasted his power and remained his legacy to Goa.[22] Native Catholics were no longer racially barred from entering the secular priesthood; nor were Hindus (of both the Old and New Conquests) persecuted in Goa for their religious beliefs or practices.[23] The bulk of Portuguese dwindling revenues during the nineteenth century were now largely the product of 'unofficial trade'[24] owing to an expanding British monopoly, the bulk of which did not contribute to the Portuguese treasury, but rather stayed in the hands of Goan merchants and middlemen – both Catholic and Hindu – who were involved in such enterprises.[25] The historian Celsa Pinto describes this unofficial trade as 'the linchpin that held together the last *relics* of the Portuguese empire which ultimately enabled the Portuguese in Asia to outlast their competitors'.[26] Lastly, the income of many Goans living in Portuguese India was now supplemented by remittances from Goan family members living in neighbouring British India, emigrants who had left Portuguese India during the British occupation of Goa, seeking better living conditions and an education under the British;[27] this in turn, helped sustain a strong Goan middle class that was both Catholic and Hindu in composition, and that spoke Portuguese and Konkani alternately. It is these two distinct Indo-Portuguese communities (Catholic and Hindu) that will be showcased during ritual in 1859.[28]

Throughout the 1800s Portugal also experienced profound political changes having to do with frequent government overturns in Lisbon[29] – which arguably left less time and energy to oversee the colonies[30] – and continued entanglements with Great Britain even after the end of its occupation of Goa. Soon after the defeat of Napoleon, starting in 1820 a new period of liberal reforms was ushered in in the metropole, and these were not without repercussions in the colony.[31] A civil war at home that was fought between 1828 and 1833 resulted in a final victory for the liberals of Portugal, who brought with them a new era of constitutional reforms and freedom of expression; a feudal legal structure was now replaced with a bourgeois capitalist one in Portugal,[32] and the majority of its citizens were now won over by the ideas of free trade, and less so by the idea of imperial expansion, ideas that had been conveniently impressed upon them by Portugal's ally and mentor – Great Britain – at a time when it clearly benefited Britain's own colonial economy in India.[33] Lastly, the year 1857 marked an important shift in Anglo-Portuguese relations: not only did the British experience their first large-scale native insurrection at this time, its epistemological repercussions for both British and Portuguese forms of colonialism in India profound and long-lasting, but the Portuguese learned a valuable lesson in moderation from their neighbours by assisting them in quelling the Mutiny – hence another reason for their expanded military budget during the second half of the nineteenth century.[34] More importantly, their active assistance renewed their position in India as a colonial power alongside the British and the protection of Portuguese sovereignty by the British in a worst-case scenario,[35] and initiated the building of new roads and telegraph lines between Portuguese India and British India, two aspects that also transformed ritual in 1859.

Just as in earlier historical moments, all of the above shifts in colonial state practices had repercussions in the realm of the church.[36] First, part of Portugal's liberal reforms of the 1820s also involved the dismantling of all remaining religious orders in the Portuguese territories, including those in Goa. This dissolution took effect in 1834 and resulted in a higher number of native secular clergy operating in

Goa.[37] Not only did this move expand on the earlier expulsion of the Jesuits in 1759, but it too would alter the missionary landscape of Goa, and result in continuing tensions between the Padroado and Propaganda, the so-called 'Goan schism'. The signing of the Concordata[38] in 1857 resulted in, among a variety of changes, renewed ties between the Vatican and Portugal, and the right of patronage on the part of the Portuguese Crown to be exercised not only in Portuguese India but also in British India,[39] historical details that, once again, will be showcased during ritual in 1859.

Thus, it is not surprising that in the midst of all these political uncertainties, Anglo-Portuguese ties and tensions, and shifts in state and church policies and practices leading up to ritual, the Governor General of Goa submitted a formal request in 1841 to have the body of Goa's patron saint transferred to Panjim shortly before its inauguration two years later as Portuguese India's new state capital. Specifically, it was because of the decay of Old Goa and the recent buildup of Nova Goa that colonial officials desired to move Xavier to symbolically shore up this new centre of Portuguese power. That the Governor was also invested in continuing the trend to 'secularize' Xavier alongside Goa itself – protecting both precious bodies in the process – makes sense in light of this larger historical context. However, despite the strong reasoning underlying his appeal, perhaps he went too far in his attempt to completely 'secularize' Goa's patron saint: in the end, he was proved wrong by the royal sense of where Xavier belonged, given past incidents as well as the fragility of his corpse. However, considering the uncertainty of the political and economic conditions of the nineteenth century, it also makes sense that in the last instance the queen stipulated in her decree that, if state funds were no longer available to fortify the Church of Bom Jesus, Xavier would be moved, no matter the cost, given his enduring historical significance for Portuguese India.[40]

The second 'Solemn Exposition' of 1859

Characterizing ritual

> In one of the earthquakes, which were frequent in Santiago, capital of Chile, the Episcopal Palace was hit. The Bishop D. Gaspar de Villarcelo was buried underneath the ruins; but when he invoked the Great Apostle of the East Indies, in the moment of collapse, promising to do something in his honour, he was saved from inevitable death; the pious prelate, buried between the ruins, he found that not only was he alive, but neither had he suffered even a minor contusion. In acknowledgement of this miracle, he composed in Latin a hymn to St Francis Xavier.

– Advertisement accompanying *The Historical Summary of the Marvelous Life, Conversions, and Miracles of St Francis Xavier*, by Felippe Neri Xavier, 1860[41]

In 1859 a Catholic Bishop in Santiago (Chile) invoked the name of Goa's patron saint at the moment he was about to be buried alive in an earthquake. He promised that if Xavier came to his rescue he would perform a pious act in his honour. Fortunately, the bishop walked away from the earthquake without a single injury. Shortly thereafter, in recognition of this 'miracle' enacted on his behalf, he composed in Latin a hymn dedicated to St Francis Xavier which was published, alongside the unusual story of how he came to write it, in the popular presses of both Portugal[42] and Goa, including inside Felippe Neri Xavier's 1859 manual on the life, miracles, and conversions of St Francis Xavier, which was publicly sold in Goa during the days of his ritualization. My discussion of the multitude of discourses and diversity of practices that characterize this 'Second Solemn Exposition' is based on information culled largely from Neri's ritual handbook and organized around different foci: setting up ritual; Xavier's corporeality; the balancing role of church and state in resurrecting Goa, including a reading of our eyewitness account; the public and the press, including emergent technologies of industrialization and communication; souvenirs, relics, miracles, and conversions; and, lastly, ritual's closing ceremonies. Each area of focus provides a way to organize the abundance of information available on this exposition,[43] the content itself affording a window on to the more general contours of ritual practice and a glimpse of the many layers of which it is comprised. In setting up my foci as overlapping and mutually constituting, I will suggest that ritual practice in 1859 is very much about the Estado da Índia showcasing certain colonial strengths to a larger and more diverse audience in the face of a ruinous state, resurrecting Xavier and Goa simultaneously, and setting up a model of a historical state in the process.

Setting up ritual: preliminary exchanges

Several exchanges between metropole and colony concerning the staging of a 'Second Solemn Exposition' of St Francis Xavier in 1859 point to some of the preliminary steps taken on the part of the Estado da Índia to realize ritual practice. I detail them here in order to suggest what was at stake for a colonial state bent on promoting Xavier's (and Goa's) resurrection. In the first of these exchanges, the Governor General of Goa writes to the king of Portugal on 28 May 1859, requesting his authorization to stage an exposition in the days following Xavier's saint day of 3 December.[44] In his response, by way of the Secretary of State of Overseas Business, the king gives his authorization (on 11 July

1859) to do so as long as the state takes the necessary precautions to ensure that the venerable remains of Xavier 'do not suffer any damage' and that proper order is maintained among the 'numerous meetings of the faithful'.[45] A second exchange, dated 19 August 1859, further elaborates on the nature of this particular exposition, suggesting that all inhabitants of India will be enthusiastically welcomed to participate in the festivities, regardless of sex, age, or religion, and that these solemnities will be unlike anything seen before and on a much grander scale.[46] Lastly, a third notice in August announces plans to print a state-commissioned book dedicated exclusively to St Francis Xavier, and the overwhelming public interest in obtaining a copy well in advance of its actual publication.[47] Together, these three exchanges – all conveniently reprinted in Neri's ritual manual – confirm that state officials were heavily invested in staging a second exposition centred on Xavier's corpse to display colonial order and power, continuing a ritual trend set up initially in 1782;[48] however, clearly a different set of colonial concerns were at stake in 1859 in order to ensure its success.

Corporeality: lost keys, the 'shrinking' corpse

In the months preceding Goa's second exposition, the Governor General set up numerous specialized committees to oversee a variety of ritual practices, the first of which involved examining the corpse of Xavier to determine whether or not he was fit for public exposure, a measure that earlier had been authorized by King Dom Pedro V of Portugal. Interestingly, the three keys to his casket that had been so carefully guarded by church dignitaries and state officials throughout the eighteenth century, and which had been placed, after the expulsion of the Jesuits, in the hands of three distinct officers in order to guard against indiscreet openings of his coffin, had now disappeared – 'no one knowing how or when exactly' in these turbulent times.[49] A new lock was quickly issued and keys placed in the desk of the Chief Secretary to Government, a desk which required its own set of four keys to be opened, thus ensuring the added protection of the precious keys to Xavier's casket.[50]

Here I reproduce for the reader the contents of the medical report which was performed on 12 October 1859, the details of which were published and circulated via a government bulletin for Goa's (reading) public two days later.

> Following in the year of the birth of our Lord Jesus Christ in 1859 on 12 October, at 10:00 am in the Church of Bom Jesus, the Professed House of the Fathers of the Jesuits, situated in the ancient city of Old Goa, where the Tomb with the body of St Francis Xavier is found, the Illustrious His Excellency Sr Visconde de Torres Novas, Governor General of the

Estado da Índia, the Interim Governor of the Archbishop of Goa, the Senate of the State, Municipal Chamber of the Advisory of the Islands, and other Corporations, Authorities, and Chiefs of Public Distributions of this State under which they are assigned, arrived, having all been invited to attend the opening of the said Tomb in order to know in which state the Body of the same Saint is found, by virtue of the authority connected by his Majesty by decree of the Ministry of Overseas Business (No. 100 of July of the past year). And then the keys that exist in the hands of the Secretariat were presented to open the coffin, in which is located the body of the said Saint, which was found dressed in sacerdotal vestment; and the doctors, comprising the Board of Health, the Physician in Residence, Eduardo de Freitas e Almeida, the Surgical Resident, José António de Oliviera, and the Surgeon of 1st Class, António José da Gama, proceeds to examine the same Body. They found the cranium with its scalp, still with hair but only a little, and completely bare on the left side. The face, all covered with withered skin and dark in colour, had an opening on the right side, communicating with the maxillary sinus on the same side, which appeared to correspond with the bruise referred to in the report of 1 January 1782. Of the front teeth only one of the lower incisors is wanting. Both the ears exist, but the right arm is wanting. The left hand, including the nails, is entire, just as it is described in the abovementioned report of 1782. The abdominal walls are covered with an integument dried up and somewhat dark in colour, the abdominal cavity not containing any intestines. The feet are covered with an integument equally dried up and dark in colour, the prominence of the tendons being distinctly marked. The fourth and fifth toes of the right foot are wanting. Some remnants of the integument and phalanges of one of these toes are in a spongy condition. In view of which they agreed that the Body and Relics of the same Saint were in a state of being able to be exposed to the public for veneration in order to excite and augment the devotion of the people and of all that is referred, I, Christovão Sebastião Xavier, Official Major of the Secretariat of this State, made this Document, which is signed by all the Corporations and above mentioned authorities. And I Joaquim Heliodoro da Cunha Rivara, Secretariat wrote this. (Signed) Visconde de Torres Novas – the Governor General, Caetano João Peres – Interim Archbishop, José de Vasconcellos Guedes de Carvalho, Interim President of the Senate of Goa. Eduardo de Freitas e Almeida, Doctor in Residence and Member of the Advisory to the Government, José António de Oliveira, Surgical Resident of this State, António José de Gama, Surgeon of the First Class, Agostinho Ferreira de Brito, Head Chief of the Military Distribution, António Luiz Lobato de Faria, Coronel of the Supreme Council, Fernando Luiz Leite de Souza e Noronha, Coronel of the Supreme Council, Francisco da Costa Mendes, Secretary of the Board of Treasury and Effective Member of the Advisory Council, António José Pereira, Canon of the See Cathedral, and Vicar General of the Archbishop, António Faustino dos Santos Crespo, Justice of the Right of the Chamber of the Islands, serving the Senate,

Candido José Mourão Garcez Palha, Chief Engineer and Inspector of Public Works, etc.[51]

With the examination of 1782 serving as a point of reference, the content of this medical report performed seventy-seven years later mirrors its predecessor in that Xavier's body is found to be in a certain state of 'corruption', but still 'fit' enough for public veneration. The purpose underlying both public displays is the same: 'to augment the devotion of the people'. However, the details of this later autopsy report are also quite distinct from the former given the changing historical circumstances. First, this medical examination is performed by three trained physicians – two specializing in surgery and thus with an intimate knowledge of the human body – and in the presence of members of Goa's Board of Health. The content of this report reveals a thorough knowledge of body parts, and their respective functions and is couched in a language of medical expertise.[52] Second, a noticeably larger audience is in attendance at this opening, which is treated much more like a semi-public event, including this time not only Governor General Torres Nova[53] and Interim Archbishop João Peres (who occupies the position of Administrator of the Church of Bom Jesus and now in charge of Xavier's management) but, in addition, members representing numerous state organizations – including the military and the Senate – as well as the Chief Engineer of Public Works, each person or group's attendance ritually significant. Present at Xavier's medical examination are two additional key figures who will continue to figure prominently in this set of ritual practices: Joaquim Heliodor Cunha de Rivara – the Secretariat and Director of the Goa Archives – and Felippe Neri Xavier – who has already been introduced as Director of Goa's Press and the author of the *Resumo Historico da Maravilhosa Vida, Conversoes, e Milagres de S. Francisco Xavier, Apostolo, Defensor, e Patrono das Índias*, which includes a copy of Xavier's autopsy report. Third, the findings of the medical report reveal that it is no longer the 'body' but the 'Body and Relics' of St Francis Xavier that are to be exposed for public view, a linguistic detail that suggests that the corruption of Xavier is now recognized and historicized in the very act of labelling them 'relics'. Lastly, there are informal lingering concerns over the height of Xavier's body as 'below the average height of a man'.[54] However, this qualifier is soon determined to be reasonable, as a result of his natural 'shrinking' over time.[55]

On 10 November 1859 Governor General Torres Nova issued a final decree from his residence in Panjim approving the festivities surrounding the 'precious mortal remains of the Apostle of India' but with several qualifications: that the colonial state should take the necessary precautions in order to ensure that Xavier's body does not suffer any damage on the occasion of his 'public veneration'; that the best possible order is maintained in the face of a large crowd of ritual participants; and, finally, that the specially designed programme be strictly adhered to during the days of the saint's exposition.[56]

Resurrecting Goa

> It seems that the ancient city of Goa [in 1859] has been raised from its ruins, alive, animated, flourishing as it was when it was an emporium of the Orient.[57]

During these turbulent times, the Estado da Índia went to elaborate and excessive lengths to resurrect Old Goa both physically and ideologically. This was achieved by setting up various commissions to oversee the implementation and management of a variety of ritual practices, and by using the role of the press to publicize the many details of ritual. These organs were set up in a manner that not only simultaneously resurrected Xavier by paying homage to him as a 'secularized' figure but also laboured hard to represent Portuguese India as harmoniously unified, politically and religiously, to an outsider public.

Thus, with Portugal's royal approval to stage an exposition now granted – the necessary (state) funds provided six months earlier in July 1859 and with a budget far exceeding past events[58] – and Xavier's corpse medically proven capable of public veneration a month earlier, colonial state officials set up numerous committees to oversee a variety of ritual practices, all of which had been formally approved by the Governor General and managed by the Municipal Council of Goa.[59] One of the first concerns was to make Old Goa – particularly since it had by now been mostly abandoned by its dwindling populace for Nova Goa – more visibly attractive for its diverse visiting public, and included directives to increase the lighting and cleanliness of the city, in an appeal to make it appear more *civilized*.[60] Colonial organizers also commissioned an orchestra to be set up in Old Goa to perform during the days of the exposition,[61] and formed a separate committee to oversee the overall improvement of the structure of the Church of Bom Jesus, Xavier's chapel, including its surrounding grounds. Candles and music were installed inside in order to create a decorative atmosphere;[62] additional directives included the cleaning – inside and out – of the coffin which housed Xavier's corpse;[63] removing the shrubs that hedged Xavier's chapel – 'with a view to render it easily accessible';[64] cleaning the pieces of silver which adorned the outside of Xavier's coffin; draping a scarlet velvet cloth newly arrived from Europe on the outside of his coffin; and placing a new damask cloth in the inside of his coffin.[65] This same commission was also put in charge of overseeing any additional 'important arrangements' deemed necessary to fortify Old Goa: these included putting a fresh coat of paint on the fronts of the houses of three neighbourhoods located on the main street leading to the Church of Bom Jesus as well as placing lights in the front windows of each of these same houses to be illuminated at night 'as it [is] done in Europe and some cities in Asia'.[66] All of these state directives were to be posted and published by the Goa National Press so as to ensure the compliance of its public with its rules and regulations both in advance of and continuing through the days of ritual.[67]

During the same month of November 1859, a different commission was set up to oversee press activities.[68] Once again, it is the Director of the Goa National Press, Felippe Neri Xavier, who is put in charge of publishing a 'popular hymn' dedicated to this saint in order to advertise the forthcoming event and to 'satisfy the desires of the devotees who solicit[ed] this publication'.[69] Copies of Neri's ritual manual,[70] alongside various other items dedicated to Xavier, were to be sold inside the Press Pavilion, a temporary structure set up directly outside the front door of the Church of Bom Jesus. An official programme for the exposition was to be printed simultaneously by Goa's National Press in Portuguese, English, and Marathi.[71] Meanwhile, Governor General Torres Nova ordered a separate committee to receive and manage the donations that they would potentially receive during the exposition,[72] and requested a battery of soldiers with artillery to fortify Goa's borders, and stand guard during the days of the exposition.[73]

With the preparations complete, on 3 December at 10 a.m. the bells in each church of Goa were rung three times while artillery was fired from the forts in and around Goa.[74] According to Neri, a moment of 'respectful silence' was witnessed immediately afterwards by all those in attendance – including the author himself as well as the visiting Father Alexis Canoz, whose eyewitness testimony I discuss next – because they were filled with such 'emotion' on the cusp of the official opening of the 'Second Solemn Exposition' of St Francis Xavier.[75]

On 30 November – a few days prior to the start of Xavier's exposition – colonial officials warmly marked the arrival of Dr Alexis Canoz, Vicar Apostolic of Madurai and Administrator of Bombay, with full civil and military honours.[76] Canoz had sailed to Goa from Bombay by way of a formal invitation from Portuguese colonial officials to witness this momentous occasion firsthand.[77] In Goa itself and throughout the festivities, Canoz was accompanied by the Reverends Gard and Charmillot, two other Vicars Apostolic representing different constituents on the Indian subcontinent who had arrived in Goa via a new road.[78] In the few days leading up to the festivities, Canoz was given a royal tour of Goa (Velha and Nova)[79] with the intention that he would preside over the 'opening ceremonies' – specifically, he was assigned the prestigious task of singing the solemn High Mass[80] – thus temporarily filling the vacant position of the Archbishopric of Goa.[81]

Canoz's meticulously recorded impressions of the ceremony were published simultaneously in a Bombay journal and in Neri's commissioned book, with the intention that they would also be circulated for a larger European audience. Here the role of the press cannot be underestimated in producing and circulating certain images of Goa in this era of new technologies of industrialization and communication. Thus, Canoz's eyewitness description of the opening ceremonies not only allows us access to the world of ritual activity but illuminates the level of investment (and anxiety) on the part of colonial officials in showcasing Goa as a spiritual haven of sorts, its religiosity represented as a colonial strength during the exposition. However, Canoz's testimony simultaneously reveals additional ritual layers, for this ecclesiastical official was also a member of the Society of Jesus who happened to be visiting Goa on the centenary of its suppression from Portuguese India.[82] His eyewitness account will also reveal continuing tensions between various religious interests competing in Goa – specifically those between the Padroado and the Propaganda, despite the signing of the Concordata in 1857.

Here I reproduce for the reader a copy of Alexis Canoz's impressions of the opening ceremonies of 3 December 1859, as they were recorded by him a week later from his home in Bombay for the *Bombay Catholic Examiner*, and reprinted courtesy of Neri.

> I make haste to communicate to you all the ineffable consolation that providence bestowed on me in a style totally unexpected, next to the tomb of St Francis Xavier, whose sacred corpse is exposed during this month to public veneration of the faithful, having been exposed the last time in 1782 ... Finally the great day of the feast of St Francis Xavier arrived, and it was solemnly announced majestically by the bells of the Cathedral, and in all the churches of the city and by the cannons of artillery. The prepared troops for this occasion marched in line preceded by their music, in order to be in front of the Church of Bom Jesus, and they took their positions on the street, where the Governor would pass; the canons of the Cathedral, and the clergy already having gone to the chapel of the Monument to wait for His Excellency. It was later that he arrived, at 10 o'clock exactly, he left the procession, and crossing the long corridor of the cloister he entered the church. The coffin was levitated underneath the canopy by six Canons covered in capes, and followed by the Governor – his position most important – and all the civil businessmen and military of the State, who had congregated for this beautiful ceremony. The procession stopped next relatively close to the

grilles of the cross, where the coffin was opened and the lid removed. Then the body of the saint, prepared in order to be exposed for view, had been placed inside the coffin, and immediately a solemn mass was sung with music, that was interrupted by a panegyric to the Apostle of India. The Interim Administrator of the Archdiocese had disposed for us a place on the platform, from where we could see the procession. It was impossible to hear even one word of the sermon because of the great distance between us and the preacher and because of the rustle of people that bustled forward and came to the sacred tomb, without paying any attention to the preacher whom they could not comprehend. I was informed that he asked for three 'Ave Marias' at the end of the sermon, one for the king, the other for the Governor, and the third for the Bishop present at the ceremony. The Goans pretended that I prayed with them for the *Padroado* which the Preacher did not mention. The Governor seemed discontent for me that I had not been offered a place of honor on the presbytery. Nevertheless, I for my part was very satisfied with what had been destined for me since I was most able to leisurely pray in the presence of the tomb of the Saint. The Mass was concluded, one of the officials of the Church came looking for me and my two companions, Father Gard and Father Charmillot, who had arrived from Belgao the preceding day, in order to introduce us into the sanctuary at the moment at which started the act of kissing the feet of the saint. I can't express to you all, my Reverend Father, the emotion and sentiments of happiness and fortune that I experienced when I touched with my lips the sacred feet, that walked in so many remote countries, treading many times in this land of India, preaching alike to so many deranged nations submerged in the darkness of idolatry the new happiness of peace and salvation. In as much as we helped in the ceremony, it was so pathetic, but I considered myself a deputy in the name of all of the Society (Jesuits), and I prayed with all the fervor of which I was capable by the Church, and its Head, in the painful circumstances, in which it is believed to be actual, for all of the Society and for that which governs it; for the extinction of the Schism and for our mission in India and China united in my heart of Madurai and Bombay; and imploring for our missionaries the apostolic spirit of St Francis Xavier and the favor of conversion for the nations of India; reciting devotedly the beautiful oration of the Apostle Saint ... Not being satisfied with my first view and kiss, I returned there in the afternoon, and on the following day where it was private, having spoken of this already to Canon Pereira, Vicar General, who was in charge of presiding over on Sunday the veneration of the saint's relics. I spoke also about this business matter to the Administrator of the Diocese, and afterwards to the Secretary of the Government, and I could thus pursue my desire. It happened that they forgot to make use of a tray that moved around by wheels in order to facilitate the daily movement of the coffin, in which rested the body, before and after the act of being kissed. The hour of my day was fixed for the operation of restituting to its place that body, and I was invited to help in the act with my two companions. You

> can imagine that I was punctual at the designated hour. There we found some qualified persons and some privileged ladies, I myself helped to raise the precious load, that was posted in the path in front of the coffin, in a manner that gave rise to a perfect occasion to contemplate the body of the Saint. Nevertheless, we could discern the features of that heroic face, that for three centuries was not enough to remove. The skin was a little darkish, the mouth a little open, under which to see the teeth; the lips, the nose, and the forehead of the head are completely distinguishable; he seemed to have some white hairs on his head connected by the skin; the head is a little raised, and rests on top of a pillow; the left arm covered with a sleeve of a tunic of precious cloth, and all the hand is bare and the shrunken fingers separated from one another. His feet conserve perfectly their form and have all their toes except the two minor of his right foot that were removed. The proper nails are visible. One of three physicians who examined the body of the saint on the 12th of last October, on the first preliminary opening informed me that he had feared disappointment, but that he promptly was pacified. He told me that he found the skin of the interior abdomen and it was without deterioration. He attributed the shortness of the corpse, that was only 4.5 feet in length, to the disappearance of various cartilages. I have given these particulars because I am certain that they will be of interest to you all, and so that you can read them, without doubt that you begrudge me the opportunity to have seen with my own eyes these relics, that have been miraculously preserved, preaching to us even now in the most eloquent manner of penitence and mortification, showing us here on earth the glory of crucified members in the service of God, in anticipation of the day of his glorious resurrection.[83]

Alexis Canoz's valuable testimony, circulated thereafter in Goa, Bombay, and parts of Europe, reveals the Estado da Índia's representation of itself on stage to a wider audience. Our visitor's account first speaks to the elaborate preparations and various committees that were organized beforehand to ensure ritual's success. Canoz highlights the 'majestic' ringing of bells in Goa's cathedrals, the firing of cannons of artillery, the marching of 'prepared' troops, and the playing of music as all contributing to this 'beautiful ceremony'. In addition, Canoz reveals the privileged position that he himself was accorded during the festivities, Goa's Governor General providing him and his two colleagues with an elevated platform to stand on – a position which affords him a 'leisurely' place to pray and view the entirety of the procession that was unfolding before his eyes. He is also given a privileged position later on during the solemnities, wherein he is allowed to assist in moving the precious coffin and corpse of Xavier.

Canoz's testimony also provides a window on to the prominent position given to state officials, particularly the Governor General, throughout the days of ritual. During the initial procession to Old Goa, every other group is assigned a particular position on the road leading to the church of Bom Jesus; each awaits 'His Excellency' to pass. It is Governor General Torres Nova who enters the church first – his position 'most important' according to Canoz[84] – followed by other state dignitaries, businessmen, and members of the military. Canoz also highlights the religiosity of this second exposition; he details musical performances, the ringing of church bells, numerous sermons dedicated to Xavier, and fervent praying on the part of the public, including Canoz himself. He also describes the overwhelming feeling of emotion and sentiment he personally felt upon touching his lips to the 'sacred feet' of Xavier. Lastly, he includes a summary of the medical findings that earlier sanctioned his public exposure, and for the benefit of those readers who might not have access to them otherwise, 'certain that they will be of interest to you all'. Nor does he want Xavier's (reading) public to 'begrudge me the opportunity to have seen with my own eyes these relics'. Canoz's testimony is unusual, relative to past eyewitness accounts (in 1554, 1624, and 1782), in that he directly appeals to his audience for sympathy and support of Xavier's exposition.

Meanwhile, Canoz's representation of this event is complicated by his dual positions as a Vicar Apostolic and member of the Jesuit order. Thus, on the one hand, Canoz's testimony reveals that, despite the signing in 1857 of the Concordata in which Portugal was given the right to oversee and manage its missions in both Portuguese India and British India (interestingly, a copy of this agreement was posted during the exposition itself)[85] tensions between the Portuguese Padroado and the Vatican Propaganda – the 'Goan Schism' as it was called – were far from resolved, not only to the extent that they were visible in the ritual arena.[86] On the other hand, he considers himself a 'deputy' of the Jesuits: while in Goa he feels compelled to write a separate letter in aid of the Jesuit cause, and addressed to the General of the Society of Jesus.[87] Within the body of this letter, he asserts the legacy of the Jesuits in Goa today, and prays for the (return of the) Society of Jesus, a religious order which, by this time, was quietly but steadfastly being reinstalled in certain posts in India, but only through the permission of the Vatican. In the remaining days before his departure, Canoz requests and is granted permission to visit several Jesuit sites in and around Goa.[88] On his last day, before setting sail for Bombay, Canoz returns to the Church of Bom Jesus to venerate Xavier's corpse one last time before sitting down for a final breakfast with Governor General Torres Nova at his residence in Nova Goa.[89]

The public and the press: accommodating diversity, technologies of industrialization and communication

We are directed finally to the square of the Church of Bom Jesus, passing by an infinity of carts, wagons, and horses, etc., which were parked in its vicinity, and in the front an armed force in great Portuguese uniform formed a square around the church and extended the length of the street which led to the Arsenal. The wide square of which we speak, the royal main road was at the side, and the long road in front were completely inundated with an immensity of people who occupied these places, placing themselves in an amphitheatre-like manner, some on the ground of the main road below, others on the steps of the square, and the majority on an elevated plane, until the wall of the centre of the Resident City it was reached, and the windows of the choir of the Temple [Church of Bom Jesus], and the contiguous house crammed full with people, this multitude including everything – men, women, children – Nationals and Strangers thrown together in this way, the religion and class to which they pertain forgotten. Christians, Gentiles [Hindus], Moors, Parsis, Gugires or Batias, Nacuas, Parias, Farazes, Chingalas, Malavares, Negros, and other diverse classes making up that great tide were distinguished by their clothing, some extravagantly dressed. The devotees of these diverse religions were invited to join to venerate the former Defender of India [Xavier] and were united in dutiful respect to the great man, whose corpse was to be seen. They came together without repugnance in this way in spite of their beliefs and inveterate prejudices, bearing in mind that the Apostle Saint in his missions, conversion, and miracles did not attend to differences in religion, class, and colour, we read in his Life Story. – F. Neri Xavier, *Resumo Historico*[90]

In 1859 the Estado da Índia continued a trend initiated in 1782 to 'secularize' the figure of Xavier. In the months preceding ritual, colonial officials had set up various committees to invite, plan, and manage the 'public' that would be in attendance at the 'Second Solemn Exposition' of St Francis Xavier; they did so in the hopes of attracting and accommodating a larger and more diverse group – diverse with regard to race, gender, and religion – and in order to contribute to the larger process of resurrection of saint and state. From the above description, it is evident that the public in attendance in 1859 was incredibly varied – representing in some sense the complexities of the Portuguese colonizing enterprise in Goa during the second half of the nineteenth century as well as its troubled links with British India.

The Portuguese first sought to encourage the attendance of a large number of ritual participants by way of new technologies of industrialization developed during this era of metropolitan liberal reform. In communicating news of the upcoming exposition of Xavier's corpse, colonial officials now relied on the telegraph that had been installed in

Goa two years earlier, and which, in turn, enabled faster communication between distant places throughout India and allowed for advance advertising of this event.[91] In addition, the port of Panjim (now Nova Goa) was utilized to receive boatloads of visitors,[92] and a new and improved road established between British India and Portuguese India enabled a larger number of people from distant locations the opportunity to see Xavier's corpse and this model Portuguese colony for the first time.[93] Interestingly, an 'industrial exposition' – the first of its kind – was staged in Goa in the days following Xavier's 'closing ceremonies', an advertisement for it conveniently included in a Bombay notice for Xavier's display in 1859.[94]

The Goa National Press had a central defining role in disseminating information regarding this second exposition to the public.[95] Not only was a complete programme of ritual's day-to-day activities as well as a pastoral letter printed on 26 November 1859 made available for free distribution[96] but the Director of Goa's press, Felippe Neri Xavier, alongside Joaquim Heliodoro Rivara da Cunha, the Secretary of State and Director of the Goa Archives, had been put in charge of recording all the ritual practices that marked this exposition for a state-commissioned commemorative book,[97] also the source material that I rely on for my analysis. Two thousand five hundred copies of this first edition were available for sale at the opening of the exposition inside the Pavilion of the National Press.[98] In Madras, an English version of Neri's ritual manual was also published, which in turn suggests an interest on the part of the Estado da Índia in publicizing and thus making accessible the details of Xavier's exposition to a larger English-speaking public located outside Goa.[99] Lastly, various presses located throughout the Indian subcontinent and Portugal published an assortment of advertisements, eyewitness accounts, summaries, etc. of the solemnities as they were taking place in Goa.[100]

Colonial officials also sought to encourage and accommodate the diversity of the public through a variety of additional ritual measures. Not only were sermons and masses delivered in a variety of languages including Portuguese and English as well as various Indian languages,[101] but facilities – mostly tents – were set up to house the many people who had travelled long distances to arrive in Goa during the days of festivities.[102] As an expanding public arrived in Goa in the first weeks of the exposition, the original programme was modified to allow those attending into the Church of Bom Jesus throughout the day up until late night and without a midday closing.[103] However, these additional measures were not enough to satisfy the public's demands to touch Xavier's corpse, according to our Director of the National Press. Neri describes the 'displeasure' that many people experienced after being turned away at the front doors of the Church of Bom Jesus, particularly since they had travelled long distances, many arriving in Goa from such far away places as the Madras Presidency in British India, and having heard incredible stories about Xavier's many miracles along the way.[104] While some members of the public were content to hear sermons that were preached for their benefit in the grounds of the church, others refused to leave Goa without at the very least a sighting of Xavier's corpse.[105] Instead, they found refuge for a few days in the vestibule of a small chapel dedicated to Xavier that was located on the now deserted grounds of the Old (Jesuit) College of St Paul. Some chose to drink water from two stagnant pools located nearby while others sang hymns and awaited entrance into the Church of Bom Jesus.[106] According to Neri, it was during this waiting period that several individuals saw an 'apparition' of Xavier washing his own feet and drinking water from these same pools of water, a 'story' that was later testified to by additional participants and noted by church and state officials.[107]

In response to such overwhelming dissatisfaction on the part of the public, the Governor General sought and gained royal approval to extend the duration of the exposition beyond its initial closing date of 1 January 1860.[108] By official decree on Christmas Day – 25 December 1859 – the exposition was extended until 8 January[109] (now thirty-seven days in its entirety) owing to an inability to accommodate the large throngs of people who, colonial officials quickly realized, had to sometimes wait up to two or three days before they were allowed in, or alternatively were turned away at the doors of the Church of Bom Jesus.[110] Just as colonial officials reportedly accommodated the public's desire to extend ritual's length, they accommodated the public's interest in obtaining copies of Neri's ritual manual, the announcement of the printing and sale of a second edition made at roughly the same time since the first run of 2,500 copies had sold out during the first twenty days of the exposition.[111]

The number of attendants was estimated to be approximately two hundred thousand persons, a remarkable five to six thousand visitors per day.[112] Both Catholic and Hindu Goans – male and female, young and old – were also in attendance at this exposition.[113] Meanwhile, many diasporic (Hindu and Catholic) Goans now living in British India had travelled to Old Goa for the purpose of renewing ties with their homeland and their patron saint.[114] Colonial subjects from Daman and Diu also attended the festivities, thus ritually linking these three 'shrinking' Portuguese enclaves surrounded by a larger British India.[115] In addition, a large group of Christian pilgrims from both India and neighbouring Sri Lanka attended the 'Second Solemn Exposition' for the first time, their participation encouraged and enabled by the newly established telegraph and road systems, and the state's accommodation of their language differences.[116] These pilgrims came not only to visit the Church of Bom Jesus but to see additional sites that Xavier had visited during his lifetime. Lastly, numerous eyewitness accounts included in the popular presses of both Portuguese India and British India reveal that a large number of visitors from various locations on the Indian subcontinent had come for the sole purpose of seeing the body of St Francis Xavier and the site that was witness to the incredible biography of his corpse.[117] Accordingly, not only were persons of various 'religious' backgrounds – Christian, Jewish, Protestant, Muslim, Parsi – in attendance, but also persons of a variety of 'national' backgrounds – British, French, Portuguese, Indian, Chinese, Mongol, etc.[118] Together, this large and diverse group of people not only confronted, imagined, and analysed each other in the arena of ritual – sometimes reinforcing and other times subverting categories of race, class, nation, and religion in the process – but, more importantly, from the perspective of the *Estado*, they were witness to the 'resurrection' of saint and state.

Colonial officials were also invested in sanctioning only certain acts of devotion during ritual, in the hopes of policing the borders of ritual activity and preventing 'indiscreet acts of veneration' focused on Xavier's corpse which might cause very real physical damage to it.[119] Members of the public were expected to follow certain rules inside the Church of Bom Jesus, restrictions that included observing silence inside the holy chapel of the saint (particularly during the recitation of rosaries) donating funds for the maintenance of this former Jesuit church, providing offerings in the name of Xavier, and following the directives of the guards stationed at the entry and exit doors of the church.[120] Colonial officials also determined that they could not elevate Xavier's coffin for a better frontal view because such an action would impede the public's view of a side altar. Instead, Xavier's coffin remained in its original position with members of the public expected to crouch down in order to see the corpse from its two sides.[121] Lastly, saint veneration was to be expressed through one simple act of devotion by members of the public: the kissing of Xavier's feet, interestingly, a practice forbidden to the general public but reserved for members of the nobility during his 'First Solemn Exposition' staged in 1782. Only now, in 1859, participants were allowed to kiss his feet 'multiple times' – despite the fragile condition of his corpse; this was considered proper veneration for a saint, rather than an act of 'indiscreet devotion', a detail which directly indexes the state's more willing acquiescence to public desires during his second exposition.[122]

Taken together, the diversity of the public present in Goa as well as the Portuguese accommodation of this diversity in ritual suggests that the 'Second Solemn Exposition' was very much about minimizing, accepting, and celebrating certain 'differences' simultaneously. On the one hand, distinctions between Christians of various sects as well as those between different European nationals were blurred during the exposition. More significantly, the differences between all Goans, regardless of caste, class, location, or religious status, were being minimized through the ritual process, an unified and idealized Indo-Portuguese 'culture' successfully represented on stage for a larger public that too was the product of various colonizing and missionizing projects throughout the Indian subcontinent. In other words, the Estado da Índia hoped to stabilize Goa's identity first and foremost as a Portuguese colony in the midst of an encompassing and encroaching British presence in India by showcasing the uniqueness and endurance of their 'culture' as a colonial and missionary legacy. On the other hand, certain differences were being magnified but accepted in the space of ritual in the hope of representing Goa through ritual as simultaneously a thriving centre of Catholic faith on the Indian subcontinent and a spiritual haven not only tolerant of people of distinct classes, races, religions, and castes but accepting of their 'differences'. In the end, it is 'diversity' – another word for 'difference' – that both defines and is defined by the public in attendance at Xavier's 'Second Solemn Exposition', and that is showcased as a uniquely Portuguese colonial strength in 1859.

Trafficking in 'supernatural commerce':[123] *souvenirs, relics, miracles, and conversions*

The Estado da Índia promoted and extended the efficacy of Xavier's corpse in serving Goa's growing spiritualism – despite his evident 'shrinking' – through a variety of methods (old and new) in the space of ritual in 1859. The saint's powers are now displaced on to both inanimate and animate objects through the power of contact and contagion: on to the former by way of 'souvenirs' and 'relics' that are sold to the public on the sidelines of ritual and the latter by way of 'miracles' of healing and acts of 'conversion' involving members of the public. Here I suggest that a diverse public was sustained through certain technologies of industrialization – the press, telegraph, and roads. Discourses of souvenirs, relics, miracles, and conversions – the above story gleaned from Neri's ritual manual serving as a typical example – were also enabled by these same technologies, since they allowed them to travel, thus taking on meaning in multiple places for numerous individuals, located inside and outside Goa, and during and after the event of ritual.

First, a special committee was organized to oversee the production of a variety of 'relics' to be sold during the days of ritual activity from inside a temporary structure set up in Old Goa for this sole purpose. However, the manner by which inanimate objects officially became 'relics' and came to be sold in the Pavilion of the National Press[124] was a process initially instigated by the public but, in the end, co-opted by the colonial state, a detail that confirms, once again, the expanding role of the public during Xavier's second exposition. On 17 November 1859 the Director of the National Press, the same Felippe Neri Xavier of earlier ritual moments, sought out and received permission from Goa's Governor General for a 'secret' opening of Xavier's tomb (separate from his medical examination) in order to render an 'accurate' drawing of his corpse, produce an official image in Xavier's 'likeness', and obtain his proper measurements to be used in producing a variety of souvenirs to be sold at the National Pavilion.[125] State permission was duly granted so long as Xavier did not 'suffer any damages' and Neri took every 'precaution' along the way.[126] This image of Xavier was later reproduced on stamps, medals, and coins which, in turn, alongside other items such as rosaries and miniature wax body parts, would be sold as 'official' souvenirs at the site of the Pavilion to members of the public, many of whom would be returning to their places of origin with these souvenirs – a trace of their experience – in hand by way of the improved road system that connected Goa to various parts of British India.[127]

Members of the public were sanctioned to kiss Xavier's feet when they filed past his corpse and casket. Interestingly, it was during this procession that members of the public first became desirous of producing their own 'relics' of Xavier by touching personal items, things found on hand such as 'handkerchiefs, coins, paper, and even cotton' to his corpse when they filed past his tomb.[128] This practice had been initially discouraged by colonial officials because it both potentially caused further damage to Xavier's already fragile corpse, and moved the authority of defining 'relics' from the state into the hands of the public.[129] Colonial officials, however, in an about face, then decided to take charge of this popular practice, touching certain items to the 'head, [left] hand, and feet'[130] of the saint's corpse in order to more carefully control, authenticate, and mediate the practice of relic worship in 1859;[131] these official souvenirs and relics were then sold at the National Pavilion.

At the same time that the efficacy of Xavier's corpse is transferred on to relic objects, this saint's powers are also displaced on to animate things by way of miracles of healing and acts of conversion. Once again, it is through the power of touch – contact with the saint's corpse –

that members of the public are cured of chronic illnesses or converted to Catholicism. Here I argue that these discourses of miracles and conversions enable the colonial state to spread Xavier's powers – and by extension Goa's powers – beyond the borders of this Portuguese colony by involving a diverse audience that includes both Catholics and non-Catholics, and is spread via the same technologies of industrialization – the press and the roads – used to promote the popularity of relic worship. The profiles of the individuals involved in these miracles and conversions will reveal yet another layer of the diversity of the Goan public (Catholic and Hindu) in attendance during ritual.

Included in Neri's ritual manual are descriptions of the many 'offerings' given in the name of Xavier in the hope of curing a variety of chronic afflictions[132] as well as eight 'healings' that took place during the exposition at the site of Xavier's corpse, all of them classified as 'miracles' not only by the Director of the National Press but by church and state officials alike after an outside commission was set up to verify their authenticity.[133] Neri provides the details of these eight miraculous healings which were widely publicized in the popular press:

> 1. João Thomaz Fernandes, son of Pedro Fernandes and Mariana Fernandes, resident of Panjim, 9 years old, born with a defective left foot. On December 13, he arrived at the Temple [Church of Bom Jesus]. He was accompanied by his mother who lifted him to kiss Xavier's feet, and in this act he felt a pain in his leg, which continued until he left the church, but he was thinking he was tired from the journey. He woke up the next day without the defect in his foot. The incident was published in the Gazettes and he was examined by doctors who recognized it as a miracle.
>
> 2. D. Maria Antonia da Costa Campos, daughter of Coronel Francisco da Costa Campos, and D. Maria Antonia de Mattos e Goes, resident of Panjim, 13 years old. She had a serious illness in 1855, loss of feeling and movement in her extremities on the right side until the lumbar region, her foot extended to her leg, it was flexed at the thigh. She tried all sorts of cures to no avail, she still couldn't walk. She kissed the feet of Xavier for the first time; afterwards she heard of the miracle of João Thomaz Fernandes, and went back again with hope to obtain an equal grace. On 26 December, she went a second time to kiss Xavier's feet; she felt a violent pain in her body (where it had suffered), she then recovered her feeling and started to walk with both feet, even today she is perfectly cured and has total movement. She changed her name to D. Maria Antonia Francisca Xavier da Costa Campos. This miracle was less publicized than the first one.
>
> 3. Maria Isabel de Sousa, daughter of Caetano de Sousa, and Luísa Maria Rodrigues, of Candolim, married, 19 years of age. She suffered from an inflammation of the uterus. On 23 December, she arrived in Old Goa, and was transported on the shoulders of someone until she reached the Temple. She was then helped by her mother; she kissed Xavier's feet

and then recovered her health completely afterwards. Upon returning to Candolim, she gave thanks to his power at her church, and her neighbours marvelled at her transformation.

4. Pedro António José da Cunha, almost 50 years old, resident of Candolim, had an attack of ___ in December 1855. He has since lived with this attack which left a lesion which made it impossible to wear shoes. He arrived at the Temple on 8 December, immediately felt better after kissing Xavier's feet, he attributes his cure to the protection of the saint.

5. Mariana Luiz, single, 60 years old, of Candolim, was paralysed for a long time. On 15 December, with difficulty she arrived at the Temple. She was standing inside the church when she felt better. She returned to her house on foot afterwards. Today, she attributes the miracle to the patronage of the Saint.

6. Humiliana Bernadina do Rosario, 34 years old, Widow of Benedito Francisco Fernandes, of Candolim, paralysed for more than 12 years with a loss of senses in her right hand. She arrived on 14 December, and, after kissing Xavier, she all of a sudden felt better; she had feeling in her right hand. Her miracle was not from natural causes according to authorities.

7. Pedro Manoel de Sousa, son of António de Sousa and Josepha Fernandes, of Tivim, 8 years age, had lesions on both legs, without free movement. He could not walk without touching hands to ground. He was carried to Xavier and he kissed his feet. It was in this act that he felt better; he walked out of the Temple to the Industrial Pavilion. It was a miracle according to the authorities.

8. Jerónimo Ferrão, son of João Ferrão and Natalia de Noronha, of Tivim, 24 years of age. He had lost all sense of reason and in this state of alienation he did not have knowledge of what he saw or did. His mother took him to Old Goa, and after kissing his feet he felt better immediately. His miracle is not attributed to a physical cause.[134]

Interestingly, in the above cases, all eight individuals, an equal number of males and females and from a range of ages, young to old, suffering from a variety of ailments,[135] are Catholic residents of Goa, a detail which suggests that these miracles were performed only on those whose 'faith' was strong enough to accept Xavier's intercession by way of contact with his corpse. Neri suggests that 'faith' in Xavier expands as a direct result of these miracles, particularly in the case of the two cured children.[136] The above profiles of these eight individuals who are ritual participants also provide a window on to the diversity of Goa's Catholic public as well as its successful and continual reproduction through ritual. In the case of Mariana Luiz it is enough to stand in the Church of Bom Jesus – this in itself a form of contact – in order for this saint's powers to take bodily effect. For the seven others, it is strictly through the act of kissing – now a state-sanctioned form of veneration – that they are cured of their sometimes chronic ailments, suggesting that their faith in both Xavier and Catholicism may have been strong but not as resilient as that of this sixty-year-old woman. Interestingly, it is the miraculous cure of João Thomaz Fernandes that renews the faith of D. Maria Antonia da Costa Campos, a young girl who returns to the Church of Bom Jesus upon hearing the news of the first case and is miraculously cured in the process. She also changes her name to include Xavier, her new name standing in as proof of her continued Catholic faith in him.

While these accounts are deemed 'miraculous' by the witnesses themselves, a group of medical practitioners is brought in to verify the veracity of their testimonies and the quality of their claims, deciding between 'prompt cures, permanent and astonishing works, and those which pass as miracles'.[137] For each of the eight cases detailed above, the appointed commission concludes that 'miraculous' agents rather than 'physical' reasons enabled their cures, their widespread publication acting both to distribute Xavier's powers to a larger (reading) audience[138] and to represent Goa – through its residents – as a place of steady Catholic faith. News of Xavier, Goa, and these 'miracles' would also travel by way of the telegraph, roads, and, of course, by word of mouth.

Alongside the eight miraculous healings that took place at the site of Xavier's corpse in 1859, seven conversions to Catholicism were witnessed by members of Goa's public. Interestingly, the efficacy of Xavier's corpse was now being displaced on to non-Catholic bodies, the majority of these acts occurring during the last week of the exposition. Once again, the details of these conversions were circulated in Goa's popular presses:

> 1. On 25 December, A negro woman of 45 years of age more or less, resident of Panjim [Nova Goa], and is now called Conceição.
> 2. On 2 January, a male gentile, originally of Madurai [British India], of 36 years of age more or less, now called João.
> 3. On 3 January, a male gentile of Sirula of Bardez [Goa], of 40 years of age more or less, and is now called Ignacio Francisco.
> 4. On7 January, a male gentile of Mapço [Goa], of 36 years of age more or less, and is now called Francisco Xavier.
> 5. On the same day, a female gentile, of Bombay [British India] of 30 years of age more or less, and is now called Anna Joaquina.
> 6. On 8 January, a male gentile, native of Siloam [Goa], of 36 years of age more or less, and is now called João Agostinho.
> 7. On the same day, a female gentile, native of Usgão of Ponda [Goa], of 34 years of age more or less, is now called Anna Francisca.[139]

In total, four male and three female individuals (were) converted to Catholicism during the exposition, his or her new Christian names provided in each case as a marker of the newly adopted religious faith.

The taking on of Xavier's name in two cases suggests his seminal role in their conversions during the days of his public display. Interestingly, unlike the eight miraculously healed persons who spanned a wide range of age groups and were all residents of Goa, these particular members of the public are all middle-aged, two of them non-residents of Goa. These two other converts to Catholicism have come to Goa for the exposition from different provinces in British India, their conversions signifying the power of Portuguese India's compelling spirituality (considered a colonial strength) in the midst of an encroaching British India as well as the linkages between them by way of new technologies of travel and communication. Together, the profiles of these seven individuals, including one 'negro woman' whose residence is Goa, not only provide a window on to the diversity of Portuguese India's and British India's non-Catholic publics but serve as a reminder of the Portuguese colonizing project which involved the constant movement of people between its various colonial outposts, in particular between India and Africa during the nineteenth century, when Portugal's 'third empire' (Mozambique and Angola) was becoming increasingly more important in the wake of the loss of Brazil and the steady decline of Goa.

Interestingly, since Xavier's corpse lacks an 'odour of sanctity' in 1859, colonial officials saw fit to incense his corpse with fragrant smells throughout the month of his solemn exposition, a ritual detail that Neri includes in his manual.[140] Here I argue that Xavier's lack of smell is directly compensated for through the power of his touch. Despite medical evidence attesting to his corruptibility and shrinking stature this same year, Xavier's saintly powers are simultaneously displaced on to both inanimate things (souvenirs and relics) and animate bodies through miracles of healing and acts of conversion. These discourses are enabled, dispersed, and circulated by means of new technologies of industrialization that conveniently crosscut Portuguese and British epistemological and physical boundaries in such a way as to reflect the nature of their troubled ties in 1859.

Closing the coffin, creating an archive

On 8 January 1860 – thirty-seven days after its opening – the 'Second Solemn Exposition' of St Francis Xavier was officially closed to the sound of ringing bells from all the cathedrals of Goa and fired artillery from the many military outposts located in and around Portuguese India.[141] The 'closing ceremonies' were led by Goa's Governor General Torres Nova. First, a last Catholic Mass was performed at the site of Xavier's coffin inside the Church of Bom Jesus in the presence of this head of state alongside his entourage of civil and military leaders.[142]

Next, the same ecclesiastical and military officials who had previously been selected to help support the canopy under which Xavier's coffin had been placed on the first day of the festivities now assisted in the official closing of the lid of his coffin at two o'clock in the afternoon.[143] Once again, the new set of keys which had been under the charge of Secretary of State Joaquim Heliodoro da Cunha Rivara and had been used to open his coffin on 3 December was now brought forth to lock his coffin, Neri pointing to the 'melancholy' that was felt by all those who were present, including himself.[144] Lastly, a final procession consisting of the same civil, ecclesiastical, and military officials who had been present on his opening day was organized to return Xavier's coffin to his rightful place inside the Church of Bom Jesus.[145] However, this procession was first preceded by smelling incense burners from which aromas spilled out on to Xavier's coffin, which itself was flanked on all sides with lit candles.[146] Interestingly, D. Maria Antonia Francisca Xavier da Costa Campos, one of the eight members of the public who had earlier been 'miraculously' healed by kissing Xavier's feet, is given the honour of directly following his corpse in the procession, a detail which suggests both the colonial weight placed on miracles and the increased visibility accorded to women during this particular exposition.[147] She is followed by the Governor General, the Interim Archbishop and other important civil and ecclesiastical dignitaries, all of them carrying 'large candles' in their hands.[148] In a final ritual act, Xavier's coffin is deposited inside his chapel and safely returned to his altar before the procession exits the Church of Bom Jesus from its south end.[149]

Neri also informs us that, on the same day of the closing ceremonies, certain objects were quietly 'deposited' inside Xavier's silver coffin before it was officially locked 'for future memory'.[150] These objects were 'archived in [Xavier's] tomb' by Joaquim Gustavo A. Peres; he had been ordered to do so by Neri and Rivara, the Directors of Goa's Press and Archives, respectively.[151] Here I include Neri's list of objects which were placed inside Xavier's coffin:

1 Copy of the 'Historical Summary of the Marvellous Life, Conversions and Miracles of St Francis Xavier' [Neri's book]
1 Hymn to St Francis Xavier
1 State Decree Approving the Opening of the Tomb of St Francis Xavier in 1859
4 Pictures of the Life of St Xavier, and a description of his Tomb
3 Miniature pictures of Xavier, two being on yellow paper
1 Measurement of the body of the saint, in silk ribbon, rose coloured
1 Measurement of the body of the saint, in silk ribbon, white
1 Measurement of the body of the saint, in silk ribbon, pink
3 Additional measurements of the body of the saint, in silk ribbon of varied colours.[152]

Seen together, these archival objects curiously not only represent the success of Xavier's 'Second Solemn Exposition' but affirm certain facts surrounding his festivities: the colonial state's official approval of Xavier's public veneration, the exact length of his corpse as it was measured prior to his display – interestingly, one of the major preoccupations during his earlier medical examination – and the finer details of ritual as they were recorded by Felippe Neri Xavier in his state-commissioned book, the most exhaustive 'archive' to date of the history of the life, miracles, and conversions of Goa's patron saint. Together, these material things ensure that, in the last instance, the richness of Xavier's ritual afterlife will not be forgotten. In other words, in 1859 the Estado da Índia is interested not only in preserving this saint's corpse and image for an abstract 'future memory' but in creating a Xaverian archive – a time capsule of sorts – in a manner that pays proper homage to Goa's most valued relic and commodity.

Conclusion

> It is said that as long as the body of St Francis does not disappear from Goa, the territory will not pass away from the hands of the Portuguese.
> – English manual for visitor to Goa, published in 1890 on the Occasion of the Fourth Solemn Exposition of St Francis Xavier[153]

In proposing a model of a historical state,[154] I am developing a larger argument about the character of Portuguese colonial rule during the latter half of the nineteenth century as compared to the British (and their turn to ethnology) during this post-Mutiny phase. In the face of a dissolute state and an uncertain future that increasingly had everything to do with worsening ties with the British in India and frequent native revolts, the Portuguese increasingly relied on ritual to showcase that they were not history-less, the 'resurrected' bodies of Xavier and Goa their enduring legacy in India. In lieu of a conclusion, I suggest that this turn to history (and historicity) on the part of the Estado da Índia not only occurred in 1859 but was established as a pattern during the latter half of the nineteenth century as its power – political, economic, and religious – continued to 'shrink' in much the same way as Xavier's corpse. The second half of the nineteenth century witnessed not only the signing of the 1878 Anglo-Portuguese treaty,[155] which in effect made Portugal a permanent 'client state' of the British,[156] but also the staging of subsequent expositions centred on Xavier's corpse and image.[157] During this period of 'dominance without hegemony' (1859–1900),[158] the Estado da Índia repeatedly turned to Xavier's ritualization, with the exposition of 1859 turned into a model of sorts for future expositions.[159] Not only would Xavier's repeated displays continue to remind India's diverse public of the historical richness and legacy of the Portuguese in Goa – including their creation of a distinct Indo-Portuguese 'culture' – but it would also set them up as the sole protectors of Catholicism – a nerve centre of spirituality – in the midst of an expanding British India that was now vying for a position as the 'nerve center of the capitalist world economy'.[160] Thus, by staging 'Solemn Expositions' not only in 1859 but also in 1878[161] and 1890,[162] ritual in effect was becoming regularized as a prop for this 'historical' state during a period when their crown, like that of their colonial counterparts in India, the British, was becoming ever more 'hollow', but under a very different set of political, economic, and religious conditions.[163] Thus, while the British would eventually quit India in 1947, the Portuguese refused to accept their 'fate'. Instead, they staged an even more elaborate exposition in 1952 to 'commemorate' the death of St Francis Xavier exactly four hundred years earlier in the hope of garnering support for Goa's newly proclaimed status as an 'overseas province' of Portugal, the topic of my next chapter.

Notes

1 D. Cottineau de Kloguen quoted in José da Fonseca, *An Historical and Archaeological Sketch of the City of Goa* (Delhi: Asian Educational Services, 1986 [1878]), p. 188.

2 Richard F. Burton, 'Old Goa as It Is', in *Goa, and the Blue Mountains; or Six Months of Sick Leave* (Berkeley: University of California Press, 1991 [1851]), pp. 68–71. Burton travelled to Goa in 1847 while on sick leave from his British army regiment stationed in Sind. The theme that recurs throughout the Goa chapters is the danger of imperial decline, and the lessons to be learned for the British.

3 João da Veiga Coutinho, *A Kind of Absence, Life in the Shadow of History* (Stamford, CT: Yagunta Press, 1997). This interest in viewing Goa as 'an object lesson in poor management and symbol of a great imperial project' was the reason underlying the British commissioning of José da Fonseca's *An Historical and Archaeological Sketch of the City of Goa*, a popular English guidebook discussed throughout this chapter.

4 Felippe Neri Xavier, *Resumo Historico da Maravilhosa Vida, Conversões, e Milagres de S. Francisco Xavier, Apostolo, Defensor, e Patrono das Índias*, 2nd edn (Nova Goa: Imprensa Nacional, 1861) p. 318, footnote 260 (*Boletim do Governo do Estado*, No. 52).

5 *Boletim do Governo do Estado*, No. 36 (Lisbon: Ministério da Marinha e Ultramar, 16 August 1841).

6 See Celsa Pinto's *Trade and Finance in Portuguese India: A Study of the Portuguese Country Trade, 1770–1840* (New Delhi: Concept Publishing Company, 1994), p. 235. Closer to home, the French also had their own colonial foothold in Pondicherry (south of Madras) from the late seventeenth century onwards.

7 See Viceroy Conde de Sarzedas's Proclamation (No. 233) to this effect, dated 5 June 1808, in Viriato A.C.B. de Albuquerque, *O Senado de Goa: Memoria Historico Archeologica* (Nova Goa: Imprensa Nacional, 1909), p. 462.

8 A. da Silva Rego, 'Os Ingleses em Goa, 1799–1813' (unpublished manuscript, 1959), later published in *Separata dos Estudos Politicos e Sociais*, Volume III, No. 1 (Lisbon, 1965), p. 13.

9 Ibid., pp. 13–28. A regiment of British troops was stationed in Murmagão during and long after the end of the occupation. It was Goa's Governor General, the Conde de Sarzedas (1807–16), who, through diplomatic channels, negotiated the withdrawal of the British forces from Goa.

10 Interestingly, it was the Hindus of Goa who forewarned the Portuguese government of the British plan to occupy Goa, information they gathered through their contacts at various courts of independent Hindu and Moslem princely states. See Maria Selma de Vieira Velho, 'Goa, a Synthesis of Indo-Portuguese Cultural Relations', in *Seminario internacional de Historia Indo-Portuguesa, 1978* (Lisboa: Instituto de Investigação Cientifica Tropical, 1985), p. 472.

11 A. da Silva Rego, 'Os Ingleses em Goa', p. 12. He states the offer was given at Rs 70,000 which was approximately valued at half a million pounds in 1839.

12 The Pinto Rebellion was instigated by two 'native' priests protesting against the government because they saw no hope for merit-based promotions for native priests under the Portuguese regime. See Joaquim Heliodoro da Cunha Rivara, *Goa and the Revolt of 1787*, ed. Charles Borges, tr. Renato da Cunha Soares (New Delhi: Concept Publishing Company, 1996).

13 See Nandkumar Kamat, 'Stagnant Economy of Portuguese Goa: A Study in Socio-psycho-pathology', in *Socioeconomic Aspects of Portuguese Colonialism in Goa: 19th and 20th Century*, ed. B.S. Shastry (Belgaum: Yarball Offset Printers, 1990), pp. 13, 19.

14 Ibid., pp. 19-20. The Ranes were a tribe who inhabited the district of Satary in the New Conquests of Goa. They had provided the bulk of the Goa army before turning against the government. Disputes continued to break out between the Portuguese government and the Ranes in 1871, 1895, and 1897.

15 See Gervase Clarence-Smith, *The Third Portuguese Empire, 1825–1975, A Study in Economic Imperialism* (Manchester: Manchester University Press, 1978), p. 5.

16 Between 1863 and 1894, 50 per cent of the colonial budget was spent on military expenses as compared to 6 per cent on church expenses. See B.S. Shastry, 'The Colonial Budgets of Portuguese Goa, 1852–1909: Some Observations', in *Socioeconomic Aspects of Portuguese Colonialism in Goa: 19th and 20th Century*, ed. B.S. Shastry (Belgaum: Yarball Offset Printers, 1990), p. 5.

17 Ibid., pp. 1-8. Starting in 1852, the Portuguese began to introduce (almost yearly) budgets – most revenues were spent on military forces, civil administration, and church establishments, but little was spent on the economic development of Goa, or the welfare of the people.

18 According to N. Kamat, the increased revenues generated through taxation were largely spent on strengthening the war machine to crush local revolts and rebellions, building lavish monument in honour of heroes, erecting statues, and constructing big parks and aristocratic mansions. The second phase of urbanization – the shifting of the capital to Nova Goa – was part of this larger scheme to fortify Goa. See his 'Stagnant Economy of Portuguese Goa', p. 14.

19 The idea of developing a 'Permanent Settlement' was about developing property relations and a strong middle class (*badralok*) to act as the landowners, hence the British entrenchment in India through the acquisition of property and property relations. See Ranajit Guha, *A Rule of Property for Bengal: An Essay on the Idea of the Permanent Settlement* (Durham, NC: Duke University Press, 1996).

20 Celsa Pinto, *Trade and Finance in Portuguese India*, p. 239. Other historians such as Gervase Clarence-Smith suggest that Portugal was already a client state of Britain even at the height of their prosperity in the eighteenth century. See his *The Third Portuguese Empire*, pp. 1–3.

21 Portuguese sovereignty in Goa was fully recognized and accepted by Great Britain. See Gervase Clarence-Smith, *The Third Portuguese Empire*, p. 3.

22 Ibid.

23 Fatima Gracias, 'Quality of Life in Colonial Goa, Its Hygienic Expression (19th–20th Centuries)', in *Essays in Goan History*, ed. Teotónio de Souza (New Delhi: Concept publishing Company, 1989), p. 186.

24 According to Celsa Pinto, this unofficial trade has been grossly underestimated in terms of generating revenues. She details a 'lively trade' in luxuries and essentials (opium, slaves, gold, ivory, textiles, tobacco) during the late eighteenth and early nineteenth centuries. Commerce in timber and spices continued to thrive beyond the mid-nineteenth century. See Celsa Pinto, *Trade and Finance in Portuguese India*, pp. 234–9.

25 Ibid., p. 234.

26 Ibid., p. 239. Emphasis mine.

27 During the second half of the nineteenth century, an important development took place in the rural economy of Goa: agricultural employment was supplanted by emigration. On the history of emigration of Goans to British India, see Fatima Gracias, 'Quality of Life in Colonial Goa, Its Hygienic Expression (19th–20th Centuries)', p. 188.

28 Gervase Clarence-Smith writes of these 'Creole' groups as Portugal's greatest colonial asset in the nineteenth century, a point not lost during ritual in 1859. See his *The Third Portuguese Empire*, pp. 3–5.

29 Ibid.

30 Ibid., p. 3.

31 Many Goans saw this as a time to air their grievances against the colonial government since a Liberal party was in power. The need for a periodical Goa press was now felt in light of this new constitutionalism – various publications emerged as a result. See Pia de Menezes Rodrigues, 'Interactive Relationship between Goa and Bombay Journalism' in *Goa's External Relations*, ed. P.P. Shirodkar (Panjim: Rajhauns Vitaran, 1992), p. 90.

32 Gervase Clarence-Smith, *The Third Portuguese Empire*, p. 7.

33 Ibid.

34 The Portuguese immediately offered their services to the British. For example, Governor General Viscount de Torres Novas facilitated the marching of British troops across the Goa territories of Daman and Diu intended to debilitate an insurrection in a section of the army in Bombay. See A. Lopes Mendes, *A Índia Portugueza, Breve Descripção das Possessões Portuguezas na Asia*, Volume 1 (Lisboa: Imprensa Nacional, 1886), p. 21. See P.P. Shirodkar, 'Insurgency, 1857 Mutiny in Western India and the Portuguese', *Researches in Indo-Portuguese History*, Volume II, ed. P.P. Shirodkar (Jaipur: Publication Scheme, 1998), pp. 168–204.

35 See A. Lopes Mendes, *A Índia Portugueza*, p. 21.

36 See Kenneth Ballhatchet, 'European Missions and Indian Society: The Archbishop of Goa, the Vicar Apostolic of Malabar and the Padroado in the Early Nineteenth Century', in *Seminário Internacional de Historia Indo-Portuguesa* (Lisboa: Instituto de Investigação Cientifica Tropical, 1978), p. 319.

37 See Carlos Merces de Melo, *The Recruitment and Formation of the Native Clergy in India, 16th–19th Century, An Historico-Canonical Study* (Lisboa: Agencia Geral do Ultramar, 1955), p. 51. See Luís Filipe F.R. Thomaz, *De Ceuta a Timor* (Lisboa: Difel, 1994), p. 262. When the orders were suppressed, many of the same religious men carried out their work now as secular priests. See Rev. M. de Sá, 'The Ecclesiastical Province of Goa', *Indo-Portuguese Review, Calcutta*, Volume 4 (Calcutta: Indo-Portuguese Association, 1922), p. 8.

38 See Cosme José Cosa, S.F.X., *A Missiological Conflict Between Padroado and Propaganda in the East* (Pilar, Goa: Pilar Publications, 1997), p. 69.

39 See Casimiro Christovão de Nazareth, *Mitras Lusitanas no Oriente, Catalogos dos Prelados da Egreja Metropolitana e Primacial de Goa e das Dioceses Suffraganeas com A Recopilação das Ordenancas por elles Emittadas, e Summario dos Factos Notaveis da Historia Ecclesiastica de Goa*, 2nd edn (Lisboa: Imprensa Nacional, 1897), p. 482.

40 Felippe Neri Xavier, *Resumo Historico*, p. 318, footnote 260 (Boletim No. 52), and p. 320 (Boletim No. 18).

41 'Advertencia', *Ladainha de S. Francisco Xavier, Acompanhada de Duas Oracões* (Nova Goa: Imprensa Nacional, 1860), p. 15.

42 It was also published in Portugal's *Nação*, No. 3 (1859).
43 The abundance or excess of information itself is an important factor in characterizing ritual in 1859.
44 Felippe Neri Xavier, *Resumo Historico*, p. 347, No. 16 (Licença, Exame do Corpo, e sua Exposição em 1859).
45 Ibid.
46 Ibid., p. 355 (Da Authorisação Regia para a Exposição de 1859, e das diligencias que se empregaram para a levar a effeito).
47 Ibid. (Da Authorisação Regia para a Exposição de 1859, e das diligencias que se empregaram para a levar a effeito). Also, an English version was printed at Madurai to accommodate an English-speaking public.
48 J.M.S Daurignac states that the exposition of 1782 did not 'inspire much enthusiasm nor did many people attend'. See J.M.S. Daurignac, *Historia de São Francisco de Xavier, Da Companhia de Jesus, Apostolo das Índias e do Japão, Protector do Oriente*, 3rd edn (Goa: No Publisher Listed, 1880), p. 246.
49 Here I quote Neri, who confusedly traces the history of two of the original keys. See Felippe Neri Xavier, *Resumo Historico*, pp. 272, 356.
50 The Secretary General at this time was Cunha Rivara, who will come up again as a 'key' figure.
51 Government Bulletin (No. 80, dated 14 October 1859) reprinted in *Memoria Historico-Eclesiastico da Arquidiocese de Goa, 1533–1933*, ed. Pe Amaro Pinto Lobo (Nova Goa, Tip. A Voz de S. Francisco Xavier, 1933), pp. 380–4. There are 46 additional signatures, including that of Neri, who was also present during Xavier's medical examination.
52 This fits with Michel Foucault's discussion of a shift in medical practices and discourses at the end of the eighteenth century, and the emergence of modern medicine occurring in the last years of the eighteenth century. See his *The Birth of the Clinic*, tr. A.M. Sheridan Smith (New York: Vintage Books, 1994), p. xii.
53 Torres Nova was Governor General of Goa between 1855 and 1861. He was 'of a firm character, a generous soul and noble', as described by A. Lopes Mendes upon meeting him. See his *A Índia Portugueza*, p. 21.
54 Neri wrote down additional details of the medical examination which were not included in the official autopsy report, reflecting on the 'shrinking' stature of Xavier. See John Castets's translation of Neri's account in his 'The Miracle of the Body of St Francis Xavier', *Indian Catholic Truth Society*, No. 13 (1925), pp. 27–9.
55 And by metaphorical extension, the Estado da Índia may be 'shrinking' in stature owing to the steady encroachment of the British.
56 Felippe Neri Xavier, *Resumo Historico*, p. 426, No. 161.
57 *Annaes do Conselho Ultramarino, Parte não Official Series II, Janeiro de 1859 a Dezembro de 1861* (Lisboa: Imprensa Nacional, 1867), p. 118.
58 Felippe Neri Xavier, *Resumo Historico*, p. 355 (Da Authorisação Regia para a Exposição de 1859).
59 Ibid.
60 Ibid., p. 422, No. 21. 'Posture of the Municipal Chamber in order to clean and light the city'. Emphasis mine.
61 Ibid., pp. 363, 392. The orchestra was conducted by the 'celebrated' Rd Cónego Joaquim António do Rosário.
62 Ibid., pp. 363–4.
63 Ibid.
64 José da Fonseca, *An Historical and Archaeological Sketch of the City of Goa*, p. 267.
65 Felippe Neri Xavier, *Resumo Historico*, Chapter 87, pp. 363–4.
66 Ibid., p. 379.
67 Ibid., p. 362.
68 Notices of the exposition were publicized in Goa via a series of publications first called the *Boletim do Governo do* Estado da Índia (1835–1907), and later changed to *Boletim Oficial do Governo Geral* (1915–35).

69 Felippe Neri Xavier, *Resumo Historico*, Chapter 87, p. 363.
70 Ibid., p. 364.
71 Ibid., pp. 365–6. For a complete copy of the official programme, see Felippe Neri Xavier, *Resumo Historico*, p. 426.
72 Ibid., p. 433. Interestingly, donations would be divided into those that were received for the 'splendour of the cult' and those that were received 'especially for the saint'.
73 Ibid., p. 434, No. 24: 'Circular para a marcha da tropa para a Cidade Velha. Military Secção Militar da Secretaria do Governo Geral em Nova Goa, 23 de Novembro de 1859'.
74 Ibid., p. 426.
75 Ibid., p. 391.
76 Ibid., 'Preparations', Chapter 87, p. 364.
77 Ibid., p. 365.
78 Ibid.
79 Ibid., p. 366. Canoz was personally attended to by Goa's Governor General, Visconde de Torres Novas.
80 According to P. Rayanna, *St Francis Xavier and His Shrine*, 2nd edn (Panjim: Imprimatur, 1982), p. 205.
81 The archbishopric was empty in 1859 owing to ongoing tensions between the Padroado and Propaganda. For additional details, see Cosme José Costa, S.F.X., *A Missiological Conflict*, pp. 70–1 (footnotes).
82 The Jesuits were slowly let back into India throughout the mid-nineteenth century, but they were allowed to come through only the Propaganda and not the Padroado. There were very few if any Jesuits operating in Goa in 1859, Canoz more than likely one of the first Jesuits to return to Goa after their expulsion on the centenary of their expulsion, nonetheless. According to the Jesuit historian Charles Borges, after their suppression, the Jesuits who returned to India were more tolerant, less powerful, more subdued, less aggressive, pro-political, more introspective, and more interested in social reform and helping the poor. They generally adopted a pro-native policy. See his unpublished paper 'Contrasting Images: The Jesuits before and after the Expulsion', *Indo-Portuguese History Conference* (Porvorim, Goa: Xavier Center for Historical Research, 6–9 September 1999).
83 Felippe Neri Xavier, *Resumo Historico*, p. 463. A copy of Canoz's testimony was also published in English in the 'St. Thomas Catholic Chronicle' of Madras, according to Felippe Neri Xavier, *Resumo Historico*, Chapter 91, p. 402.
84 Ibid., p. 366.
85 Ibid., p. 403.
86 Ibid., pp. 488–92.
87 On 10 December 1859 Canoz wrote a letter to the General of the Society of Jesus. See J.M.S. Daurignac, *Historia de São Francisco de Xavier*, p. 225.
88 Ibid.
89 Felippe Neri Xavier, *Resumo Historico*, p. 486.
90 Ibid., pp. 381–3. Note his use of the word 'temple' instead of church, which I suggest is part of the trend to 'secularize' the festivities of 1859 to include participants of all religions, not just Christianity.
91 The telegraph was established between Belgao and Goa on 13 February 1857, and was a joint effort between the Governor of the Presidency of Bombay and the Governor General of Goa. See A. Lopes Mendes, *A Índia Portugueza*, p. 21.
92 Felippe Neri Xavier, *Resumo Historico*, p. 494. For example, the *Victoria* had three daily trips with frequent departures and return trips.
93 These improved roads were the precursor to a railway line that was established between Mormugão and British India as part of the Anglo-Portuguese treaty of 1878. See Teresa Albuquerque, 'The Anglo-Portuguese Treaty of 1878: Its Impact on the People of Goa', *Indica*, Voume 27, No. 2 (September 1990), p. 117.
94 Felippe Neri Xavier, *Resumo Historico*, p. 494. For additional details on this industrial exposition as well as its location within a larger historical context of colonial expositions (both Portuguese and British) during the second half of the nineteenth

century, see Filipa L. Vicente, 'A exposição do corpo sagrado de S. Francisco Xavier e as exposições industriais e agrícolas em Goa', *Oriente* (December 2002), pp. 55–66, and her 'Exposiçoes coloniais na Índia Portuguesa e na Índia Britânica (séculos XIX e XX)', *Oriente* (April 2004), pp. 70–88.

95 The press in 1859 was a voice piece of government practices and policies, and involved heavy Portuguese censorship rules and regulations. See Pia de Menezes, 'Interactive Relationship between Goa and Bombay Journalism', p. 90.

96 See Newman Fernandes, *St Francis Xavier and Old Goa, An Historical Guide* (Panjim: Koinia Publications, 1994), p. 42.

97 For additional details on both figures, see António de Meneses, 'Felippe Neri Xavier, Historiografo e Homen Publico, 1801–1875', *Harpa Goesa*, No. 7 (December 1974), pp. 29–32.

98 Felippe Neri Xavier, *Resumo Historico*, p. 355.

99 *Annaes do Conselho Ultramarino*, p. 118

100 Felippe Neri Xavier, *Resumo Historico*, Chapter 91, pp. 400–2.

101 Ibid., p. 533.

102 Ibid., p. 366.

103 Newman Fernandes, *St Francis Xavier and Old Goa*, p. 42.

104 Felippe Neri Xavier, *Resumo Historico*, Chapter 93, p. 411.

105 Ibid.

106 Ibid.

107 Ibid., footnote 327. Neri notes another apparition wherein a person saw Xavier's resurrection, a ritual detail that evokes Goa's resurrection, one of the larger themes of this chapter.

108 Ibid., p. 493.

109 Ibid.

110 Ibid., p. 366.

111 Ibid., p. 355. I first came across a second edition of Neri's book in the private family collection of Mr Percival Noronha, who graciously allowed me to make a photocopy of it in its entirety.

112 Ibid., p. 494.

113 Ibid.

114 Ibid. There was much fluidity between Goans living in Panjim and Bombay, many returning 'home' (via the new roads) for holidays and special events.

115 Ibid., p. 494.

116 Ibid., p. 363.

117 *Archivo Pittoresco: Semanario Illustrado*, Volume III (Lisboa: Typographia de Castro & Irmão, 1860), p. 185.

118 These distinct religious groups and nationalities are described in *Archivo Pittoresco: Semanario Illustrado*, p. 185.

119 Felippe Neri Xavier, *Resumo Historico*, p. 426.

120 Ibid. Newman Fernandes states that the donations were a sizeable amount, almost enough to pay for the expenses incurred during the staging of the exposition. See his *St Francis Xavier and Old Goa*, p. 42.

121 Felippe Neri Xavier, *Resumo Historico*, p, 388, footnote 315.

122 Ibid.

123 Ines Županov, 'The Prophetic and the Miraculous in Portuguese Asia: A Hagiographical View of Colonial Culture', *Santa Barbara Portuguese Studies*, Volume II (1995), p. 139. She describes the Jesuit monopoly in Asia as being 'supernatural commerce'.

124 Felippe Neri Xavier, *Resumo Historico*, p. 443.

125 Ibid., p. 364.

126 Ibid.

127 Susan Stewart discusses how souvenirs serve to authenticate the experience of the viewer, serving as a trace of that experience. The souvenir 'moves history into private time'. See her *On Longing, Narratives of the Miniature, the Gigantic, the Souvenir, the Collection* (Durham, NC: Duke University Press, 1993), pp. 134–8.

128 Felippe Neri Xavier, *Resumo Historico*, p. 356. Cotton may very well have been a foreign import to Goa from British India.
129 Ibid., p. 408.
130 Ibid., p. 366.
131 Ibid., p. 408.
132 Ibid., p. 539, No. 40. An official committee was also set up to oversee votive offerings. Many of these kinds of item were also sold at the Pavilion of the National Press as souvenirs, and included gold and silver emblems, coins, silver, copper, paper, jewels, and miniatures (such as a small baby Jesus, with body parts in gold and or silver, or wax body parts). See *Annaes do Conselho Ultramarino*, p. 118.
133 Ibid., p. 496.
134 Ibid., p. 561.
135 Interestingly, the majority of the cures are directed at the legs and/or the same body part(s) of Xavier's that were venerated and touched to produce relics.
136 Felippe Neri Xavier, *Resumo Historico*, Chapter 91, p. 403.
137 Felippe Neri Xavier, *Resumo Historico*, p. 496.
138 These eight miraculous healings were also reproduced in gazetteers, almanacs, religious literature, etc, but often in less detail and more summary form. See Amaro Pinto Lobo Pe, ed., *Memória Histórico-Eclesiástico da Arquidiocese de Goa, 1533–1933* (Nova Goa: Tip. A Voz de S. Francisco Xavier, 1933), pp. 380–4.
139 These details reproduced in *Annaes do Conselho Ultramarino*, p. 118, and in *Memoria Historico-Eclesiastico da Arquidiocese de Goa*, p. 382.
140 Felippe Neri Xavier, *Resumo Historico*, p. 388, footnote 313. Interestingly, in 1866, the same Cunha Rivara, Secretary General and Director of Archives, describes the ecclesiastics in India as having lost their 'odour of sanctity' by their excessive ambition and by their interference in state matters. Cunha Rivara quoted in J.A. da Costa, *A History of Goa* (Mapusa, Goa: Ramakant Printers, 1982), p. 195. That is, by metaphorical extension, properties associated with Xavier's corpse were actively ascribed to other political and religious bodies.
141 Felippe Neri Xavier, *Resumo Historico*, Chapter 92, p. 409. These same auditory and visual markers also signified the beginning of ritual.
142 Ibid., p. 407.
143 Ibid., p. 408.
144 Ibid., p. 409.
145 Ibid., p. 407.
146 Ibid.
147 Ibid., p. 408. The status of women (and thus their visibility in public arenas) would greatly improve in Portuguese India with the passing of the Civil Code in 1870. See Pratima Kamat, 'Some Legal Aspects of the Socio-Economic Life of Women in Portuguese Asia', in *Goan Society Through the Ages*, ed. B.S. Shastry (New Delhi: Asian Publication Series, 1987).
148 Ibid., p. 409.
149 Ibid., pp. 407, 409. The acts of entering and exiting were restricted to the southern door owing to the heavy military presence standing guard inside and outside the Church of Bom Jesus.
150 Ibid., p. 538.
151 Ibid. No additional information on Peres is available.
152 Ibid. These measurements were of Xavier's height.
153 English manual for visitors to Goa, entitled *Guide to the City of Old Goa: A Handbook for Visitors to the Exposition of the Sacred Body of St Francis Xavier, Apostle of the Indies, During the Month of December 1890* (Bombay: The Bombay Circulating Library Printing Press, 1890), p. 35.
154 See Nicholas B. Dirks, Part III: 'The Ethnographic State', in his *Castes of Mind: Colonialism and the Making of Modern India* (Princeton: Princeton University Press, 2001), pp. 127–227. Dirks's frame not only provides a larger contextual and comparative arena within which to view the role of the Portuguese in India in the latter half of the nineteenth century, but also how the British increasingly viewed

them (the Portuguese) as ethnological subjects alongside their Indian counterparts; this characterization also helps to understand the nature of Anglo-Portuguese ties during this same time frame.

155 See Teresa Albuquerque's 'The Anglo-Portuguese Treaty of 1878', pp. 117–18.

156 For example, the Prince of Wales (later King Edward VII) went on an 'official tour' of Goa in 1875. See António de Menezes, *Historical Notes on Goa* (Nova Goa: Publication Casa J.P. Fernandes, 1878), pp. 106-9. The year 1881 also marked the beginning of public discussions centred on 'the Colonial Question' in Portugal; that is, whether or not and how the Portuguese should maintain their colonies. See António José de Seixas, *A Questão Colonial Portugueza* (Lisboa: Typographia Universal, 1881), p. 5.

157 Interestingly, an attempt to stage an exposition as early as 1864 failed even though Portugal's king had given his permission. See 'Varia Variorum', *O Oriente Portuguez*, Volume 7 (1910), p. 296. This failed exposition reinforces my argument concerning the Estado's increasing reliance on ritual to display its sense of historicity. In other words, it is important to recognize the significance of the non-event. See Nicholas Dirks, 'Ritual and Resistance: Subversion as Social Fact', in *Contesting Power: Resistance and Everyday Social Relations in South Asia*, eds D. Haynes and G. Prakash (Berkeley: University of California Press, 1991).

158 Here I suggest the application of Ranajit Guha's famous term for the British during this same time frame to the Portuguese in India. See Ranajit Guha, *Dominance Without Hegemony: History and Power in Colonial India* (Cambridge, MA: Harvard University Press, 1997).

159 Viriato A.C.B. Albuquerque would take over Neri's role for subsequent expositions of Xavier (1878 and 1890).

160 As described in Celsa Pinto, *Trade and Finance in Portuguese India*, p. 239.

161 Xavier's 'Third Solemn Exposition' was staged between 3 December 1878 and 6 January 1879. For additional details, see Viriato A.C.B. Albuquerque, *A Exposição do Venerando Corpo do Apostolo das Índias, S. Francisco Xavier, em 1878* (Nova Goa, Tipographia da Cruz, 1879).

162 Xavier's 'Fourth Solemn Exposition' was staged between 3 December 1890 and 1 January 1891. For additional details, see Viriato A.C.B. Albuquerque, *Exposição do Venerando Corpo do Glorioso Apostolo das Índias, S. Francisco Xavier, em 1890, Memoria Historico-Descriptiva, Illustrada com Estampas* (Nova Goa, Imprensa Nacional, 1891).

163 I adopt the idea of a 'hollow crown' from Nicholas Dirks, but suggest its application to the Portuguese in India. See his *The Hollow Crown: Ethnohistory of an Indian Kingdom*, 2nd edn (Ann Arbor, MI: University of Michigan Press, 1993).

CHAPTER SIX

Commemoration (1952)

Introduction

> As the ritual articulations of myths, commemorations play an important part in creating a *usable* national history.[1]

> Goa may be a minor pimple but it is a pimple that disfigures the face of Hindustan. – Dr Lohia, Goan Freedom Fighter, 1946[2]

In December 1952 ceremonies took place in a multitude of cities to commemorate[3] the death of St Francis Xavier exactly four hundred years earlier on the island of Sancian (China). These celebrations took place in Pamplona (Spain) – his place of birth; Vatican City (Italy) – where he received his Jesuit orders and was canonized; Lisbon (Portugal) – under whose royal crown he went to Goa; Paris (France) – where he had been educated; Tokyo (Japan) – where he had missionized, and of course Goa (India) – where his corpse lay in state. While all of these locations mark significant points during this saint's biography in life, each becomes a ritual site for commemorating Xavier on the four-hundred-year anniversary of his death. In this chapter I take as my central focus the practice of commemoration, focusing on Xavier's tenth 'Solemn Exposition' that was staged in Old Goa from 3 December 1952, until 6 January 1953, under the auspices of the Estado da Índia. These multiple investments in Xavier's ritualization also took place at a time when the continued status of Goa as a Portuguese colony was being negotiated in an international context; as will become evident in the following ritual analysis, many considered the fate of Goa to lie in Xavier's left hand – again, his right hand having been preserved at the Vatican since 1622.

In this chapter I develop a model of commemoration in order to characterize the exposition held in 1952, but also to suggest that this momentous celebration was the culmination of a series of expositions

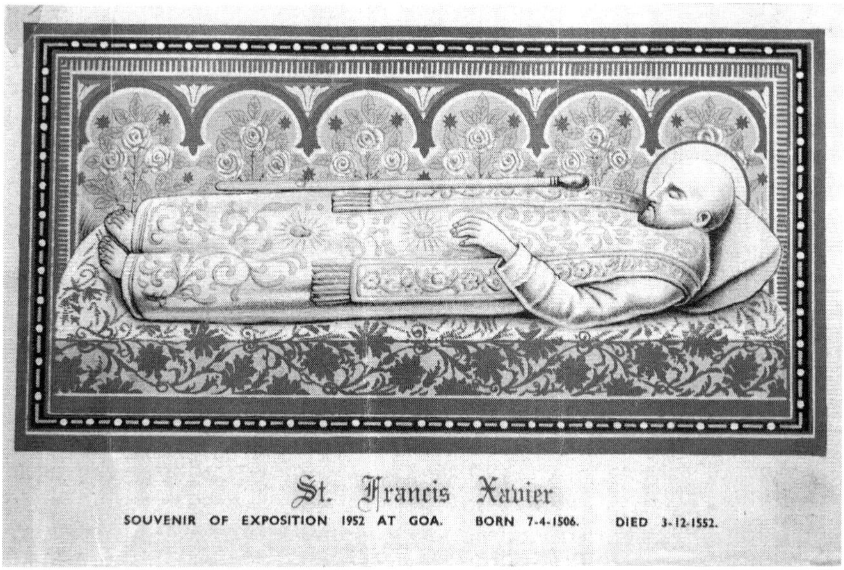

Figure 7 Souvenir of Exposition 1952 at Goa

(1910, 1922, 1931, 1942) that were staged in Goa by colonial officials during this period to 'commemorate' certain dates in the life, times, and afterlife of Xavier. I first turn to the character of a 'failed' celebration in 1906 (one organized to commemorate the quatercentenary of Xavier's birth in 1506) in order to explore the Estado da Índia's initial development, refinement, and increasing reliance on a discourse and materiality of commemoration to enact and display colonial power under certain governmental regimes and historical circumstances during the first half of the twentieth century. The exposition of 1952 then represents the last in this series of commemorations of this saint's biography – fittingly, a commemoration of (Xavier's) death exactly four hundred years earlier. It was staged during a time when Portugal was increasingly put on the defensive about its ethical right to maintain Goa as an 'overseas province' in the midst of a newly independent Indian nation-state (1947) – that is, just as its own possible 'death' was in sight.

My exploration of the tenth exposition dedicated to Xavier also attends to the centrality of his corpse (and condition) in sanctioning the act of commemoration. It is at this time that Xavier's long-standing label of 'incorrupt body' is formally replaced with that of 'sacred relics' by Portuguese colonial and religious officials during his medical examination. I will suggest that commemoration is utilized by the Estado da Índia in order to replace or compensate for the lack of efficacy on the part of Xavier's physical body. While the unique and miraculous powers of Xavier's corpse had been successfully displaced – through the power of touch – on to other bodies (both animate and inanimate) in spite of his corrupted state during his exposition in 1859, this was less a guarantee almost one hundred years later.

By 1952, Portuguese colonial officials turned towards ritually signifying that which was materially real and stable in order to successfully harness Xavier's image to their own colonial agenda: certain momentous (read successful) events in the life, times, and death of their patron saint were being inscribed and institutionalized for collective memory through the process of commemoration. Given the very real horrors of two recent world wars and the struggle for Indian independence, which involved the violence of Partition as recently as 1947–48, commemoration was a more ritually secure option, since it reaffirmed both Portugal's historical commitment to Goa – through the figure and biography of Xavier – and Prime Minister António Oliveira Salazar's 'one-nation theory', in which Goa was no longer considered a colony but rather a natural extension of Portugal – that is, as one crucial part of the whole. However, commemoration this time would also unwittingly open itself up to the 'hazards of representation' precisely because it was tied to particular imperialist and nationalist struggles.[4]

Just as ritual on the quatercentenary of Xavier's death was defined by certain investments on the part of various nation-states that had a stake in reproducing Xavier's biography on stage, the requisite public in 1952 was no longer just a Goan one. I will suggest that, in this era of European decolonization, the staging of an exposition in Old Goa was, on the one hand, about continuing to define Goa as a spiritual haven (with Catholic, Hindu, and Muslim pilgrims from across India in attendance), this time not in the face of an encroaching secularized British India (as was the case in 1859), but in the midst of a religiously diverse, tolerant and independent Indian Union that was simultaneously negotiating Goa's future with Portugal. On the other hand, the Estado da Índia's investment in ritual in 1952 was also about showcasing Goa as an 'overseas province' of Portugal with indisputable cultural, historical, and political links to its motherland to an even larger public that exceeded the boundaries of India. Relatively new technologies to enhance communication and travel such as the aeroplane, telephone, radio, and international press were utilized for the express purpose of enabling a larger seeing, reading, and listening public not only to take part in the solemnities, but to witness these ritual bonds between metropole and colony, and affirm the (Portuguese) case of Goa in an international context. In this chapter I rely on a certain type of source material for my ritual analysis. Not unlike prior ritual moments, a manual commissioned by the Estado da Índia and compiled by Francisco Xavier da Costa was produced concurrently with Xavier's tenth exposition and made available for sale to members of the public, with excerpts in both Portuguese and English provided. I also rely on the power of the press (Goan, Indian, and Portuguese) to record informational details and personal impressions, as well as its centrality as a forum for determining the fate of Xavier's corpse, and hence the (colonial) future of Goa.

In the last section of the chapter – in lieu of a conclusion – I briefly turn to the 'extraordinary' exposition that was staged in 1961 by the Estado da Índia in the face of its own demise, that is, in light of encroaching Indian troops bent on 'liberating' Goa from more than four hundred and fifty years of Portuguese colonial rule. I suggest that this particular set of ritual practices 'failed', not only because it lacked a commemorative force (1961 was not a ritually significant year in Xavier's biography) but also because it was staged for explicitly political reasons: it was hastily organized to garner support for Portugal's continued colonial hold over Goa. In praying at the feet of its patron saint in 1961 – by now a familiar ritual practice (the *posse*) that Portuguese colonial officials had turned to on so many previous occasions, most successfully in 1683 and most recently in 1952 – the Estado da Índia attempted to save Goa from yet another Indian 'invasion'. However, just as the colonial state could not defy the inevitable decomposition of a saint's corpse, it could not defy its own, particularly in this era of global decolonization. Fittingly, the Portuguese laid down their arms on 18 December 1961, in the midst of Xavier's exposition, which in turn was immediately suspended. As Sebastiam Gonçalves, an appointed official Jesuit biographer of Goa's patron saint whose completed manuscript had been put on the same Lisbon-bound ship as our would-be saint's amputated right arm in the year 1615, had so prophetically suggested, Xavier would prove to be more valuable in death than in life.

Building a model of commemoration (1906–42)

> We thought to celebrate with modest pomp in this year [1906] the 4th centenary of the birth of St Francis Xavier – Goa's Archbishop, 1906[5]

The year 1906 witnessed a proposal on the part of the Archdiocese of Goa to commemorate, for the first time, the birth of St Francis Xavier in Goa on his quatercentenary.[6] Here I briefly explore the reasons why this particular celebration surrounding Xavier was postponed to the following year, outlining in the process a more general model of commemoration that I will suggest was modified and/or expanded upon with each successive commemoration (1910, 1922, 1931, 1942), culminating in the Tenth 'Solemn Exposition' held in Goa in December 1952.

In its series of regularly published annual decrees, the Archdiocese of Goa includes one for the year 1906 entitled 'Exposing the Motives why the Project to celebrate the Fourth Centenary of the Birth of the Illustrious and Reverend St Francis Xavier were Renounced', and then postponed to the following year on his feast day of 3 December (1907).[7] It becomes apparent that certain conditions were not satisfied on the part of the Archdiocese of Goa to initiate proceedings to stage a commemorative event with 'modest pomp'. Thus, what was originally viewed as a 'natural' and 'public' act is now renounced precisely because of the secular-ness of the month of April – the supposed month of Xavier's birth. This fact alone motivates the Archbishop to suggest that a sacred feast such as the one proposed for 1906 should be postponed until 3 December 1907, to coincide with Xavier's holy saint's day.[8] It is important that the fourth centenary of Xavier's birth should not be confused with the centenary celebrations of 'simple illustrious men', for Xavier is anything but that to church, state, and public in Goa. Even celebrations that include sumptuous acts are not a fitting tribute to Goa's patron saint according to the Archbishop. Neither are celebrations that appear outwardly religious deemed appropriate. Instead, any commemoration pertaining to Xavier's day of birth must have religion and religiosity at its ideological centre. The Archbishop also lists the 'excessive rigours of the climate' in Goa during the month of April as yet another reason underlying his desire to postpone the fourth centenary celebrations of Xavier's birth. In the end, it is with both regret and reason that the Archdiocese renounces its plans, but maintains the idea to 'celebrate his next feast with the most splendour that it is accustomed to'.[9]

The above conditions underlying the postponed celebration of 1906 provide the basic building blocks for a (future) model of commemorative rituals centred on the biography of Xavier. The example of 1906 illuminates that certain idealized qualifications had to be met before the Archdiocese, with the permission of both the king of Portugal and the Governor General of Goa, would commit itself to staging a centenary event in Portuguese India. Not only was the biographical date in question in need of verification before any such planning could take place, but such celebrations were required to be public by nature, with no expense spared, and with religiosity at their core; they were also to be staged on or near Xavier's saint's day of 3 December. Together, these specific conditions point to the defining characteristics necessary for Xavier's commemoration to take place successfully according to colonial and religious officials alike.

Curiously, the year 1906 also witnessed the production of a controversial medical thesis whose subject matter was Xavier's corpse. A student at the Goa Medical School by the name of L.M. Julio Frederico Gonçalves submitted his thesis entitled 'The Miracles of St Francis Xavier are not Miracles, nor are they of St Francis Xavier', shortly thereafter receiving his medical degree before emigrating to Portugal.[10] The production and approval of his graduate thesis first indicates that there was a growing body of published materials that were critical of Xavier – including the condition of his corpse – and his legacy during this period of frequent metropolitan changes in government and burgeoning nationalist struggles focused on the demise of colonialism the world over, a point that is further developed in relation to the commemoration of 1952. Alternatively, Gonçalves's thesis suggests an expanding interest in viewing Xavier's corpse as less a miraculous phenomenon than a fascinating medical specimen to be studied, and gestures towards my continued focus in earlier chapters on medical forensics and diagnosis. This second point is also examined in more depth in relation to his tenth exposition. The development of a distinctive type of state medical report – one that promoted 'accuracy' and 'authenticity' in relation to 'body parts' above all other characteristics – was integral to a model of commemoration, since it simultaneously allowed his corpse to represent the biography of Xavier, only in an alternative public format. Later expositions – staged in 1910, 1922, 1931, and 1942 – were envisioned precisely because of the ritual potential of Xavier's biography – simultaneously a sign of the success of the Estado da Índia – and were enacted in Goa under varying historical conditions and governmental regimes in metropole and colony in order to generate and reinforce collective memory. In other words, colonial officials increasingly relied on the certainty of Xavier's biography (in life and death) in increasingly uncertain times (1906–42).

The first half of the twentieth century witnessed the remarkable end of the Portuguese monarchy (1910), a period of republicanism (1910–26), and the advent of the Salazar dictatorship (1928–74). The repetition of ritual approximately every ten years also signified an increasingly less powerful colonial state that increasingly relied on the power of ritual. Meanwhile, these celebrations dedicated to Xavier continually connected other metropoles – in particular Portugal and Spain – and organizations – in particular the Society of Jesus and the Vatican – to Goa, and were very much shaped by larger world events, such as the Second World War and the struggles for national independence on the Indian subcontinent. Thus, in the midst of all these global changes, the Estado da Índia celebrated, through the staging of a series of commemorative expositions focused on Xavier's corpse, the reconquest of Goa under Affonso de Albuquerque in 1510 (1910), Xavier's canonization in 1622 (1922), the *posse* in 1683 (1931), Xavier's arrival in Goa in 1542 (1942),[11] and, lastly, Xavier's death in 1552 (1952). It is to this last set of ritual practices that I now turn.

1952: commemorating Xavier's death

> The chequered course of India's history during the past 200 years or more has left certain foreign possessions in various parts of the country. These possessions continued for this long period because India herself was under alien domination. With the establishment of independence in India, the continued existence of foreign possessions became anomalous and opposed to the conception of India's unity and freedom. Therefore, it has become necessary for these possessions to be politically incorporated in India. The Indian National Congress trusts that this change will be brought about by peaceful methods and the friendly cooperation of the Governments concerned. The Congress realised that during this long period administrative, cultural, linguistic, educational, and judicial systems have grown up in these possessions which are different from those prevailing in the rest of India. Any changeover must therefore take these factors into consideration and allow for a gradual adjustment which will not interfere with the life of the people in the areas concerned. The Congress would welcome the present cultural heritage of these possessions to be continued so far as the people of these possessions desire, and for a measure of autonomy to be granted wherever possible so as to enable the people of these possessions to maintain their culture and institutions within the larger framework of India. – Resolution of the Indian National Congress on foreign possessions in India, December 1948[12]

The tenth 'Solemn' Exposition of St Francis Xavier was staged in Old Goa in December 1952 to commemorate the death of Goa's patron saint exactly four hundred years earlier on 3 December 1552. Commemoration was directly tied to the biography of Xavier, as had been the case in proposing celebrations for 1906 (birth), 1922 (canonization), and 1942 (arrival in Goa). Thus, not only does the exposition of 1952 witness an expanding discourse of commemoration: it represents the culmination of this series of commemorative rituals staged in the twentieth century, enacting and sometimes perfecting many of those practices proposed but not fully realized at earlier ritual moments. Despite the elaborateness of the festivities in 1952, commemoration also proved to be elusive in the hands of the Estado da Índia given the corruptibility of Xavier's corpse, the nature of commemoration this time around (death), and the dramatically different historical circumstances – in particular the independence of India in 1947 and its growing concern

– as evidenced in the above statement – about what to do with these so-called other 'foreign possessions', Goa included. Commemoration – as a discourse and material practice – was particularly vulnerable to the 'hazards of representation' in 1952 because it had the potential to signify the culmination of so many colonial processes connecting saint and state, not only that of Xavier's biography, corporeality, and miraculous powers, but also that of the entire history of his ritualization and, finally, of Portuguese colonialism itself. As will become evident, this set of ritual practices presented itself as 'the end' at all these different levels even as colonial officials tried to postpone this same end through the continuing intercession of their faithful political, religious, and spiritual figurehead. Thus there was always a tension between accepting (and thus commemorating) the end of saint and state, and denying that same end by representing Xavier's tenth exposition as a last stand against Portugal's enemies. In other words, by 1952 two very different colonial sensibilities were constantly in play. In the following analysis I adopt a thematic approach to explore this set of ritual practices, the details themselves indicative of the power and prestige of the Estado da Índia at a moment when it was, not coincidentally, facing its own imminent death.

Ritual preparations, renovations and adopting (new) technologies

> Within three years – on 3 December 1952 – will also occur the fourth centenary of the death of St Francis Xavier. It has not been difficult to start, from right now, to think about the organization of a great commemorative programme that will be of interest to the Catholic world, especially the Catholic people of the Orient, a great number of whom are of the Roman Catholic faith, first from the island of Sanchian, of the Chinese, where the great Saint died, and afterwards, to Goa, where they venerate his mortal remains, reaffirming their belief in the doctrine that he preached ... The prestige that Portugal enjoys in the Far Orient, which comes to it from the superior services provided for these people, is well manifested. There will be no cost to maintain this prestige that today, more than ever, should be staged as the foundation of an intense affirmation of moral force. And, in this capital, Portugal continues with its clean reputation, respected and admired by all the people of the world that never will repeat the case of the commemoration of St Francis Xavier.[13]

By now a pattern had been established wherein expositions dedicated to Xavier were scheduled approximately every ten years throughout the twentieth century. However, unlike earlier commemorative expositions which were organized at most one year in advance of the actual celebrations, plans for commemorating Xavier's death in 1952 were initiated as early as 1949 – as evidenced in the above colonial government bulletin – and continued up until the opening ceremonies on 3 December 1952. Such elaborate and advance planning on the part of the Estado da Índia suggests both its continued reliance on Xavier to enact and represent colonial power in Goa and the ritual weight given to marking the anniversary of Xavier's death – as compared to other moments in his biography – since it so perfectly epitomized commemoration, and at an acute historical moment nonetheless (1952). Thus, by September 1949, the planning of a tenth exposition was well under way, particularly since a commemoration of this type and scale would never be 'repeated', at least not in the foreseeable future. This celebration would unite the Catholic world of the Orient through the figure of Xavier, at the same time affirming Portugal's privileged and specialized position as a 'moral force' in the Orient to a larger audience, and as my analysis will suggest, during a time when it perhaps needed this affirmation the most.

These 'preparatory works' in advance of the staging of the tenth exposition also involved elaborate renovations of the many religious buildings in Old Goa starting in 1951, on a scale that was unprecedented, one that far exceeded past expositions.[14] The Portuguese colonial government appointed an architect by the name of Baltasar de Castro to oversee this project, which included complete renovations of both the inside and outside of the Chapel of St Catherine (the See Cathedral) and minor renovations to the front of the Convent of St Francis of Assisi.[15] Colonial officials also relied on a number of technologies, both old and new, to enhance travel and communication not only between metropole and colony but between Goa and numerous other parts of the world, and within the space of ritual itself. In a pattern similar to past commemorative expositions, regular steamboat services between Bombay and Goa were made available on a daily basis during the days of the exposition.[16] Members of the public could now rely on an extensive railway system that had been built in earlier days to connect British India and Portuguese India.[17] For the first time, microphones were set up in Old Goa for the many speeches and masses that were to be delivered during the days of the exposition,[18] while numerous telegrams were received by Goa's Governor General from many heads of state who expressed their support for the upcoming celebrations.[19] Pope Pius XII was also scheduled to deliver a radio speech to be broadcast in Portuguese on the first day of the exposition.[20] A Goan radio station and direct telephone lines between Lisbon and Goa were also inaugurated in 1952 prior to the opening of the tenth exposition.[21] Lastly, with the advent of flying, it was now possible for persons from distant lands to travel to Goa to take part in Xavier's tenth exposition. Members of the international press were specially invited to attend the festivities in Old Goa, their coverage producing multiple testaments to the successes (and failures) of this set of ritual practices in 1952.[22] The mobilization of all these relatively new technologies in the ritual arena on the part of the Estado da Índia also suggest the changing times, post-Second World War industrialization, numerous investments in Xavier's biography from nation-states and organizations located outside Goa, the diversity of the public in attendance, and, finally, the degree to which the Estado da Índia was invested in commemoration, all continuing themes of this chapter.

The travelling exhibition of Xavier's right arm in 1949

> In 1949, commemorating the fourth centenary of the arrival of the first Catholic missionary, St Francis Xavier, in Japan, an international pilgrimage was organized and all of Japan made elaborate preparations for the centenary. The arm was carried through the principal centres of missionary activity of the Saint during his lifetime including the column of 26 martyrs at Nagasaki, Kagoshima, Yamaguchi, Hiroshima, Kobe, Osaka, Nara, [and] Kyoto. This arm which cured so many sick, helped thousands of unfortunate, baptised several hundreds of persons, absolved countless people, even revived the dead. It will be possible to fill up an entire volume if one goes on relating the many benefits.[23]

At the same time that civil and ecclesiastical officials in Goa were busily preparing Xavier's corpse for the grandest commemorative exposition yet, the right arm of Xavier, which had been surgically removed and sent to the Vatican as part of his canonization proceedings in 1614 where it remained encased in a reliquary, was now a travelling exhibition in 1949, its stopovers including Portugal, Goa, and Japan. It was first flown from Rome to Lisbon, where a small ceremony took place in the presence of two Ministers, of War and Foreign Affairs, respectively, and the Reverend Dr Mauricio dos Santos, a Jesuit who delivered a speech in honour of the saint, stating 'that the right arm of Xavier was raised up in order to bless us all'.[24] Xavier's right arm was then placed on a second plane, one that also carried a number of Catholic pilgrims from Rome, Portugal, and Spain, all destined for the 'Golden Goa' of old times.[25] It was here that Xavier's right arm was to be remarkably reunited with the rest of his corpse (three hundred and thirty-five years later), if only for a day,[26] before it was flown to Japan, where celebrations took place in multiple Japanese cities tied to Xavier's biography. The festivities started on 15 August 1949, and lasted fifteen days in the presence of the Japanese Emperor to commemorate the fourth centenary of this Jesuit missionary's arrival in Kagoshima in the year 1549.[27]

Xavier's medical examination: from 'incorruptible corpse' to 'sacred relics'

The miracle [of Xavier's corpse] is over; it could not be eternal. – Goa's Archbishop Costa Nunes, 1952[28]

Prior to the staging of ritual practice in 1952, Xavier's corpse was placed on the autopsy table to assess whether or not he was fit for public veneration on the fourth centenary of his death. This was by now an all-too-familiar ritual practice – such standard medical reports had been also issued with the festivities of 1910, 1931, and 1942; once again the saint's corpse was sanctioned for public display. However, the details of the procedure that was performed by medical doctors would result in a dramatically different set of conclusions.

Xavier's medical examination took place as early as 23 June 1951, one and a half years in advance of his proposed exposition. Here I reproduce for the reader the details of this remarkable autopsy report:

Document of the Exam of the Venerable Body of St Francis Xavier. (Confidential). On the 23rd of June 1951, at 8:30, upon the invitation of His Excellency Reverend Patriarch of the Indies, D. José da Costa Nunes, in the Sacristy of the Basilica of the Bom Jesus, the doctors António Luís de Sousa Sobrinho, Director of the Services of Health and Hygiene of the Estado da Índia, and João Manuel Pacheco de Figuereido, Director of the Medical and Surgical School of Goa, met in order to proceed to examine the venerable Body of St Francis Xavier that was closed inside the coffin of wood arranged on a table. The seals were broken and the coffin was opened by His Excellency Reverend the Patriarch, His Excellency in Charge of General Government, Dr. Manuel Marques de Abrantes Amaral and His Excellency the Reverend Archbishop Coadjutor (Assistant) D. José Vieira Alvernaz, Archbishop of Anazartha, being present also the Reverend Canon Aires Franklin de Sa, Administrator of the Basilica, who observed that the Body of the Saint was found dressed in his sacerdotal vestments with the head flexed towards the thorax and the left forearm and hand with its fingers half flexed, resting transversally across the chest. The objective of the exam was directed in first place to those accessible regions, that is, those not covered by the vestments, like the head, left hand, and the feet.

HEAD: The occipital and parietal left sides are denuded [bare] but perfectly conserved. The parietal and frontal sides present themselves dressed in dry withered skin with some signs of destruction on them and there are seen a few rare hairs attached to the body by skin, where they appear to be encrusted. The side presents a perforation underneath the right arch. The prominence of the molar regions and that of the ocular globes is conserved, being able to distinguish the eyelids of the right eye. The small nose is well conserved, being the right nasal bone dislocated backwards and the earlobe of the same side a little worn out. The orifices of the nasal passages are visible. The relief of the mouth is conserved, the lips half open, with the musculature and skin in the direction of destruction, leaving to see the distinctiveness of the inferior incisors, small and regular, being the second left one dislocated backwards. Rare hairs of the beard on the left side being, like on the head, attached with skin to the body. The right ear is conserved. The outer lobe of the right ear doesn't exist, noting in the temporal maximillary region, of the same side, in consequence of the destruction of skin, three large orifices, one of which the major one, corresponds to the location of the implantation of the outer lobe. Across these orifices are clearly visible the bones.

LEFT HAND: Resting with palm side on the chest, with the fingers half-flexed, muscular substances and conserved skin. Dorsal side: some flexible tendons are distinguishable, being most clear and prominent at the extension of the index finger. Only the thumb finger has a nail.
Palm Side: some flexible tendons are clearly distinguishable, with little flexibility of the veins.

LEFT FOOT: Dorsal side. Conserved masses of muscles, the tendons distinctive and the skin withered. The first and fifth toes are complete and with nails; absent are the digital bones on the second toe; the third toe is reduced to a plain morsel of cutaneous (pertaining to the skin) place; it is missing the bones and the fourth toe doesn't have skin on the dorsal side. The sole of the foot is very well conserved, as well as the muscular masses that cover the heel that is on the path of destruction.

RIGHT FOOT: Of reformed aspect and in forced extension. The heel is dislocated inside. It does not have the last four toes. By the opening, the result is that they don't exist, the insteps are visible, the muscle masses conserved, minus the posterior part which is destroyed in part and with faded skin. Some tendons are distinguishable, the big toe is prominent and without a nail. The major part of the skin of the sole is conserved.

Accordingly, by determination of His Excellency, the Reverend Patriarch, the vestments that covered the anterior part of the body were removed and he observed:

1. The head was disarticulated, completely free resting on a pillow cushion and the cranial cavity empty.

2. The left hand is articulated (joined) with the two bones of the forearm, maintaining the wholeness and articulation of the wrist. The bones of the forearm are losing their covered skin, of which was noted the third inferior, with small pieces of destruction.

3. Maintained whole is the tibia joint of both sides of the inferior members, like on the forearm, the bones – tibia and fibula – on both sides, are covered in skin, with zones of destruction, only on the third inferior.

4. The left tibia and fibula, in the superior extremity, are still conserved.

5. The two femurs, have regressed to some small pieces of skin, and the kneecaps are jointed with the bones of the leg for half the length.

6. Deposited in the central part of the coffin we found the following bones: a bone of the sternum, two clavical bones, the left omoplate, the

humerus, 2 fragments of the ribs, 21 vertebrae (4 cervical, 12 dorsal, and 5 lumbar) the sacrum, and the two iliac bones with only 5 lumbar vertebra and the last dorsal jointed.

7. Various discolored pieces of skin, of which 5 were large, seeing clearly that the major was of the buttocks region. In order to reconstitute the skeleton, all the existing portions and those already mentioned were collected in order on a table, being for this end to arrange a wire in the vertebrae cavities to connect them. Reconstituting the skeleton by juxtaposing the bones, it was observed that the Body of the Saint, measured from the extremity of the first toe of the left foot to the top of the head, was 171 centimeters in length, and 162 centimeters when measured from head to the heel. Finally, all the parts of the Body, in appropriate order, but not jointed, and the 5 pieces of skin, were placed in the coffin and covered by the vestments that had been removed by reason of the exam. We declare that the Body doesn't present any sign of putrefaction, nor of a bad smell. In the duration of the exam, several photographs were taken by J.P. Guerra.

From this exam, the minutes of this present act are drawn that is signed by us. Old Goa, Basilica of Bom Jesus, on the 23rd of June 1951. Signed: António Luís de Souza Sobrinho, João Manuel Pacheco de Figueireido and José Vieira Alvernaz, Archbishop of Anarta. [29]

The details of this medical examination – parts of which were kept confidential – evidence several interrelated themes concerning the condition of Xavier's corpse in 1952, themes that mark both similarities and differences in style and content from past medical examinations. First, the same balance of civil and ecclesiastical leaders and medical doctors witnessed at earlier examinations is also maintained throughout the proceedings of 1952. Not only were the seals verified before being broken to ascertain whether or not his coffin had been illegally opened prior to examination, but the autopsy was performed jointly by Archbishop Nunes and several certified medical doctors and in the presence of the Governor General of the Estado da Índia and the Administrator of the Church of Bom Jesus. Second, the objective of this examination was to explore in detail the condition of Xavier's corpse, with a continuing focus on body parts, including both those covered and those not by his priestly vestments. Similar conclusions are drawn concerning the evident deterioration of certain body parts since his last exposition – the emphasis on the missing outer earlobe in 1952 is one such example – whereas others remain well conserved. Xavier's corpse is found to be in a state of in between-ness: it is neither completely desiccated – still no signs of putrefaction or bad smells are evident – nor perfectly preserved – many pieces of skin are discoloured or withered – just as had been the case at earlier ritual moments. Third, this autopsy report is couched in the language of medical expertise and scientific accuracy, suggesting in the process that Xavier's corpse is increasingly treated as a scientific specimen by 1952, a discourse that first emerged in 1906 with the production of a medical thesis on Xavier. Fourth, there is a repeated concern with Xavier's authenticity via his height, a concern that had first been expressed in 1859, but that has also arisen intermittently throughout the time frame of this chapter. By 1952 his corpse had been measured once again from head to toe to determine whether his height corresponded to past estimates by his official biographers who had described his stature in life. The medical report of 1952 thus picks up where recent ones left off, determining the condition of Xavier's body by way of similar practices and foci, only many years later and in more exhaustive detail.

However, there are also departures from past examinations, particularly the fact that many details of Xavier's autopsy report are kept confidential. The medical doctors in charge – in this case, Sobrinho and Figueireido – adopt new medical practices that are indicative of modernizing medical techniques. First, a man by the name of J.P. Guerra is employed to take photos of the corpse throughout the duration of the medical examination, a practice never performed before for medical purposes. Second, after removing Xavier's vestments, his head is found to be disarticulated: 'completely free resting on a pillow cushion', separate from the rest of his body. It is this medical statement that is the most outstanding, for it is after this discovery that his corpse is labelled a 'skeleton', his bones arranged on a table, and a wire placed through his multiple bodily cavities in an attempt to 'reconstitute' his corpse. Lastly, his many body parts, along with any existing portions of skin, are placed inside his coffin, and thereafter covered with his sacerdotal vestments. While Xavier had been readied multiple times before in preparation for ritual exposure, this is the first time that such a practice of reconstituting his corpse becomes part of the medical proceedings, or at least is (publicly) acknowledged as such.[30]

The above medical findings, in turn, resulted in the production of two qualifiers to ritual practice in 1952. First, Patriarch Nunes made the careful decision to replace Xavier's label of 'incorruptible body' with that of 'sacred relics' for the exposition in 1952.[31] Even though his body was found to be in parts, it was still considered precious – several relics were then produced out of a dried piece of skin found hanging from one of his legs.[32] Second, it was decided by the Pope that upon the completion of the tenth exposition, his 'sacred relics' would be encased in glass to prevent any further deterioration, a suggestion that had also been made in the case of the expositions of 1931 and 1942 but never implemented. Perhaps it is because death is at the centre of commemoration in 1952 that the famous words of the Archbishop quoted at the outset of this section are deemed acceptable at this time: 'The miracle is over, it could not be eternal.'

Ritual contours: harnessing the old and new

> The celebrations of the fourth centenary of the death of St Francis Xavier, whose body was finally brought to Goa, do not constitute the only stirring testimony of veneration to the Great Apostle that endures where it is conserved by people of diverse faiths to which he preached; the celebrations will be a splendid demonstration also of the fidelity of Portuguese India to the tradition and glory of the name Portugal.[33]

The many activities that made up this thirty-five-day commemorative exposition were largely overseen by Archbishop Costa Nunes, and the newly arrived Governor General, Paulo Bénard Guedes,[34] a 'balancing' of church and state displayed once again in the space of ritual. Numerous 'esteemed' guests – both civil and ecclesiastical – from abroad were specially invited for this momentous occasion.[35] In addition, the same Francisco Xavier da Costa of earlier expositions (1900, 1910, 1922, 1931, 1942) was put in charge of producing a manual that recorded all of ritual's rich details, only for the first time both English and Portuguese texts were included – a detail that suggests both the strength and popularity of the English language on the Indian subcontinent, including within Goa, and the accommodation of a more diverse public in the space of ritual.

Reportedly, this public numbered 817,000 persons – the highest total to date[36] – each serving as a witness to the fourth centenary of Xavier's death. For the first time, a one-kiss-per-person rule was strictly enforced owing to the fragility of Xavier's corpse,[37] and in light of the fact that 'this would be the last occasion on which it would be permitted to kiss the foot of the Apostle directly', a pronouncement made public by Patriarch Nunes himself.[38] In addition, numerous donations and offerings, in the form of both money and wax, were received during the days of the exposition,[39] and several 'extraordinary facts' were circulated via the Goa press.[40] In addition, the supply and distribution of food in Old Goa were undertaken by a private company, which also ran a restaurant during the days of the exposition inside the Patriarchal Palace for the express purpose of accommodating all of Goa's many esteemed visitors.[41] Lastly, a 'Cultural and Artistic Exhibition' was staged at the Institute of Vasco da Gama in Goa to coincide with the days of the exposition: here the 'Portugueseness' of Goa – and by extension, Salazar's 'one-nation theory' – is reinforced through a seamless display of paintings, sculptures, and ceramics by numerous metropolitan artists, alongside many Goan ones.[42]

Portuguese and Indian investments in Xavier: reviving the posse, *protecting Goa*

Goa is the transplantation of the Occident in Oriental territories, and the expression of Portugal in India. – António de Oliveira Salazar, 1956[43]

I should like to tell the people of Goa how we all sympathize with them in this struggle and how we are all following it with anxious interest. For us, Goa is as much a part of India as any other part, and the freedom of India inevitably includes the freedom of the people of Goa. Goa cannot be separated from India. So any struggle for freedom there becomes part of our own struggle. – Prime Minister of India, J. Nehru, 21 July 1946[44]

Portugal's investment in Xavier's commemoration is marked by the centrality of the *posse* ceremony during the tenth exposition, a ritual practice that had also defined past commemorative expositions (1931, 1942) staged under Salazar's dictatorship,[45] and which was now revived once again in order to bless the newly arrived Governor General of the Estado da Índia.[46] What had been originally planned for an earlier date was now postponed and performed instead on the day of the closing ceremonies, 6 January 1953.[47] At this time, Governor General Paulo Bénard Guedes was handed Xavier's 'symbolic' staff of command by Patriarch Nunes in a 'traditional' ceremony,[48] with Nunes pointing out that Xavier would once again protect Goa from 'enemy invasions', thus ensuring a government of 'firmness, rectitude, justice, peace, and progress'.[49]

Situating the revival of *posse* within a larger historical context reveals the significance of this ritual act's centrality to the tenth exposition of 1952. First, while Salazar's Estado Novo had survived the Second World War (Goa becoming a major exporter of iron ore in the postwar period)[50] soon after the end of British colonization in India (1947), starting in the 1950s Salazar began to promote two theories concerning Goa's (Portuguese) status in India to counter arguments such as the one made by India's Prime Minister Jawaharlal Nehru cited at the outset of this section.[51] Two additional factors – France's willingness to pull peacefully out of Pondicherry, also a colonial enclave located amidst an independent India, and a growing independence movement in Goa itself, a movement not without its own set of concerns and contradictions – played a central role in pushing Salazar to promote his own theory of nationhood.[52] Since Portugal's prestige was still very much tied up with that of its colonies, Salazar first promulgated the 'one-nation theory' in which he projected an image of Goa as an 'expression of Portugal in India' and an 'overseas province of Portugal'.[53] Salazar argued that 'if geographically Goa is India, socially and in religion and culture Goa is Europe', hence, it must be preserved as a 'memorial of the West in the East',[54] the figure of Xavier no doubt playing a role in determining Goa's commemorative status.[55] Second, this dictator propounded a legal theory based on Portugal's 'four centuries old sovereignty' over Goa, claiming a legal right to rule Goa on the basis of precedent.[56] Thus, commemoration in 1952 only strengthens Salazar's argument against Nehru, a case built less on economics, and more on history and culture, one that he was also forced to defend in front of the United Nations.[57] Salazar, a former economist himself, made public statements asserting that Goa's continual financial drain on Portugal's economy did not deter its obligations to its overseas province.[58] Lastly, another reason for Portugal's resistance to granting freedom to Goa had everything to do with its more profitable African colonies, the fear being that Goa's integration into the Indian nation-state would be the 'open sesame' for African decolonization, a point that I will suggest was not lost during ritual activity.[59] Meanwhile, as Salazar was building a case for Portugal, utilizing the space of ritual as well to reinforce his argument, Prime Minister Nehru was working through diplomatic channels to resolve the 'Goa problem', including plans for the Consul of the Indian Union to attend the upcoming festivities in Portuguese India.[60] Nehru's tactics would dramatically change after France's complete withdrawal from India in 1954, a point to be discussed in relation to the last colonial exposition of 1961.

Given Salazar's promotion of a 'one-nation theory' which defined metropole and colony as one territory, it is no surprise then that numerous commemorative acts were simultaneously organized in Portugal to mark the fourth centenary of Xavier's death. Not only was a statue of Xavier commissioned in order to be displayed in Lisbon, but the Municipal Council of this same city named one of its principal avenues after Goa's patron saint during the days of the exposition in Old Goa.[61] In addition, an 'Exposition of Missionary and Sacred Art' had been staged in Lisbon in 1951, an exhibition which included numerous Xaverian objects – three ivory sculptures of Xavier from Goa, one of his sandals, a box containing silver from the covering of his original casket in the Church of Bom Jesus, and an 'oriental box containing relics of the saint' – of which certain less prized items then travelled to Madrid for public display.[62]

Thus, given these changing historical circumstances – Salazar's development of a 'one-nation theory' to absolve Portugal's role in maintaining colonies in an era of decolonization, the demise of British colonialism in India five years earlier, a foreseeable end to French colonialism in Pondicherry, an ever-expanding anti-Portuguese campaign in the Goan, Indian, and international contexts, and, finally, the looming threat of a possible invasion by a newly independent

Indian government under Prime Minister Nehru[63] – colonial officials turned to the *posse* and Xavier's intercession in the hopes of doing more than just blessing the arrival of Goa's newest Governor General. Colonial officials would also rely on a heightened Portuguese military and police presence during the days of the exposition to further protect saint and state.[64] Perhaps it is no surprise, then, that during the last years of Portugal's colonial regime in Goa it was common to refer to St Francis Xavier pitifully as an 'official of the Portuguese Overseas Ministry'.[65]

Promoting religiosity

> Should the coming Xaverian celebrations succeed in creating in us this spirit of proselytization, we shall have paid to St Francis Xavier the homage he would most appreciate. – Archbishop José Costa de Nunes, 7 September 1952[66]

In the midst of these multiple investments in Xavier and his powers of state on the fourth centenary of his death, it is also important to look at how religiosity was promoted within the space of ritual. It had been under Salazar's Estado Novo that the infamous 'Acto Colonial' had been passed, and a new Constitution (1933) written, one which brought the Catholic Church under its confidence to explicitly promote the imperialist designs of the new 'fascist' state,[67] and which would be showcased in 1952. Faith is repeatedly enacted and promoted during the days of the exposition, a Roman Catholicism that is promoted not only through speeches, including a live fifteen-minute radio sermon delivered in Portuguese by Pope Pius XII on the opening day of the festivities,[68] but also by means of a variety of additional ritual activities which were reprinted in Francisco Xavier da Costa's 'Programme of the Religious Services in the Old City of Goa'.[69] These (daily) practices included the ringing of bells in all the churches and cathedrals of Old Goa on the mornings of the opening and closing festivities, the assigning of prestigious positions to Goa's many religious leaders and students during the 'inaugural' procession which involved moving Xavier's corpse to the nearby See Cathedral in front of fifty thousand 'devotees',[70] as well as during the days of the exposition, and the frequent chanting of the 'Litany of Saints'.[71] Additional daily ritual activities consisted of the singing of hymns, in Latin, Portuguese, and Konkani,[72] the recitation of sermons and other 'acts of devotion' dedicated to the exemplary Christian life of Xavier,[73] the hearing of confessions in a multitude of languages,[74] and, finally, the performance of numerous Catholic communions and masses inside the See Cathedral, including a grand Pontifical Mass which took place on the opening day of the festivities, in front of the colonial state's most esteemed guests.[75] Additional masses were performed inside all the churches of Old Goa while numerous Catholic pilgrims were accommodated inside these same churches.[76] Remarkably, in the end, over three thousand Masses took place during the days of Xavier's exposition.[77] Finally, in order to allow members of the public sufficient time and space for the 'kissing of Xavier's relics', the See Cathedral remained open from 6 a.m. until 7 p.m. on a daily basis, and sometimes, if necessary, 'during the night'.[78] Together, all of these ritual practices transformed not only the See Cathedral which temporarily housed Xavier's corpse but Old Goa itself into a centre of Catholic religiosity during the month-long exposition.

Portuguese colonial officials also invited numerous Catholic bishops from India and Ceylon[79] to take part in the exposition, reinforcing Goa's position as a centre for Catholic faith and pilgrimage. In addition, six Archbishops – representing Bombay, Karachi (Pakistan), Delhi, Verapoly, Dacca (East Pakistan), and Goa and Daman – were given the privilege of carrying Xavier's corpse during the inaugural procession to the See Cathedral.[80] Additional guests from the African subcontinent were also invited; for example, the Apostolic Prefect of Zanzibar was specially invited to Goa from Nairobi because of his 'urgent desire' to kiss the body of Xavier.[81] On 10 December eighty African soldiers – presumably transported from either Mozambique or Angola, Portugal's largest and most profitable African colonies at this time – were baptized by the same Cardinal Legate.[82] Their collective baptism signifies not only Portugal's larger (Catholic) empire outside Asia but also the strong historical ties between Portuguese India and Portuguese Africa through colonialism and Catholic missionary work, as well as the militarization of Goa during the days of the exposition.

At the same time that the Estado da Índia promoted Xavier's role as an agent of Catholicism, it also represented the space of ritual as one of religious tolerance. Accordingly, it was suggested that the Catholics of Portuguese India must proselytize not by active conversion but rather by example; only then could the process of Catholic evangelization take place without damage to the religious diversity of both Goa's and India's population.[83] Thus, even though the message of Xavier had not changed over the years, it could now be interpreted differently; that is, the circumstances had shifted such that in 1952 a different kind of response was necessary, a response that included freedom of religious ideology and practice in the face of a more 'secular' but religiously diverse Indian nation-state.[84] Archbishop Nunes himself sustained this belief throughout the days of the exposition, stating during a pastoral speech that 'different periods of time call for different modes of action. To judge remote epochs with the criteria of present times is to misunderstand things.'[85]

Restoring the Jesuits

> It was notable the services of the Priests, Scholastics, and Brothers of the Company of Jesus [the Jesuits] who, in great number, and alternating themselves in pairs of two every two hours, organized and admitted the pilgrims to kiss and to give them, touched to the Venerable Relics, religious articles. – Francisco Xavier da Costa, 1952[86]

Thus far, I have suggested that the Jesuits had steadily encroached upon the Goan scene thoughout the twentieth century, their increasing presence visible at past commemorative expositions of Xavier as well. During his tenth exposition, members of this religious order are given a prominent yet restricted position owing to their past strong biographical ties to Xavier, and are assigned certain ritual practices to manage in order to enhance the religiosity of Goa and strengthen Xavier's commemorative powers in the process.

By 1952, the Jesuits had been legally operating in Goa for approximately twenty years since, under the dictates of Salazar's legislation of a new Constitution in 1933, they had been allowed to return to all Portuguese territories, including Goa. The role of the Jesuits during the tenth exposition is prescribed by Archbishop Costa Nunes himself.[87] During the inaugural procession to the See Cathedral, it is Pe Walter Mathias, Superior of the Jesuits of Goa, who directs the thousands of people lined up on either side of Xavier's coffin by way of a microphone, a new technology that helps to ensure the order of the procession.[88] Members of the Society of Jesus are also put in charge of organizing the large number of Catholic pilgrims who have come to Old Goa to renew their faith – including their reception, organization in orderly lines, admission inside the See Cathedral, Mass ceremonies, and, finally, the regular posting of 'lost and found' items discovered throughout the days of the exposition.[89] On a daily basis, two Jesuit priests are stationed inside the See Cathedral to preside over the 'any indiscreet acts of devotion' centred on Xavier's 'sacred relics' while two other non-ordered ecclesiastics are put in charge of ensuring that pilgrims did not touch or kiss anything beyond Xavier's toe, and only once at that.[90]

With the central ritual activities, including the veneration of Xavier's corpse, taking place inside the See Cathedral, the Jesuits are also put in charge of overseeing the management of the Church of Bom Jesus. Members of this religious order are responsible for arranging on a daily basis Catholic masses, confessions, and communions inside this former Jesuit Baroque-styled church.[91] Several 'illustrious' Jesuits were invited as guests to participate in the commemoration of Xavier in 1952 – including Pe Domingos Alves Mauricio, Representative of the

Provincial of the Society of Jesus in Portugal, Fr Eugene De Valcount Lockwood, who came to Goa from as far away as the United States,[92] and nine Jesuit priests from Australia;[93] these visitors were specially accommodated inside the Church of Bom Jesus. Together, all of these sanctioned religious activities suggest that the Jesuits were given an expanded yet circumscribed role during the days of the exposition, a role that also enforces their historical ties to the Church of Bom Jesus and Goa's patron saint.

Accommodating difference and distance

> In view of a large number of Pilgrims coming in from the Indian Union, Pakistan, Ceylon, Malaya, Far East, Persian Gulf, Africa, and parts of Europe, a religious service will be organized to meet the requirements of each group of Pilgrims. – *Pictorial Review and Guide to Goa*, 1952[94]

The persons who visited Old Goa during the days of the tenth exposition far exceeded, in both number and diversity, the attendant public at past commemorative rituals centred on Xavier. The accommodation of such a wide range of publics by the Estado da Índia has everything to do with the nature of commemoration in 1952, and the larger historical circumstances in which ritual was imbricated. The difficulty of commemorating Xavier's death at a moment when both the miracle of his corpse was declared over and their own political 'death' was close at hand was not lost on Portuguese colonial officials. However, with the hope perhaps that they could contribute to the forestalling of such an 'end' through Xavier's display, Portuguese colonial officials staged the most elaborate exposition that they had ever attempted, one which recognized the expanding role of different publics in determining ritual's success.

Civil and ecclesiastical leaders first extended invitations to diverse publics – Goan and non-Goan, Indian and European, Portuguese and Spanish, Catholic and Hindu, male and female, religious and secular[95] – to visit Old Goa during the month-long celebrations in the hopes of representing Goa less as a colony but rather as an 'overseas' province of Portugal in accordance with Salazar's 'one-nation theory'. This process of producing a large (seeing) public was enabled by several factors: the harnessing of new technologies (the aeroplane, the railway, transatlantic shipping) which made such long-distance travel possible and increased the speed of travel, the accommodation of many of these same visitors in Old Goa itself, and finally, the translation of many of the principal ritual acts into a variety of languages (English, as well as various Indian indigenous languages, including Goan Konkani) for those coming from different linguistic and cultural backgrounds.[96]

Here I provide a brief overview of the diversity of these publics, as they were detailed by Francisco Xavier da Costa in his ritual manual. Included were approximately ten thousand members (mostly children and teenagers) of two Catholic organizations – Catholic Action and Catholic Youth of Goa – who were assigned to visit Old Goa on 8 December.[97] Diasporic Goans arriving from other parts of the Indian subcontinent included a large number of Goans from Bombay, home of the largest Goan community outside Goa itself,[98] and from Karachi (Pakistan), also home to a sizeable Goan community.[99] Interestingly, in 1952 the number of Goans who travelled to Portuguese India from abroad surpassed all earlier expositions.[100] Visiting Indian pilgrims included eight hundred Parsees from Ahmedabad, who travelled together, two young Muslim boys, who later expressed their desire to convert to Catholicism, five hundred Catholics from Trichur who were accompanied by their bishop and fifty priests, an 'extraordinary number' of Hindus and Muslims accompanied by their families, two Hindu princesses – the Maharanis of Bharia and Sawantvadi – and, finally, sixty Indian students from the St Francis Xavier School accompanied by their teachers.[101] Lastly, the fourth centenary of Xavier's death also witnessed the influx of an unprecedented number of Catholic pilgrims from all over the world, including residents of Pakistan, Ceylon, Malaya, the Persian Gulf, the Far East, Africa, and Europe.[102] Da Costa's compilation of 'foreign visitors' to Goa lists a thousand pilgrims each from Ceylon and Karachi (Pakistan), an unspecified number from Daman (Portuguese territory near Bombay), and nine hundred pilgrims from Europe who arrived in Old Goa by ship.[103] In order to accommodate these diverse publics, Portuguese colonial officials had to embody diversity in the space of ritual itself.

Goa's political and religious leaders also invited members of the foreign press to help produce a reading public, one that was not necessarily located in Portuguese India, but that still participated by proxy. A large group of journalists, representing numerous publishers, were invited by Portuguese colonial officials as 'illustrious guests' to report on the festivities centred in Old Goa.[104] This public consisted of foreign journalists from India, the UK, the USA, Brazil, Spain, and France and represented such daily newspapers and magazines as *Life International*, *The New York Times*, *O Globo* (Brazil), *The Daily Telegraph* (London), and wire services such as Reuters, and the BBC, among others.[105] Nor did Portugal miss this opportunity to represent the Goan celebrations in the metropolitan press: it sent its own set of eight journalists representing such Portuguese daily newspapers as *Diário de Lisboa*, *Diário Popular*, and *Comércio do Porto*.[106] These journalists were accommodated in the newly inaugurated Hotel Mandovi located in nearby

Panjim (Nova Goa),[107] and were expressly invited to an opening reception hosted by Goa's Governor General Guedes.[108] Thus, the attendance of members of the international press at this tenth exposition helped to produce and circulate numerous eyewitness accounts of ritual and in a multiplicity of languages beyond the borders of Goa to a Xaverian 'imagined community',[109] which, despite its location or diversity, was unified by a spiritual figure. Thus, in harnessing commemoration to a larger political agenda – one of promoting Portuguese nationalism and imperialism by actively producing a multi-tiered public (simultaneously a seeing, listening, and reading one) – the Estado da Índia turned innocent bystanders into 'ritual participants'[110] who both constituted and were constituted by the 'Goa problem'.

Producing and preserving commemorative objects

> To the tourist or pilgrim of Faith we dedicate these pages illustrated with religious monuments of Old Goa that attest to the eloquence of its architecture and statues, of its frescos and pictures, of its sculptures and paintings, of its precious stones, and epitaphs, the epic of Faith transplanted by seafarers, missionaries and soldiers in the territories of the Levant, distinguishing an ideal and a glorious epoch – the rebirth of five hundred years of Portugueseness.– *Old Goa, An Historical Guide*, 1952[111]

In a manner similar to past celebrations, the tenth exposition also witnessed the production of a variety of commemorative objects honouring Goa's patron saint. However, by 1952, the number and type of material objects endowed with commemorative powers had increased, as well as the places of their circulation. Portuguese colonial officials first produced a variety of postage stamps to commemorate Xavier on the fourth centenary of his death. On 23 December 1952 three commemorative stamps were issued by the Estado da Índia to coincide with the days of the exposition.[112] These three stamps, two of which are focused on his corporeality, index Xavier directly; one is an image of a statue of the saint, a second is of his famed silver casket, and a third is of his right arm encased in a reliquary.[113] These stamps were not only circulated in Old Goa but also travelled to those sites in Asia where Portugal had remaining colonies – India (Daman and Diu), Macau, and Timor – their circulation contextualizing Goa and its patron saint within a larger Portuguese empire that was facing decolonization and numerous nationalist movements.[114] The practice of producing commemorative stamps helped mark the fourth centenary of Xavier's death, but also expanded Xavier's commemorative powers by their circulation within and beyond Goa's borders. Interestingly, on the very same day – 23 December 1952 – that these three stamps were issued by the Estado da Índia to circulate in Portuguese Asia, a series of four Xaverian stamps were issued by Salazar to circulate in Portugal.[115] Once again, metropole and colony(s) were intimately linked, only this time not through Xavier's well-travelled body parts but through the simultaneous production of commemorative stamps.

Our ritual expert Francisco Xavier da Costa also details several 'extraordinary facts',[116] including the remarkable story of a young Goan woman who, after being paralysed for over a year, and thus not able to travel to Old Goa for the exposition, asked another Catholic woman to carry a Xaverian commemorative stamp to the site of his corpse in order to ask for his intercession, which she performed successfully, returning the 'blessed' stamp to its owner upon her return. This paralysed woman then touched this same stamp to her own body, healing herself in the process, an act that was represented as 'ingenious' in the press.[117] This story, in turn, reinforces the indexical power of these commemorative stamps even as it inserts a note of caution into Xavier's corporeal powers in 1952.[118] Lastly, in a parallel move that continued the trend of relying on images of Xavier to act as proxies for his 'sacred relics', Portuguese colonial officials produced a series of postcards and Goa guidebooks (available in both Portuguese and English) to commemorate Xavier on the fourth centenary of his death,[119] both practices indexing the emergence of Goa as an international proto-tourist site and the commemoration of Portuguese India that was taking place alongside that of its patron saint.[120]

Refuting 'false rumours'

> The enemy propaganda has circulated in the foreign press the following false rumours: that the Jesuit priests sold relics of St Francis Xavier and that they received money from Masses and Offerings. – Francisco Xavier da Costa, 1952[121]

Interestingly, Francisco Xavier da Costa dedicates a separate section in his ritual manual to 'false rumours';[122] in both their individuality and totality, these rumours inextricably shaped ritual at the same time that they help to expose the vulnerabilities of church and state precisely at a moment when they were particularly vulnerable to what da Costa calls 'enemy propaganda'.[123] Analysing them at face value allows me to explore them as a window on to what in fact was happening in 1952. On the one hand, in their prodigious efforts to successfully represent Goa as an 'overseas province' of Portugal in the space of ritual to members of the foreign press, Portuguese colonial officials tried to quell any negative rumours; that is, they attempted to stop their paths of circulation by labelling them 'unfounded' or 'false'. On the other hand, they allowed certain select rumours to proliferate because their circulation strengthened their ritual cause. In the end, the Estado da

Índia failed to account for the resilience of rumour, and thus underestimated the defining role of the public – including the foreign press – in the face of larger historical circumstances.

Significantly, several rumours that circulated during the tenth exposition were centred on Xavier's corpse, which in turn implicated other (colonial) bodies. One such rumour suggested the removal of Xavier's 'sacred relics' by colonial officials prior to ritual activity because of the poor condition of his corpse, a rumour 'without the slightest foundation' that Archbishop Nunes purposely counters in his pastoral speech, thus assuring the roused public that, in fact, Xavier's corpse was located in Goa and would be exposed to the public as further proof, a rumour reminiscent of earlier times and expositions (1782), only on this occasion directed not at the Jesuits but rather at the state.[124] Another circulating rumour, however, did involve the Jesuits, and concerned their unauthorized selling of Xaverian powders and relics, a rumour that was countered by statements involving the Goa police and the public in preventing such acts of 'exploitation'. [125] Yet another circulating rumour indicated that this would be the last time that members of the public would be allowed to 'kiss the foot of the Apostle directly'.[126] Instead of being discounted by colonial state officials, this particular rumour was allowed to proliferate, thus ensuring the popularity of this exposition precisely because of the fragility of Xavier's corpse and promoting the idea that this was potentially the last time such a sacred act would be allowed. The wider appeal of this rumour was a powerful one, for members of the public who participated in this ritual in 1952 were thus potentially part of history-in-the-making. Lastly, a widespread rumour suggested that many foreigners, returning to their homes, experienced much 'grief' from not having been able to kiss Xavier's 'sacred relics', despite the Estado da Índia's extension of the closing date to 6 January.[127] This rumour was labelled 'false' by colonial officials in an attempt to demonstrate their every effort to accommodate large and diverse public(s) in the space of ritual; da Costa goes so far as to point out that two shiploads of pilgrims from Bombay, arriving on the day of the closing ceremonies, had been given special permission by Archbishop Nunes to kiss Xavier's relics despite it being one day after the end of the festivities.[128] Together, these rumours (including those labelled false) which were directed variously at Xavier's corpse, colonial officials, and the Catholic Church (both the Archdiocese and the Jesuits) suggest the expanding power of rumour and the hazards of representation in 1952. These rumours also indicate the very real condition of this saint's body parts, the colonial state's anxiety surrounding this fact and their subsequent investment in preserving his 'sacred relics', the state's dependence on its public to ensure the exposition's success at a time when public opinion perhaps mattered most, and finally, the metonymic quality of his corpse; that is, Xavier stands in for the Estado da Índia such that commemoration potentially signifies two deaths in 1952.

Closing the ceremony, encasing Xavier's 'sacred relics'

> Some time after the celebration of the fourth centenary of the death of the Saint, the Engineer Ettore Brandizzi came to Goa to compose the Relics and place them, on 2 February of 1955 in an urn of crystal and silver, which was sealed on the 13th day of this same year. – Dr J.M. Pacheco de Figuereido, 1977[129]

The closing ceremony for Xavier's tenth exposition was staged on 6 January 1953.[130] On the morning of this day, at 9 a.m., Patriarch Nunes arrived alongside Governor General Guedes at the See Cathedral to oversee this set of ritual practices, which were performed in front of a specially 'reserved' public.[131] First, the Archbishop handed Xavier's historic baton to Goa's head of state in the 'traditional and symbolic' *posse* ceremony described in an earlier section.[132] Second, the closing Pontifical Mass was performed by Patriarch Nunes. Thereafter, he gave an 'eloquent panegyric' to Goa's patron saint, including a lecture on Xavier's biography, focusing in particular on the ten years that Xavier spent missionizing in Asia.[133] Both the Mass and the lecture were amplified by Nunes's use of a microphone.[134] Third, Xavier's 'sacred relics' were incensed before his casket was locked with the colonial set of three keys and the standard seals put in place.[135] It was then placed on the altar of the sacristy of the See Cathedral.[136] Lastly, the silver casket was carried in procession on the shoulders of four assistant prelates and two canons who reportedly had 'tears in their eyes'; accompanied by lit candles and devotional singing (in Konkani), they placed him in his chapel located inside the historic Church of Bom Jesus.[137] The commemoration of Xavier on the fourth centenary of his death had now officially come to a close.

Meanwhile, Portuguese colonial officials did not lose sight of Pope Pius XII's final order to encase Xavier's sacred relics in a 'crystal glass urn' following the end of the tenth exposition in order that Goa's patron saint be 'more effectively preserved'.[138] Following the Vatican's request, this 'crystal glass urn' was first made in Rome by the Casa Brandizzi company, and then sent to Goa in pieces, arriving there on 30 January 1955,[139] accompanied by an Italian engineer by the name of Ettore Brandizzi, who proceeded to 'place in order' the bones of Xavier while expressly not touching his face, hand, and feet.[140] According to J.M. Pacheco de Figueiredo – the doctor in charge of performing

Xavier's medical examination in 1951 and who recorded his memories of the Italian engineer's visit to Goa[141] – at this time Archbishop Costa Nunes refused Brandizzi the option of employing 'wax' or 'some sort of plastic substance' to improve the condition of Xavier's face.[142] It reportedly took almost two weeks – from 2 to 13 February 1955 – to complete the careful transfer of Xavier's relics to the new crystal glass urn inside the Church of Bom Jesus,[143] his old wooden coffin and set of three keys eventually placed nearby, inside a newly created museum dedicated to Xaverian cult objects.[144] Xavier's 'sacred relics' were now permanently sealed and preserved for an unforeseen future. Yet, despite these many precautionary measures, this was not the end of his ritualization in death.

By way of a conclusion: the 'extraordinary' exposition of 1961

> The modern state, embedded as it is within the universal narrative of capital, cannot recognize within its jurisdiction any form of community except the single, determinate, demographically enumerable form of the nation. It must therefore subjugate, if necessary by the use of state violence, all such aspirations of community identity. These other aspirations in turn, can give to themselves a historically valid justification only by claiming an alternative nationhood with rights to an alternative state. – Partha Chatterjee, 1993 [145]

> Mr. Nehru today warned that India could no longer tolerate the actions of the Portuguese authorities in Goa and would have to take adequate steps to give them an effective reply ... India had been waiting patiently for over 13 years to settle the issue of Goa peacefully through negotiations. – *The Statesman*, 2 December 1961[146]

Less than ten years after the close of the tenth exposition in Goa, the Estado da Índia harnessed Xavier once again in an attempt to pray for his intercession in the face of an 'impending' Indian invasion, and to garner public support for Portugal's continued colonial hold over Goa. This impromptu exposition was organized to take place during the month of December 1961. Despite the fact that it was not a commemoratively significant year in the biography of Xavier, Portuguese colonial officials turned to his ritualization, adopting and adapting the model of commemoration they had perfected over the years – staging once again the now familiar *posse* ceremony – precisely because of the dire political circumstances in which they found themselves.

Briefly, in the period between the last exposition of 1952 and the staging of this 'extraordinary' exposition – the newly anointed name given to unscheduled expositions such as this one in 1961[147] – the larger historical circumstances had changed dramatically such that Prime Minister Nehru was no longer interested in continuing diplomatic negotiations to resolve the 'Goa Problem'.[148] First, in 1954, France had pulled out of Pondicherry after peaceful negotiations.[149] Second, the Indian government's continuing economic blockade of Portugal, implemented in 1954 as a result of France's withdrawal from India, had greatly affected Goa's economy, stimulating both emigration abroad and resentment on the part of many (Catholic) Goans toward the Indian Union.[150] Third, Salazar continued to enforce his 'one-nation theory' wherein Goa was considered an 'overseas province' of Portugal; that is, he continued to mobilize this form of neo-colonialism in the face of growing opposition at both international and local levels.[151] Fourth, Goa's expanding independence movement continued to agitate against Portuguese colonial rule, mobilizing members of India's (including Goa's) public through speeches, demonstrations, rallies, publications, and small acts of Gandhian-influenced *satyagraha*.[152] Lastly, Nehru himself, in 1958, made certain commitments regarding Goa's future status after its successful incorporation into the Indian Union, commitments that would protect its autonomy and certain fundamental rights guaranteed by the Constitution of India, including freedom of religion and worship.[153] In accommodating the 'desires' of the people, Nehru also singled out Goa's patron saint, pledging this same year to 'preserve the tomb of St Francis Xavier, a sacred Roman Catholic shrine'.[154] Salazar responded by suggesting that Portugal would not negotiate 'over a territory it viewed as an integral part of its country'.[155]

Thus, amidst these escalating tensions between Salazar and Nehru and their competing ideas of nationhood,[156] that is, as the 'storm clouds of war hovered over Goa',[157] Portuguese colonial officials staged the eleventh 'Solemn Exposition' of St Francis Xavier's 'sacred relics'.[158] Even though a ritual manual modelled on Francisco Xavier da Costa's earlier ones was lacking for 1961 – owing no doubt to the haste with which this exposition was organized – the details of this event were widely circulated via the Goan, Indian, and Portuguese presses. The subdued festivities commenced on 14 December[159] with the hope that, through the intercession of Goa's patron saint, Portuguese India might be saved from integration into the Indian nation-state. Earlier, Portuguese authorities had ordered all the houses located on the 10km road between Panjim and Old Goa to be whitewashed in preparation for the upcoming exposition.[160] Meanwhile, Salazar had sent a specially appointed minister from Lisbon to inaugurate the festivities in Goa.[161]

On the opening day of the festivities, Xavier's relics were first removed from his 'permanent' crystal glass urn – interestingly, this ritual act took place in direct opposition to Pope Pius XII's earlier mandate to preserve his relics inside this protective casing – and exposed for public display, the chosen venue not the See Cathedral as had been the case in 1952 but rather the Church of Bom Jesus, his original home.[162] Next, the acting Governor General, Manuel António Vassalo e Silva, deposited his staff of command at the feet of the Saint, 'praying that Xavier should assume control and Goa should be saved from an attack by Indians'.[163] In contrast to past commemorative expositions – in particular the previous tenth exposition of 1952 – the public at this event was initially restricted to Portuguese colonial officers and military troops,[164] a ritual detail that suggests several points: the unusual circumstances under which this exposition was staged; the unease with which this exposition was staged by Portuguese colonial officials as well as their continuing investments in saint and state and their mutually imbricating roles; the prominence of ritual acts in representing and enacting political processes; and, finally, the defining role of the public in shaping the contours of ritual. On the fifth day of Xavier's public display – 18 December – Xavier's eleventh exposition was interrupted by the entry of the Indian Army into Portuguese India – these troops had been sent by Nehru to 'liberate' Goa in a campaign named 'Operation Vijay'.[165] On this very same day, Portuguese military officers laid down their arms without a single shot being fired. After four hundred and fifty-one years, Portuguese colonial rule in India was now officially over.[166]

That it was rumoured during these last days of the exposition that Salazar had ordered Xavier's corpse, including his 'precious' silver casket which was considered a 'masterpiece of Goan craftsmanship', to be transferred to Lisbon to mark the end of Portuguese sovereignty in India suggests once again the intertwined histories of Xavier and the Estado da Índia and the power of rumour as a force of history.[167] However, that it was also rumoured (and reported in the press) that members of Goa's public resisted all attempts on the part of the Portuguese to remove Xavier's 'sacred relics' from Old Goa on the eve of its liberation[168] suggests the defining role his (changing) image and corpse had in individual lives despite the fact that he was initially a manufactured product of Portuguese colonialism.[169] Thus, Xavier remained inside the Church of Bom Jesus, the site where he had lain in state for the last three hundred years and was solemnly venerated one last time, with reportedly both Goans and members of the Indian Army in attendance.[170] Thereafter, his 'sacred relics' were quietly returned to their glass casing.[171] Remarkably, this was the first time in the history of Xavier's many expositions that ritual activity was not extended, but rather suspended as a result of larger political circumstances.[172]

Governor General Vassalo e Silva departed from Goa soon thereafter, fittingly enough, neither with Xavier's 'sacred relics' nor with his 'precious silver casket', but with his staff of command, the same gem-studded baton that had staved off an earlier Indian 'invasion' in 1683, and that had been used in countless ritual acts of state (the *posse*) thereafter – including his commemoration as recently as 1952 – but that was now rendered useless as a political tool, though no doubt it still had a considerable historical and commodity value.[173] In much the same way that Goa's last outgoing Governor General feared adverse reactions from Catholics if he chose to remove Xavier's precious casket, India's Prime Minister feared adverse reactions from all Goans if he did not continue the tradition of safeguarding this prized possession. One year later, in 1963, and true to his earlier pledge to preserve Xavier's tomb after Goa's integration in the Indian Union, Prime Minister Nehru visited the former Portuguese colony to pay homage to Xavier, whose 'sacred relics' had helped determine Goa's (and thus India's) fate.[174]

The (failed) exposition of 1961 represents in some sense the 'death' that had been prophesied by the Estado da Índia in 1952 with Xavier's tenth exposition even as it continued to rely on the power of commemoration to forge a viable future in increasingly uncertain times. When colonial officials were unsuccessful in their one last attempt to 'package' history[175] in 1961 through the political, religious, and spiritual figure of Xavier, they had to finally accept the 'death' not only of the miracle of his corpse that they had in fact publicly announced in the space of ritual in 1952 but also of all the other colonial processes that were imbricated in the history of this saint and that they had put off in the hope that he would intercede on their behalf in spite of his corrupted state: the 'death' of the biography of his corpse as well as that of his ritualization in Goa, and, finally, the 'death' of Portuguese colonialism itself.

Notes

1 Maria Bucur and Nancy Wingfield, 'Introduction' to *Staging the Past: The Politics of Commemoration in Habsburg Central Europe, 1848 to the Present*, eds M. Bucur and N. Wingfield (West Lafayette, IN: Purdue University Press, 2001), p. 2.

2 Sushila Sawant Mendes, 'Dr. Lohia and Goa's Freedom Struggle', in *Essays in Goan History*, ed. Teotónio de Souza (New Delhi: Concept Publishing Company, 1989), p. 179.

3 'Commemorate: 1. to call to remembrance by a ceremony, etc., to honor by some act of respect or affection intended to preserve the memory of a person or event. 2. to preserve the memory of; to serve as a memorial to.' See *Webster's New Universal Unabridged Dictionary*, 2nd edn (New York: Simon and Schuster, 1983), p. 363.

4 See Webb Keane, *Signs of Recognition, Powers and Hazards of Representation in an Indonesian Society* (Berkeley: University of California Press, 1997).

5 Pe. R.J. Theodoro Martins, *Collection of Diocese Decrees of the Archdiocese of Goa. 1900–1911, Authorized by his Excellency and Reverend Archbishop Primary Patriarch of the Oriental Indies* (Nova Goa: Typ. Arthur & V. Inc., 1912), pp. 299–301. Year of 1906 Official Rites/Business/Work, No. 65.

6 Ibid.

7 Ibid.

8 Ibid.

9 Ibid.

10 L.M. Júlio Frederico Gonçalves, *Os Milagres de S. Francisco Xavier não são Milagres nem são de S. Francisco Xavier* (Graduate thesis, Goa Medical School, 1906). I was unable to locate a copy of this thesis in either Goa or Portugal. For a brief biographical sketch of Gonçalves see Alexio Manuel Costa (ed.), *Dicionário Literatura Goesa (Volume 3)* (Macau: Instituto Cultural de Macau, Fundação Oriente, 1997). According to Costa, Gonçalves received his medical degree in 1906 but redid his medical degree in Lisbon, completing it in 1910. Interestingly, on 11 December 1906, one Dr Josico Noronha, MD, and Professor of the Medical School of Poona, presented a paper at a medical conference, taking objection to Gonçalves's thesis by arguing that Xavier's corpse defied the laws of nature, and was therefore miraculous. See 'The Miracles of St Francis Xavier in the Face of Science', *A Voz de S. Francisco Xavier*, Ano. 1, No. 27 (8 March 1932), p. 272.

11 Because of limited space, I do not delve into the ritual details of these other expositions. See Francisco Xavier da Costa, *Exposições do Venerando Corpo de S. Francisco Xavier em 1900–1910–1922* (Nova Goa: Tip. Bragança and Co., 1924); Francisco Xavier da Costa, *Exposição do Venerando Corpo de S. Francisco Xavier em 1931* (Nova Goa: Tip. A Voz de S. Francisco Xavier, 1935); Francisco Xavier da Costa, *Resumo Histórico da Exposição das Sagradas Relíquias de S. Francisco Xavier em 1952* (Bąstora, Goa: Tipographia Rangel, 1954), p. 241 (Appendix reproduces the details of the Ninth Exposition of Xavier held in 1942).

12 Shantishree Pandit D.N.B., 'The Parliament and Foreign Policy in India: Its Policy Towards Goa (1952–1961)', in *SocioEconomic Aspects of Portuguese Colonialism in Goa: 19th and 20th Centuries*, ed. B.S. Shastry (Belgaum: Yarbal Offset Printers, 1990), p. 174.

13 'A Proxima Exposição do Corpo de S. Francisco Xavier', *Boletim Geral das Colonias*, Ano XXV, Nos 290–1 (Agosto–Setembro, 1949), p. 182.

14 Newman Fernandes, *St Francis Xavier and Old Goa, An Historical Guide* (Panjim: Koinia Publications, 1994), p. 59.

15 Ibid., pp. 59–60. The pavements in Old Goa were also asphalted at this time.

16 Ibid.

17 Ibid.

18 Francisco Xavier da Costa, *Resumo Histórico da Exposição das Sagradas Relíquias de S. Francisco Xavier em 1952*, p. 101.

19 *Noticias do Estado da Índia*, No. 64 (Segunda Quinzena de Março de 1953), pp. 25–7.

20 P. Rayanna, *St Francis Xavier and His Shrine*, p. 210.

21 Silvia M. de Mendonça-Noronha, 'The Economic Scene in Goa, 1926–1961', in *Goa Through the Ages Volume II. An Economic History*, ed. Teotónio de Souza (New Delhi: Concept Publishing Company, 1987), p. 277.

22 António de Menezes, 'Expositions of St Francis Xavier', *Goa Travel and Tourism*, Volume II, No. 3 (January 1986), p. 7.

23 António de Menezes, 'The Miraculous Arm', *Globo* (February 1974), pp. 10–11.

24 No author listed, 'Relíquia de S. Francisco Xavier', *Boletim Geral das Colonias*, Ano XXV, No. 289 (July 1949), pp. 93–4.

25 Ibid.

26 Ibid.

27 Ibid. See also Domingo José Soares Rebelo, *São Francisco Xavier: Luminar da Missionação e das Descobertas Portuguesas* (Alcobaça: Press not listed, 1995), p. 209.

28 Francisco Xavier da Costa, *Resumo Histórico da Exposição das Sagradas Relíquias de S. Francisco Xavier em 1952*, p. 149.

29 Unpublished manuscript copy of Xavier's medical report of 1951 (Porvorim, Goa: Xavier Centre for Historical Research). While da Costa references the fact that such a medical examination took place and that Xavier's relics were deemed fit for public veneration, he does not include its details in his published ritual manual for 1952. See his *Resumo Histórico da Exposição das Sagradas Relíquias de S. Francisco Xavier em 1952*, pp. 149–52. Newman Fernandes's summary of the finding of Xavier's examination in 1952 is similar, based on this same unpublished report. See his article, 'The Body of St Francis Xavier', *Renovação*, No. 22 (16–30 November 1994), pp. 421–6. Pacheco de Figueiredo, one of the above official examiners, refers to this report in later interviews and articles. See his article, 'A Medical and Historical Study: The Sacred Relics of St Francis Xavier', *Navhind Times* (2 May 1976), p. 5. Interestingly, it has been suggested that Pacheco de Figuereido was requested by colonial officials to state that Xavier's corpse evidenced 'insignificant alterations' in his exposed parts. The report was also sent for approval to Pope Pius XII who added that such a scientific explanation for the conservation of Xavier's corpse was unnecessary. See *Boletim Geral do Ultramar*, Ano XXVIII, No. 330 (Dezembro 1952), pp. 29–31.

30 In the past, Xavier's coffin was typically cleaned at the end of an exposition, and his corpse was assessed for any damages. According to a story that was told to me by an informant, the practice of fixing up Xavier's corpse was typically handed down through the generations to the eldest son of one prominent Goan family. Fieldnotes, Candolim, Goa (8 September 1999).

31 Francisco Xavier da Costa, *Resumo Histórico da Exposição das Sagradas Relíquias de S. Francisco Xavier em 1952*, pp. 7–13. To label Xavier's corpse 'relics' is also to commemorate Xavier.

32 See Carmo Azevedo, 'A Miracle No More', *Goa Today* (November 1984), p. 13.

33 *Boletim Geral do Ultramar*, Ano XXVIII, No. 330 (December 1952), p. 1.

34 Newman Fernandes, *St Francis Xavier and Old Goa, An Historical Guide*, pp. 59–63.

35 Ibid.

36 Francisco Xavier da Costa, *Resumo Histórico da Exposição das Sagradas Relíquias de S. Francisco Xavier em 1952*, p. 119.

37 Ibid., pp. 53–6.

38 Ibid., pp. 7–13.

39 Ibid., p. 152.

40 *Noticias do Estado da Índia*, No. 64 (Segunda Quinzena de Março de 1953), pp. 8–9.

41 Newman Fernandes, *St Francis Xavier and Old Goa, An Historical Guide*, pp. 59–63.

42 'Mostruario de Arte Metropolitano', *Boletim Geral do Ultramar*, Ano XXVIII, No. 330 (December 1952), p. 57. At this public exhibit, 68 Portuguese artists displayed a total of 171 works, alongside 66 paintings by Goan artists.

43 António Salazar, 'Portugal, Goa e a União Indiana', *Noticias do Estado da Índia*, No. 137 (Segunda Quinzena de Abril de 1956), p. 4.

44 Nehru quoted in Lourdes Bravo da Costa Rodrigues, 'Goa and Indian Leaders', in *Goa's External Relations*, ed. P.P. Shirodkar (Panjim: Prabhakar Bide, 1992), p. 103.

45 For additional biographical details on Salazar, see António Costa Pinto, *Salazar's Dictatorship and European Fascism: Problems of Interpretation* (New York: Columbia University Press, 1995).

46 Newman Fernandes, *St Francis Xavier and Old Goa, An Historical Guide*, pp. 59–63.

47 Ibid. See also Francisco Xavier da Costa, *Resumo Histórico da Exposição das Sagradas Relíquias de S. Francisco Xavier em 1952*, pp. 137–9.

48 Ibid.

49 Nunes quoted in Francisco Xavier da Costa, *Resumo Histórico da Exposição das Sagradas Relíquias de S. Francisco Xavier em 1952*, pp. 137–9.

50 Silvia M. de Mendonça-Noronha, 'The Economic Scene in Goa, 1926–1961', p. 284.

51 By 1952, Gandhi had been assassinated (1948), and Nehru was focused on transforming India into an independent nation-state. See P.P. Shirodkar, *Goa's Struggle for Freedom* (Panjim: Mrs Sulabha P. Shirodkar, 1999), p. 79.

52 Whereas T.B. Cunha (1891–1958) is known as the father of Goan independence because he established the Goa Congress in 1928, Dr Ram Manohar Lohia is known for instigating the Civil Disobedience Campaign in Goa, adopting a tactic used by Gandhi. Thousands of people attended the meeting called by Lohia at Margão on 18 June 1946, in defiance of prohibitory orders from the Portuguese government. Soon after, jails were flooded with 'satyagrahis' who protested against Portugal's continued colonial hold over Goa. For additional details see Sushila Sawant Mendes, 'Dr. Lohia and Goa's Freedom Struggle', pp. 175–9. See also P.P. Shirodkar, *Goa's Struggle for Freedom*, pp. 78–9.

53 Pratima Kamat, *Farar Far: Local Resistance to Colonial Hegemony in Goa, 1510–1912* (Panaji, Goa: Institute Menezes Bragança, 1999), p. 283. Salazar's agenda was furthered by the 'theory of Lusotropicalismo' proposed by Gilberto Freyre, a Brazilian sociologist who travelled throughout several Portuguese colonies in Asia and Africa in 1952, observing race relations. His findings concluded that the Portuguese were non-racist, the best kind of colonizers, since there was less hatred between colonizer and colonized. See his seminal work, *The Masters and the Slaves: A Study of Development of Brazilian Civilization*. In 1952, Salazar seized this theory as 'scientific proof' that Portuguese colonialism was 'good to think'. Also, beginning in 1952, restrictions were placed on all non-Portuguese foreigners, including all non-Goan Indians, residing in Portuguese territories. See P.P. Shirodkar, *Goa's Struggle for Freedom*, pp. 77–8.

54 Salazar quoted in Pratima Kamat, *Farar Far*, p. 283.

55 Xavier's shrine indeed becomes one of the things ensured by Nehru in 1958 that Goa will be allowed to maintain and will be respected after Goa's incorporation into the Indian Union. See Arthur Rubinoff, *The Construction of a Political Community, Integration and Identity in Goa* (New Delhi: Sage Publications, 1998), p. 42.

56 Pratima Kamat, *Farar Far*, p. 283.

57 Ibid., pp. 283–4.

58 Ibid.

59 Ibid.

60 *Boletim Geral do Ultramar*, Ano XXVIII, No. 330 (December 1952), p. 8.

61 'El Centenario de la Muerte de San Francisco Javier en Todo el Mundo', *De Nuestra Vida*. Ano XVI, No. 81 (Special edition dedicated to Xavier) (Lima, March 1953), p. 29.

62 Dr Luís Chaves, 'As Tradições e Lendas Portuguesas de S. Francisco Xavier', in *Archivum Historicum Societatis Iesu*, Volume XXII (Roma: AHSI, 1953), p. 103.

63 P.P. Shirodkar, *Goa's Struggle for Freedom*, p. 79. As part of his change in tactics in resolving the 'Goa Problem', Nehru contemplated the use of force.

64 *Boletim Geral do Ultramar*, Ano XXVIII, No. 330 (December 1952), p. 8.

65 Fr Lucio Da Veiga Coutinho, 'A Puzzling Epithet', *Goa Today* (December 1994), p. 22.

66 Francisco Xavier da Costa, *Resumo Histórico da Exposição das Sagradas Relíquias de S. Francisco Xavier em 1952*, p. 53.

67 Silvia M. de Mendonça-Noronha, 'The Economic Scene in Goa, 1926–1961', pp. 282–3.

68 Francisco Xavier da Costa, *Resumo Histórico da Exposição das Sagradas Relíquias de S. Francisco Xavier em 1952*, pp. 104–5. His speech was later translated into a variety of languages representing the diversity of India – Konkani, Malayalam, Tamil, Kanada, and Telegu – thus making it accessible to an even wider, multi-tiered public.

69 Ibid., pp. 63–5.

70 Newman Fernandes, *St Francis Xavier and Old Goa, An Historical Guide*, pp. 59–63.

71 Francisco Xavier da Costa, *Resumo Histórico da Exposição das Sagradas Relíquias de S. Francisco Xavier em 1952*, pp. 63-5.

72 Ibid., pp. 63–5, 67–8.

73 Ibid., pp. 63–5.

74 Ibid., pp. 117–18.
75 Ibid., pp. 63–5.
76 'Pictorial Review and Guide to Goa' ('Official Programme for the Exposition of St Francis Xavier'), *'Goa Today' Souvenir of the Exposition of St Francis Xavier, 3rd December 1952*, ed. Luís das Dores Silva (Bombay: Western India House, 1952), p. 15.
77 Francisco Xavier da Costa, *Resumo Histórico da Exposição das Sagradas Relíquias de S. Francisco Xavier em 1952*, pp. 118, 152.
78 Ibid., pp. 63–5.
79 Francisco Xavier da Costa, *Resumo Histórico da Exposição das Sagradas Relíquias de S. Francisco Xavier em 1952*, pp. 119–20.
80 Newman Fernandes, *St Francis Xavier and Old Goa, An Historical Guide*, p. 59.
81 *Noticias do Estado da Índia*, No. 64 (Segunda Quinzena de Março de 1953), pp. 22–4.
82 P. Rayanna, *St Francis Xavier and His Shrine*, p. 210. No additional details are available on the attendance of this sizeable group of African soldiers.
83 Francisco Xavier da Costa, *Resumo Histórico da Exposição das Sagradas Relíquias de S. Francisco Xavier em 1952*, pp. 49–53.
84 One of the main tenets of the newly created Indian Constitution was freedom of religion and worship. See Shantishree, 'The Parliament and Foreign Policy in India: Its Policy Towards Goa (1952–1961)', p. 178.
85 Francisco Xavier da Costa, *Resumo Histórico da Exposição das Sagradas Relíquias de S. Francisco Xavier em 1952*, pp. 7–13.
86 Ibid., pp. 118–19.
87 Ibid., pp. 117–18.
88 Ibid., pp. 101–3.
89 Ibid.
90 Ibid., pp. 74–5.
91 Ibid., pp. 117–18.
92 Ibid., pp. 122–3. Da Costa includes these two Jesuits in his list of 'illustrious' visitors to Goa.
93 *Noticias do Estado da Índia*, No. 64 (Segunda Quinzena de Março de 1953), pp. 22–4.
94 'Pictorial Review and Guide to Goa', p. 15 ('Official Programme for the Exposition of St Francis Xavier').
95 Francisco Xavier da Costa, *Resumo Histórico da Exposição das Sagradas Relíquias de S. Francisco Xavier em 1952*, pp. 65–7. For an expanded discussion of Xavier's popularity amongst a female public, see Paulo Durao, 'As Mulheres no Epistolario de S. Francisco Xavier', *Boletim do Instituto Vasco da Gama* (December 1952), p. 64.
96 António de Menezes, 'Expositions of St Francis Xavier', p. 8.
97 Francisco Xavier da Costa, *Resumo Histórico da Exposição das Sagradas Relíquias de S. Francisco Xavier em 1952*, pp. 65–7.
98 Newman Fernandes, *St Francis Xavier and Old Goa, An Historical Guide*, pp. 59–63. For additional information on the Goan Bombay community, see Silvia M. de Mendonça-Noronha, 'The Economic Scene in Goa, 1926–1961', p. 282.
99 Ibid. According to estimates there were approximately fourteen thousand Goans living in Karachi by the year 1961, which in turn suggests that in 1952 there was a sizeable group living there. See *The Statesman* (19 December 1961), p. 21.
100 Francisco Xavier da Costa, *Resumo Histórico da Exposição das Sagradas Relíquias de S. Francisco Xavier em 1952*, p. 123.
101 'Cronica da Exposição', *Noticias do Estado da Índia*, No. 64 (Segunda Quinzena de Março de 1953), pp. 22–4.
102 'Pictorial Review and Guide to Goa', p. 15 ('Official Programme for the Exposition of St Francis Xavier').
103 Francisco Xavier da Costa, *Resumo Histórico da Exposição das Sagradas Relíquias de S. Francisco Xavier em 1952*, pp. 120–1.
104 Ibid., pp. 122–3. Relevant is Foucault's idea of 'governmentality' wherein the press is one example of a modern technique of the art of government; it functions as

an arena in which governments can express their views at the same time that they use this space to mark support (or public opinion) for these same views. See his 'Governmentality' in *The Foucault Effect: Studies in Governmentality*, ed. G. Burchell, C. Gordon, and P. Miller (Chicago: University of Chicago Press, 1995), pp. 87–104.

105 The list of presses is compiled from Francisco Xavier da Costa, *Resumo Histórico da Exposição das Sagradas Relíquias de S. Francisco Xavier em 1952*, pp. 122–3; *Boletim Geral do Ultramar*, Ano XXVIII, No. 330 (December 1952), p. 43; and António de Menezes, 'Expositions of St Francis Xavier', p. 8.

106 Francisco Xavier da Costa, *Resumo Histórico da Exposição das Sagradas Relíquias de S. Francisco Xavier em 1952*, pp. 122–3. The press in Portugal was heavily censored by the Salazar dictatorship. These newspapers were largely voice pieces for government propaganda.

107 *Boletim Geral do Ultramar*, Ano XXVIII, No. 330 (December 1952), p. 46.

108 Ibid., p. 43.

109 Benedict Anderson, *Imagined Communities* (London: Verso, 1983), p. 6.

110 Maria Bucur and Nancy Wingfield, 'Introduction', *Staging the Past*, p. 1.

111 'Introduction' to *Velha-Goa, Guia Histórico* (Editado por Ocasião da Exposição das Reliquias de S. Francisco Xavier pelo Quarto Centenario da Sua Morte, 1552–1952). Reproduced in 'Colecção de Divulgação e Cultura', No. 25 (Panjim, Goa: Edição da Repartição Central de Estatica e Informação, 1952).

112 Newman Fernandes, *St Francis Xavier and Old Goa, An Historical Guide*, pp. 59–63.

113 Ibid.

114 Domingo Teles, 'Datas Historicas da Vida e Morte de S. Francisco Xavier e das Pessoas e factos a ele Associados', *Separata do Boletim do Instituto Menezes Bragança*, No. 143 (1984), pp. 11–12.

115 Ibid.

116 *Noticias do Estado da Índia*, No. 64 (Segunda Quinzena de Março de 1953), pp. 8–9.

117 Ibid.

118 Ibid. Nine cases of healings were reported during the exposition of 1952, and included the one described above as well as additional cases such as the curing of a Catholic girl's tuberculosis, the recovery of a Hindu woman who was mute, a young Catholic's boy's recovery from paralysis, and the healing of a young Parsi girl from Poona (India). Interestingly, instead of being labelled 'miracles' as had been the case during past expositions, in 1952 they were instead treated more cautiously and referred to as 'extraordinary facts' by colonial state officials, which in turn suggests the limited scope prescribed to Xavier's corporeal powers in 1952.

119 Newman Fernandes, *St Francis Xavier and Old Goa, An Historical Guide*, pp. 59–63.

120 See, for example, the 'Pictorial Review and Guide to Goa', and a French travel guide book to Goa by Rémy: *Goa, Rome of the Orient*, tr. Lancelot C. Sheppard (London: Arthur Barker Ltd, 1957).

121 Francisco Xavier da Costa, *Resumo Histórico da Exposição das Sagradas Relíquias de S. Francisco Xavier em 1952*, p. 123.

122 Ibid., 'Boatos Falsos'.

123 Ibid.

124 Ibid., pp. 7–13.

125 Ibid., p. 123.

126 Ibid., pp. 7–13. Interestingly, this same rumour had circulated prior to the exposition of 1942 for similar reasons.

127 Ibid., p. 123.

128 Ibid., pp. 137–9.

129 Dr J.M. Pacheco de Figueiredo, 'Tentativa de um Estudo Medico-Historico', p. 120.

130 Francisco Xavier da Costa, *Resumo Histórico da Exposição das Sagradas Relíquias de S. Francisco Xavier em 1952*, pp. 137–9.

131 Ibid.

132 Ibid.
133 Ibid.
134 Ibid. This detail suggests the continuing theme of harnessing new technologies to amplify ritual.
135 Ibid. These are standard 'closing' measures: the incensing supplements his odour of sanctity, the locking of his casket ensure his future protection, and the seals ensure that any future openings would be exposed.
136 Ibid.
137 Ibid.
138 Ibid., pp. 7–13.
139 Moreno de Souza, S.J., 'A Guide to Bom Jesus Basilica, The Shrine of St Francis Xavier' (Basilica do Bom Jesus, Velha Goa: Imprimatur, 1996), p. 10.
140 Newman Fernandes, 'The Body of St Francis Xavier', p. 426.
141 Dr J.M. Pacheco de Figueiredo, 'Tentativa de um Estudo Medico-Historico', p. 120.
142 Ibid.
143 Ibid.
144 See Moreno de Souza, S.J., 'A Guide to Bom Jesus Basilica, The Shrine of St Francis Xavier'.
145 Partha Chatterjee, *The Nation and Its Fragments* (Princeton, NJ: Princeton University Press, 1993), p. 238.
146 *The Statesman,* 2 December 1961.
147 According to Mario Cabral e Sa. See his 'The Unsolved Mystery', *Goa Today,* Volume XXIX, No. 1. (August 1994), p. 46.
148 See Shantishree, 'The Parliament and Foreign Policy in India: Its Policy Towards Goa (1952–1961)', p. 176.
149 Ibid.
150 Silvia M. de Mendonça-Noronha, 'The Economic Scene of Goa, 1926–1961', p. 263.
151 Ibid. See also António Salazar, 'Portugal, Goa e a União Indiana', *Noticias do Estado da Índia,* No. 137 (Segunda Quinzena de Abril de 1956), p. 7.
152 The centre of Goa's independence movement was based in Bombay, since all Goans suffered political repression in Goa itself. The mouthpiece of the 'Goa Liberation Council' was the *Goan Tribune,* which had been established in 1956. See Pia de Menezes Rodrigues, 'Interactive Relationship between Goa and Bombay Journalism', in P.P. Shirodkar, ed. *Goa's External Relations* (Panjim: Prabhakar Bide, 1992), p. 99.
153 Arthur Rubinoff, *The Construction of a Political Community, Integration and Identity in Goa,* p. 42.
154 Ibid.
155 Ibid. Salazar quoted in Arthur Rubinoff.
156 Here Nehru is ascribing to Chatterjee's idea of a modern nation-state, whereas Salazar is advocating a case for the exceptionalism of Goa to remain a colony of Portugal.
157 Rajan Narayan, *Goencho Saib: The Life and Mission of St Francis Xavier* (Panjim: Tata Press Limited), pp. 58–9.
158 P. Rayanna, *St Francis Xavier and His Shrine,* p. 212. There were also unconfirmed reports that Xavier's corpse had been displayed to pilgrims as recently as March 1961 in order to publicize the civil war in Angola. See Carlos Alexandre de Morais, *Cronologia Geral da Índia Portuguesa,* Instituto Cultural de Macão (Macau: Impressão Tipographia Welfare, 1993), p. 321.
159 Ibid.
160 As reported in 'Exposition of Saint's Body in Goa', *The Statesman,* 8 December 1961.
161 Ibid.
162 P. Rayanna, *St Francis Xavier and His Shrine,* p. 212.
163 Newman Fernandes, *St Francis Xavier and Old Goa, An Historical Guide,* p. 63.
164 According to Rayanna, no one from the Indian Union or any other country was allowed to attend the festivities in 1961. See his *St Francis Xavier and His Shrine,*

p. 212. One journalist I spoke with remembers that there were a large number of pilgrims in attendance amidst a heightened sense of tension. Interview, Panjim (7 July 1999).

165 For additional details on 'Operation Vijay', see P.P. Shirodkar, *Goa's Struggle for Freedom*, pp. 77–9.

166 Ibid. Also liberated alongside Goa were Daman (near Bombay) and Diu (Gujarat), two other Portuguese enclaves located inside the borders of the Indian nation-state.

167 Carmo Azevedo, 'Bits and Pieces about St. Xavier', *Goa Today* (November 1984), p. 17. One journalist remembers the speculation in 1961 concerning whether or not the body of Xavier had been removed by the Portuguese on the eve of their departure. Interview Panjim (7 July 1999).

168 'Goa Returns to Normal', *The Statesman*, 21 December 1961.

169 This is one of the larger points developed throughout this book – that Xavier's changing image and corpse slowly transcend the categories applied to them by those in power and become as much a part of everyday life in Goa such that the public increasingly shapes the contours of his ritualization, and, in the end, determines his fate as the place where ties of descent meet ties of the land.

170 P. Rayanna, *St Francis Xavier and His Shrine*, p. 250.

171 Ibid., p. 212. I spoke with numerous ritual participants who remembered the Portuguese attempt to smuggle Xavier out of Goa in 1961. Interviews, Panjim (September 1999 to April 2000). Accordingly, members of the public had taken it upon themselves to post guards to protect Xavier during the night after his 'sacred relics' were returned to his glass casing.

172 Ibid. Xavier's eleventh exposition had been initially scheduled for 14–31 December 1961. However, when the Indian army entered Goa on 18 December, the exposition was terminated that same day.

173 Carmo Azevedo, 'Bits and Pieces about St. Xavier', p. 17.

174 Ibid.

175 Michel-Rolph Trouillot elaborates a model of commemorations as 'packaging history'. See his *Silencing the Past: Power and the Production of History* (Boston: Beacon Press, 1995), pp. 3–5. The postcolonial context did not in fact signal the death of Xavier's ritualization (in death), for he would continue to be exposed publicly, albeit in relation to a different set of (postcolonial) political, economic, and religious agendas.

CHAPTER SEVEN

Conclusion: Xavier and the Portuguese colonial legacy

> In colonialism, then, the local is that which is produced by a transcendent discourse: after the fact of conquest. Nonetheless, the fact of conquest must itself be located. – Vicente Rafael, 1993[1]

> It has been said more than once that India has two most beautiful mausoleums – the Taj Mahal at Agra and (on a smaller scale) the silver casket of St Francis Xavier in Goa – P. Rayanna, S.J., 1982[2]

In December 2004 government officials in Goa staged the sixteenth exposition of the 'sacred remains' of St Francis Xavier. While it took place amidst a dramatically different context, it followed the Portuguese colonial pattern established in the twentieth century of displaying his corpse at ten-year intervals. That Xavier's body continues to be exposed for public view in postcolonial Goa (1964, 1974, 1984, 1994, 2004) not only suggests the emergence of this ritual practice out of the very historical conditions discussed in this book but underscores some of the conceptual investments of this historical anthropology project: to 'translate' saint veneration to a colonial context; to examine the spiritual and the material aspects of colonialization and missionization; to look at the production of a relational triad of church, state, and public at five different historical moments through the lens of ritual; to delve into the space of ritual as a practical and discursive field that actively produces the 'local'; to analyse ritual as an ethnographic event located in historical time, and as a site of continuity and change; to explore the interim of ritual as a site for the negotiation of different epistemologies of 'faith'; to document the physical decay of a corpse over four hundred years; and, finally, to tell the biography of a (colonial) state through the biography of a saint in life *and death*.

To emphasize Xavier's dual role as an agent of church and state in the production of the 'local' under Portuguese colonial rule also intimates his continuing role in Goa's postcolonial imaginary of itself.[3]

Throughout the research process, which took me first to Portugal and then to Goa, I encountered Xavier not only in the archives and the field but in the extraordinary and the everyday, which, in turn, suggests that he is very much entrenched in Goa's landscape today precisely because of his seminal role in Portuguese India's past as a religious, political, and spiritual figure. I interviewed a woman who had prayed to the saint before the birth of each of her three children, and encountered numerous Goans of diverse backgrounds and different generations who have consigned the dates of Xavier's biography and expositions to memory. Other Goans I met regularly visit his mausoleum and shrine located inside the Church of Bom Jesus in Velha Goa. I also traced 'stories' – some more fantastic than others – concerning Xavier, including one that revived an earlier debate concerning the replacement of his corpse with that of another on the eve of his exposition in 1782, and a second story that suggested that a prominent Catholic Goan family had been assigned the secret task of 'fixing up' Xavier's corpse prior to each of his postcolonial expositions. I also spoke to a woman whose family had previously owned an authenticated piece of Xavier's skin that was unfortunately now lost and, finally, interviewed a Jesuit Superior who believes that Xavier's expositions should be discontinued and his corpse quietly buried.

I spent time with a group of Goan journalists, many of whom are also amateur historians who together maintain Goa's patron saint – now a controversial figure for both Hindu and Christian Goans alike – as a topic of lively debate in the newspapers. I attended a conference on the 'historical ties' between Goa and Portugal, and was invited to view the private library of a Catholic Goan whose collection includes many first and second edition biographies of Xavier, including a rare copy of Felippe Neri Xavier's invaluable book that provides the basis for my fifth chapter on resurrection. I also visited the newly established Goa branch of the Fundação Oriente, a Portuguese cultural institution located in downtown Panjim, which is invested in promoting Goa's 'Portuguese-ness' through exhibits, exchange programmes, and Portuguese language lessons. I wandered through the streets of Fontainhas, one of Goa's oldest neighborhoods and a fine example of Portuguese colonial architecture and urban planning, both catching glimpses of Portugal's faded glory and getting caught up its nostalgia for all things 'Portuguese'.

I frequently visited Old Goa, taking part in the guided tours of the Church of Bom Jesus, which houses the body of Xavier, in order to see how this Indian state's colonial and Catholic past is being represented and packaged for Goans and tourists alike. I also dealt with the Goa branch of the Archaeological Survey of India, a national institution

Figure 8 The Thirteenth Exposition of the body of St Francis Xavier 1974 at Goa

that is now the official keeper of Goa's Christian and Hindu past(s), and which, after much red tape, gave me permission to film and photograph in and around Old Goa, including inside the Church of Bom Jesus. I both participated in and filmed the set of ritual activities which comprised Xavier's feast day of 3 December 1999, taking note of the diversity of participants and the kinds of devotional practices that took place at the foot of his ornate silver casket. I collected Xaverian memorabilia from Old Goa, including posters from his past expositions, miniatures of his corpse, and moulds of his (right) arm, leg, and foot cast in wax and plastic. I frequently paid homage to Xavier himself, directed by placards carefully placed inside the Church of Bom Jesus to stand on a certain step on the main altar in order to get the best possible view of his corpse located fifty feet up inside his Italian mausoleum. Lastly, this saint's involvement in the production of the 'local' under Portuguese colonial rule intimates his continuing role in India's postcolonial representation of Goa. Here I end my reflections by turning to the prophetic writings of the postcolonial writer Salman Rushdie, for even *he* does not forget Goa's role in the making of this nation-state.

In his now famous *Midnight's Children*, a story of India's partition, the character of Saleem Sinai relates the sudden disappearance of his old Goan nursemaid, Mary Pereira, in 1958 to his patient assistant, Padma.[4] He writes:

> Ask her [Mary Pereira] how she went home to the city of Panjim in Goa, how she told her ancient mother the story of her shame! Ask how her mother went wild with the scandal (appropriately enough it was a time for old folk to lose their wits)! Ask: did daughter and old mother go into the streets to seek forgiveness? Was that not the one time in each ten years when the mummified corpse of St Francis Xavier (as holy a relic as the Prophet's hair) is taken from its vault in the Cathedral of Bom Jesus and carried around the town? Did Mary and old distraught Mrs. Pereira find themselves pressing up against the catafalque; was the old lady beside herself with grief for her daughter's crime? Did old Mrs. Pereira, shouting, 'Hai! Ai-hai! Ai-hai-hai!' clamber up on to the bier to kiss the foot of the Holy One? Amidst uncountable crowds, did Mrs. Pereira enter a holy frenzy? Ask! Did she or didn't she, in the clutches of her wild spirit, place her lips around the big toe on St Francis' left foot? Ask for yourself: did Mary's mother bite the toe right off? ... And is this also true: were the papers making it up when they wrote that the old lady had been miraculously punished; when they quoted Church sources and eye-witnesses, who described how the old woman was turned into solid stone? No? Ask her if it's true that the Church sent a stone-statue figure of an old woman around the towns and the villages of Goa, to show what happened to those who misbehave with the saints? Ask: was

> this statue not seen in several villages simultaneously – and does that prove fraud, or a further miracle?[5]

In recounting the story of Mary Pereira to Padma, Rushdie simultaneously tells the tale of Goa's colonial past. Firstly, in the above passage, it is her name itself which represents Portuguese India; 'Mary Pereira' signifies both her Portuguese ancestry and her conversion to Catholicism, the dual processes that typically characterized the Portuguese colonial enterprise. It is also pertinent that Mary Pereira lives in Bombay, but makes frequent visits to Goa, including during the time of year when festivities surrounding Xavier's corpse are regularly staged, a detail that highlights the history of a Goan emigrant community that left Portuguese India starting in the nineteenth century in order to seek better living conditions in nearby British India, often as domestic workers or *ayahs* as in the case of Mary Pereira above, but one that also maintained strong ties with its homeland through (the help of) Xavier.

Similarly, in the above passage, it is a mother and daughter (as opposed to a father and son) who turn to Xavier to seek forgiveness for the daughter's shame, a feature that highlights the fact that Goa's patron saint was popularly a focal point for female veneration throughout its colonial history. Rushdie also informs us that Mary Pereira's visit to Goa coincides with the one time every ten years that the 'mummified' corpse of Xavier is removed from the Church of Bom Jesus and carried around town, a detail that reveals the manner by which Xavier's corpse, despite its poor condition, was regularly exposed at ten-year intervals throughout the twentieth century. It is Mary Pereira's mother who, in a frenzy of devotion, and amidst 'uncountable crowds', climbs on top of the bier to kiss Xavier's foot, a description that reveals both the kinds of devotional practices that developed around Xavier's corpse throughout the history of his expositions and the crucial role of the public in engaging in ritual practices centred on Xavier. In an aside, Rushdie tells us that Xavier's foot is as holy a relic as the Prophet's hair, a detail that not only translates this Catholic saint's exchange value for a wider audience but also indexes the religious diversity of India. Interestingly, Mary Pereira's spirited mother bites the saint's toe off, a detail that is of course reminiscent of the infamous story of Isabel de Carom, a lady of Portuguese nobility, who reportedly performed the same act on Xavier during his first public display in 1554. Mary's mother is 'miraculously' punished for her impious act, an event that, in turn, highlights the fact that supernatural powers were often attributed to Xavier throughout the colonial period.

Rushdie also informs us that there were eyewitnesses, newspaper stories, and church sources documenting this remarkable event, a detail that affirms the importance of a variety of persons and source materials for both giving credibility to and preserving a multitude of stories related to Xavier. That the Church used the unlawful biting off of Xavier's toe by Mary's mother as a lesson for prescribing certain (read 'correct') behaviours around saints indexes the historical role of various Catholic institutions in Goa in mediating veneration practices. Circulating stories of how the 'old woman' turned into a stone statue which was seen in more than one place at the same time suggest the power of rumour as a force of (Goan) history. The author's chosen setting of the year 1958 for Mary Pereira's visit to her homeland is significant in terms of revealing Goa's precarious political position vis-à-vis Portugal and India; this was the height of the period in which Prime Minister Nehru put diplomatic pressure on Portugal's dictator Salazar to 'quit' Goa precisely because it lay within the territorial boundaries of the Indian nation-state.

Finally, when our narrator Saleem asks whether or not these unusual events prove fraud or a further miracle, he poses the same question that has been repeated throughout Goa's colonial past with regard to Xavier's body. The power of Rushdie's writings lies in his ability to transform history into a cyclical process. Thus, in the same way that the character of Saleem represents newly independent India, Mary Pereira represents (post) colonial Goa. In the end, Rushdie leaves his reader with a distinct impression of Goa in which its 'Portuguese' past and 'Indian' present are both indelibly shaped by the figure and corpse of Xavier, a postcolonial discourse that escapes neither history nor the nation-state.

Notes

1 Vicente Rafael, *Contracting Colonialism: Translation and Christian Conversion in Tagalog Society Under Early Spanish Rule* (Durham, NC: Duke University Press, 1993), p. 35.

2 P. Rayanna, S.J., *St Francis Xavier and His Shrine*, 2nd edn (Panjim, Goa: Imprimatur, 1982), p. 192.

3 I follow Vicente Rafael in emphasizing that the 'local' under colonialism foreshadows the contours of the postcolonial condition. See his *Contracting Colonialism*, p. xiii.

4 Here I follow the pattern adopted throughout this book of exploring different genres of source materials as a way to look at changing representations of saint and state – in this case I am looking at postcolonial Indian literature.

5 Salman Rushdie, *Midnight's Children* (New York: Penguin, 1980), pp. 337–8.

Figure 9 Souvenir of the Exposition 1964

BIBLIOGRAPHY

Travelogues

Baldeus, Philip. *A Description of the East India Coasts of Malabar and Cormandel with their Adjacent Kingdoms and Provinces, & of the Empire of Ceylon and of the Idolatry of the Pagans in the East Indies* (New Delhi: Asian Educational Services, 1996 [1672]).

Barbosa, Duarte. *The Book of Duarte Barbosa*, ed. Mansel Longworth Dames (New Delhi: Asian Educational Services, 1989).

Burton, Richard F. *Goa, and the Blue Mountains; or Six Months of Sick Leave* (Berkeley: University of California Press, 1991 [1851]).

Camões, Luís de. *The Lusiads*, tr. William Atkinson (New York: Penguin, 1952).

Careri, Gemelli and M. de Thevenot. *Indian Travels of Thevenot and Careri: Being the Third Part of the Travels of M. De Thevenot into the Levant and the Third Part of the Voyage Round the World by Dr. John Francis Gemelli Careri*, ed. Surendranath Sen (New Delhi: National Archives of India, 1949).

Carré, Abbé. *The Travels of the Abbé Carré in India and the Near East, 1672 to 1674*, Volume I (New Delhi: Asian Educational Services, 1990).

De Kloguen, Denis L. Cottineau. *An Historical Sketch of Goa* (New Delhi: Asian Educational Services, 1995 [1831]).

Della Valle, Pietro. *The Pilgrim, The Travels of Pietro Della Valle*, ed., tr. George Bull (London: Hutchinson, 1989 [1652]).

Della Valle, Pietro. *The Travels of Pietro Della Valle in India*, ed. Edward Grey, Volume 1 (New Delhi: Asian Educational Services, 1991 [1652]).

Fryer, John. *A New Account of East India and Persia, Being Nine Years Travel, 1672–1681*, Volume 3, ed. William Crooke (New Delhi: Asian Educational Services, 1992).

Godinho, Manuel. *Intrepid Itinerant: Manuel Godinho and His Journey from India to Portugal in 1663*, ed. John Correia-Afonso (Delhi: Oxford University Press, 1990).

Hamilton, Alexander. *A New Account of the East Indies, Being the Observations and Remarks of Capt. Alexander Hamilton, From the year 1688–1723; Trading and Traveling by Sea and Land, to Most of the Countries and Islands of Commerce and Navigation, Between the Cape of Good Hope and the Island of Japan*, Volume 1 (New Delhi: Asian Educational Services, 1995).

Hutt, Anthony. *Goa, A Traveller's Historical and Architectural Guide* (New Delhi: Scorpion Publishing United, 1988).

Mandelslo, John Albert. *Mandelslo's Travels in Western India (1638–9)*, ed. M.S. Commissariat (London: Oxford University Press, 1931).

Manrique, Sebastião. *The Land of the Great Image: Being the Experiences of Friar Manrique in Arakan*, ed. Maurice Collins (New Delhi: Asian Educational Services, 1995).

Manucci, Niccolao. *Storia do Mogor, or Mogul India, 1653–1708*, Volume III, tr. William Irvine (Calcutta: Editions Indian, 1966).

Oaten, E.F. *European Travellers in India, During the Fifteenth, Sixteenth and Seventeenth Centuries, the Evidence Afforded by Them with Respect to Indian Social Institutions, and the Nature and Influence of Indian Governments* (New Delhi: Asian Educational Services, 1991 [1909]).

Penrose, Boies. *Goa–Rainha do Oriente, Goa–Queen of the East* (Lisboa: Commissão Ultramarina, 1960).

Pinto, Fernão Mendes. *The Travels of Mendes Pinto*, ed., tr. Rebecca Catz (Chicago: University of Chicago Press, 1989).

Rémy [Gilbert Renault]. *Goa, Rome of the Orient*, tr. Lancelot C. Sheppard (London: Arthur Barker Ltd, 1957).

Tavernier, Jean-Baptiste. *Travels in India by Jean-Baptiste Tavernier*, Volume 1, ed. William Crooke (New Delhi: Munshiram Manoharlal Publishers Pvt Ltd, 1995).

Van Linschoten, John Huyghen. *The Voyage of John Huyghen Van Linschoten to the East Indies, 1598*, Volume 1, ed. Arthur Coke Burnell (New Delhi: Asian Educational Services, 1988).

Government printed sources

Albuquerque, Reverend Manuel João Socrates de. *Sumário Chronólogico de Decretos Diocesanos do Arcebispado de Goa desde 1775 até 1922* (Bastora, Goa: Typografia Rangel, 1922).

Albuquerque, Viriato A.C.B. *A Memoria da Exposição do Venerando Corpo de S. Francisco Xavier em 1878* (Goa: Imprensa Nacional, 1879).

Albuquerque, Viriato A.C.B. *O Senado de Goa: Memoria-Histórico Archeologica* (Nova Goa: Imprensa Nacional, 1909).

Albuquerque, Viriato A.C.B. *Exposição do Venerando Corpo do Glorioso Apostolo das Índias, S. Francisco Xavier, em 1890, Memoria Histórico-Descriptiva, Illustrada com Estampas* (Nova Goa: Imprensa Nacional, 1891).

Annaes do Conselho Ultramarino, Parte nao Official Series II, Janeiro de 1859 a Dezembro de 1861 (Lisboa: Imprensa Nacional, 1867).

Anuário da Arquidiocese de Goa para 1914 e 1923. Coordenado com autorisação de S. Exa. Revdma. o Sr. Arcebispo Primaz Patriarca das Índias Orientais (Nova Goa: Tip. Arthur & Viegas, 1923).

Anuário da Arquidiocese de Goa e Damao, 1933. Coordenado com autorisação de S. Exa. Revdma. o Sr. Arcebispo Primaz Patriarca das Índias Orientais (Nova Goa: Tip. Arthur & Viegas, 1932).

A Voz de S. Francisco Xavier, Ano I, No. 10 (10 November 1931).

A Voz de S. Francisco Xavier, Ano II, No. 20 (17 January 1933).

A Voz de S. Francisco Xavier, Ano IV, No. 21 (30 January 1935).

Boletim da Filmoteca, Nos 30/1, 40/1, 48 (Lisbon: Instituto de Investigações Cientifica Tropical e Centro de Estudos de Historia e Cartografia Antiga, 1987).

Boletim do Governo do Estado, No. 36 (1841), Nos 80 and 93 (1859) (Lisbon: Ministerio da Marinha e Ultramar).

Boletim Eclesiastico da Arquidiocese de Goa, No. 7 (January 1953), No. 8 (February, 1953).

Boletim Geral do Ultramar, Ano XXVIII, No. 330 (December 1952).

Bragança, Menezes (ed.). *A Índia Portuguesa*, Volume Segundo (Nova Goa: Imprensa Nacional, 1923).

Colecção de Divulgação e Cultura, No. 22 (Panjim, Goa: Edição da Repartição Central de Estatica e Informação, 1951).

Colecção de Divulgação e Cultura, No. 25 (Panjim, Goa: Edição da Repartição Central de Estatica e Informação, 1952).

Comemorações Centenarias: Programa Oficial (Lisboa: Comissão Executiva dos Centenarios do Governo de Portugal, 1940).

De Melo, Carlos Merces. *The Recruitment and Formation of the Native Clergy in India, 16th–19th Century, An Histórico-Canonical Study* (Lisboa: Agencia Geral do Ultramar, 1955).

De Nazareth, Casimiro Christovão. *O Calendario Eclesiástico e Liturgica de Goa para o Anno de 1868* (Nova Goa: Imprensa Nacional, 1867).

De Nazareth, Casimiro Christovão. *O Calendario Eclesiástico e Liturgica de Goa para O Anno de 1874* (Nova Goa: Imprensa Nacional, 1873).

De Nazareth, Casimiro Christovão. *Mitras Lusitanas no Oriente, Catalogos dos Prelados da Egreja Metropolitana e Primacial de Goa e das Dioceses Suffraganeas com A Recopilação das Ordenancas por elles Emittadas, e Summario dos Factos Notaveis da Historia Ecclesiástica de Goa*, 2nd edn (Lisboa: Imprensa Nacional, 1897).

De Seixas, António José. *A Questão Colonial Portugueza* (Lisboa: Typographia Universal, 1881).

Godinho, John. 'The Exposition in 1782', *Boletim do Governo*, No. 94 (1863).

Ladainha de S. Francisco Xavier, Acompanhada de Duas Orações (Nova Goa: Imprensa Nacional, 1860).

Lobo, Pe Amaro Pinto (ed.). *Memória Histórico-Eclesiástico da Arquidiocese de Goa, 1533–1933* (Nova Goa: Tip. A Voz de S. Francisco Xavier, 1933).

Martins, Pe R.J. Theodoro. *Collection of Diocese Decrees of the Archdiocese of Goa. 1900–1911, Authorized by his Excellency and Reverend Archbishop Primary Patriarch of the Oriental Indies* (Nova Goa: Typ. Arthur & V. Inc., 1912).

Mendes, A. Lopes. *A Índia Portugueza, Breve Descripção das Possessões Portuguezas na Asia*, Volume 1 (Lisboa: Imprensa Nacional, 1886).

'The Miracles of St Francis Xavier in the Face of Science', *A Voz de S. Francisco Xavier*, Ano. 1, No. 27 (8 March 1932).

'Mostruario de Arte Metropolitano', *Boletim Geral do Ultramar*, Ano XXVIII, No. 330 (December 1952).

Noticias do Estado da Índia, No. 57 (December 1952).

Noticias do Estado da Índia, No. 64 (Segunda Quinzena de Março de 1953).

O Oriente Portuguez, Volume 12, Nos 9 and 10 (1915) (Nova Goa: Imprensa Nacional).

Pereira, A.B. de Bragança. *S. Francisco Xavier, Esboço Histórico* (Publicação

Comemorativa da Exposição do Corpo do Apostolo das Indias pelo 4o Centenario da sua Morte). Reproduced in *Colecção de Divulgação e Cultura*, No. 24 (Panjim: Edição da Repartição Central de Estatistica e Informacão, 1952).
Pereira, AB de Bragança, (ed). *A Índia Portuguesa, Volume Primeiro* (Nova Goa: Imprensa Nacional, 1923).
Primeira Publicação apos 160 Anos do Manuscrito Inedito de José Caeiro Sobre os Jesuitas do Brasil e da Índia na Perseguição do Marques de Pombal (Academia Brasileira de Letras, Baia: Escola Tipografica Salesiana, 1936).
'Proceedings of the Inauguration and Installation of the Xaverian Study', *O Oriente Portuguez*, Volume 4 (Nova Goa: Imprensa Nacional, 1907).
'A Proxima Exposição do Corpo de S. Francisco Xavier', *Boletim Geral das Colonias* Ano XXV, Nos 290–291 (August–September 1949).
'Reliquia de S. Francisco Xavier', *Boletim Geral das Colonias*. Ano XXV, No. 289 (July 1949).
Rivara, J.H. da Cunha (ed.). *Arquivo Portuguez Oriental*. Fasciculo 1, Part 2, Fasciculo 2, Fasciculo 4 (Nova Goa: Imprensa Nacional, 1876).
Salazar, António. 'Portugal, Goa e a União Indiana', *Noticias do Estado da Índia*, No. 137 (Segunda Quinzena de Abril de 1956).
'Sam Francisco Xavier, Chitranim Jivit', *A Voz de S. Francisco Xavier*, Ano II, No. 27 (7 March 1933).
'Varia Variorum', *O Oriente Portuguez*, Volume 7 (Nova Goa: Imprensa Nacional, 1910).
'O Venerando Corpo de S. Francisco Xavier', *A Voz de St Francis Xavier*, Ano I, No. 14 (3 December 1931).
Xavier, Felippe Neri. *Resumo Histórico da Maravilhosa Vida, Conversões, e Milagres de S. Francisco Xavier, Apostolo, Defensor, e Patrono das Índias*, 2nd edn (Nova Goa: Imprensa Nacional, 1861).

Biographies of Xavier, Xaverian literature, Goa guide books

Afonso, Francisco Correia. *The Spirit of Xavier* (Bangalore: Good Shepherd Convent Press, 1922).
Afonso, Vincent Correia. 'Xavier in Kunkolistan' (unpublished manuscript).
Albuquerque, Viriato A.C.B. *A Exposição do Venerando Corpo do Apostolo das Índias, S. Francisco Xavier, em 1878* (Nova Goa: Tipographia da Cruz, 1879).
Azevedo, Carmo. 'Sources for a History of St Francis Xavier in Portuguese, Konkani and English', Paper presented at a 'Seminar on St Francis Xavier: Issues for Today', Xavier Centre of Historical Research, Porvorim, Goa, 13 November 1994.
Cano, Domingo Manfredi. *San Francisco Javier, Un Español de Leyenda*, ed. Luís de Caralt (Barcelona: No Publisher Listed, No Publication Date Listed).
Da Costa, Francisco Xavier. *Exposiçao do Venerando Corpo de S. Francisco Xavier em 1931* (Nova Goa: Tip. A Voz de S. Francisco Xavier, 1935).
Da Costa, Francisco Xavier. *Exposições do Venerando Corpo de St Francis*

Xavier em 1900–1910–1922 (Nova Goa: Tip. Bragança & Co, 1924).

Da Costa, Francisco Xavier. *Resumo Histórico da Exposição das Sagradas Relíquias de S. Francisco Xavier em 1952* (Bastora, Goa: Tipographia Rangel, 1954).

Da Costa, Francisco Xavier. S. *Francisco Xavier em Goa* (Nova Goa: Tip. Bragança & Co, 1922).

Daurignac, J.M.S. *Historia de São Francisco de Xavier, Da Companhia de Jesus, Apostolo das Índias e do Japao, Protector do Oriente*, 3rd edn (Goa: No Publisher Listed, 1880).

Daurignac, J.M.S. *S. Francisco Xavier, Apóstolo das Índias*, 6th edn (Braga: Livraria Apostolado da Imprensa, 1880).

D'Cruz, F. Mervyn (ed.). *Goa and St Francis Xavier. A Guide Book to Old Goa, Incorporating Articles on the Life and Philosophy etc. of St Francis Xavier* (Madras: Hogarth Press, 1931).

'Dedication', in *Manual Xaveriano* (Basilica do Bom Jesus,Velha Goa: Imprimatur, 1956).

De Lucena, João, S.J. *Historia Da Vida do Padre S. Francisco de Xavier, e do que Fizeram na Índia Os Mais Religiosos da Companhia de Jesu* (Lisboa: Oficina de António Gomes, 1600).

De Souza, Francisco, S.J. *Oriente Conquistado a Jesu Christo pelos Padres da Companhia de Jesus, da Provincia de Goa* (Lisboa: Valentim Da Costa Deslandes, 1710).

De Souza, Moreno, S.J. 'A Guide to Bom Jesus Basilica, The Shrine of St Francis Xavier' (Basilica do Bom Jesus, Velha Goa: Imprimatur, 1996).

Documenta Indica, Volume *XIV*, eds Joseph Wicki and John Gomes (Roma: IHSI, 1979).

Escalada, Francisco, S.J. *Guia Histórico-Artistica del Castillo de Javier y Sus Contornos* (Pamplona: Casa Editorial de G. Huarte, 1919).

Faber, Rev. Fr. F.W. ed. *The Life of St Francis Xavier: Apostle of Índia and Japan*, tr. from the Italian of Rev. Fathers D. Bartoli and J.P. Maffei of the Society of Jesus, 9th edn (Madras: CNT Institute Press, 1923).

Fernandes, Newman. *St Francis Xavier and Old Goa, An Historical Guide* (Panjim: Koinia Publications, 1994).

Fonseca, José da. *An Historical and Archaeological Sketch of the City of Goa* (Delhi: Asian Educational Services, 1986 [1878]).

Fragoso, Humiliano Preito de José Joaquim. *Inçenso e Myrrha a S. Francisco Xavier Pelo Tricentenario da Sua Canonisação* (Nova Goa: Tip. Braganca & Co., 1922).

Furtado, Aquino Dos Remedios. *An Illustrated Guide to Goa* (Panjim: published by author, 1922).

Gonçalves, L.M. Júlio Frederico. *Os Milagres de S. Francisco Xavier não são Milagres nem são de S. Francisco Xavier* (Graduate thesis, Goa Medical School, 1906).

Gonçalves, P. António B. *O IV Centenario da Morte de St Francis Xavier Conferencia* (Macau: Press not listed, 1953).

Gonçalves, Sebastiam, S.J., *Primeira Parte da Historia Dos Religiosos da Companhia de Jesus e do que fizeram com a divina graça na conversão*

dos infieis a nossa sancta fee Catholica nos reynos e provincias da Índia Oriental, Volume I, ed. Joseph Wicki, S.J. (Coimbra: Atlantida, 1957).
Guide to the City of Old Goa: A Handbook for Visitors to the Exposition of the Sacred Body of St Francis Xavier, Apostle of the Indies, During the Month of December 1890 (Bombay: The Bombay Circulating Library Printing Press, 1890).
Lembrança do Quarto Centenario da Morte de S. Francisco Xavier, 1552–1952 (Porto: Livraria Apostolado da Imprensa, 1952).
Martins, Rocha. *O Apostolo das Índias, S. Francisco Xavier* (Lisboa: Agencia Geral das Colonias, 1942).
Menezes, António de. *Historical Notes on Goa* (Nova Goa: Publication Casa J.P. Fernandes, 1878).
Pais, Alex. A. *A Pilgrim's Guide to the Shrine of St Francis Xavier at Goa* (Mangalore: KM Book Press, 1922).
'Pictorial Review and Guide to Goa', *'Goa Today' Souvenir of the Exposition of St Francis Xavier, 3rd December 1952*, ed. Luís das Dores Silva (Bombay: Western India House, 1952).
Rayanna, P., S.J. *St Francis Xavier and His Shrine*, 2nd edn (Panjim, Goa: Imprimatur, 1982).
Rebelo, Domingo José Soares. *São Francisco Xavier: Luminar da Missionação e das Descobertas Portuguesas* (Alcobaça: Press not listed , 1995).
Schurhammer, Georg. 'Die Heiligsprechung Franz Xavers' in *Varia I* (Lisboa: Centro de Estudos Históricos Ultramarinhos, 1965).
Schurhammer, Georg. 'Festas em Goa no Ano 1624', *Varia I* (Roma: Institutum Historicum, 1965).
Schurhammer, Georg, S.J. *Francis Xavier: His Life, His Times*, tr. M. Joseph Costelloe, Volumes I–IV (Roma: The Jesuit Historical Institute, 1977).
Schurhammer, Georg. 'Mejico Y Javier: Un Documento Inedito sobre Su Culto', *Varia I* (Lisboa: Centro de Estudos Históricos Ultramarinhos, 1965).
Schurhammer, Georg. 'St Francis Xavier and India', *Varia I* (Lisboa: Centro de Estudos Históricos Ultramarinos, 1965).
Schurhammer, Georg. 'The Church of St. Paul, Malacca', *Xaveriana* (Lisboa: Centro de Estudos Históricos Ultramarinos, 1964).
Teixeira, Manuel, S.J., 'Vita S. Francisci', in *Monumenta Xaveriana*, Tomus Secundus (Matriti: Typis Gabrielis Lopez del Horno, 1912).
Tercer Centenario de la Canonizacion de San Ignacio de Loyola y San Francisco Javier, 1622–1922. Relacion de las Festas que Para Celebrarlo ha Organizado la Compania de Jesus en Madrid (Madrid: Tipografia Catolica, 1922).
Valignano, Alessandro, S.J., 'Vita S. Francisci', in *Monumenta Xaveriana*, Tomus Primus (Matriti: Typis Augustini Avrial, 1899–1900).

Periodicals/newspaper articles

Anuário de S. Francisco Xavier, Ano IV (1960).
Archivo Pittoresco: Semanario Illustrado, Volume III (1860).
Azevedo, Carlos de. 'Um Artista Italiano em Goa', *Review Garcia de Orta*, Numero Especial (1956).

Azevedo, Carmo. 'A Miracle No More', *Goa Today* (November 1984).

Azevedo, Carmo. 'Bits and Pieces about St. Xavier', *Goa Today* (November 1984).

Azevedo, Carmo. 'Commercialization of a Sacred Veneration', *Navhind Times* (19 November 1994).

Azevedo, Carmo. 'Expositions: From Sacred Veneration to Tourist Attraction', *Goa Today* (February 1985).

Azevedo, Francisco de Simas Alves. 'O Brasao de Armas bordado na Casula de St Francis Xavier', *Hidalguia*, Numero 16 (May–June 1956).

Barbosa, Alexandre M. 'Off to a Ritualistic Start', *Goa Today*, Volume XXIX, No. 5 (December 1994).

'The Case of Goa', *Goa Freedom Movement Publications* (Rome: Vatican City, November 1964).

Castets, John. 'The Miracle of the Body of St Francis Xavier', *Indian Catholic Truth Society*, No. 13 (1925).

Chaves, Dr Luís. 'As Tradições e Lendas Portuguesas de S. Francisco Xavier', *Archivum Historicum Societatis Iesu*, Volume XXII (Roma: AHSI, 1953).

Coutinho, Fr Lucio Da Veiga. 'A Puzzling Epithet', *Goa Today* (December 1994).

Cruz, Caetano. 'History of the Expositions', *The Herald* (21 November 1984)

Da Silva, William R. 'Exposition of a Beleaguered Community', *Goa Today* (December 1994).

De Mello, Alfredo Froilano. 'When the Twain Did Meet', *Goa Today* (December 1994).

De Souza, Moreno. 'Are the Relics at Old Goa not St. Xavier's?' *Goa Today* (July 1984).

De Souza, Moreno. 'When Did Francis Die?' (unpublished manuscript) sent to *The Examiner* (1994).

Durao, Paulo, S.J. 'As Mulheres no Epistolario de S. Francisco Xavier', *Boletim do Instituto Vasco da Gama* (December 1952).

'El Centenario de la Muerte de San Francisco Javier en Todo el Mundo', *De Nuestra Vida*. Ano XVI, No. 81 (Special edition dedicated to Xavier), Marzo (Lima 1953).

'Exposition of Saint's Body in Goa', *The Statesman* (8 December 1961).

Fernandes, Newman. 'The Body of St Francis Xavier', *Renovação*, No. 22 (16–30 November 1994).

Figueiredo, A.J. Frederico Gonçalves de. 'Uma Festa e Uma Viagem', *Illustração Goana, Periodico Litterario*, Primeiro Anno, No. 1 (1864).

Figueiredo, Dr J.M. Pacheco de. 'A Medical and Historical Study: The Sacred Relics of St Francis Xavier', *Navhind Times* (2 May 1976).

Figueiredo, Dr J.M. Pacheco de. 'Tentativa de um Estudo Medico-Histórico', *Memorias da Academia das Ciencias de Lisboa*, Tomo XXI (Lisboa: Academia das Ciencias de Lisboa, 1977).

'Goa Returns to Normal', *The Statesman* (21 December 1961).

Menezes, Anton. 'The Miraculous Arm', *Globo* (February 1974).

Meneses, António de. 'Felippe Neri Xavier, Historiógrafo e Homen Público, 1801–1875', *Harpa Goesa*, No. 7 (December 1974).

Menezes, António de. 'Expositions of St Francis Xavier', *Goa Travel and Tourism, Volume II*, No. 3 (January 1986).

Menezes, Armando. 'A Saviour of Souls', *Goa Today*, Volume XXIX, No. 5 (December 1994).

Noronha, Jorge de Abreu. 'A New Dimension to the Inquisition', *Goa Today*, Volume XXIX, No. 5 (December 1994)

'Pictorial Review of Goa, Souvenir of the Exposition of St Francis Xavier', *Goa Today* (December 1952).

Rodrigues, Francisco. 'St Francis Xavier: Duas Exposições de Seu Corpo em 1744 and 1751', *Revista de Historia*, No. 47–48 (July–December 1923).

Sa, Mario Cabral e, 'The Unsolved Mystery', *Goa Today*, Volume XXIX, No. 1 (August 1994).

Schurhammer, Georg. 'Historical Research into the Life of Francis Xavier in the Sixteenth Century', *Revista de Historia*, No. 47–48 (July–December 1923).

Statesman, The (2 December 1961).

Statesman, The (19 December 1961).

Teles, Domingo. 'Datas Historicas da Vida e Morte de S. Francisco Xavier e das Pessoas e factos a ele Associados', *Separata do Boletim do Instituto Menezes Bragança*, No. 143 (1984).

Thomaz, Luís Filipe Ferreira Reis. 'O Cristianismo e As Tradições Pagas na India Portuguesa', *Separata das Actas do Congresso Internacional de Etnografia*, Volume IV (10–18 July 1963).

Waugh, Evelyn. 'Goa: The Home of a Saint', *Month* (December 1953).

Wicki, Joseph. 'S. Francisco Xavier Subdito da Coroa Portuguesa', *Portugal em Africa*, Volume 9, No. 54 (1952).

Secondary sources

Agnew, Jean-Christophe. *Worlds Apart: The Market and the Theater in Anglo-American Thought, 1550–1750* (Cambridge: Cambridge University Press, 1986).

Albuquerque, Teresa. 'The Anglo-Portuguese Treaty of 1878: Its Impact on the People of Goa', *Indica*, Vol. 27, No. 2 (September 1990).

Albuquerque, Teresa. *Goa: The Rachol Legacy* (Bombay: Wenden Offset Private Ltd, 1997).

Alden, Dauril. *The Making of an Enterprise, The Society of Jesus in Portugal, Its Empire and Beyond, 1540–1750* (Stanford: Stanford University Press, 1996).

Ames, Glenn J. *Renascent Empire?: The House of Braganza and the Quest for Stability in Portuguese Monsoon Asia, ca. 1640–1683* (Amsterdam: University of Amsterdam Press, 2000).

Amin, Shahid. *Event, Metaphor, Memory: Chauri Chaura, 1922–1992* (Berkeley: University of California Press, 1995).

Anderson, Benedict. *Imagined Communities* (New York: Verso, 1983).

Antony, Philomena S. 'Missionary Expansion: Cultural and Agricultural Contacts between Colonial Goa and Brazil', in *Discoveries, Missionary Expansion and Asian Cultures*, ed. Teotónio de Souza (New Delhi: Concept Publishing Company, 1994).

Appadurai, Arjun. *Modernity at Large: Cultural Dimensions of Globalization* (Minneapolis: University of Minnesota University Press, 1996).

Asad, Talal. *Genealogies of Religion: Discipline and Reasons of Power in Christianity and Islam* (Baltimore: Johns Hopkins University Press, 1993).

Axel, Brian (ed.). *From the Margins, Historical Anthropology and Its Futures* (Durham, NC: Duke University Press, 2002).

Azevedo, Carmo. 'The Casados', in *Goan Society Through the Ages*, ed. B.S. Shastry (New Delhi: Asian Publishing Services, 1987).

Baden-Powell, B.H., *The Land Systems of British India*, 3 Volumes (Oxford: Clarendon Press, 1892).

Bakhtin, M.M. *The Dialogic Imagination: Four Essays*, ed. M. Holquist, tr. C. Emerson and M. Holquist (Austin: University of Texas Press, 1981).

Bakhtin, M.M. *Rabelais and His World*, tr. H. Iswolsky (Bloomington: Indiana University Press, 1984).

Ballhatchet, Kenneth. 'European Missions and Indian Society: The Archbishop of Goa, the Vicar Apostolic of Malabar and the Padroado in the Early Nineteenth Century', in *Seminário Internacional de Historia Indo-Portuguesa* (Lisboa: Instituto de Investigação Cientifica Tropical, 1978).

Barkey, Karen. *Empire of Difference: The Ottomans in Comparative Example* (Cambridge: Cambridge University Press, 2008).

Bastos, Cristiana. 'Race, Medicine and the Late Portuguese Empire: The Role of Goan Colonial Physicians', *Journal of Romance Studies*, Volume 5, No. 1 (2005).

Bell, Catherine. *Ritual: Perspectives and Dimensions* (New York: Oxford University Press, 1997).

Bell, Catherine. *Ritual Theory, Ritual Practice* (New York: Oxford University Press, 1992).

Birmingham, David. *Concise History of Portugal* (Cambridge: Cambridge University Press, 1993).

Blusse, Leonard and George Winius. 'The Origin and Rhythm of Dutch Aggression against the Estado da Índia, 1601–1661', in *Indo-Portuguese History, Old Issues, New Questions*, ed. Teotónio de Souza (New Delhi: Concept Publishing Company, 1985).

Borges, Charles. 'Contrasting Images: The Jesuits before and after the Expulsion', *Indo-Portuguese History Conference* (Porvorim, Goa: Xavier Center for Historical Research, 6–9 September 1999).

Borges, Charles. *The Economics of the Goa Jesuits, 1542–1759, An Explanation of Their Rise and Fall* (New Delhi: Concept Publishing Company, 1994).

Borges, Charles. 'Religious Orders and Estado da India in Goa: A Balancing Act', in *Goa's External Relations*, ed. P.P. Shirodkar (Panjim: Dr Wolfgang de Silva Marg printers, 1992).

Borges, Charles. 'Some Popular Religious Expressions in 16th Century Catholic Goa', in *Souvenir of the Laying of the Foundation of the Extension to the Holy Family Church, 8th September, 1991* (Porvorim, Goa, manuscript).

Bourdieu, Pierre. *Outline of a Theory of Practice*, tr. Richard Nice (Cambridge: Cambridge University Press, 1977).

Bowen, John. *Religions in Practice: An Approach to the Anthropology of Religion*, 2nd edn (Boston: Allyn and Bacon, 2002).

Boxer, Charles. *Four Centuries of Portuguese Expansion, 1415–1825; A Succinct Survey* (Berkeley: University of California Press, 1969).

Boxer, Charles. *Portuguese India in the Mid-Seventeenth Century* (New Delhi: Oxford University Press, 1980).

Boxer, Charles. *The Portuguese Seaborne Empire, 1415–1825* (New York: Alfred Knopf, 1969).

Brading, D.A. *Mexican Phoenix, Our Lady of Guadalupe: Image and Tradition Across Five Centuries* (Cambridge: Cambridge University Press, 2001).

Brown, Peter R. *The Cult of Saints: Its Rise and Function in Latin Christianity* (Chicago: University of Chicago Press, 1981).

Bucur, Maria and Nancy Wingfield (eds), *Staging the Past: The Politics of Commemoration in Habsburg Central Europe, 1848 to the Present* (West Lafayette, IN: Purdue University Press, 2001).

Burton, Antoinette. *Dwelling in the Archive. Women Writing House, Home, and History in Late Colonial India* (Delhi: Oxford University Press, 2003).

Cameron, Averil. *The Later Roman Empire, AD 284–430* (Cambridge, MA: Harvard University Press, 1993).

Cannadine, David and Price, Simon (eds), *Rituals of Royality: Power and Ceremonial in Traditional Societies* (Cambridge: Cambridge University Press, 1987).

Chakrabarty, Dipesh. 'Postcoloniality and the Artifice of History: Who Speaks for 'Indian' Pasts?' *Representations*, No. 37 (Winter 1992).

Chakrabarty, Dipesh. *Provincializing Europe: Postcolonial Thought and Historical Difference* (Princeton: Princeton University Press, 2000).

Chakravarti, Ananya. *The Empire of Apostles: Jesuits in Brazil and India* (Unpublished PhD, University of Chicago, 2012).

Chatterjee, Partha. *The Nation and Its Fragments* (Princeton: Princeton University Press, 1993).

Chaturvedula, Nandini. *Imperial Excess: Corruption and Decadence in Portuguese India (1660–1706)* (Unpublished PhD, Columbia University, 2010).

Chaudhuri, K.N. *Trade and Civilization in the Indian Ocean* (New York: Cambridge University Press, 1985).

Chauhan, R.S. 'Marketing in Goa During the 16th Century', in *Goan Society Through the Ages*, ed. B.S. Shastry (New Delhi: Asian Public Services, 1987).

Clarence-Smith, Gervase. *The Third Portuguese Empire, 1825–1975, A Study in Economic Imperialism* (Manchester: Manchester University Press, 1978).

Clarke, David. 'Invoking the Body's Presence', *The American Journal of Semiotics*, Volume 9, No. 1 (1992).

Coates, Timothy. *Convicts and Orphans: Forced and State-Sponsored Colonizers in the Portuguese Empire, 1550–1755* (Stanford, CA: Stanford University Press, 2001).

Coates, Timothy. 'State Sponsored Female Colonization in the Estado da Índia, ca. 1550–1750' *Santa Barbara Portuguese Studies*, Volume II (1995).

Coelho, Victor. 'Connecting Histories: Portuguese Music in Renaissance Goa', in *Goa and Portugal: Their Cultural Links*, eds C. Borges and H. Feldman (New Delhi: Concept Publishing Co, 1997).

Coelho, Victor. 'Kapsberger's Apotheosis ... of Francis Xavier (1622) and the Conquering of India', in *Genre, Nationhood and Sexual Difference*, eds R. Dellamora and D. Fischlin (New York: Columbia University Press, 1997).

Cohn, Bernard. *An Anthropologist Among the Historians and Other Essays* (Delhi: Oxford University Press, 1987).

Cohn, Bernard. *Colonialism and Its Forms of Knowledge* (Princeton: Princeton University Press, 1996).

Cohn, Bernard. 'Representing Authority in Victorian India', in his *An Anthropologist Among the Historians and Other Essays* (Delhi: Oxford University Press, 1987).

Comaroff, Jean. *Body of Power, Spirit of Resistance: The Culture and History of a South African People* (Chicago: Chicago University Press, 1985).

Comaroff, Jean and John. *Ethnography and the Historical Imagination* (Boulder: Westview Press, 1992).

Correia-Afonso, John. *Jesuit Letters and Indian History, 1542–1773*, 2nd edn (Bombay: Oxford University Press, 1969).

Correia-Afonso, John. 'Manuel Godinho's Alternatives to the Carreira da India', *Indo-Portuguese History, Old Issues, New Questions*, ed. Teotónio de Souza (New Delhi: Concept Publishing Company, 1985).

Cosme, José Costa, S.F.X. *A Missiological Conflict Between Padroado and Propaganda in the East* (Pilar, Goa: Pilar Publications, 1997).

Costa, Alexio Manuel ed. *Dicionário Literatura Goesa (Volume 3)* (Macau: Instituto Cultural de Macau, Fundação Oriente, 1997).

Coutinho, João da Veiga. *A Kind of Absence, Life in the Shadow of History* (Stamford, CT: Yagunta Press, 1997).

Couto, Diogo do. *Black Legend of Portuguese India: Diogo do Couto, His Contemporaries and the Soldado Pratico. A Contribution to the Study of Political Corruption in the Empires of Early Modern Europe*, XCHR Studies, Series, No. 3 (New Delhi: Concept Publishing Company, 1982)

Crone, V.D. *The Discovery of the East* (New York: St. Martin's Press, 1972).

Cruz, Maria Augusta Lima. 'Notes on Portuguese Relations with Vijayanagara, 1500–1565', in *Santa Barbara Portuguese Studies*, Volum II (1995), pp. 13–14.

Da Costa, J.A. *A History of Goa* (Mapusa, Goa: Ramakant Printers, 1982).

Das Gupta, Ashin and M.N. Pearson (eds), *India and the Indian Ocean: 1500–1800* (Calcutta: Oxford University Press, 1987).

Davis, Natalie. *Fiction in the Archives* (Stanford: Stanford University Press, 1987).

D'Costa, Anthony. *The Christianization of the Goa Islands, 1510–1567* (Bombay: Imprimatur, 1965).

De Barros, Joseph. 'Discoveries and Martyrs of Missionary Expansion in the East', in *Discoveries, Missionary Expansion and Asian Cultures*, ed. Teotónio de Souza (New Delhi: Concept Publishing Company, 1994).

De Matos, Artur Teotodoro. 'Assets and Income of the Religious Orders in Goa at the End of the 16th Century', in *Discoveries, Missionary Expansion and Asian Cultures*, ed. Teotónio de Souza (New Delhi: Concept Publishing Company, 1994).

De Menezes, Pia. 'Interactive Relationship between Goa and Bombay Journalism' in *Goa's External Relations*, ed. P.P. Shirodkar (Panjim: Prabhakar Bhide and Rajhauns Vitaran, 1992).

Derrida, Jacques. *Archive Fever: A Freudian Impression*, tr. Eric Prenowitz (Chicago: University of Chicago Press, 1996).

De Sá, Bailon. 'The Genesis of Portuguese Discoveries and Their Influence on Indian Culture', in *Discoveries, Missionary Expansion and Asian Cultures*, ed. Teotónio de Souza (New Delhi: Concept Publishing Company, 1994).

De Sá, Rev. M. 'The Ecclesiastical Province of Goa', *Indo-Portuguese Review, Calcutta*, Volume 4 (Calcutta: Indo-Portuguese Association, 1922).

De Souza, Teotónio. 'Bibliographical Essay', in *Medieval Goa: A Socio-Economic History* (New Delhi: Concept Publishing Co., 1979).

De Souza, Teotónio. 'Christianization and Cultural Conflict in Goa, 16th–19th Century', in *Congresso Internacional de Historia, Missionação Portuguesa e Encontro de Culturas Actas*, Volume IV (Braga: Universidade Catolica Portuguesa, 1993).

De Souza, Teotónio. 'Hindu Dominance of Goan Economy', *Indica*, Volume 12, No. 1 (March 1975).

De Souza, Teotónio. 'Urban Topography and Demography', in *Medieval Goa: A Socio-Economic History* (New Delhi: Concept Publishing Co., 1979).

De Souza, Teotónio (ed.). *Essays in Goan History* (New Delhi: Concept Publishing Company, 1989).

De Souza, Teotónio (ed.). *Goa Through the Ages Volume II. An Economic History* (New Delhi: Concept Publishing Company, 1987).

De Souza, Teotónio (ed.). *Jesuits in India: In Historical Perspective* (Macau: Instituto Cultural de Macau, 1992).

De Souza, Teotónio (ed.). *Discoveries, Missionary Expansion and Asian Cultures* (New Delhi: Concept Publishing Company, 1994).

De Souza, T.R. 'The Portuguese in Asia and their Church Patronage', in *Western Colonialism in Asia and Christianity*, ed. M.D. David (Bombay: Himalaya Publishing House, 1988).

Delooz, Pierre. 'Towards a Social Study of Canonized Sainthood in the Catholic Church', in *Saints and Their Cults: Studies in Religious Sociology, Folklore and History*, ed. Stephen Wilson (Cambridge: Cambridge University Press, 1983).

Dirks, Nicholas B. 'Annals of the Archive: Ethnographic Notes on the Sources of History', in *From the Margins: Historical Anthropology and its Futures*, ed. Brian Keith Axel (Durham, NC: Duke University Press, 2002).

Dirks, Nicholas B. *Castes of Mind: Colonialism and the Making of Modern India* (Princeton: Princeton University Press, 2001).

Dirks, Nicholas B. 'The Crimes of Colonialism. Anthropology and the Textualization of India' in *Colonial Subjects: Essays on the Practical History of Anthropology*, eds P. Pels and O. Salemink (Ann Arbor, MI: University of Michigan Press, 1999).

Dirks, Nicholas B. *The Hollow Crown: Ethnohistory of an Indian Kingdom*, 2nd edn (Ann Arbor, MI: University of Michigan Press, 1993).

Dirks, Nicholas B. 'Ritual and Resistance: Subversion as Social Fact', in

Contesting Power: Resistance and Everyday Social Relations in South Asia, eds D. Haynes and G. Prakash (Berkeley: University of California Press, 1991).

Disney, Anthony. 'The Portuguese Empire in India, 1550–1650, Some Suggestions for a less Seaborne, More Landbound Approach to Its Socio-economic History', in *Indo-Portuguese History, Sources and Problems*, ed. J. Correia -Afonso (Delhi: Oxford University Press, 1991).

Disney, Anthony. 'The Viceroy Count of Linhares at Goa, 1629–1635', in *Seminario Internacional de Historia Indo-Portuguesa, 1978* (Lisboa: Instituto de Investigação Cientifica Tropical, 1985).

D'Souza, Carmo. *Legal System in Goa, Volume II: Laws and Legal Trends (1510–1969)* (Calangute, Goa: Agnelo D' Souza, no year of publication).

Douglas, Mary. *Natural Symbols* (New York: Random House, 1973).

Durkheim, Emile. *Elementary Forms of the Religious Life* (New York: The Free Press, 1912).

Eaton, Richard. *Sufis of Bijapur, 1300–1700: Social Roles of Sufis in Medieval India* (Princeton: Princeton University Press, 1978).

Eisenstein, Elizabeth. *The Printing Press as an Advent of Change: Communication and Transformations in Early Modern Europe* (Cambridge: Cambridge University Press, 1979).

Fabian, Johannes. *Out of Our Minds: Reason and Madness in the Exploration of Central Africa* (Berkeley: University of California Press, 2000).

Fernandes, James. *Bwiti: An Ethnography of the Religious Imagination in Africa* (Princeton: Princeton University Press, 1982).

Fernandes, Jason Keith. *Citizenship Experiences of the Goan Catholics* (Unpublished PhD, ISCTE – Instituto Universitário de Lisboa, 2013).

Foot, John. 'The Dead Duce', *History Today*, Volume 49, Issue 8 (August 1999).

Foucault, Michel. *The Archeology of Knowledge and the Discourse on Language*, tr. A.M. Sheridan (New York: Pantheon, 1972).

Foucault, Michel. *The Birth of the Clinic*, tr. A.M. Sheridan (New York: Vintage Books, 1994).

Foucault, Michel. *Discipline and Punish: The Birth of the Prison*, tr. A.M. Sheridan (New York: Vintage, 1979).

Foucault, Michel. 'Governmentality', in *The Foucault Effect: Studies in Governmentality*, eds G. Burchell, C. Gordon, and P. Miller (Chicago: University of Chicago Press, 1995).

Foucault, Michel. *History of Sexuality*, Volume 1, tr. R. Hurley (New York: Vintage, 1972).

Foucault, Michel. *The Order of Things: An Archaeology of the Human Sciences* (New York: Vintage Books, 1973).

Foucault, Michel. 'The Subject and Power', in *Michel Foucault: Beyond Structuralism and Hermeneutics*, eds Hubert L. Dreyfus and Paul Rabinow, 2nd edn (Chicago: University of Chicago Press, 1983).

Frykenburg, R. (ed.); *Land Control and Social Structure in Indian Society* (Madison: University of Wisconsin Press, 1969).

Geary, Patrick. *Furta Sacra: Thefts of Relics in the Central Middle Ages* (Princeton: Princeton University Press, 1978).

Geertz, Clifford. *The Interpretation of Cultures* (New York: Basic Books, 1973).
Geertz, Clifford. *Negara: The Theatre State in Nineteenth Century Bali* (Princeton: Princeton University Press, 1980).
Ginzburg, Carlo. *The Cheese and the Worms* (Baltimore: Johns Hopkins University Press, 1982).
Gluckman, Max. 'Gossip and Scandal', *Current Anthropology*, Volume 4, No. 3 (June 1963).
Gluckman, Max. *Order and Rebellion in Tribal Africa* (London: Cohen and West, 1963).
Gluckman, Max. *Politics, Law and Ritual in Tribal Society* (Oxford: Basil Blackwell, 1965).
Goody, Jack. 'Against Ritual: Loosely Structured Thoughts on a Loosely Defined Topic', in *Secular Ritual*, eds S. Moore and B. Myeroff (Amsterdam: Van Gorcum and Company, 1977).
Gracias, Fatima. 'Quality of Life in Colonial Goa, Its Hygienic Expression (19th–20th Centuries)', in *Essays in Goan History*, ed. Teotónio de Souza (New Delhi: Concept Publishing Company, 1989).
Guha, Ranajit. *Dominance Without Hegemony: History and Power in Colonial India* (Cambridge, MA: Harvard University Press, 1997).
Guha, Ranajit. *A Rule of Property for Bengal: An Essay on the Idea of the Permanent Settlement* (Durham, NC: Duke University Press, 1996).
Hamilton, Carolyn, Verne Harris, Jane Taylor, Michele Pickover, Graeme Reid and Razia Saleh (eds). *Refiguring the Archive* (Cape Town: David Philip, 2002; Dordrecht, Netherlands: Kluwer Academic Publishers, 2002).
Hansen, Thomas and Finn Stepputat (eds). *States of Imagination: Ethnographic Explorations of the Postcolonial State* (Durham, NC: Duke University Press, 2001).
Helgerson, Richard. 'Camões, Hakluyt, and the Voyages of Two Nations', in *Colonialism and Culture*, ed. N. Dirks (Ann Arbor, MI: University of Michigan Press, 1992).
Hespanha, António Manuel. *As Vésperas do Leviathan* (Lisboa: Almedina, 1994).
Hillman, David and Carla Mazzio (eds). *The Body in Parts: Fantasies of Corporeality in Early Modern Europe* (New York: Routledge, 1997).
Hocart, A.M. 'The Temple of the Tooth in Kandy', *Memoirs of the Archaeological Survey of Ceylon*, Volume IV (London: Luzac and Company, 1931).
Holt, John. *Buddha in the Crown, Avalokitesvara in the Buddhist Traditions of Sri Lanka* (New York: Oxford University Press, 1991).
Ifeka, Caroline. 'The Image of Goa' in *Indo-Portuguese History, Old Issues, New Questions*, ed. Teotónio de Souza (New Delhi: Concept Publishing Company, 1985).
Jorissen, Engelbert. '16 March 1554, Reflections of a Mid-Sixteenth Century Scene in Goa', in *Goa and Portugal, Their Cultural Links*, eds C. Borges and H. Feldmann (New Delhi: Concept Publishing Company, 1997).
Kamat, Nandkumar. 'Stagnant Economy of Portuguese Goa: A Study in Socio-psycho-pathology', in *Socioeconomic Aspects of Portuguese Colonialism in Goa: 19th and 20th Century*, ed. B.S. Shastry (Belgaum: Yarball Offset Printers, 1990).

Kamat, Pratima. *Farar Far: Local Resistance to Colonial Hegemony in Goa, 1510–1912* (Panaji, Goa: Institute Menezes Bragança, 1999).

Kamat, Pratima. 'Some Legal Aspects of the Socio-Economic Life of Women in Portuguese Asia', in *Goan Society Through the Ages*, ed. B.S. Shastry (New Delhi: Asian Publication Series, 1987).

Kantorowicz, Ernst. *The King's Two Bodies* (Princeton: Princeton University Press, 1957).

Kaplan, Caren. *Questions of Travel: Postmodern Discourses of Displacement* (Durham, NC: Duke University Press, 1996).

Keane, Webb. *Signs of Recognition, Powers and Hazards of Representation in an Indonesian Society* (Berkeley: University of California Press, 1997).

Kopytoff, Igor. 'The Cultural Biography of Things: Commoditization as Process', in *The Social Life of Things: Commodities in Cultural Perspective*, ed. Arjun Appadurai (New York: Cambridge University Press, 1986).

Kulkarni, A.R. 'Portuguese in the Deccan Politics: A Study of the New Marathi Documents from Lisbon', in *Indo-Portuguese History, Old Issues, New Questions*, ed. Teotónio de Souza (New Delhi: Concept Publishing Company, 1985).

Lach, Donald. *Asia in the Making of Europe*, Volume I (Chicago: University of Chicago Press, 1994).

Leach, Edmund. *Culture and Communication* (Cambridge: Cambridge University Press, 1976).

Liu, Yi. 'Clergy, Nobility and Crown in Decadência' *História* [online], Volume 24, No. 1 (2005).

Lopes, Maria de Jesus dos Mártires. *Epistolario de Um Açoriano na Índia, D. António Taveira da Neiva Brum da Silveira (1750–1775)* (Ponta Delgada, Azores: University of Azores, 1983).

Lopes, Maria de Jesus Mártires. *Goa Setecentista: Tradição e Modernidade (1750–1800)* (Lisboa: Centro de Estudos dos Povos e Culturas de Expressão Portuguesa Universidade Católica Portuguesa, 1996).

Lopes, Maria de Jesus dos Mártires. 'Teaching Methods in Goa (1750–1800)', in *Discoveries, Missionary Expansion and Asian Cultures*, ed. Teotónio de Souza (New Delhi: Concept Publishing Company, 1994).

MacPherson, Kenneth. 'A Secret People of South Asia: The Origins, Evolution and Role of the Luso-Indian Goan Community from the Sixteenth to Twentieth Centuries', *Itinerario*, Volume XI, No. 2 (1987).

Madureira, Luís. 'Tropical Sex Fantasies and the Ambassador's Other Death: The Difference in Portuguese Colonialism', *Cultural Critique*, No. 28 (Autumn 1994).

Martínez, Tomás Eloy. *Santa Evita*, tr. Helen Lane (Barcelona: Seix Barral, 1995).

Mascarenhas, Mira. 'The Church in Eighteenth Century Goa', in *Essays in Goan History*, ed. Teotónio de Souza (New Delhi: Concept Publishing Co, 1989).

Mathew, K.S. 'Church Economics in 16th Century Goa', in *Goa: Cultural Trends*, ed. P.P. Shirodkar (Panaji: Casa Packmaster, 1998).

Mathew, K.S. *Portuguese and the Sultanate of Gujarat (1500–1573)* (Delhi: Mittal Publications, 1986).

Maxwell, Kenneth. *Pombal: Paradox of the Enlightenment* (Cambridge:

Cambridge University Press, 1995).

Mendes, Sushila Sawant. 'Dr. Lohia and Goa's Freedom Struggle', in *Essays in Goan History*, ed. Teotónio de Souza (New Delhi: Concept Publishing Company, 1989).

Mendonça-Noronha, Silvia M. de. 'The Economic Scene in Goa, 1926–1961', in *Goa Through the Ages Volume II. An Economic History*, ed. Teotónio de Souza (New Delhi: Concept Publishing Company, 1987).

Messick, Brinkley. *The Calligraphic State: Textual Domination and History in a Muslim Society* (Berkeley: University of California Press, 1996).

Mignolo, Walter. *The Darker Side of the Renaissance: Literacy, Territoriality, and Colonization* (Ann Arbor, MI: University of Michigan Press, 1995).

Moraes, George. 'Contribution of Cunha Rivara to Indian Historiography', in *Seminário Internacional de Historia Indo-Portuguesa, 1978* (Lisboa: Instituto de Investigação Cientifica Tropical, 1985).

Morais, Carlos Alexandre de. *Cronologia Geral da Índia Portuguesa*, Instituto Cultural de Macão (Macau: Impressão Tipographia Welfare, 1993).

Muir, Edward. *Civic Ritual in Renaissance Venice* (Princeton: Princeton University Press, 1981).

Mundadan, A. Mathias. *History of Christianity in India*, Volume I (Bangalore: Theological Publications in India, 1983).

Narayan, Rajan. *Goencho Saib: The Life and Mission of St Francis Xavier* (Panjim: Tata Press Limited).

Neill, Stephen. *A History of Christianity in India, The Beginnings to AD 1707* (Cambridge: Cambridge University Press, 1984).

Nevett, Albert, S.J., *John de Britto and His Times* (Anand: Gujarat Sahitya Prakash, 1980).

Nolan, M. and S. Nolan, *Christian Pilgrimage in Modern Western Europe* (Chapel Hill: The University of North Carolina Press, 1989).

Oriente (Dezembro 2005; special issue dedicated to topic of Xavier on the quincentenary of his birth).

Osswald, María Cristina. *Jesuit Art in Goa between 1542 and 1655: From Modo Nostro to Modo Goano* (PhD thesis, Instituto Universitário Europeu, Florence: 2003).

Oxford American Desk Dictionary and Thesaurus, The, 2nd edn (New York: Berkeley Books, 2001).

Pearson, Michael. 'Corruption and Corsairs in Sixteenth Century Western India: A Functional Analysis', in his *Coastal Western India* (New Delhi: Concept Publishing Company, 1981).

Pearson, Michael. 'The Crowd in Portuguese India', in his *Coastal Western India* (New Delhi: Concept Publishing Company, 1981).

Pearson, Michael. 'The Goa Rendas 1600–1700', in *Mare Luso-Indicum*, Tome II (Paris: Librairie Minard, 1973).

Pearson, Michael. 'The Port City of Goa: Policy and Practice in the 16th Century', in his *Coastal Western India* (New Delhi: Concept Publishing Company, 1981).

Pearson, Michael. *The Portuguese in India* (Cambridge: Cambridge University Press, 1987).

Pemberton, John. *On the Subject of 'Java'* (Ithaca, NY: Cornell University Press, 1994).

Pereira, Claudia. 'The Gawada of Goa: A Debate on Status', *Oriente*, No. 6 (2003).

Perez, Rosa Maria. *The Tulsi and the Cross: Anthropology and the Colonial Encounter in Goa* (New Delhi: Orient Blackswan, 2012).

Pinto, António Costa. *Salazar's Dictatorship and European Fascism: Problems of Interpretation* (New York: Columbia University Press, 1995).

Pinto, Celsa. *Goa: Images and Perceptions, Studies in Goan History* (Goa: Prabhakar Bhide, 1996).

Pinto, Celsa. *Trade and Finance in Portuguese India: A Study of the Portuguese Country Trade, 1770–1840* (New Delhi: Concept Publishing Company, 1994).

Pinto, Paulo Jorge Sousa. 'Purse and Sword: D. Henrique Bendahara and Portuguese Melaka in the Late 16th Century', *Santa Barbara Portuguese Studies*, Volume II (1995).

Pinto, Rochelle. *Between Empires: Print and Politics in Goa* (Oxford: Oxford University Press, 2007).

Poole, Stafford. *Our Lady of Guadalupe: The Origins and Sources of a Mexican National Symbol, 1531–1797* (Tucson: University of Arizona Press, 1995).

Pratt, Mary Louise. *Imperial Eyes: Travel Writing and Transculturation* (London: Routledge, 1992).

Priolkar, A.K. *The Goa Inquisition* (Bombay: Bombay University Press, 1961).

Priolkar, A.K. *The Printing Press in India, Its Beginnings and Early Development* (Bombay: Marathi Samshodhana Mandala, 1958).

Rafael, Vicente L. *Contracting Colonialism: Translation and Christian Conversion in Tagalog Society under Early Spanish Rule* (Durham, NC: Duke University Press, 1993).

Rego, A. da Silva, 'Os Ingleses Em Goa, 1799–1813' (unpublished manuscript, 1959), later published in *Separata dos Estudos Politicos e Sociais*, Volume III, No. 1 (1965).

Rego, A. da Silva, *Portuguese Colonisation in the 16th Century: A Study of the Royal Ordinances* (Johannesburg: Witwatersrand University Press, 1959).

Rivara, Joaquim Heliodoro. *Goa and the Revolt of 1787*, ed. Charles Borges, tr. Renato da Cunha Soares (New Delhi: Concept Publishing Company, 1996).

Robinson, Rowena. *Conversion, Continuity and Change: Lived Christianity in Southern Goa* (New Delhi: Sage Publications, 1998).

Rodrigues, Lourdes Bravo da Costa. 'Goa and Indian Leaders', in *Goa's External Relations*, ed. P.P. Shirodkar (Panjim: Prabhakar Bide, 1992).

Rodrigues, Pia de Menezes. 'Interactive Relationship between Goa and Bombay Journalism', in *Goa's External Relations*, ed. P.P. Shirodkar (Panjim: Rajhauns Vitaran, 1992).

Rowe, Katherine. 'God's Handy Work, Divine Complicity and the Anatomist's Touch', in *The Body in Parts: Fantasies of Corporeality in Early Modern Europe*, eds D. Hillman and Carla Mazzio (New York: Routledge, 1997).

Rubin, Miri. *Corpus Christi: The Eucharist in Late Medieval Culture* (New York: Cambridge University Press, 1991).

Rubinoff, Arthur. *The Construction of a Political Community, Integration and Identity in Goa* (New Delhi: Sage Publications, 1998).

Ruiz, Teofilo. 'Elite and Popular Culture in Late Fifteenth Century Castilian Festivals: The Case of Jaen', in *City and Spectacle in Medieval Europe*, eds B. Hanawalt and K. Ryerson (Minneapolis: University of Minnesota Press, 1994).

Rushdie, Salman. *Midnight's Children* (New York: Penguin, 1980).

Russell-Wood, A.J.R. *The Portuguese Empire, 1415–1808: A World on the Move* (Baltimore: Johns Hopkins University Press, 1998).

Saldanha, Arun. *Psychedelic White: Goa Trance and the Viscosity of Race* (Minneapolis: University of Minnesota Press, 2007).

Sanders, Paula. *Ritual, Politics and the City in Fatimid Cairo* (Albany: SUNY Press, 1994).

Santos, Boaventura de Sousa. 'Between Prospero and Caliban: Colonialism, Postcolonialism, and Inter-Identity', *Luso-Brazilian Review*, Volume 39, No. 2, Special Issue, *Portuguese Cultural Studies* (Winter 2002).

Santos, Catarina Madeira. *Goa É A Chave De Toda a Índia Perfil: Político Da Capital do Estado Da Índia* (Lisboa: Comissão Nacional para as Comemorações dos Descobrimentos Portugueses, 1999).

Scammel, G. 'England, Portugal and the Estado da Índia, c. 1500–1635', in *Seminário Internacional de Historia Indo-Portuguesa* (Lisbon: Instituto de Investigação Cientifica Tropical, 1985).

Schneider, Jane. 'Rumpelstiltskin's Bargain: Folklore and the Merchant Capitalist Intensification of Linen Manufacture in Early Modern Europe', in *Cloth and Human Experience*, eds A. Weiner and J. Schneider (Washington, DC: Smithsonian Institution Press, 1989).

Scott, David. *Formations of Ritual: Colonial and Anthropological Discourses on the Sinhala Yaktovil* (Minneapolis: University of Minnesota Press, 1994).

Scott, Joan. 'The Evidence of Experience', in *Questions of Evidence: Proof, Practice and Persuasion Across the Disciplines*, eds James Chandler, Arnold Davidson, and Harry Harootunian (Chicago: University of Chicago Press, 1994).

Shantishree, Pandit, D.N.B. 'The Parliament and Foreign Policy in India: Its Policy Towards Goa (1952–1961)', in *SocioEconomic Aspects of Portuguese Colonialism in Goa: 19th and 20th Centuries*, ed. B.S. Shastry (Belgaum: Yarbal Offset Printers, 1990).

Shastry, B.S. 'The Colonial Budgets of Portuguese Goa, 1852–1909: Some Observations', in *Socioeconomic Aspects of Portuguese Colonialism in Goa: 19th and 20th Century*, ed. B.S. Shastry (Belgaum: Yarball Offset Printers, 1990).

Shastry, B.S. 'Marques de Pombal and the Jesuits of Goa', in *Jesuits in India: In Historical Perspective*, ed. Teotónio de Souza (Macau: Instituto Cultural de Macau, 1992).

Shastry, B.S. 'Sources of Income and Items of Expenditure of the Church in Goa (c.1510–1800 AD): A Note', in *Goan Society Through the Ages*, ed. B.S. Shastry (New Delhi: Asian Publication Series, 1987).

Shirodkar, P.P. 'British Occupation of Go (1799–1815)', *Researches in Indo-*

Portuguese History, Volume 1, ed. P.P. Shirodkar (Jaipur: Publication Scheme, 1998).

Shirodkar, P.P. 'Evangelization and Its Harsh Realities in Portuguese India', in *Discoveries, Missionary Expansion and Asian Cultures*, ed. Teotónio de Souza (New Delhi: Concept Publishing Company, 1994).

Shirodkar, P.P. *Goa's Struggle for Freedom* (Panjim: Mrs Sulabha P. Shirodkar, 1999).

Shirodkar, P.P. 'Insurgency, 1857 Mutiny in Western India and the Portuguese', in *Researches in Indo-Portuguese History*, Volume II, ed. P.P. Shirodkar (Jaipur: Publication Scheme, 1998).

Shirodkar, P.P. 'Socio-Cultural Life in Goa During the 16th Century', in *Goa and Portugal: Their Cultural Links*, eds C. Borges and Helmut Feldmann (New Delhi: Concept Publishing Company, 1997).

Shirodkar, P.P. (ed.). *Goa: Cultural Trends* (Panaji: Casa Packmaster, 1998).

Stallybrass, Peter. 'Footnotes' in *The Body in Parts: Fantasies of Corporeality in Early Modern Europe*, eds D. Hillman and C. Mazzio (New York: Routledge, 1997).

Stallybrass, Peter and Allon White. *The Politics and Poetics of Transgression* (London: Methuen & Co, 1986).

Steensgard, Niels. *The Asian Trade Revolution of the Seventeenth Century: The East India Companies and the Decline of the Caravan Trade* (Chicago: University of Chicago Press, 1974).

Stein, Burton. *The Making of Agrarian Policy in British India, 1770–1900* (Delhi: Oxford University Press, 1992).

Stewart, Susan. *On Longing, Narratives of the Miniature, the Gigantic, the Souvenir, the Collection* (Durham, NC: Duke University Press, 1993).

Stokes, Eric. *The English Utilitarians and India* (Oxford: Oxford University Press, 1959).

Stoler, Ann. *Along the Archival Grain: Epistemic Anxieties and Colonial Common Sense* (Princeton: Princeton University Press, 2009).

Stoler, Ann and Fred Cooper (eds). *Tensions of Empire: Colonial Cultures in a Bourgeois World* (Berkeley: University of California Press, 1997).

Stoller, Paul. *The Taste of Ethnographic Things* (Philadelphia: University of Pennsylvania Press, 1989).

Subrahmanyam, Sanjay. *The Career and Legend of Vasco da Gama* (New Delhi: Cambridge University Press, 1997).

Subrahmanyam, Sanjay. 'Commerce and Conflict: Two Views of Portuguese Melaka in the 1620's', *Journal of South East Asian Studies*, Volume XIX, No. 1 (March 1988).

Subrahmanyam, Sanjay. 'Commerce and State Power in Eighteenth Century India: Some Reflections', *South Asia Research*, Volume 8, No. 2 (November 1988).

Subrahmanyam, Sanjay. *Explorations in Connected History: Mughals and Franks* (New Delhi: Oxford University Press, 2005).

Subrahmanyam, Sanjay. *Improvising Empire, Portuguese Trade and Settlement in the Bay of Bengal, 1500–1700* (Delhi: Oxford University Press, 1990).

Subrahmanyam, Sanjay. 'Introduction: The Portuguese and Early Modern Asia', in *Sinners and Saints: The Successors of Vasco da Gama*, ed. Sanjay Subrahmanyam (Delhi: Oxford University Press, 1998).

Subrahmanyam, Sanjay. 'The Kagemusha Effect, the Portuguese, Firearms, and the State in Early Modern South India', *Moyen Orient & Océan Indien*, Volume IV, No. 4 (Paris: Société d'Histoire de l'Orient, 1987).

Subrahmanyam, Sanjay. 'Palavras do Idalção: Un Encontro Curioso em Bijapur no Ano de 1561', *Cadernos do Noroeste*, Volume 1, Nos 1–2 (2001).

Subrahmanyam, Sanjay. *The Portuguese Empire in Asia, 1500–1700* (New York: Longman Publishing, 1993).

Subrahmanyam, Sanjay. 'The Viceroy as Assassin: The Portuguese, the Mughals and Deccan Politics, c.1600', *Santa Barbara Portuguese Studies*, Volume II (1995).

Subrahmanyam, Sanjay. 'The Viceroy as Assassin: The Portuguese, the Mughals and Deccan Politics', in *Sinners and Saints: The Successors of Vasco da Gama*, ed. Sanjay Subrahmanyam (Delhi: Oxford University Press, 1998).

Subrahmanyam, Sanjay (ed.). *Sinners and Saints: The Successors of Vasco da Gama* (Delhi: Oxford University Press, 1998).

Subrahmanyam, Sanjay and Luís Filipe F. R. Thomaz. 'Evolution of Empire: The Portuguese in the Indian Ocean during the Sixteenth Century', in *The Political Economy of Merchant Empires*, ed. J. Tracey (Cambridge: Cambridge University Press, 1991).

Tambiah, Stanley. 'The Magical Power of Words', *Man* Volume 3, No. 2 (June 1968).

Thomaz, Luís Filipe F.R., *De Ceuta a Timor* (Lisboa: Difel, 1994).

Thomaz, Luís Filipe F.R. 'Factions, Interests and Messianism: The Politics of Portuguese Expansion in the East, 1500–1521', *The Indian Economic and Social History Review*, Volumn 28, No. 1 (1991).

Trexler, Richard. *Public Life in Renaissance Florence* (Ithaca, NY: Cornell University Press, 1980).

Trouillot, Michel-Rolph. *Silencing the Past: Power and the Production of History* (Boston: Beacon Press, 1995).

Tumarkin, Nina. *Lenin Lives!: The Lenin Cult in Soviet Russia* (Cambridge, MA: Harvard University Press, 1997).

Turner, Victor. *Dramas, Fields and Metaphors: Symbolic Action in Human Society* (Ithaca, NY: Cornell University Press, 1974).

Turner, Victor. *Forest of Symbols: Aspects of Ndembu Ritual* (Ithaca, NY: Cornell University Press, 1967).

Turner, Victor. *The Ritual Process: Structure and Anti-Structure* (Harmondsworth: Penguin Books, 1974).

Velho, Maria Selma de Vieira. 'Goa, a Synthesis of Indo-Portuguese Cultural Relations', in *Seminário internacional de Historia Indo-Portuguesa, 1978* (Lisboa: Instituto de Investigação Cientifica Tropical, 1985).

Verdery, Katherine. *The Political Lives of Lives of Dead Bodies: Reburial and Post-Socialist Change* (New York: Columbia University Press, 1999).

Vicente, Filipa L. 'A exposição do corpo sagrado de S. Francisco Xavier e as exposições industriais e agrícolas em Goa', *Oriente* (December 2002).

Vicente, Filipa L. 'Exposiçoes coloniais na Índia Portuguesa e na Índia Britânica (séculos XIX e XX)', *Oriente*, No. 8 (April 2004).

Vicente, Filipa L. *Other Orientalisms: India Between Florence and Bombay, 1860–1900* (New Delhi: Orient Blackswan, 2012).

Viswanathan, Gauri. *Outside the Fold: Conversion, Modernity, and Belief* (Princeton: Princeton University Press, 1998).

Walker, Timothy. 'The Early Modern Globalization of Indian Medicine: Portuguese Dissemination of Drugs and Healing Techniques from South Asia on Four Continents, 1670–1830'. *Portuguese Literary and Cultural Studies*, No. 19 (2010).

Warner, Michael. *Publics and Counterpublics* (New York: Zone Books, 2005).

Weber, Max. *The Sociology of Religion*, tr. Ephraim Fischoff (New York: Beacon Press, 1963 [1922]).

Webster's New Universal Unabridged Dictionary, 2nd edn (New York: Simon & Schuster, 1983).

Weiner, Annette and Schneider, Jane (eds). *Cloth and the Human Experience* (Washington: Smithsonian Institution Press, 1989).

Wicki, Joseph, S.J., 'Duas Cartas Oficiais de Vice-Reis da India: 1561 e 1564', *Studia* (January 1959).

Wicki, Joseph, S.J. 'The Portuguese Padroado in India in the Sixteenth Century, and St Francis Xavier', in *Christianity in India: A History in Ecumenical Perspective*, eds H.C. Perumalil and E.R. Hambye (Alleppey: Prakasam Publications, 1972).

Williams, Lea E. 'Inauspicious Ambience: The Historical Setting of Early Luso-Chinese Contacts', in *Indo-Portuguese History: Old Issues, New Questions*, ed. Teotónio de Souza (New Delhi: Concept Publishing Company, 1985).

Williams, Raymond. *Marxism and Literature* (New York: Oxford University Press, 1977).

Wilson, Stephen (ed.). *Saints and Their Cults: Studies in Religious Sociology, Folklore and History* (Cambridge: Cambridge University Press, 1983).

Winius, G.D. 'Millenarianism and Empire, Portuguese Asian Decline and the "Crise de Conscience" of the Missionaries', *Itinerario*, Volume XI, No. 2 (1987).

Xavier, Ângela Barreto. *A Invenção De Goa* (Lisboa: Imprensa de Ciências Sociais, 2008).

Xavier, P.D. 'The Church and Society in 16th Century Goa', in *Goa: Cultural Trends*, ed. P.P. Shirodkar (Panaji: Casa Packmaster, 1998).

Xavier, P.D. *Goa: A Social History, 1510–1640* (Panji: Vitaran Rajhauns, 1993).

Xavier, P.D. 'Some Aspects of the Finances of the College of St. Paul, 1700–1750', in *Goan Society through the Ages*, ed. B.S. Shastry (New Delhi: Asian Publication Services, 1987).

Županov, Ines. 'Aristocratic Analogies and Demotic Descriptions in the Seventeenth Century Madurai Mission', *Representations*, Volume 41 (Winter 1993).

Županov, Ines. *Disputed Mission: Jesuit Experiments and Brahmanical Knowledge in Seventeenth-century India* (New Delhi: Oxford University Press, 1999).

Županov, Ines. 'The Prophetic and the Miraculous in Portuguese Asia: A Hagiographical View of Colonial Culture', *Santa Barbara Portuguese Studies*, Volume II (1995).

INDEX